MAXIMIZE
YOUR TRAINING

MAXIMIZE
YOUR TRAINING

Insights from Leading Strength and Fitness Professionals

Edited by Matt Brzycki

MASTERS PRESS

NTC/Contemporary Publishing Group

Library of Congress Cataloging-in-Publication Data

Maximize your training : insights from leading strength and fitness professionals /
   edited by Matt Brzycki.
       p.   cm.
    Includes bibliographical references and index.
    ISBN 0-8442-8317-7
    1. Weight training.   2. Bodybuilding.   I. Brzycki, Matt, 1957– .
  GV546.M33   1999
  613.7′1—dc21   99-13968
                                         CIP

Cover design by Nick Panos
Cover photograph, top: Copyright © Stewart Cohen/Tony Stone Images;
bottom: Copyright © David Madison/Tony Stone Images
Interior design by Hespenheide Design
Picture research by Elizabeth Broadrup Lieberman

Published by Masters Press
A division of NTC/Contemporary Publishing Group, Inc.
4255 West Touhy Avenue, Lincolnwood (Chicago), Illinois 60712-1975, U.S.A.
Copyright © 2000 by Matt Brzycki. All rights reserved.
No part of this book may be reproduced, stored in a retrieval system,
or transmitted in any form or by any means, electronic, mechanical,
photocopying, recording, or otherwise, without the prior written permission
of NTC/Contemporary Publishing Group, Inc.
Printed in the United States of America
International Standard Book Number: 0-8442-8317-7

00   01   02   03   04   05   CU   15   14   13   12   11   10   9   8   7   6   5   4   3   2

Contents

Preface

This book was created by a total of 37 authors. If not for the collective efforts of these ladies and gentlemen, the book would not have become a reality. I want to thank all of them for their time and toil in writing their chapters and in making this unique and valuable contribution to the strength and fitness community.

All of the authors are either very well established in their respective specialties or are up-and-coming professionals. They have a variety of backgrounds in strength and fitness including seven widely known researchers and educators with doctoral degrees (Cedric X. Bryant, Ralph N. Carpinelli, Ted Lambrinides, James A. Peterson, W. Daniel Schmidt, Wayne L. Westcott, and Richard Winett); one prominent medical doctor (M. Doug McGuff); three respected practitioners who are strength and conditioning coaches at the professional level with Major League Baseball (Sam Gannelli, San Diego Padres), the National Basketball Association (Shaun Brown, Boston Celtics), and the National Football League (Jeff Friday, Baltimore Ravens), as well as 10 collegiate strength and conditioning coaches from Stanford University (Michael Bradley), Penn State (Chip Harrison, Jeremy Scott, and John Thomas), Southeast Missouri State University (Tom Kelso), the University of Detroit (Jim Kielbaso), Michigan State University (Ken Mannie and Tim Wakeham), the University of Notre Dame (Mickey Marotti), and the University of Miami (Kevin C. Tolbert). Several authors may best be described as pioneers (Brian D. Johnston and Ken E. Leistner). Others have carved, or are beginning to carve, their own niche in the strength and fitness field (Tony Alexander, Rocco Castellano, Jan Dellinger, Frank Furgiuele, Daniel I. Galper, Kristi D. Graves, Chris Green, Bill Piche, Rachael E. Picone, Liza Rovniak, Steve Weingarten, Bob Whelan, and Jessica A. Whiteley). Despite having varied backgrounds, their messages share a common theme: Strength and fitness programs should be practical, efficient, productive, comprehensive, and, above all, safe.

These distinguished strength and fitness professionals have teamed up to share several centuries' worth of their insights in this book to help maximize your training.

Matt Brzycki
October 1998

This chapter was prepared with a sense of profound gratefulness to the Almighty for instilling in this writer a boundless appreciation for strength and then allowing him remarkable opportunities to associate with so many of His physically gifted creations.

Might and Muscle: Antiquity to Arnold

Jan Dellinger, A.A.
York® Barbell Company, Inc.
York, Pennsylvania

Great physical strength has been mythologized by mankind in legend, lore, and literature since the beginning of recorded history. Odes to athletes, soldiers, gladiators, and other possessors of inordinate physical prowess abound from Ancient Greece and Rome. Nordic cultures have many favorite sons of Conan whose tales of exceptional strength and valor have lived on over centuries. Similarly, the Bible carries references to individuals of incredible strength, size, and power, notably the Nazarite Samson, the colossal Philistine Goliath, and the Mighty Men of Israel—the elite personal guard of King David.

In fact, regardless of the historical period, possessors of extreme physical strength have been accorded high status and social acclaim in their culture. Upon the death of these gifted persons the pinnacles of their strength achievements were enumerated on the headstones of their graves. One of the oldest such memorials was found in contemporary Yugoslavia, dating back to the second century B.C. and detailing the weightlifting feats of Pomponius Secundinus.

The British, in particular, were meticulous in recognizing and remembering their strength icons. Dated May 22, 1742, the headstone of Richard Joy—a.k.a. the "Kentish Samson"—carries an extensive commemoration of his muscular prowess.

The "icon" characterization is by no means an exaggeration of the celebrity that elite-caliber strongmen enjoyed in bygone days. Because the upper crust of many societies were just as curious about the limits of man's physical strength as average folks were, strength stars often gave command performances for the ruling nobility. Richard Joy's feats of strength enthralled King William III of England in the late 1600s; Joy subsequently became a regular source of entertainment for the court of Queen Anne.

Rulers of certain cultures firmly comprehended the need for regular physical exercise in promoting maximum functionality and efficiency, and they took steps to mandate participation among their subjects. As far back as 3500 B.C., Chinese emperors required the populace to exercise daily. By the close of the Chou dynasty (approximately 300 B.C.), certain strength standards (as measured by prescribed weightlifting maneuvers using stones) were part of the entrance test for military service.

As time went on, many of the European royalty developed an interest in personal fitness, thereby giving certain high-profile strongmen a greater presence in the royal courts. As a personal trainer to world leaders, no one will ever rival Louis Attila (born Louis Durlacher). To say that Attila had European friends in high places would be quite an understatement for he served as the fitness instructor to France's Baron Rothschild, King George of Greece, Crown Prince Frederick (who became the King of Norway), the prince of Wales (who became King Edward of England), Princess Dagmar (who ultimately reigned as the Empress of Russia and was the mother of Czar Nicholas), the children of Denmark's King Christian, and numerous of Britain's nobles.

Attila's knowledge and charm proved just as winning on this side of the Atlantic. Upon opening a physical culture studio in New York City in 1894, he immediately attracted Big Apple luminaries to his establishment and was accepted into their elite social circles. Two years thereafter, when Attila embarked on his only matrimonial venture (at the age of 54)—marrying an 18-year-old client named Rosa Sanders—the ceremony was held at City Hall and presided over by Mayor Strong. Moreover, New York City newspapers declared the wedding to be one of the most prominent social events of 1896.

The list of legendary strength stars who were Attila's pupils was just as stellar as his roster of fitness clients among nobles. It would seem virtually impossible that one of Attila's protégés could outdo the old master in terms of winning friends and influence in lofty places, but one just may have. Due to the exceptional impact he registered as a strongman and showman in England at music halls and vaudeville theaters, and later here in America with the Ziegfeld Follies, Eugen Sandow was accepted as an equal by nobility, politicians of the highest rank, and renowned public figures worldwide. Far from a charismatic "muscular conversation piece," the Prussian powerhouse was a reform-minded activist who used his lofty contacts and considerable personal fortune to introduce much-needed services in Britain's public schools—services such as regular medical and dental checkups, school lunch programs for underprivileged children, regular physical education, and classes in health and hygiene.

A vivid example of the widespread acceptance and respect Sandow commanded is chronicled in David Webster's *The Iron Game*—must reading for anyone with even the slightest interest in the general topic of strength and those extraordinary individuals who comprise its heritage: "Great kings, presidents and emperors from all over the world sought his [Sandow's] friendship and exchanged gifts. His book, *Life Is Movement*, was received with great enthusiasm by no less than nine kings and queens and many more princes. Presidents William Taft and Woodrow Wilson, the clergy, physicians and people from all walks of life acclaimed this work. . . ."

BACK TO THE FUTURE

Just how far back in time does recognition of the value of resistance exercise extend? Interior walls of Egyptian tombs carry illustrations denoting the practice of swinging exercises employing stone or lead weights. Archeological examination of ruins in ancient India show that this culture engaged in similar forms of physical conditioning. Moreover, mosaics on Sicilian architecture dating back to the third century A.D. depict both males and females using weights.

Perhaps more important to us today is the fact that by the middle of the sixteenth century, progressive schools in France and Germany were starting to view physical education via weight training as part of a more effective broad-based public school curriculum. In the ensuing 150 years or so, the concept that resistance exercise held therapeutic benefits continued to surface. Published in 1728, John Paugh's book, *A Physiological, Theoretic and Practical Treatise on the Utility of Muscular Exercise for Restoring the Power of the Limbs*, showcased actual dumbbell exercises. And by the latter part of the 1700s, a German named Johann Besedow opened an academy for the in-depth study of physical education. Among the courses offered was a regimen of lighter exercises using sandbags.

Milo of Crotona (Greece) is often given credit for discovering the Overload Principle of progressive resistance exercise, thanks to his practice of back-squatting and lifting a bovine from calfhood until it had grown to a bull. Of course, as the animal matured in size and strength, Milo's muscular strength increased strikingly in compensation.

While Milo may have stumbled onto this fundamental tenet of physiology, Iron Game historians typically credit Archibald MacLaren with being the first to articulate and seriously scrutinize the concept during the mid-1860s. Possessing degrees in medicine and gymnastics—a common academic background for those interested in physiology in that day—the Scotsman's private salon in Oxford, England, provided him plenty of opportunity to engage in trial and error. MacLaren was supremely methodical in his experimental endeavors, even taking before-and-after photos of subjects to measure progress.

In reading about MacLaren and his research methods, one can come away with the impression that he viewed his mission as finding the definitive training method for maximum productivity. In fact, he authored highly publicized papers assessing the various known systems of bodily exercise of the time. Ironic, isn't it, that almost 150 years after MacLaren, the physiology-research community has grown to untold numbers producing incomprehensible amounts of data and yet we still can't conclusively determine the most productive weight training procedures?

Nonetheless, MacLaren's drive, tenacity, and vision ultimately caught the attention of the British government, which hired him to oversee the physical training of its army. The weight training portion of his program for preparedness consisted of eight exercises with dumbbells and seven with a barbell. These movements remained a staple in the training of the British military for years until Eugen Sandow became Great Britain's national fitness role model. He upgraded MacLaren's program somewhat by giving greater depth and meaning to the Overload Principle. Iron Game historians also tend to put a star next to MacLaren's name because he is considered the first instructor who actually demanded genuine effort or exertion from his pupils when exercising.

MUSCULAR CHRISTIANITY

Often with cultural trends, a singular phenomenon can incubate simultaneously in several different parts of the world. While interest in attaining physical strength was clearly in vogue in Europe in the mid-nineteenth century, America was on the verge of a similar explosion. Several factors coalesced to create this strength-friendly climate. For one, Old World textbooks on exercise written in the preceding century were translated and published in the United States. Also, as Europeans immigrated to the United States, they brought their cultural pastimes and passions with them. Note the massive influx of Germans in 1848 who were, as a group, fond of lifting heavy dumbbells and Indian clubs. Of course, this prompted the need for commercial gymnasiums and other styles of service clubs where recreational fitness activities were offered in large urban population centers.

As people made the transition from a vigorous agricultural lifestyle to a more sedentary city existence, many believed that Americans were starting to decline both physically and morally. Social reformers who shared this belief initiated what became known as the Muscular Christianity movement.

At the same time, itinerant professional strongmen were just beginning to appear with circuses and at variety entertainment venues.

THE AMERICAN SAMSON

As these powerful social forces united, Dr. George Barker Windship—a nationally known health reformer—supplied the movement with a prominent figure to rally around. A Harvard-trained physician, Windship lectured widely on the value of good health. However, his major thrust was radically different from other speakers of the day who typically espoused light calisthenics, vegetarianism, and moderation in all pursuits of life. Instead Windship stressed the need to maximize the human body's physical strength as comprehensively and symmetrically as possible. He also provided standard tips concerning hygiene, nutrition, and ventilation. As a matter of fact, Windship adopted the motto "strength is health."

The good doctor's myriad lectures contained considerable information on the extraordinary long-term advantages associated with the practice of systematic weight training. His exercise prescription included staunch recommendations for the use of the heaviest weights possible in accordance with one's present level of conditioning and the directive to increase resistance whenever possible. Additionally, exercise periods were best to be of limited duration, not to exceed one hour. And the last of Windship's maxims was that obtaining sufficient rest before engaging in the next bout of weight exercise was of pivotal importance.

Windship's actual exercise selection could only be labeled as the epitome of abbreviated training, focusing initially (in 1854) almost exclusively on very short-range leg and back movements like the hand-and-thigh lift, harness lift, hip lift, and their close cousin the partial deadlift. One need not be extremely grounded in Iron Game history to recognize that this cadre of movements was a page directly out of the book of eighteenth-century strongmen. From the beginning, the huge poundages these partial movements permitted simply captivated Windship, fulfilling him emotionally as well as physically.

In 1858 Windship incorporated the use of heavy dumbbell training into his repertoire. Although at first a pair of 50-pound dumbbells was beyond his capabilities in the overhead press, within three years the 5′7″, 150-pound physician could press overhead a pair of 100s simultaneously to arms' length. No, these statistics on Windship are not a misprint. In light of his smallish size, how curious it seems that he was widely recognized as the American Samson (not to mention his reputation as the strongest man in the world).

Enigmatic though he was, Dr. Windship's lectures were erudite and insightful. However, the real catalyst of his renown was his post-lecture lifting exhibitions where he handled weights ranging from 1,200 to 1,800 pounds depending upon the particular movement demonstrated. Also, he would occasionally engage in a head-to-head strength contest with a worthy local opponent.

Windship's cultural impact crescendoed in the 1860s as the short-range, heavy-duty style of partial deadlift (sometimes done straddling the bar)—which became popularly known as the health lift—resonated with the American public. Predictably, copycat marketers sprang up. Not only did Windship and his imitators usher in an explosion of for-profit studios devoted to the health lift in major metropolitan areas, but similar strength-testing machines appeared in parlors, offices, and schools everywhere.

One of Windship's coattail riders, David Butler, deserves a quick mention. Like Windship, he resided in Boston, promoted the health lift—although he utilized the commercial phrase *centerlifting*—manufactured machines for its practice, suggested that the movement be done with ultraheavy weights, and recommended its practice to both sexes. However, the regimens he promoted at his gymnasiums were arguably more rounded and contained elements that were unique and progressive for that time. For example, three of the four phases of a Butler workout consisted of four successively heavier single-repetition attempts with a generous rest in between exertions. In the case of the health or centerlift, the downtime between single lifts was five minutes.

Even on the commencing pulley exercise—which was deemed a warm-up—the progression was the same. Of course, the health lift (second in the sequence) and the one-hand jerk with a dumbbell (the third movement) were done similarly. Trainees were instructed to increase the weight at each station in successive workouts, which in the case of the health lift was a 5- to 10-pound increment.

Realizing that tangible results would keep the public coming back and that all things have at least temporary limits, Butler counseled his pupils in fundamental poundage cycling. Using the health lift as an example, when practitioners reached a poundage plateau they were to reduce their training weight by 50 to 100 pounds and gradually start increasing the poundage again over the weeks until they had gone beyond their former ceiling.

And what became of the health-lift craze? It was steaming along quite well until the ever-enigmatic Dr. Windship died suddenly of a massive stroke in September 1876 at the age of 42. Opponents of heavy lifting seized on the occurrence to publicly debunk the "strength is health" philosophy with scare tactics. This was sufficient to cripple the health-lift industry/movement, prompting many dyed-in-the-wool lifters to question the longevity factor associated with strength training. Very probably Windship's abrupt passing gave rise to the longstanding myth that strongmen die young.

Wrapping up this passage on Dr. Windship, he is deserving of the Father of American Weightlifting moniker that has been attached to his name. At the same time, his equipmental introductions—verifiable via government patent—solidify his position as a true American original. These vanguard items would include: a graduating plate-loading dumbbell capable of expedient adjustment from 8 to 101 pounds in half-pound increments; a device for partial movements allowing the weight to be raised via a yoke or handle for the hands and later a multi-station gym that featured a lifting platform for the partial movements, cables for exercising the chest, a rowing unit, and a chin bar. Windship also developed a hydraulic strength training device utilizing air pressure for resistance.

Although this may appear to be a considerable amount of space devoted to Windship, it by no means plumbs the full depths of his achievements and impact. Hence, additional examination is recommended. The most complete single source on Windship I have ever encountered is found in the Volume 3, number 1 (September 1993) issue of *Iron Game History*. (This publication can be obtained through the Todd-McLean Collection, Department of Kinesiology, Room 107, Anna Hiss Gym, A2000, The University of Texas, Austin, TX 78712.)

WEIGHTLIFTING COMPETITIONS

To twentieth-century strength devotees, the phrase *weightlifting competition* connotes a contest involving the performance of either the Olympic lifts (snatch and clean and jerk) or the powerlifts (bench press, squat, and deadlift) using a barbell. However, historical documentation shows that weightlifting competitions took place as far back as the sixth century B.C. in Greece, employing slabs of stone or boulders, which were lifted in various ways or sometimes hoisted overhead and thrown for distance.

Within many cultures of the world, the tradition of rock or stone lifting has been passed down through the ages. Even at the dawn of the twentieth century, it was very popular among the French-speaking provinces of Canada. Of course, the Germanic cultures embraced the art of stone lifting, excelling at deadlifting slabs in excess of 500 pounds while utilizing only one or two fingers (in the case of the more prodigious practitioners). And the custom of stone lifting remains strong to this day in the Basque quarter of Spain.

When it comes to exhibiting heroic strength with huge stones, the Scottish have no equal. This culture's most renowned strength implements are the legendary Dinnie Stones—a pair of ultrachallenging boulders whose combined weight reaches 785 pounds. They are named after their initial master Donald Dinnie. Matching prowess via the stones has been a part of the Highland Games format for nearly two centuries with much honor and reward going to the champions.

Stone lifting has received renewed exposure in more recent times thanks to its inclusion in televised professional strongman contests. In fact, at one of these titanic showdowns, contestants were required to escort the Dinnie Stones over the five-yard-long bridge that Donald is said to have carried them across . . . but the contemporary strongmen did it against the clock!

So when did structured lifting competitions begin using weights of a kind we today would recognize? Historian David Webster, author of *The Iron Game*, gave credit as follows: "It was in Central Europe, however, that weightlifting as a sport was initiated . . . Britain seems to have taken the lead in March, 1891, when the first ever international championships were organized in London. Competitors from Italy, Belgium, Britain and Germany took part and this competition was decided by repetition lifting rather than on an aggregate total as is now the custom." Furthermore, the contested lifts involved only dumbbells.

Amateur weightlifting was part of the 1896 Olympic Games format. However, a decided dearth of contestants—only two contested lifts and a tie for first at the Games in Athens—left such a poor impression that the sport was not part of the Olympics again until 1904 in St. Louis. Unfortunately, the competition again did not inspire much enthusiasm.

Ironically, support for weightlifting was much better at an outlaw (unsanctioned by the International Olympic Committee) event staged by the country of Greece in 1906. By comparison, a veritable cavalcade of talented strongmen from

Austria, Belgium, Denmark, France, Germany, and, of course, the host country took part. Greatly aiding this sudden interest in competitive weightlifting was no doubt the quantity and quality of powerhouses coming out of the "beer garden" cultures, which spawned a strong mix of sports and socialization.

In spite of—or perhaps because of—this highwater showing, the sport of weightlifting was omitted from the quadrennial games of 1908 and 1912. Then, all global athletic contests were interrupted by World War I, resuming again in 1920 with the Olympics in Belgium. This seemed the precise fresh start that weightlifting needed. However, its likelihood of prospering was greatly enhanced thanks to the formation of the International Weightlifting Federation, which gave the activity much needed organization, standardization, and stability. Contested lifts at the time included the one-hand snatch, one-hand clean and jerk (with the opposite hand), and the two-hand clean and jerk, all done with a barbell. The three classic Olympic lifts—the press, snatch, and clean and jerk—were adopted at the 1928 Olympics and remained the established order until the 1976 Games when the press was dropped from the format.

Barbells with revolving sleeves made their debut at the 1928 Olympics. Hence, some of the numbers attributed to star lifters of this turn-of-the-century time look somewhat wanting by today's standards. Lest one doubts the degree of body power these ancestral strongmen possessed, get yourself a nonrevolving globe barbell of less than 7 feet in length and see how much you can elevate overhead.

THE GOLDEN AGE OF PROFESSIONAL STRONGMANISM

Of course many of these early-twentieth-century goliaths abandoned the world of amateur competitive weightlifting in favor of the more lucrative touring professional strongman circuit. Many amassed handsome fortunes and, as noted earlier, gained wide social acceptance. America was indeed a land of opportunity for this high-profile group.

It goes without saying that traditional lifting movements and feats were part of the standard strongman repertoire. However, because this occupation was rightly viewed as another form of entertainment, flamboyant showmanship and resplendent attire were almost as important to performers as inordinate strength. Predictably, climactic finale feats became more colossal (and dangerous) over time. For example, various supporting feats using automobiles were quite dramatic. Of course, one-upmanship was always in vogue so the next wrinkle was to lie on one's back while leg pressing support ramps across which a vehicle loaded with passengers would be driven. While such a feat was showstopping to be sure, at least two strongmen performers sustained broken legs when the ramps that they were supporting collapsed during a presentation. It would seem that some of these strongmen believed in the adage "No guts, no glory!"

One other point worth making is that not all of the performers were men. Estonia's Maria Loorberg was a major hit with circuses and carnivals in several Russian provinces in the early 1900s thanks to her ability to juggle a pair of 72-pound dumbbells simultaneously, lift a 145-pound man in each hand and—while in the laying leg press position—support on her feet a total of 1,986 pounds of live weight.

The tiny country of Belgium produced two professional strongwomen of note as well. "Athleta," as noted by historian David Willoughby in the February–March 1983 edition of *IronMan* magazine, possessed a biceps measurement of just over 16½ inches, a neck of 17½ inches, and a best in the clean and jerk of just over 200 pounds. She gave birth to a trio of lovely, although somewhat smaller, daughters who also toured professionally on the strength circuit.

Although records concerning Gertrude Leandros—Belgium's other gal powerhouse from that time period—are not as revealing, she nevertheless was most noted for the many different ways, as well as the ease, with which she routinely lifted her 132-pound stage partner. Making this feat all the more incredible was the fact that at her zenith, Ms. Leandros weighed a scant 28 pounds more than her partner.

Not to be outdone, the United States had its own distaff strength stars. Josephine Blatt's signature was a backlift with 20 grown men employed as resistance. Stop and think: That adds up to at least 3,000 pounds.

Unquestionably, though, the empress of all turn-of-the-century strongwomen was Kati Brumbach Sandwina. Inheriting her predisposition for extreme size and strength from her father—who himself hailed from a long line of Bavarian professional strongmen—Kati was 6′1″ and at her zenith weighed between 210 and 220 pounds. She possessed a biceps measurement of 16 inches, a waist of 27 inches, calves stretching the tape to 17 inches, thighs measuring 27 inches, and wrists and ankles of 8 and 11 inches respectively. The power that flowed from this package was so incredible that she was without peer among her professional counterparts. No touring strongman of her bodyweight could match her in standard weightlifting feats or tests involving odd objects. Officially, the great Kati did a *one-arm* clean and jerk with 177 pounds and a two-arm clean and jerk with 286 pounds. This latter number was by no means her true limit as she subsequently did 310 in good form during an exhibition.

Extraordinary as these performances seem, her most astounding feat was the daily shouldering of a 1,200-pound cannon off the back of a wagon prior to carrying it around the center ring of the Barnum and Bailey Circus. This never failed to elicit thunderous applause from the audience.

Renowned on every continent, Sandwina retired in 1941 at the age of 57, whereupon she and her husband opened a bar and grill in Queens, New York. Even into her middle 60s, she would entertain patrons on Saturday nights by bending stout iron bars into pretzels and doing repetition handstand presses without any assistance to maintain her balance. Small wonder that when Sandwina was in her prime, many traveling strongmen instructed their managers never to book them in the same city—no matter how large the city—against her. (For those interested, a thorough profile of Kati Sandwina can be found in the December 1965 issue of *Strength & Health* magazine.)

As the mid–nineteenth century became a heyday for strength training activities in the United States, interest in other related forms of heavy athletics peaked as well. This led naturally to the need for some organization and structure regarding these increasingly popular events. Working in conjunction with the already well-established Caledonian Societies (professional Scottish Highland Games athletes) a trio of weightlifters (W. B. Curtis, John Babcock, and Henry Buermeyer) founded the New York Athletic Club (NYAC) in 1868. While this organization came into existence for the express purpose of promulgating the acceptance of track and field sports, the NYAC was America's first native athletic club.

Because the Scottish-style games enjoyed tremendous support in many pockets of North America—typically drawing crowds of up to 20,000–30,000 spectators—the NYAC quickly developed a friendly rivalry with the New York Caledonian Society. Aside from the fact that this alliance marked the introduction of formal track and field competitions in this country, it's significant to note that the Amateur Athletic Union (AAU), a broad-spanning sports sanctioning body of international scope even today, sprang from this early cooperative effort.

Fast-forwarding approximately 100 years from the aforementioned period, weightlifting and weight training had developed an image problem among many sectors of the American public. Reviewing just some of the history outlined here would suggest this turn of events to be improbable: the legacy of professional strongmanism that thrived through at least the first quarter of the twentieth century; the leadership role that weightlifters had assumed in the overall organization of amateur athletics and the acceptance of heavy weightlifting as a training adjunct for at least power-type athletic events; America's enduring penchant for physical improvement, which at a minimum embraced light to moderate dumbbell training; and, as has been demonstrated, the public enthusiasm which has expanded periodically to include ultraheavy training, à la the partial movement craze of the Windship era. Furthermore, the 1940s and 1950s were a boom period for Olympic-style weightlifting in America; in fact, the last such distinguished bright spot.

Perplexing as this seems in light of history, stigmas and negative stereotypes had become attached to the good name of weight training. Again, longevity of the serious practitioner was a frequent issue. Critics apparently contended that the strain of heavy lifting overburdened the heart and, in the long run, lowered life expectancy.

However, in no realm of American society was the bias against weight training so rife and the naysayers so staunch as among the fraternity of athletic coaches. Of course, their complaints were based strictly on functional considerations. The two main fears expressed centered on a deterioration of flexibility from the use of weights—a condition commonly referred to as *muscle-bound*—and the loss of natural speed thanks to a supra-hypertrophied state of musculature.

Thanks to mountains of physiological research, we now know that such accusations were the complete opposite of the actual truth. However, do not underestimate the power and clout such adversarial stances exerted on the general public, especially when harbored by prestigious institutions like the medical and athletic coaching communities.

BARBELLS ON CAMPUS

So how did sports and society journey from this valley of ignominy to the uncontested acceptance that weight training enjoys today? Like many cultural trends, the renaissance of weight training began on college campuses across America. Around the middle of this century, younger, more progressive researchers specializing in human physiology as well as collegiate physical educators, began to question the negative party line.

Of course, the great discovery concerning resistance exercise was made in slightly different ways from university to university. And in the interest of full disclosure, it must be pointed out that some researchers entered their investigations figuring to prove the negatives correct after all. Yet, in fairness, once their inaccurate beliefs were dispelled by the scientific method, these individuals became some of the staunchest weight training advocates anywhere. Just such a scenario is part of the history behind the acceptance of barbells in physical education and athletics at the State University of Iowa. Two highly regarded research-minded professors at the school named Dr. C. H. McCloy and Dr. Arthur Wendler put weight training under the microscope in 1943, fully expecting to prove that over time, innate flexibility and coordination were spoiled by its practice. After absorbing the scant literature available at the time on the subject, they assumed the role of guinea pigs and embarked on a rigorous weight training schedule to experience the results firsthand.

McCloy and Wendler may have commenced as doubters but their progress was so compelling that they were fervent converts in short order. Their zeal for systematic barbell exercise grew into a passion to explore the full range of benefits it could produce. Perhaps more importantly, their pioneering scientific scrutiny of progressive resistance exercise ushered in a dynamic era of weight-training activity on the Hawkeye campus. By the late 1950s, eight classes in weight training were offered each semester for academic credit. Mastery of the Olympic lifts was also a part of the curriculum. An adapted program of physical education addressed the needs of students in special circumstances (i.e., post-operative conditions, physical handicaps, and corrective and therapy situations). Competitive lifting was part of the intramural athletics program, and barbells and dumbbells became a substantial part of the recreational fitness program for the student body. Weight training was thoroughly integrated into the training programs of all varsity sports. In short, the efforts of McCloy and Wendler inspired generations of graduate students to specialize in the area of physiological research. By the way, if the late Dr. McCloy's name seems familiar to readers, it may be because he authored a book entitled *Weight Training for Athletes.*

To reiterate, the circumstances under which weight training was accepted varied from campus to campus. However, in almost every case there was at least one highly respected figure present pressing the cause. At the University of Notre Dame, this pivotal person was unquestionably Father B. H. B. Lange. In many ways he was the quintessential spokesperson for weight training. This strongman/priest exuded physical robustness and power well into his later years. Moreover, his extensive academic laurels and professional acumen brought credibility to any position or cause he championed.

Father Lange's commanding presence slowly began winning the important folks on campus over to weights as early as 1922. It's seldom remembered that Knute Rockne was also Notre Dame's head track coach at that time. Rockne, a long-time friend of Lange's, became convinced that barbell work, if intelligently applied, enhanced athletic ability. Hence, he turned his field athletes over to Lange for expert instruction.

In 1935, Lange took over an old unwanted building on campus and stocked it with what in that day was a startling array of equipment. Most of it he built with his own hands. There were also tons of iron plates and steel bars that he purchased with his own money or acquired via donations. Over the ensuing 25 years—despite receiving absolutely no official endorsement of any kind from Notre Dame University—Lange estimated that more than 6,000 regular trainees passed through the doors of his iron den. Included in this number were athletes from a wide spectrum of varsity sports. They were referred to Father Lange by their coaches even though his facility was not attached to the athletic department in any way.

Finally in 1960—following the lead of several other major universities—Notre Dame formally recognized the value of weight training, incorporating it into the physical education curriculum—and the university gave Father Lange a brand-new facility to boot.

The *esprit de corps* that Father Lange brought to Notre Dame, higher education, and weight training prompts much admiration—more than can be documented in a solitary chapter. The strength coaching profession truly should regard him as a founding father.

The first college campus in America to make barbells and dumbbells available to students may have been the University of Texas at Austin. Back in 1913, a wealthy alumnus bought a couple of barbell sets and some dumbbells from the Milo Barbell Company in Philadelphia (the driving force in American weightlifting circles during the early 1900s) and donated them to the university. Initially it was a very small circle who availed themselves of the donated iron, but numbered among this in-crowd was a varsity wrestler and handball player named Roy McLean. Noting that his athletic proficiency improved as his physical prowess with the weights improved, McLean instituted the school's first classes in weight training when he was named assistant director of physical training and athletics at the school in 1919.

However, McLean found it anything but a cakewalk when it came to spreading his zeal for progressive resistance exercise among the school's athletic population. Virtually en masse, the Longhorn coaches put their collective foot down and vehemently prohibited their players from using barbells and dumbbells. A rebel with a cause, McLean persisted, keeping meticulous records on the students in his classes as well as on some athletes that he inveigled to train in secret. McLean soon was able to silence any coaching critic with the hard evidence. Weight training then exploded at the school.

Since the green light was given to weight training at the University of Texas, McLean's name has been synonymous with weight training activities at the school. In fact, a fabulous library and museum devoted to the history of the Iron Game was built there and bears the name of the late physical educator along with that of one of his pupils, Dr. Terry Todd.

Suffice it to say that by the mid- to late 1950s, colleges and universities from coast to coast were implementing resistance-exercise programs to enhance athletic performance, to augment for-credit physical education courses, rehabilitation, and therapy; and to provide positive after-school recreation.

Still, in researching this spread of weight training across America's campuses, it appeared that Louisiana State University (LSU) had virtually no peer in embracing it so completely. Like most major institutions of the time, the folks in Baton Rouge recognized the potency of the new strength and conditioning dimension, incorporating it immediately into conditioning classes, recreational activities, and across-the-board athletic training; meaning that basketball players, baseball players, and short- and long-distance runners were using weights to improve their athletic performance right along with the field athletes and football players. Hence, it was not unusual to find athletes from finesse sports who could put up some good numbers in the basic barbell-dumbbell exercises.

At LSU, though, weight training reached an altogether higher level than it had at other major universities. So rampant was the use of weights on campus that small weight rooms were installed in every dorm—a practice virtually unheard of in the 1950s. Granted, this step was implemented to save school property from damage as students frequently smuggled weights into their rooms to train after hours; however, the fact that school administrators opted to offer a structured alternative—as opposed to taking the easy way out and ordering a ban on all weights in dorms—indicates a very progressive mind-set.

Formal Olympic weightlifting meets and odd-lift contests took place regularly on campus. The LSU Olympic lifting team reached such a level of accomplishment that they were a major force in open AAU-sanctioned events. Some of these platform powerhouses were student athletes who only performed the Olympic lifts to augment their sports performance. They were not even full-time Olympic lifters. By the same token, there were LSU grads who went on to national weightlifting honors.

Also doing much to promote and advance the pro weight environment at LSU was a dynamic research program spearheaded by Dr. Francis A. Drury, Dr. Jerry Barham, and others such as athletic trainer Martin Broussard who possessed a seemingly insatiable desire to be on the cutting edge of all aspects of the exciting new vista. As a matter of fact, Drury and company once engaged in a pilot program with Dr. John Ziegler and Bob Hoffman—founder of the York® Barbell Company—studying the possibilities of using isometric contractions (static exercise) to build strength. Viewed by many as the next great step in the evolution of strength training, isometric exercise fascinated many noted researchers. Dr. McCloy of the State University of Iowa also performed extensive studies on this subject matter, particularly with regard to rehabilitation cases—including those involving heart attack patients.

Another name at the center of the weight training revolution at LSU in the 1950s was Alvin Roy, though, ironically, he was not a staff member at the school. Undoubtedly a strength and conditioning coach with a pedigree, this Baton Rouge fitness-center operator was setting up programs for high schools, colleges, and individuals long before it was fashionable. By the early 1960s alone, Roy had gotten thriving strength and conditioning programs up and running for footballers at Georgia Tech, University of Florida, LSU, University of Alabama, Southern Louisiana College, and University of Mississippi just to name a few. During that same time frame, he served as the personal trainer to such nationally known athletes as 1958 Heisman Trophy winner Billy Cannon—who ran a 9.4-second 100-yard dash when he weighed 215 pounds—NFL All-Pro running back Jim Taylor of the Green Bay Packers, and NBA all-star Bob Pettit.

In addition to serving as the conditioning coach with numerous NFL teams, there's no way of telling exactly how many young men Alvin Roy guided to their physical pinnacle—just as there's no way of determining how many he inspired to make strength coaching their life's work.

OF STRENGTH AND HEALTH

No discussion of the ebb and flow of progressive resistance exercise within the American culture would be complete without mention of Robert Collins Hoffman, who functioned as a very high-profile point man in the culturewide campaign to restore weight training to a bona fide fitness medium. Indeed, his drive and intensity in defense of weights seemed to increase exponentially in the face of criticism from naysayers.

Hoffman's singleness of purpose may have sprung from the fact that, as a young man, he had personally experienced the profound effect of resistance training on his own athletic performance. He was very much a crusader.

Hoffman promoted weight training through his publication *Strength & Health* magazine. *S&H*, as it became known in Iron Game circles, served as a rallying point for all supporters of the weight training movement, courting and reporting the phenomenon as it advanced across the American landscape—especially as it moved through institutions of higher learning. Around 1960, this magazine introduced a new column entitled "Barbells on Campus" to chronicle the explosion. Alumni of colleges and universities large and small who desire to trace the weight training heritage of their alma mater might very well be able to do so via back issues of *S&H*. For example, of the schools previously spotlighted, the University of Texas is featured in the January 1960 issue; Notre Dame, April 1960; State University of Iowa, June 1960; and Louisiana State University, July 1960.

Also detailed within the pages of *S&H* are scads of personal weight training histories of professional and amateur athletes from just about every sport imaginable. True aficionados of strength training will find the comparisons between conditioning programs from, say, the 1950s and those of similar sports in the 1970s or 1980s quite revealing. There are also offerings from noted researchers and physical educators. For example, there are articles by Notre Dame's Father Lange in issues from 1947 to 1949.

Those who wish to investigate the roots of modern-day athletic strength training but who don't have access to a collection of *Strength & Health* magazine can experience much of the flavor and sense of profound discovery by perusing Bob Hoffman's book *Better Athletes Through Weight Training*.

THE JONES ERA

By the dawning of the 1970s, the question of whether or not athletes, and to a large extent the general populace, should train via progressive resistance exercise had become passé. Thanks in large part to the emergence of Nautilus® exercise machines and the writings and presentations of the firm's founder Arthur Jones, the relevant question was now how did people ever train without them?

Exercise machines were not really new, for in the 1830s, James Chiosso had built large units employing shrouded weight stacks and pulleys that permitted the performance of curls, squats, cable crossovers, and other movements commonly done by modern-day weight trainers. As such, Chiosso's creations were the forerunners of today's selector circuit units. Further, Universal® multi-station weight machines predate Nautilus® equipment.

Merely offering the exercise public another equipmental alternative was far from Jones's full intent. He set out to challenge the status quo and conventional practices regarding strength training. In order to back his assertions, Jones funded research and development to a hefty tune and he was not shy about publicizing the findings. Suddenly many new concepts, terms, and considerations were creeping into the parlance of the strength training community. "Strength curve," "pre-stretch," "inroads," "metabolic conditioning," and "speed of movement" were just some of the newfound topics of conversation in physiology circles. However, of even greater magnitude, Jones was the first in modern times to introduce the concept of variable resistance via machines.

As one might imagine, many in the established exercise community found Jones and his pronouncements contradicting just about every ideal that they held sacrosanct more than a little irritating. And in keeping with his irascible nature, Jones never shied away from criticizing what he believed were outdated, inefficient, and, in some cases, injury-inducing procedures that had been passed along as gospel. The battlelines were quickly drawn.

Admire him or despise him, during his heyday at Nautilus®, Jones rates as an unqualified success in terms of bringing his machines and ideas to the attention of the public at large. There's no question that promises of noticeable results via thrice-weekly 20-minute workouts brought many to commercial workout facilities who probably would not have come otherwise. Moreover, Jones's success in establishing the Nautilus® name worldwide was extraordinary, as countless commercial workout facilities bearing the corporate moniker and utilizing the one-set-to-failure and allied principles began to spring up everywhere. These trends and techniques also found considerable acceptance among professional athletes and sports teams.

Especially during the heyday of Nautilus®, Arthur Jones undeniably exerted a dramatic impact on the overall vitality of progressive resistance exercise. And much like Bob Hoffman, who was possibly this century's foremost advocate of free-weight exercise, Jones was an enormous force in creating and shaping the contemporary fitness industry.

AN AGE OF INFORMATION

The latter part of the twentieth century is commonly described as an age of information. Technological sophistication has certainly changed the face of the educational process regarding weight training. Whereas trainees in the early part of the twentieth century had to rely on train-by-mail instructors, today's trainees can train via the Internet, as there is an enormous amount of quality conditioning information on the World Wide Web.

The overwhelming demand for qualified weight training guidance has spawned another kind of relevant information outlet: service organizations. The first such organization dates back to approximately 1977. The National Strength and Conditioning Association (NSCA) was originally based in Lincoln, Nebraska, but in more recent times has relocated to Colorado Springs, Colorado. Initially, this organization consisted of an amalgam of high-profile college strength coaches and researchers who foresaw the increasing acceptance of weight training throughout our culture. They also saw the corresponding opportunities this acceptance would present and sought to bring maximum credibility to this specialized type of coaching or instructional position. Soon educational criteria were established and certification programs became available. Later on, the NSCA broadened its scope by offering certification opportunities for personal fitness trainers.

Other organizations large and small have followed the lead of the NSCA and offered certification programs to our credentials-conscious society. One particularly noteworthy example is the American College of Sports Medicine.

Sages contend that one should consult history when attempting to predict the future. What does the past foretell about the state of strength/fitness conditioning training in the twenty-first century? On one hand, a glance at the traditional amateur iron sports in America causes one to wonder: Olympic weightlifting is expanding to include a women's competitive program worldwide. Yet, the number of competitors in the United States (of all ages and both sexes) still totals less than 2,000. Powerlifting enjoys much better numbers but suffers from organizational splits, thanks to issues of steroid testing, allowable competition gear, international affiliation, judging standards, and that old demon known as politics in general. And then there's bodybuilding. If the direction and stability of professional bodybuilding is any indication, what does it say when Arnold Schwarzenegger—one of bodybuilding's own legendary figures who is not far removed from the sport at all—suggests in print that the physiques of certain current male luminaries are examples of muscular mass run amok (or words to that effect) and that a continuation of this trend will kill bodybuilding commercially. If memory serves, this same complaint has dogged women's bodybuilding from the start. Now, it has spilled over to the men.

Take heart, though, as all is not bleak on the contest front—especially for athletically inclined women. Fitness contests featuring competitors who possess a very balanced physical package of agility, flexibility, and strength appear to have a very promising future.

There's no escaping the fact that in this society, trends—or more precisely, the longevity of trends—are judged and measured by their ability to generate dollars. On this score, the fitness field appears quite secure in its role as a multimillion-dollar industry. Of course, its close cousin, the nutrition/supplement industry, is even more fiscally healthy, qualifying as a multibillion-dollar entity.

Yes, there's a fair amount of volatility on the corporate fitness front with many of the larger firms striving for growth by acquisition via the assimilation of smaller or moderate-sized companies. Still, there's no logical reason to believe strength and fitness conditioning activities will subside in the twenty-first century. They have become too much a part of our cultural lifestyle.

Perhaps the bigger question is how will technological advances impact the art of strength and fitness training? Will they be viewed as upgrades or encroachments? That's the fun thing about the strength and fitness community: It's a big tent full of eclectic opinions. Some will clamor for virtual exercise, while others will try to lift virtually anything that's heavy!

REFERENCES

Drury, F. A., M. Broussard, A. Roy, and B. Hoffman. 1962. *Functional Isometric Contraction for Football.* York, PA: Bob Hoffman Foundation.

Todd, J. 1993. Strength is health: George Barker Windship and the first American weight training boom. *Iron Game History* 3 (1): 3–14.

Wayne, R. 1997. Even Arnold is disgusted! *Muscular Development* (December): 176.

Webster, D. 1976. *The Iron Game—an Illustrated History of Weightlifting.* Printed by John Geddes (Printers).

Willoughby, D. 1983. "What Is a Strongwoman Physique?" *IronMan* 42 (3): 34–35.

This chapter is dedicated to my wife, Kim, and our daughters, Kristin and Rebecca.

2

Strength Training Q & A: What the Research Says

Ted Lambrinides, Ph.D.
Director of Exercise Science
Thomas More College
Krestview Hills, Kentucky

Questions abound in strength training. This chapter covers some questions—and answers—that are of special interest.

What effect does strength training have on metabolism?

To answer this question, the term *metabolism* must first be defined. According to the *Dictionary of Sport and Exercise Science* (Anshel 1991), metabolism is defined as "chemical changes that utilize energy and result in tissue and compound building (anabolism) or breakdown of substrates and release of energy (catabolism)." There are three ways in which strength training can alter metabolism: the workout session itself, the post-workout oxygen consumption, and the addition of new muscle mass.

The Workout Session

Muscles that contract under heavy loads require energy. They also produce heat as a by-product. While metabolism is increased by strength training, the exact amount varies depending upon the amount of muscle mass involved in an exercise and the level of resistance used. Obviously, a squat or leg press utilizes a greater amount of muscle mass than a bicep curl and, consequently, will have a greater energy cost. The metabolic rate (or energy expenditure) has been estimated to vary from 5 to 10 calories per minute, depending upon whether large or small muscle groups are involved in the exercise. Hunter and his colleagues (1988) investigated the influence of the resistance load on metabolic rate. Seventeen subjects performed a bench press at intensities ranging from 20 to 80 percent of a one-repetition maximum (1-RM). They found that the economy of the weight training exercise decreased as the resistance load increased. This indicates that there is less muscular efficiency with heavier weights and/or that stabilizing muscles participate more, which in turn increases the energy utilization during exercise. For example, the subjects used almost 12 times as much energy (calories) doing one repetition with 80 percent of the 1-RM as opposed to one repetition with 20 percent of the 1-RM—even though the work only increased by a magnitude of four. Within each bench-press load (20–80 percent) there was a strong correlation between the work performed and the energy expended. This finding is in agreement with research performed by Kuehl, Elliot, and Goldberg (1990), who found that the caloric expenditure during resistance training correlates with the total weight lifted. Hunter and his colleagues (1988) indicate that those individuals who are interested in body-composition changes should train at 60–80 percent of a 1-RM. The metabolic rate is higher at increased loads, which causes a greater number of calories to be utilized.

The Post-Workout Oxygen Consumption

There are several factors that influence the excess post-exercise oxygen consumption, including the resynthesis of creatine phosphate in the muscle, lactate removal, restoration of muscle and blood oxygen stores, increased body temperature, post-exercise elevation of the heart rate and breathing, and elevated hormone levels. Elliot, Goldberg, and Kuehl (1992) examined the post-exercise oxygen consumption of strength training exercise. Metabolic rate was measured for nine subjects after 40 minutes of cycling (at 80 percent of an individual's maximal heart rate), 40 minutes of circuit training (with 50 percent of an individual's 1-RM × 15 repetitions × 4 sets), 40 minutes of heavy resistance lifting (with 80–90 percent of an individual's 1-RM × 3–8 repetitions × 3 sets) and a control interval. All forms of exercise increased the metabolic rate immediately after exertion. For circuit training and heavy resistance lifting, the increase was also significant 30 minutes after exertion. The absolute total increment in caloric use after exertion was comparable among circuit training, heavy lifting, and cycling. However, cycling was less effective than both forms of weight training.

The energy cost or calories "burned" during the post-exercise period is relatively small. Some researchers have commented that the post-exercise effect is so negligible that it does not have a major role in weight control, i.e., it is not an efficient way to lose adipose tissue (body fat). However, the data of these same researchers suggest that the extra oxygen consumption following each of a typical monthly series of 15 exercise sessions (50 minutes at 50 percent of maximal oxygen uptake) could lead to a cumulative loss of 1 kilogram of adipose tissue; if such a rate of fat loss were sustained for 12 months, the individual concerned could have trimmed a not-so-insignificant 12 kilograms (or about 26.4 pounds) of fat from his or her body.

The other factor to consider during the post-exercise period is the fuel utilized. Strength training tends to use carbohydrate during the actual workout session. After a workout, however, more fat is used to meet the energy demands of the body. The more carbohydrate used during exercise, the more fat used after exercise. Research performed by Brooks and Gaesser (1980) as well as Bahr and Sejersted (1991) confirms that as the intensity of the exercise increases, there is a proportionate increase in fat utilization during the recovery phase. Recent research at Colorado State University (Melby et al. 1993) examined the effect of resistance training on post-exercise energy expenditure and resting metabolic rate. The study concluded that strenuous strength training could elevate metabolic rate for extended periods and that this enhanced metabolism is due to the oxidation of body fat.

The Addition of New Muscle Mass

It is well established that properly performed high-intensity strength training stimulates the development of muscle mass. The additional muscle mass alters metabolism in two ways. First, the resting metabolic rate is increased when one gains muscle mass. While the energy expenditure per pound of lean body mass does not change, the addition of more muscle mass means a larger energy expenditure or higher metabolism at rest.

Second, the more muscle mass one has, the greater the post-exercise oxygen consumption. When strength-trained individuals were compared to nontrained individuals, there was no difference in post-exercise oxygen consumption per pound of muscle. However, since strength training individuals have more muscle mass, they use more calories during the post-exercise period.

Conclusion: Strength training increases energy expenditure during a training session. The high-intensity or anaerobic nature of strength training is indicative of a high utilization of carbohydrates during a workout session. During the post-exercise recovery period, energy expenditure is elevated for a duration ranging from 2 to 15 hours. The increased energy demands are obtained by utilizing more calories—and a good portion of these calories come from fat stores.

The addition of muscle mass on an individual will cause an increase in the number of calories that are utilized at rest. So it is comforting to know that while one is exerting through a high-intensity workout, the hard work will result in a faster metabolism that continues to use calories even after the workout.

What effect does resistance training have on the cardiovascular system?

Resistance training can have many beneficial effects on the cardiovascular system. In studies performed on cardiac rehab patients, resistance training has been shown to increase time to exhaustion on the treadmill and stationary cycle and lower the product of the heart rate and blood pressure (i.e., heart rate × blood pressure) during activities such as holding a weighted object (e.g., a suitcase or briefcase) or walking while performing isometric exertion (McCartney et al. 1991; Goldberg, Elliot, and Kuehl 1994). Weak muscles contracting with a large percentage of their peak force can develop a sufficient internal pressure to limit local perfusion. Thus, in individuals with a compromised cardiovascular system, the skeletal muscles have a greater potential for improvement than the myocardium.

Research performed by Marcinik and coworkers (1991) at the University of Maryland showed that strength training substantially increased the lactate threshold. Additional research has shown that strength training has the potential to increase endurance performance, particularly that requiring fast-twitch fiber recruitment (Hickson, Rosenkoetter, and Brown 1980). These data do not demonstrate any negative performance effects of adding strength training to ongoing endurance training regimens.

What effect does resistance training have on blood cholesterol levels?

Evidence from epidemiological studies has demonstrated that low concentrations of total cholesterol and low-density lipoprotein (LDL) cholesterol and high levels of high-density lipoprotein (HDL) cholesterol are associated with a decreased prevalence of coronary artery disease (CAD). Clinical investigations have also demonstrated a reduced incidence of CAD when plasma LDL levels are reduced or HDL levels are increased.

Cholesterol is present in the body and serves many important functions; it is a component of cell membrane and nerve fibers and is required for the production of steroid hormones, bile acids, and vitamin D. In addition to that which is ingested, the body synthesizes approximately 1,000 milligrams of cholesterol each day. In fact, on the average, 65–70 percent of the cholesterol in the body is produced by the body itself. The biosynthesis of cholesterol occurs in nearly all cell types, but the liver and small intestine mucosa are the primary organs that produce cholesterol.

Triglycerides and cholesterol do not circulate freely in the plasma. They are carried in the bloodstream and bound to a protein; together they form a lipoprotein. The partitioning of cholesterol into its lipoprotein fractions is of great importance. The total cholesterol level represents the cholesterol contained in different lipoproteins, namely very low-density lipoproteins (VLDL), low-density lipoproteins, and high-density lipoproteins. The distribution of cholesterol among these various lipoproteins may be a more powerful predictor of heart disease than simply the total blood cholesterol level. The plasma total cholesterol is only weakly related to the risk of CAD and the best predictor may be the ratio of HDL to LDL or HDL to total cholesterol. The total cholesterol/HDL ratio is frequently used diagnostically. For example, two individuals may each have a blood cholesterol level of 240 milligrams per deciliter (mg/dl). If one of them has an HDL level of 80 mg/dl, then the total cholesterol/HDL ratio is 3.0, which represents average risk. If the other person has an HDL level of 24 mg/dl, the total cholesterol/HDL ratio is 10.4—more than twice the average risk. LDL and VLDL encourage cholesterol to remain in the circulation network by transporting it throughout the body to the cells, including the smooth muscle cells of the arterial walls, which frequently leads to narrowing of the arteries. The portion of total cholesterol in LDL is the primary atherogenic component of total blood cholesterol. The HDL apparently serves as a cholesterol scavenger by removing cholesterol from the periphery—including the arterial walls—and returning it to the liver, where it can be excreted as bile acids. The HDL may also interfere with the binding of LDL to the cell membrane. Because of the contrasting roles of these types of lipoprotein, HDL is frequently referred to as good cholesterol.

With this overview of cholesterol in mind, we must now examine how strength training can influence the various lipoproteins.

Research Showing a Positive Effect on Cholesterol Levels

In a study by Goldberg and associates (1984), eight women (mean age 27) and six men (mean age 33) who previously had been sedentary participated in a 16-week program of progressive resistance weight training. They used strength training machines three times a week on nonconsecutive days. Sessions lasted 45–60 minutes using a training protocol of three sets of 6–8 repetitions. The women demonstrated a 9.5 percent reduction in cholesterol, a 17.9 percent decrease in LDL cholesterol, a 4.8 percent increase in HDL cholesterol, and a 28.3 percent decrease in triglycerides. Ratios of total cholesterol/HDL cholesterol, and LDL/HDL were reduced 14.3 percent and 20.3 percent, respectively. Among men, LDL cholesterol was reduced 16.2 percent, HDL cholesterol was increased 15.8 percent, and there was an insignificant change in triglycerides. Ratios of total cholesterol/HDL cholesterol and LDL/HDL were lowered 21.6 percent and 28.9 percent, respectively.

Blessing and his colleagues (1987) utilized 33 male volunteers with an average age of approximately 45. All had lived relatively sedentary lives for several years prior to the study. They were divided into three groups: weight trainers, joggers, and controls. The weight-training group trained with three sets of 10 repetitions for weeks 1 through 6 and three sets of 5 repetitions for weeks 7 through 12. Both experimental groups increased lean body mass and decreased fat weight with no change in body weight. Serum HDL increased and total cholesterol/HDL ratio decreased significantly in both experimental groups compared to controls.

Ullrich, Reid, and Yeater (1987) studied 25 men before and after supervised weight training three times each week for eight weeks. The subjects' HDL increased significantly with training from 38.8 to 44.1 mg/dl, and calculated LDL decreased from 132 to 121 mg/dl. Triglyceride values were unchanged. The percentage of fat decreased by 4.6 kilograms after training. Maximal oxygen consumption increased significantly from 45.2 to 49.2 milliliters per kilogram per minute (ml/kg/min).

Hurley and his coworkers (1988) examined 11 healthy untrained males (average age 44) to determine the effects of 16 weeks of high-intensity strength training on the risk factors of CAD. The subjects trained three times per week on nonconsecutive days utilizing one set of 8–12 repetitions for the upper body and one set of 15–20 repetitions for the lower body. The training program resulted in a 13 percent increase in HDL, a 5 percent reduction in LDL, and an 8 percent decrease in the total cholesterol to HDL ratio.

Research Showing No Effect on Blood Cholesterol Levels

Kokkinos and his associates (1988) examined 38 healthy untrained males (average age 21) to determine the effects of 10 weeks of low- and high-repetition resistance training on lipoprotein profiles. Subjects were assigned to one of three groups: a low-repetition group that trained with 4–6 repetitions, a high-repetition group that trained with 14–16 repetitions, or an inactive control group. The number of sets was adjusted to equalize workloads. Muscular strength increased significantly in both training groups as indicated by the increase in a 1-RM test. Fat-free weight increased significantly in both training groups. Neither of the groups changed significantly in any of the cholesterol measures.

Kokkinos and his colleagues (1991) observed 16 untrained males (average age 46) to determine the effects of 20 weeks of strength training on lipoprotein profiles and post-heparin lipase activity. All subjects had abnormal lipoprotein profiles and at least two other risk factors for CAD. The training program resulted in strength increases of 50 percent in the upper body and 37 percent in the lower body, as measured by a 1-RM test. There were no significant changes in total cholesterol, HDL, or LDL levels.

Why are there conflicting findings?

It must be mentioned that several factors can influence cholesterol values other than exercise. Diet is one aspect that is sometimes not accounted for in some research studies. Diets that are high in saturated fat have been shown to increase blood cholesterol and triglycerides. Thus, if this component is not controlled in a study it can distort the results of the research. It is unlikely that a high intensity strength training program would offset the negative cholesterol effects of a person eating pure lard. Diet is an important factor in the total plan to lower one's cardiovascular risk factors. Exercise should not be viewed as a panacea for all health problems.

Another factor that can be attributed to a study failing to show a reduction in cholesterol levels is the starting level of the subjects. Kokkinos and his associates (1988) used healthy, young, lean subjects whose initial cholesterol values were approximately 140 mg/dl, which is quite low. Even aerobic exercise training does not appear to affect cholesterol levels when the initial values are low. In all likelihood, it can be concluded that increased physical activity is more effective in lowering cholesterol when the subject's initial levels are high.

When training studies show increased lean body mass, decreased percentage of body fat, and decreased total body fat, improvements in blood lipids generally follow. There is a close relationship between leanness and blood cholesterol and it is possible that a loss of body fat may be necessary for beneficial alterations in cholesterol values. Kokkinos and his colleagues (1991) trained individuals for 20 weeks and found no significant increases in lean body mass or decreases in percentage of body fat. Personally, I find this hard to believe. I can only speculate that the supervision was poor and/or these individuals were not progressing properly and exercised with the intensity of a cadaver.

In conclusion, if your cholesterol values are in a low-to-normal range, don't expect major changes from your strength training program. If you have a large percentage of body fat and have high cholesterol levels, you can lose some body fat by reducing your caloric intake and consuming a diet that provides about 60–65 percent carbohydrates, 20–25 percent fats, and 12–15 percent protein. And by all means, strength train hard enough to induce muscular growth. Strength training can help any individual achieve and maintain a healthy cardiovascular system.

What is the relationship between strength training, hormonal levels, and training results?

The topic pertaining to how different strength training programs influence one's natural hormonal levels has gained considerable attention during the past several years. Some researchers think (prematurely I might add) that by properly manipulating the strength training program variables one can stimulate hormonal increases that will lead to superior physiological adaptations. The hormones that are generally examined in research studies are testosterone, growth hormone, and insulin-like growth factor.

Testosterone and Training

Many believe that the large muscle mass and hypertrophy resulting from weight training are related to high levels of testosterone. If this is correct then the more testosterone an individual has, the greater the potential increase in size and strength. Unfortunately, this popular idea is not supported by scientific research. Fahey and his coworkers (1976) found that correlations among serum testosterone, body composition, and muscular strength were insignificant in both high school and college men and women.

Training increases serum levels of testosterone. Both endurance training and strength training have been shown to increase testosterone levels. A study by Jensen and associates (1991) compared the changes in testosterone concentrations after separate single sessions of endurance and strength training in a group of individuals who were experienced in both forms of training. The endurance exercise consisted of 90 minutes of running performed at a relative perceived exertion of 16.9. (Relative perceived exertion is a scale used to measure the intensity of exercise.) The strength training exercise also lasted 90 minutes and was composed of nine exercises (the squat, bench press, leg extension, behind-the-neck press, seated bicep curl, seated calf raise, dip, leg curl, and chin-up). These exercises were performed at 80 percent of a 1-RM for three sets of 8 repetitions each. A two-minute rest was allowed between the series. The mean rating of perceived exertion for the strength training session was 15.9.

A 37 percent increase in testosterone concentrations after 90 minutes of endurance training is comparable to that found in other studies—although some investigators have noted an unchanged testosterone concentration after exercises of the same duration. After the strength training session, a 27 percent increase in testosterone concentration was found.

Other researchers have found increases after a strength training session while Hakkinen and his associates (1988a) found testosterone concentrations that were increased, decreased, or unchanged in the same persons following strength training on different days. In both endurance training and strength training, testosterone concentrations returned to the resting level two hours after training and did not differ significantly from the morning value for the rest of the day. The results from this study and others indicate that a rapid return to normal values of testosterone concentration takes place after a single session of physical training.

This particular study did not find any significant differences between the changes in testosterone concentrations after endurance and strength training, either directly after the session or in the hours following. This is interesting since there are large differences in muscle adaptation to these two types of training. Strength training, as performed in this study, is known to increase muscle mass, while endurance training is a poor stimulus for muscle hypertrophy. The lack of any difference in testosterone response between the two types of training makes it unlikely that testosterone is of any major importance for the differences in muscle adaptation.

In spite of large differences between individuals, the correlation between individual changes in testosterone concentration after strength training and endurance training was very high. This indicated that the degree of testosterone change was individual.

When examining hormonal responses to exercises, several things must be kept in mind. A rise in hormone concentration in the blood during exercise could be interpreted as an increased output of the hormone by its endocrine gland source; a decreased destruction of the hormone (perhaps because of reduced blood flow to the liver or kidneys); or a decreased uptake of the hormones by its target tissues. Even if it was demonstrated that the rise in hormone concentration was caused by increased production, the total adaptive effect of this increased hormone production may be insignificant if the production rates do not remain elevated long enough to allow the greater hormone levels to have any substantial effect on the target tissues. Thus, one must use great caution in the interpretation of changes in blood or urine levels of hormones with exercise.

In terms of the effects of several weeks or months of training on resting testosterone levels, the results of the research are mixed. Hakkinen and his coworkers (1991) examined male weightlifters during two separate but equal three-week strength training periods and found that the free testosterone level fell during the third week of the program with two sessions a day but not during the program with one session a day. Seidman and colleagues (1991) observed 35 untrained males who performed aerobic exercise for 18 weeks and discovered that testosterone levels rose at 6 weeks, fell at 12 weeks, and returned to pretraining baseline at 18 weeks.

A decrease in resting testosterone concentrations has been noticed in endurance athletes undergoing a period of intensive training. This has also been observed in strength training athletes undergoing intensive training. Some researchers view this as a sign of overtraining. Once these athletes reduced their intensities and volume of exercise, however, their resting testosterone levels returned to normal values.

Growth Hormone and Training

As with testosterone, there is an increase in growth hormone following bouts of aerobic exercise and strength training. The increases in growth hormone during aerobic exercise are positively correlated with exercise intensity. VanHelder and associates (1986) reported an increase of 145 percent in growth hormone when subjects exercised at 40 percent of their VO_2 max (maximum oxygen intake) on a bicycle ergometer. Farrell and his coworkers (1986) found a 166 percent increase when exercising at 70 percent of VO_2 max on a bicycle ergometer. Kraemer and his colleagues (1990 and 1991) showed that strength training caused increases in growth hormone. Kraemer and his associates (1990) found that subjects who used 75–85 percent of their 1-RM with short rest intervals between sets produced greater increases in growth hormone than those who used very heavy weights for few repetitions with long rest intervals between sets.

Some research suggests that well-trained individuals have a blunted growth hormone response during exercise while other research suggests that well-trained individuals have a greater increase in growth hormone levels during exercise than their untrained counterparts. Hakkinen and his coworkers (1988b) had a group do strength training for 24 weeks and found significant improvement in their strength but no changes in their growth hormone levels. In a nine-week study, Bartels and coworkers (1989) also failed to notice an increase in growth hormone although the subjects significantly increased their strength and lean body mass.

While the aforementioned research focused on the endogenous increases in growth hormone, a study by Yarasheski and associates (1992) examined the use of exogenous growth hormone on individuals undergoing a strength training program. In this study, 16 men (aged 21–34) were randomly assigned to a strength-training-plus-growth-hormone group or to a strength-training-plus-placebo group. For 12 weeks, both groups trained all of their major muscle groups in an identical fashion while receiving 40 micrograms of recombinant human growth hormone or a placebo. Fat-free mass and total body water increased in both groups but more in the growth hormone group. The group that received the growth hormone experienced a greater increase in whole-body protein synthesis rate and whole-body protein balance but not in the protein synthesis rate of their quadriceps, their muscle strength, and the circumferences of their torso and limbs. In this study, strength training with or without growth hormone resulted in similar increments in muscular size and strength and muscle protein synthesis, indicating that (1) the larger increase in fat-free mass with growth hormone treatment was probably due to an increase in lean tissue other than skeletal muscle and (2) resistance training supplemented with growth hormone did not further enhance muscle anabolism and function.

The role of growth hormone in muscle growth is still unclear. The Yarasheski study further clouds the issue. It is assumed by some that as growth hormone increases, the size and strength of muscles increases. Until more research is performed, it is premature to view the growth hormone responses to exercise with any clear-cut cause-and-effect relationship.

Somatomedin-C (Insulin-like Growth Factor I) and Training

A brief explanation of somatomedin-c (sm-c) is in order before examining its response to exercise. Sm-c is a polypeptide, which is thought to be synthesized and released by the liver only when stimulated by growth hormone. Once it is released by the liver into the blood, it then binds to receptors found on the plasma membrane of the muscle cell and carries out the growth-promoting effects attributed to growth hormone.

Kraemer and his colleagues (1991) found that different strength training programs effected sm-c in different ways both during and after the exercise session. A program using fewer repetitions with heavy resistance brought about significant elevations in sm-c levels only during the recovery period. A program using a greater number of repetitions with less resistance and shorter rest intervals caused significant increases in sm-c levels during exercise and recovery.

Bartels and associates (1989) found an increase in sm-c concentrations (growth hormone and insulin did not increase) after a nine-week strength training program in which the subjects consumed a high-calorie diet. The subjects increased strength and lean body mass significantly. The authors concluded that

Movements that work the hips, legs, upper back, and shoulders will stimulate the greatest increases in muscular growth. (photo by Steve Lipofsky)

SM-C deserves further study as a possible mediator of gains in muscle mass during resistance training.

Kraemer and his coworkers (1991) noticed a gender difference in the response of SM-C to strength training. Age-matched men and women performed the same strength training program; equal resistance was determined relative to individual 1-RMs. Women demonstrated increases in SM-C concentrations both during and up to 60 minutes after exercise. Men showed no increases in SM-C during exercise but increases were noted for up to 90 minutes following exercise.

While the research that has been conducted to date is interesting and has helped to shed additional light on the responses and adaptations to exercise, it is clear that many factors influence the hormonal changes in exercise, such as emotional state, environmental conditions, and carbohydrate supply. To gain muscle mass, one must train hard using multi-joint movements for the majority of exercises. Movements that work the hips, legs, upper back, and shoulders will stimulate the greatest increases in muscular growth. The exercises must use resistance that is heavy enough for volitional fatigue to occur within a given repetition range (e.g., 6–9, 8–12, 12–15, and 15–20). The amount of rest between sets should be short—about one minute. Subjects with a low-to-normal percentage of body fat need to increase their caloric intake. Further, adequate rest is necessary to allow for physiological adaptations and to avoid overtraining. Individuals who train hard with basic multi-joint exercises, consume enough well-balanced calories, and get adequate rest between workouts will increase muscle mass. That's a fact. Whether this is due to testosterone, growth hormone, or SM-C is unknown, and it should not matter anyway to the average trainee looking for results. If you are a competitive weightlifter, the neural adaptations that are necessary to contest a 1-RM appear to be better stimulated by training with longer rest intervals between sets.

At this point in time, it is premature to anguish over which workouts will give you the best hormonal release. As the research discussed earlier has shown, endurance training increases testosterone and growth hormone as does strength training—yet the physiological adaptations from these two types of exercise are different. Research by Bunt and colleagues (1986) indicates that women have greater increases in growth hormone than men, yet women do not experience greater increases in tissue growth.

The relationship between hormonal changes and exercise is complex and has the potential to answer some puzzling training questions in the future.

Should I perform fast repetitions to become fast?

The best recommendation comes from a study by Voigt and Klausen (1990) who showed that even though heavy resistance training by itself does not improve the speed of a skilled unloaded movement, it does enhance movement speed if it is combined with sport-specific training. The key to improvement in any sport is to practice the specific sport skills and get into excellent physical condition.

How intense or hard should one train?

Intensity is basically related to effort or exertion. With cardiovascular training, one's heart rate is generally an accurate gauge of intensity. However, intensity is difficult to measure relative to strength training. At any rate, the workouts need to be organized to increase one's effort/intensity output by increasing the resistance used and/or the repetitions performed. Ultimately, the success of a program comes down to each individual's ability to work hard and this usually means performing maximal voluntary contractions. This is clearly illustrated by Kraemer and Fleck (1988) who write: "Maximal voluntary contractions refers to an indi-

Ultimately, the success of a program comes down to each individual's ability to work hard. (photo by Kevin Fowler)

vidual's attempt to recruit as many fibers as possible for the purpose of developing force." A maximal voluntary contraction does not necessarily mean performance of a 1-RM; it could refer to the last repetition of an 8-RM—that is, performing the maximal possible weight for 8 repetitions—at which point maximal force is being developed by the muscle in a fatigued state. One characteristic that all successful weight training programs share is the inclusion of maximal voluntary contractions at some point in the program.

REFERENCES

Ades, P. A., D. L. Ballor, T. Ashikaga, J. L. Utton, and K. S. Nair. 1996. Weight training improves walking endurance in healthy elderly persons. *Annuals of Internal Medicine* 124 (6): 568–572.

Anshel, M. H., ed. 1991. *Dictionary of the sport and exercise sciences*. Champaign, IL: Human Kinetics.

Bahr, R., and O. M. Sejersted. 1991. Effect of intensity of exercise on excess postexercise O_2 consumption. *Metabolism* 40 (8): 836.

Bartels, R. L., D. R. Lamb, V. M. Vivian, J. T. Snook, K. F. Rinehart, J. P. Delaney, and K. B. Wheeler. 1989. Effect of chronically increased consumption of energy and carbohydrate on anabolic adaptations to strenuous weight training. In *The theory and practice of athletic nutrition: Bridging the gap*, report of the Ross symposium, ed. A. C. Grandjean and J. Storlie, 70–80. Columbus, OH: Ross Laboratories.

Blessing, D., M. Stone, R. Byrd, D. Wilson, R. Rozenek, D. Pushparani, and H. Lipner. 1987. Blood lipid and hormonal changes from jogging and weight training of middle-aged men. *Journal of Applied Sport Science Research* 1: 25–29.

Bosselaers, I., B. Buemann, O. Victor, and A. Astrup. 1994. Twenty-four hour energy expenditure and substrate utilization in bodybuilders. *American Journal of Clinical Nutrition* 59 (1): 10–12.

Brooks, G. A., and G. A. Gaesser. 1980. End points of lactate and glucose metabolism after exhausting exercise. *Journal of Applied Physiology* 49 (6): 1057–1069.

Bunt, J. C., R. A. Boileau, J. M. Bahr, and R. A. Nelson. 1986. Sex and training differences in human growth hormone levels during prolonged exercise. *Journal of Applied Physiology* 61 (5): 1796–1801.

Deschenes, M. R., W. J. Kraemer, C. M. Maresh, and J. F. Crivello. 1991. Exercise-induced hormonal changes and their effects upon skeletal muscle tissue. *Sports Medicine* 12 (2): 80–93.

Drinkwater, D. J. 1989. Leanness not fitness is associated with highest levels of high density lipoproteins in master athletes. *Medicine and Science in Sports and Exercise* 21: 2 (abstract).

Elliot, D. L., L. Goldberg, and K. S. Kuehl. 1992. Effect of resistance training on excess post-exercise oxygen consumption. *Journal of Applied Sport Science Research* 6 (2): 77–81.

Fahey, T. D., R. Rolph, P. Moungmee, J. Nagel, and S. Mortara. 1976. Serum testosterone, body composition, and strength of young adults. *Medicine and Science in Sports and Exercise* 8 (1): 31–34.

Farrell, P. A., A. B. Gustafson, T. L. Garthwaite, R. K. Kalkhoff, A. W. Cowley, Jr., and W. P. Morgan. 1986. Influence of endogenous opioids on the response of selected hormones to exercise in Humans. *Journal of Applied Physiology* 61 (3): 1051–1057.

Goldberg, A. L., J. D. Etlinger, D. F. Goldspink, and C. Jablecki. 1975. Mechanism of work-induced hypertrophy of skeletal muscle. *Medicine and Science in Sports and Exercise* 7 (3): 185–198.

Goldberg, L., D. L. Elliot, and K. S. Kuehl. 1994. A comparison of the cardiovascular effects of running and weight training. *Journal of Strength and Conditioning Research* 8 (4): 219–224.

Goldberg, L., D. L. Elliot, R. W. Schutz, and F. E. Kloster. 1984. Changes in lipid and lipoprotein levels after weight training. *Journal of the American Medical Association* 252 (4): 504–506.

Gore, C. J., and R. T. Withers. 1990. Effect of exercise intensity and duration on postexercise metabolism. *Journal of Applied Physiology* 68 (6): 2362–2368.

Hakkinen, K. 1989. Neuromuscular and hormonal adaptations during strength and power training: A review. *Journal of Sports Medicine and Physical Fitness* 29: 9–26.

Hakkinen, K., and A. Pakarinen. 1991. Serum hormones in male strength athletes during intensive short term strength training. *European Journal of Applied Physiology* 63 (3–4): 194–199.

Hakkinen, K., A. Pakarinen, M. Alen, H. Kauhanen, and P. V. Komi. 1987. Relationships between training volume, physical performance capacity and serum hormone concentrations during prolonged training in elite weightlifters. *International Journal of Sports Medicine* (Supplement) 8: 61–65.

Hakkinen, K., A. Pakarinen, M. Alen, H. Kauhanen, and P. V. Komi. 1988a. Neuromuscular and hormonal responses in elite athletes to two successive strength training sessions in one day. *European Journal of Applied Physiology* 57 (2): 133–139.

———. 1988b. Neuromuscular and hormonal adaptations in elite athletes to strength training in two years. *Journal of Applied Physiology* 65 (6): 2406–2412.

———. 1988c. Daily hormonal and neuromuscular responses to intensive strength training in one week. *International Journal of Sports Medicine* 9 (6): 422–428.

Hetrick, G., and J. Wilmore. 1979. Androgen levels and muscle hypertrophy during an eight week weight training program for men/women. *Medicine and Science in Sports and Exercise* 11: 102.

Hickson, R. C., M. A. Rosenkoetter, and M. M. Brown. 1980. Strength training efforts on aerobic power and short-term endurance. *Medicine and Science in Sports and Exercise* 12 (5): 336–339.

Hunter, G., L. Blackman, L. Dunnam, and G. Flemming. 1988. Bench press metabolic rate as a function of exercise intensity. *Journal of Applied Sport Science Research* 2 (1): 1–6.

Hurley, B. F., J. M. Hagberg, A. P. Goldberg, D. R. Seals, A. A. Ehsani, R. E. Brennan, and J. O. Holloszy. 1988. Resistive training can reduce coronary risk factors without altering vo_2 max or percent body fat. *Medicine and Science in Sports and Exercise* 20 (2): 150–154.

Jensen, J., H. Oftebro, B. Breigan, A. Johnsson, K. Ohlin, H. D. Meen, S. B. Stromme, and H. A. Dahl. 1991. Comparison of changes in testosterone concentrations after strength and endurance exercise in well-trained men. *European Journal of Applied Physiology* 63 (6): 467–471.

Kay, C., and R. J. Shepard. 1969. On muscle strength and the threshold of anaerobic work. *Internationale Zeitschrift fur angewandte Physiologie einschliessich Arbeitphysiologie* 27: 311–328.

Kokkinos, P. F., B. F. Hurley, P. Vaccaro, J. C. Patterson, L. B. Gardner, S. M. Ostrove, and A. P. Goldberg. 1988. Effects of low- and high-repetition resistance training on lipoprotein lipid profiles. *Medicine and Science in Sports and Exercise* 20 (1): 50–54.

Kokkinos, P. F., B. F. Hurley, M. A. Smutok, C. Farmer, C. Reece, R. Shulman, C. Charabogos, J. Patterson, S. Will, and J. Devane-Bell. 1991. Strength training does not improve lipoprotein-lipid profiles in men at risk for CHD. *Medicine and Science in Sports and Exercise* 23 (10): 1134–1139.

Kraemer, W. J., and S. J. Fleck. 1988. Resistance training: Basic principles (part 1 of 4). *Physician and Sportsmedicine* 16 (3): 165.

Kraemer, W. J., A. C. Fry, B. J. Warren, M. H. Stone, S. J. Fleck, J. T. Kearney, B. P. Conroy, C. M. Maresh, C. A. Weseman, N. T. Triplett, and S. Gordon. 1992. Acute hormonal responses in elite junior weightlifters. *International Journal of Sports Medicine* 13 (2): 103–109.

Kraemer, W. J., S. E. Gordon, S. J. Fleck, L. J. Marchitelli, R. Mello, J. E. Dziados, K. Friedl, E. Harman, C. Maresh, and A. C. Fry. 1991. Endogenous anabolic hormonal and growth factor responses to heavy resistance exercise in males and females. *International Journal of Sports Medicine* 12 (2): 228–235.

Kraemer, W. J., L. J. Marchitelli, S. E. Gordon, E. Harman, J. E. Dziados, R. Mello, P. Frykman, D. McCurry, and S. J. Fleck. 1990. Hormonal and growth factor responses to heavy resistance exercise protocols. *Journal of Applied Physiology* 69 (4): 1442–1450.

Kuehl, K., D. Elliot, and L. Goldberg. 1990. Predicting caloric expenditure during multi-station resistance exercise. *Journal of Applied Sport Science Research* 4 (3): 63–67.

Marcinik, E. J., J. Potts, G. Schlabach, S. Will, P. Dawson, and B. F. Hurley. 1991. Effects of strength training on lactate threshold and endurance performance. *Medicine and Science in Sports and Exercise* 23 (6): 739–743.

McCartney, N., R. S. McKelvie, D. R. Haslam, and N. L. Jones. 1991. Usefulness of weightlifting training on improving strength and maximal power output in coronary artery disease. *American Journal of Cardiology* 67 (11): 939–945.

Melby, C., C. Scholl, G. Edwards, and R. Bullough. 1993. Effect of acute resistance exercise on postexercise energy expenditure and resting metabolic rate. *Journal of Applied Physiology* 75 (4): 1847–1853.

Powers, S. K., and E. T. Howley. 1995. *Exercise physiology: Theory and application to fitness and performance.* Dubuque, IA: W. C. Brown Publishing.

Seidman, D., E. Dolev, P. A. Deuster, R. Burstein, R. Arnon, and Y. Epstein. 1991. Androgenic response to long-term physical training in male subjects. *International Journal of Sports Medicine* 11 (6): 421–424.

Ullrich, I. H., C. M. Reid, and R. A. Yeater. 1987. Increased HDL-cholesterol levels in a weight training program. *Southern Medical Journal* 80 (3): 328–331.

VanEtten, L., K. Westerterp, and F. Verstappen. 1995. Effect of weight training on energy expenditure and substrate utilization during sleep. *Medicine and Science in Sports and Exercise* 27 (2): 188–193.

VanHelder, W., K. Casey, R. C. Goode, and W. M. Radomski. 1986. Growth hormone regulation in two types of aerobic exercise of equal oxygen uptake. *European Journal of Applied Physiology* 55 (3): 236–239.

Viru, A. 1992. Plasma hormones and physical exercise: A review. *International Journal of Sports Medicine* 13 (3): 201–209.

Voigt, M., and K. Klausen. 1990. Changes in muscle strength and speed for an unloaded movement after various training programs. *European Journal of Applied Physiology* 60 (5): 370–376.

Webb, P. 1981. Energy expenditure and fat-free mass in men and women. *American Journal of Clinical Nutrition* 34 (9): 1816–1826.

Weinsier, R. L., Y. Schutz, and D. Bracco. 1992. Reexamination of the relationship of resting metabolic rate to fat-free mass and to the metabolically active components of fat-free mass in humans. *American Journal of Clinical Nutrition* 55 (4): 790–794.

Yarasheski, K. E., J. A. Campbell, K. Smith, M. J. Rennie, J. O. Holloszy, and D. M. Bier. 1992. Effect of growth hormone and resistance exercise on muscle growth in young men. *American Journal of Physiology* 262 (3 pt 1): E261–E267.

I dedicate this chapter to my son, Hunter.

3

The Basics of Muscle Contraction: Implications for Strength Training

Tom Kelso, M.S., C.S.C.S.
Strength and Conditioning Coach
Southeast Missouri State University
Cape Girardeau, Missouri

Understanding the technical aspects of muscle contraction is a prerequisite for anyone who intends to conduct a safe and practical strength training program. Although it can be overwhelming and confusing, it is important to seek the most logical use of the facts to give credibility to the program and make it simple to implement.

Many of the strength training philosophies and methods used today have been influenced by tradition, muscle-strength research, hands-on experience with athletes, and personal experimentation. Individual athletes and athletic teams have experienced both success and failure by using a variety of these strength training methodologies. To label one approach as best is unrealistic and impossible. Strength training is only an adjunct in the grand scheme of athletic competition. There are many other factors that influence winning and losing. Proper coaching, natural ability/talent, game strategy, mental preparation, conditioning, and nutrition all have an impact; some have greater significance than strength training itself.

All other factors being equal, properly performed strength training may be the key to success for certain individuals. But keep in mind its overall impact and singleness of purpose: to increase muscular strength. While increasing strength doesn't guarantee a championship season, it does ensure that an athlete will compete with a more functional musculoskeletal system. Hopefully, this will prevent or minimize the potential for injury (the primary objective) and complement skill execution relative to various force-output expressions required to perform skills properly. But it is important not to make strength training into anything more than its purpose.

This chapter will present many undeniable facts based upon the research findings regarding muscle contraction. These ideas can be applied in the weight room. There are, however, some aspects of muscle contraction that are still unclear and thus debatable. In such cases, the information presented is based upon common sense and conjecture. The intent is to provide useful, sound information that can assist anyone in making rational decisions on strength training and create an awareness that there are plenty of productive methods beyond those used in the traditional approach.

OVERVIEW OF MUSCLE CONTRACTION

There are many factors influencing muscle contraction and resultant force output. According to Bigland-Ritchie, Bellemare, and Woods (1986), the entire process is dependent upon

1. excitatory drive to the higher motor centers (motivation/effort)
2. balance between excitatory and inhibitory pathways converging on lower motor neuron pools
3. changes in spinal motor neuron excitability
4. integrity of electrical transmission from nerve to muscle
5. integrity of electrical transmission over the muscle
6. excitation and contraction coupling
7. energy supplies to the muscle
8. accumulation of metabolites that may interfere with metabolic and electrical events

Coupled with these factors are the following morphological (structural) dependents of force output, as noted by Edgerton and his associates (1986):

1. muscle cross-sectional area
2. muscle mass
3. muscle fiber length
4. muscle fiber type
5. interconnection between fibers (sarcomeres in either series or parallel alignment)
6. attachment of fibers to tendons
7. attachment of tendons to bones

Research scientists have determined conclusively that there are many more intricacies related to these components—and they have also concluded there is much we do not know. For those involved in the strength training of athletes, a practical use of the known facts is necessary for productive programs. The following overview will highlight the basics of muscle contraction that are applicable to strength training.

Muscle Fibers/Motor Units

Muscle tissue consists of many microscopic components, all of which contribute in some fashion to the contractile process. But in simple terms, muscle can be viewed as a bundle of contractile elements called muscle fibers. For the muscle fibers to contract and generate force, they must receive a stimulus from the central nervous system (CNS). A group of muscle fibers that is attached to the CNS by a motor nerve is called a motor unit. The motor unit is the functional element of muscle contraction (Wilmore and Costill 1988).

Fiber Types

The muscle fibers of the motor units can be categorized based upon their work output potential. At one end of the spectrum are the fibers that have a high endurance potential and are best suited for extended low-level work during daily activities. At the other end are the fibers with limited endurance potential but high force-generating ability that is needed for high-level work. It has also been determined that there are fibers that exist between these two extremes that have some of the characteristics of each (Green 1986).

Some of the classification systems which have been devised based upon work-output potential include the following:

1. slow twitch and fast twitch (Green 1986)
2. red and white (Devries 1980)
3. slow oxidative, fast oxidative glycolytic, and fast glycolytic (Green 1986)
4. Type I, Type IIa, and Type IIb (Green 1986)
5. slow fatigable, fast fatigue-resistant, and fast fatigable (Faulkner and White 1990)

For all practical purposes—and to keep it simple—the classification system of Types I, IIa, and IIb will be used in all forthcoming discussions in this chapter. It is further delineated to reveal the general characteristics of each (Devries 1980).

Type I: high aerobic capacity, low anaerobic capacity:
- small in size
- fatigue resistant
- low force capacity

Type IIa: medium aerobic capacity, medium anaerobic capacity:
- large in size
- fatigable
- medium force capacity

Type IIb: low aerobic capacity, high anaerobic capacity:
- large in size
- most fatigable
- high force capacity

Regardless of the classification system, the important thing to remember is that motor units possess different characteristics due to the nature of their fiber types. In the forthcoming discussion, the terms *muscle fiber(s)* and *motor units(s)* are used interchangeably, i.e., Type I muscle fiber(s) = Type I motor unit(s).

Recruitment Principles

For a muscle to contract and apply force, it must have some form of input relative to the desired force output. This input is provided by the CNS. Depending upon the task at hand, signals are sent through the CNS network to the muscles and force is then applied. Whenever a motor unit is activated, every muscle fiber within it contracts maximally. If a motor unit is not activated, then none of the attached fibers contract. This is called the "all-or-none principle."

Furthermore—regardless of the desired force output—motor units are activated (or recruited) in order of their size (Palmieri 1983; Sale 1986; Wilmore and Costill 1988). The Size Principle of Recruitment suggests that during any activity, the smaller Type I motor units are always recruited first. As the demands of the activity increase, the intermediate Type IIa motor units are recruited to assist. When the demands become extreme, the larger Type IIb motor units are recruited to complete the task.

Fiber-Type Percentage

The genetic endowment of fiber-type percentages can vary. Each person's percentage is dictated at birth and is unalterable. Some people may have a higher percentage of Type IIa and IIb fibers; others may have a higher percentage of Type I. The important thing to remember is that different fiber-type ratios do exist from person to person.

In general, though, the average person has roughly 50 percent Type I fibers and 50 percent Type II fibers distributed throughout the body. More specifically, the average muscle contains approximately 50 percent Type I, 25 percent Type IIa and 25 percent Type IIb (Wilmore and Costill 1988). But as stated previously, some individuals may be endowed with more or less of one type compared to the norm (Perrine 1986). One person may have a Type I:IIa:IIb fiber ratio of 45/25/30 percent; another may have a ratio of 55/30/15 percent. Such individuals may be unique but they do exist.

Neurological Ability

The type and percentage of fibers are not the only factors affecting work output potential. Neurological ability may also play a significant role in strength training.

Neurological ability is the inherent capability to activate a given number of motor units in a given effort. Individuals may be able to exert a great deal of force not only because they possess a high percentage of Type II motor units but also because they can activate a large percentage of their overall motor units regardless of the type. In this case, their neurological ability is high. Low neurological ability is just the opposite: In a given effort, a small percentage of overall motor units can be activated regardless of type. In this case, less relative force can be displayed.

Assuming an average person can activate 50 percent of the total available motor units, someone with a high neurological ability may be able to activate 55–60 percent. Conversely, low neurological ability may allow for recruitment of only 40–45 percent of the total available motor units. (This often-neglected neurological factor and its ramifications will be examined more closely later in this chapter.)

Force Requirement

The Size Principle of Recruitment dictates the order of activation of the motor units, but the key to the magnitude of the recruitment is the amount of force required (Devries 1980; Westcott 1987). The lower the force, the fewer the number of motor units activated; the higher the force, the greater the number of motor units activated.

During a low-force activity such as walking, the motor units recruited to perform the work are of the smaller type. As the demand for more force increases—as in working up to a full sprint—larger motor units are activated to assist the smaller motor units. In activities that require extreme force, such as intense strength training, a very large number of motor units are activated and contribute to the force output in an all-or-none manner (Roundtable 1985)—an important point to remember.

This phenomenon can be best understood by using other examples involving everyday activities. When a person bends down to pick up a heavy object, a great deal of force must be consciously exerted to perform the task, which involves many motor units. On the other hand, folding a piece of paper requires very little force and thus fewer motor units. Conscious efforts can also be misleading. Someone who picks up an object that is perceived to be heavy but is actually light is surprised when the object is nearly thrown into the air. The explanation is simple: Too many motor units were mistakenly called upon to perform the task.

Degree of Force

To produce the correct amount of force during a specific task, the motor units must also contract in harmony. Otherwise the muscle contractions will be sporadic, haphazard, and uncoordinated. The intramuscular coordination, or synchronization, of motor units occurs as a result of mental concentration and focus, as when a person psychs up for an exertion. This might be a low-demand effort that requires precise timing combined with a lower force output, such as shooting a free throw; or it might be a high-demand effort that requires precise timing but with a higher force output, such as powerlifting. The focus is on activating the proper muscles in sequence (developed through skill practice) and in recruiting the proper number of motor units in those muscles to first initiate and then complete the effort with precision.

Fatigue and Continuance of Force Options

Another consideration in the recruitment process is fatigue of the motor units. The endurance capacity of muscle fibers—for the sake of simplicity either high, moderate, or low—effects the force output potential. As previously activated motor units fatigue—and if the existing level of force output is desired—the CNS has options at its disposal to continue the force output. These options are dependent upon the type, amount, and magnitude of the desired force and, according to Palmieri (1983), include the following:

1. the number of units recruited per unit of time
2. the frequency of activation of the units
3. the type of units recruited

Therefore, if more force is needed to perform a task the CNS can:

1. stimulate working units more rapidly
2. recruit more of the same type of units
3. recruit larger units

Take running as an example. As the name implies, long-distance running can be performed for a longer duration than all-out sprinting. The lower level demand of long-distance running is fueled by the more enduring Type I motor units. But if the running pace is increased, Type I units must be stimulated more rapidly; more Type I units must be recruited; or the larger Type IIa units must be recruited. Fatigue then becomes more likely at this faster pace due to the greater involvement of Type I units and the activation of the less enduring Type IIa units. When an all-out sprint is performed—requiring the stimulation of more motor units (i.e., more Type IIa and possibly Type IIb)—the onset of fatigue comes much sooner.

Speed Factor

The magnitude of recruitment is also influenced by the speed of movement. Fewer motor units are involved when a light object is moved relatively quickly than when a heavier object is attempted to be moved quickly (Palmieri 1983; Green 1986; Westcott 1987; Wilmore and Costill 1988). The light object can be moved relatively quickly but requires less force and fewer motor units; the heavy object requires more force to move it, so more motor units must be activated. As the demand increases, the Type II units must be recruited. However, the speed of movement naturally decreases. Common sense also suggests that a heavy object, relatively speaking, cannot be moved relatively quickly. This is depicted in Figure 3.1.

As mentioned, the Type I motor units are capable of rapid contractions. It stands to reason then that some of the Type II motor units may not necessarily contribute to low-force/high-speed contractions relative to the Size Principle of Recruitment. Rather, it may be the impetus of only the Type I units (Green 1986). Figure 3.2 shows the theoretical relationship of motor unit involvement to force and speed requirements.

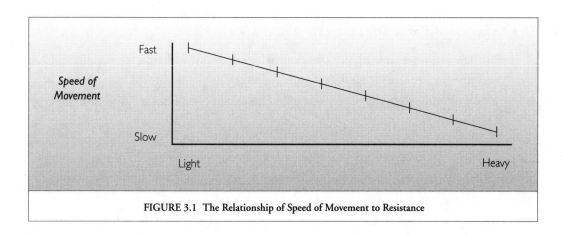

FIGURE 3.1 The Relationship of Speed of Movement to Resistance

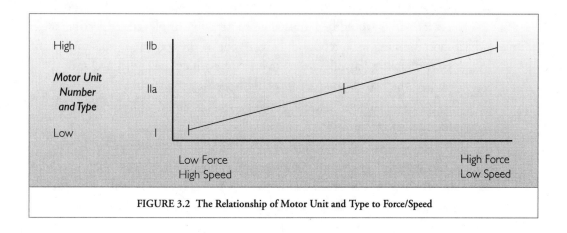

FIGURE 3.2 The Relationship of Motor Unit and Type to Force/Speed

FUNCTIONAL CONTRACTIONS

Muscles contract and generate force in different ways. Their expression of force also varies.

Types of Contractions

There are three ways that muscles can contract and produce force. Dynamically, a concentric contraction occurs when a muscle shortens against a load. An example of this occurs when extending the hip, knee, and ankle joints during a vertical jump. The gluteal, quadriceps, and calf muscles contract by shortening, which results in force applied to the ground to perform the jump. Also dynamically, an eccentric contraction occurs when a muscle lengthens against a load. For instance, lowering a weight slowly from the flexed—or bent-arm—position of a bicep curl will cause the biceps to lengthen against the load. Finally, an isometric contraction occurs when a muscle contracts statically—it produces force but no joint movement. For example, pushing against an immovable object or maintaining a static squat position requires muscle force but no angular joint motion.

The Creation of Force Output

When it comes to athletics, functional contractions—that is, the application of concentric, eccentric, and isometric expressions—are the essence of muscular force. From a functional standpoint, muscular force can be expressed in the following ways:

1. The activation of a maximum number of motor units—all firing rapidly and in synchronization—to exert maximum force in one all-out effort. This would be a muscular contraction expressed during the last do-or-die repetition in a strength training exercise or an attempt to move a very heavy object.
2. The attempt to activate a maximum number of motor units *as quickly as possible*. This would be a muscular contraction displayed by putting a shot, jumping for a rebound, driving out of the starting blocks in a sprint race, or spiking a volleyball. Provided the athlete has practiced and refined the coordinated effort of the specific activity—that is, motor learning/specificity of the skill—it allows for more explosive efforts during such skill executions.
3. A more prolonged activation of motor units over a given period of time. This would be a muscular contraction expressed in extended submaximal efforts such as performing an eight-repetition set in a strength training exercise, rowing a shell, or holding a heavy object for as long as possible.

These three examples depict specific contractions that are functionally different but are very much related. They originate from the same system but are expressed differently. Much confusion exists today because of the failure to understand this relationship.

THE STRENGTH CONTINUUM

The three preceding examples of expressing muscle force traditionally have been labeled as (1) muscular strength, (2) muscular power, and (3) muscular endurance. It is a mistake to think that these three expressions of muscle force are totally separate from each other and must be built differently. The fact of the matter is that they are simply different expressions of force output originating from the same system of muscle activation. And it is the muscular-strength expression depicted in example 1 that governs the entire system of muscle activation.

A closer look at the process of muscle activation illustrates this relationship. On one side is the totally relaxed state of the muscle (i.e., no involvement of motor units) and on the other is the expression of muscle force as defined in example 1 (i.e., a buildup to a maximal and synchronous involvement of motor units). If the logic behind the order of recruitment is applied, both power and endurance fall within the confines of the expression of strength.

A power contraction is a recruitment of motor units—depending upon force/speed requirements—in a quick burst. For instance, jumping off the ground is a power movement that can be accomplished with the involvement of relatively few motor units since the body weight is light and the force requirement is low.

By way of comparison, a football lineman blocking an opponent with an explosive initial thrust—also considered a power movement—requires more motor units to perform the task for two main reasons: the movement of the body weight itself (as in the jumping example) and the force needed to ward off the opponent. Furthermore, if the opponent becomes more difficult to move, a further recruitment of motor units must take place and the event moves closer to a strength expression. The expression of power actually can be considered a mini-strength expression relative to the amount of force required.

An endurance contraction is a submaximal recruitment effort that depends upon the length of time the force is needed. Theoretically, the force requirements during an endurance contraction could be very close to maximal or they could be very extended. The activation of motor units can vary greatly depending upon the extent of the force required. If the force is near maximal, there may be many motor units contracting and firing rapidly, as in the expression of maximal strength—but not to the extent that it inhibits further force output. An example of this would be a three-repetition effort in a strength training exercise. It is near maximal yet more extended than a 1-repetition maximum (1-RM) effort. On the other hand, a very extended exertion, such as performing 50 push-ups, will require the activation of motor units via the order of recruitment: first by increasing the firing rate of the working motor units, then by recruiting more of the same type of motor units, and finally by recruiting a larger type as fatigue takes its toll. Again, endurance can also be considered a mini-strength expression but spread out over a longer period of time.

It should now be clear how the maximum strength expression encompasses the power and endurance contraction processes. Training to develop the activation of motor units characteristic of a maximal strength expression can undoubtedly enhance the expression of both muscular power and muscular endurance. Therefore, the goal of strength training should be the progressive recruitment, overload, and adaptation of the maximum number of muscle fibers within the confines of one's genetic potential.

The intricate factors of muscle contraction can best be understood if they are viewed on a continuum: low force to high force, few motor units to many motor units, Type I motor units to Type IIb motor units, a prolonged activation of motor units to a quick burst of motor units, and less fatigable to more fatigable. This concept is a strength continuum on which both power and muscular endurance reside.

MUSCLE CONTRACTION IN STRENGTH TRAINING

A simple and practical way to understand the technical aspects of muscle contraction and show the strength/endurance and strength/power relationships is to use basic examples from the weight room. This method shows what is occurring, why it is occurring, and what the end result of muscle contraction is in various situations. A number of factors have an impact on the results, including the intensity of effort by the trainee, the type of device used to contract against, the magnitude of resistance, the number of repetitions performed, and the speed of movement. For our purposes the terms *weight* or *resistance* throughout the rest of the chapter mean the same thing—that is, light weight = light resistance.

Achieving/Avoiding Muscular Fatigue

Intensity of effort is one of the key elements in strength training. For strength to improve, an overload must be imposed on the muscles. Proper overload means extreme effort during each set of an exercise. The greater the effort, the greater the return. For this to remain true, each set must be taken to the point of momentary muscular fatigue or failure where the recruitment of all fiber types is still attempted. Depending upon individual genetic capabilities, the maximum number of fibers capable of being utilized during the performance of the set will have been recruited, fatigued, and, therefore, overloaded.

Regardless of the weight and repetitions used, anytime an exercise is halted prior to the point of momentary muscular fatigue—that is, if more repetitions are possible but not attempted—a maximal recruitment of fibers will not occur. This is plain common sense. For example:

1. Stopping at 10 repetitions when 15 are possible means that the fibers capable of being activated on the 5 neglected repetitions will not be maximally overloaded. Not completing the 5 possible repetitions means that a reserve remains and the intensity of effort is less than maximal.

2. Stopping at 5 repetitions when 6 are possible again means that some fibers capable of being activated on the sixth repetition will not be maximally overloaded. This, too, means that the intensity of effort is less than maximal. However, it is more intense than the previous example where 10 repetitions were obtained though 15 were possible.

The bottom line is that the closer one gets to achieving the maximum possible number of repetitions, the greater the muscle-fiber involvement; the greater the muscle-fiber involvement, the greater the overload.

STRENGTH TRAINING DEVICES

Many devices—including machines, free weights, and other objects—can induce strength gains. Any device can work if it allows the muscles to produce force and if it is used with safe technique. For instance, suppose that four athletes performed a compound (multi-joint) movement for the chest, shoulders, and triceps and that each athlete used one of the following devices: a barbell, dumbbells, a selectorized machine, and parallel bars for dips. Examine these situations:

Athlete 1/barbell: used 250 pounds as the resistance and performed 8 repetitions in a controlled manner to the point of momentary muscular fatigue. A ninth repetition was attempted but not obtained.

Athlete 2/dumbbells: used 95-pound dumbbells as the resistance (one in each hand) and performed 7 repetitions in a controlled manner to the point of momentary muscular fatigue. An eighth repetition was attempted but not obtained.

Athlete 3/selectorized (weight-stacked) machine: used 160 pounds as the resistance and performed 11 repetitions in a controlled manner to the point of momentary muscular fatigue. A twelfth repetition was attempted but not obtained.

Athlete 4/dips on parallel bars: used 70 pounds of weight attached to a dipping belt as the resistance (plus body weight) and performed 8 repetitions in a controlled manner to the point of momentary muscular fatigue. A ninth repetition was attempted but not obtained.

In all four examples—regardless of the athlete performing the exercise, the amount of resistance, and the device being used—the chest, shoulders, and triceps were maximally overloaded each time. Maximum muscular tension/fiber recruitment occurred through its natural process, extreme effort was put forth, and the goal of performing as many repetitions as possible all led to the maximum overload. Therefore, all four devices were effective when used as described. What, then, are the requirements of an effective strength training device? They are as follows:

1. The device must produce tension within the muscles. It must create the demand for maximum force output so that a maximum number of muscle fibers can be overloaded.
2. The device must allow the muscles to be worked through their natural range of movement. If the muscles act on a joint in a certain plane of motion, contraction of the fibers should occur against the resistance through this plane.
3. In conjunction with 1 and 2, the device must permit all of this to take place in the safest manner possible. If it places too much stress on the joints—or if it provides too much ballistic activity and violates the two previous requirements—its use should be questioned.
4. If possible, the device should be adjustable in terms of the magnitude of resistance that it provides. Some way of varying poundage by specific increments is necessary. This will facilitate progression relative to weight increases (although progression could still be maintained through repetition increases).

Applying unbiased logic to these four requirements makes it obvious that there are many devices that can be used effectively in a strength training program. The devices do not need to be sophisticated or costly.

The Practicality of Machines

Considering the four requirements of an effective strength training device, there are many machines on the market today that are more practical than free weights. Because muscles require maximum loading/fiber involvement and full range of motion (ROM) in a safe manner, one is required to push to the limit during an exercise. In some free-weight exercises, working to the absolute limit cannot be done safely. A loss of balance or the fatigue in an assisting muscle group may require the exercise to be discontinued at the point when further muscle fiber involvement would occur. Halting the exercise at this point will not allow for maximum overload.

This is the advantage of some machines: They allow the trainee to push to the limit without the danger of losing balance or terminating the exercise because of weak-link muscle groups. Without the dangers of falling weights (e.g., in a barbell bench press) or the inability to ascend (e.g., in a barbell squat), a related machine exercise can be safer and more productive in the long run. This is especially the case when one lacks a training partner.

Free weights are excellent strength training tools. But many machines are beneficial in terms of productivity and safety, especially in view of the fact that machines can be excellent tension-producing devices.

In the final analysis, ask yourself these questions. Is it possible to observe two individual athletes or teams in competition and determine what devices they trained with based upon their performance? If so, can you explain the success or failure of those individuals or teams that used all machines, a combination of machines and free weights, or all free weights in their training?

IMPACT OF THE MAGNITUDE OF RESISTANCE/REPETITIONS

It is important to understand that the resistance/repetitions used in the following examples are significant enough to be productive for strength training whether classified as *light* or *heavy* resistance (weight) or *high* or *low* repetitions. These are relative designations. For instance, a heavy weight might be 85–90 percent of a 1-RM and a light weight might be approximately 60–65 percent of a 1-RM; high repetitions could be 15–20, and low repetitions could be 3–5. In all cases, the resistance and potential time under tension can be sufficient for proper strength training. But in comparison, the resistance/repetitions in one is heavier/higher and the other is lighter/lower, thus their relative classifications.

Light/Heavy Weight

In general, when a light weight (relative to a heavy weight) is lifted, the initial tension (i.e., total fiber involvement) is lower. When you lift a light weight, the demand isn't as great as with a heavier weight. With the lower demand, the CNS recruits fewer fibers. However, keep in mind that a large percentage of fibers is involved because a significant demand is placed upon the muscles. As the weight is then lifted for ensuing repetitions, however, fatigue takes its toll. The fibers are stimulated more rapidly. More of the same type are recruited, and the larger types are then activated to continue the task. Because of this, a relatively light weight—provided that it is lifted for an adequate number of repetitions—does involve a high percentage of overall muscle fibers.

In general, when a heavy weight (relative to a light weight) is lifted, the initial tension is greater. Naturally, this is because more fibers are required for this heavier demand. As this heavier weight is lifted for subsequent repetitions, the fibers are again stimulated more rapidly, more of the same type are recruited, and the larger types are recruited to continue the task. However, fatigue develops much sooner as compared to the lighter weight. Since a greater percentage of more fatigable fibers was recruited initially—namely, IIa or IIa and IIb—their reserve is depleted and fewer are then available to continue the task. Again, this simply shows the reality of why a heavy weight cannot be lifted as many times as a relatively lighter weight.

High/Low Repetitions

The discussion of repetitions is similar to the previous examples because resistance and repetitions are directly related. In general, relatively higher repetitions require the use of relatively lighter weights and relatively lower repetitions require the use of relatively heavier weights. Therefore, the muscle contraction that occurs when performing high and low repetitions is comparable to the previous examples of relative heavy/light weights.

THE RELATIONSHIP OF MUSCULAR STRENGTH TO MUSCULAR ENDURANCE

The popular opinion about resistance/repetitions has been to do light weight/high repetitions for the development of muscular endurance and heavy weight/low repetitions for the development of muscular strength. Although this is the prevailing notion, it has no validity. What level on the resistance/repetitions continuum develops maximum endurance while avoiding strength? Likewise, where is the resistance/repetition cut-off point where muscular strength is optimally developed at the expense of muscular endurance?

In reality, the qualities of muscular strength and muscular endurance are directly related. When one increases strength, endurance increases as well. As muscle fibers in the motor units become stronger, fewer are needed to sustain a submaximal work output along the strength continuum. This also means that there is a greater reserve available to extend the submaximal effort (Stone et al. 1984). Contrary to conventional wisdom, muscular strength and muscular endurance are not trained separately.

One of the virtues of proper strength training is the ability to recruit more fibers gradually over time and overload/develop the entire pool of fibers recruited. Each time this occurs, the newly recruited fibers—as well as those previously recruited—are stimulated and, fatigued; as a result, they improve the quality of their inherent characteristics. Simply put, consistent hard, progressive training increases the ability to recruit more fibers for a given task and improves each fiber's natural quality. Therefore, more force can be generated and sustained for a longer period.

Strength/Endurance Example 1

Suppose that an athlete has a 1-RM of 400 pounds (a maximum strength test) and—at this level of maximum strength—can perform 300 pounds (75 percent of the 1-RM) for 9 repetitions (a maximum endurance test). Following an eight-week period of progressive strength training, the athlete obtains a new 1-RM of 425 pounds. At this new level of strength, the athlete can probably still perform 9 repetitions with 75 percent of the 1-RM—now approximately 319 pounds. If the original 75 percent of the 1-RM (300 pounds) is used for the endurance test, the athlete would naturally perform more than 9 repetitions. Therefore, not only does strength increase, but endurance does as well. And the increase in endurance is proportional to the increase in strength.

The opposite of this phenomenon is also true. Suppose that an athlete with the ability to do 400 pounds for a 1-RM and 300 pounds for 9 repetitions does not perform any strength training during a five-week period. After the five weeks, the 1-RM will have decreased. At this point, suppose the athlete has a 1-RM of 360 pounds and can do 270 pounds (75 percent of 360 pounds) for 9 repetitions. If the original 75 percent of the 1-RM (300 pounds) is used for the endurance test, the athlete would naturally perform fewer than 9 repetitions. Therefore, when strength decreases, so does endurance. And the decrease in endurance is proportional to the decrease in strength.

Strength/Endurance Example 2

Perform a simple test. Determine your 1-RM on the bench press. Rest five minutes, then take 40 percent of the 1-RM and do a set of maximum repetitions to muscular fatigue. The number of repetitions with 40 percent of a 1-RM will vary but should be extraordinarily high with this relatively light weight—probably more than 30. Following this endurance test, rest for 2–3 minutes and then attempt to lift the original 1-RM. At this point, it will certainly be difficult if not impossible. If you cannot do this weight, try 95 percent of the original 1-RM. If you still cannot, try 90 percent. The point: It is rare to use 40 percent of a 1-RM as the resistance in strength training. But this example proves that performing an unusually high number of repetitions using a relatively light weight eventually recruits and fatigues a percentage of the Type II fibers that are activated in maximal or near-maximal efforts. Therefore, if doing a high number of repetitions with 40 percent of a 1-RM can do this, then using a resistance that only allows 10, 12, or 15 repetitions—traditionally viewed as endurance-only resistance—can be very productive for developing strength (and, of course, endurance).

Strength/Endurance Example 3

Try another test. This one will take you six weeks. Determine a 1-RM as in the Strength/Endurance Example 2. Again rest five minutes but now use 70 percent of the 1-RM and perform a set of maximum repetitions to muscular fatigue. The number of repetitions with 70 percent of a 1-RM will vary but should be about 10–15 or more. Record the result for future reference. For the next six weeks, bench press two times per week (Monday and Thursday or Tuesday and Friday) and only do 2–3 sets of 3–6 repetitions to muscular fatigue. (You can do one or two warm-up sets if you prefer.) As a suggestion, you can use one of the following options:

Option 1: 2 weeks of 2 or 3 sets x 6 repetitions
2 weeks of 2 or 3 sets × 4 repetitions
2 weeks of 2 or 3 sets × 3 repetitions

Option 2: 3 weeks of 2 or 3 sets × 6 repetitions
3 weeks of 2 or 3 sets × 3 repetitions

Option 3: Day 1: 2 or 3 sets × 4–6 repetitions
Day 2: 2 or 3 sets × 3–5 repetitions (each week)

Option 4: 6 weeks of 2 or 3 sets × 3–6 repetitions any way you like

Regardless of how you do it, bench press only twice per week. Furthermore, always work to muscular fatigue and always attempt to increase the resistance in the next identical workout once you achieve the target repetitions. In other words, train infrequently, train hard, and train progressively.

Following the last workout of week six, rest for 3 to 4 days. At this point, repeat the endurance test using the same weight as in the previous test with 70 percent of the 1-RM. The result? You should be able to obtain more repetitions than in the test you took six weeks earlier. The point? Even though training with low repetitions and heavy resistance (the conventional periodization method of developing only muscular strength)—and in a manner far removed from the high repetitions and light weight typically endorsed as being only for muscular endurance—there was an improvement in muscular endurance.

How? By working intensely to recruit, fatigue, and overload the maximum number of muscle fibers—accomplished by using heavy resistances—then recovering fully and repeating the procedure in a progressive manner. Over time, more fibers were able to be recruited because progression occurred (more are then available for submaximal efforts, i.e., there are more in the pool). Also, the inherent fatigue capacity of each fiber type was enhanced by repetitively exhausting them in the sets done to muscular fatigue each workout over the six-week period.

Strength/Endurance Example 4

Try one more test. This one will also take you six weeks. Determine a 1-RM as in the aforementioned examples. Over a six-week period, again do the bench press as in the previous format. Only this time, do 1–2 sets of 10–15 repetitions to muscular fatigue. As a suggestion, you can use one of the following:

Option 1: 2 weeks of 1 or 2 sets × 15 repetitions
2 weeks of 1 or 2 sets × 12 repetitions
2 weeks of 1 or 2 sets × 10 repetitions

Option 2: 3 weeks of 1 or 2 sets × 15 repetitions
3 weeks of 1 or 2 sets × 10 repetitions

Option 3: Day 1: 1 or 2 sets × 12–15 repetitions
Day 2: 1 or 2 sets × 10–12 repetitions (each week)

Option 4: 6 weeks of 1 or 2 sets × 10–15 repetitions any way you like

Following the last workout of week six, rest three to four days. At this point, test for another 1-RM. It should be greater than the one you did six weeks earlier. Even though training with high repetitions and light resistance (the conventional periodization method of developing only muscular endurance)—and in a manner far removed from the low repetitions and heavy resistance traditionally endorsed as being only for muscular strength—there was an improvement in muscular strength.

How did this occur? Again, by working intensely to recruit, fatigue, and overload the maximum number of muscle fibers—accomplished this time by using lower (yet still significant) resistances—then recovering fully and repeating the procedure in a progressive manner, there was an improvement in muscular strength. Over time, more fibers were again able to be recruited since progression occurred (more are then available for maximal efforts, i.e., there are more in the pool). Also, the inherent fatigue capacity of the Type IIb fibers (their recruitment needed for the maximal effort) was maximized by repetitively exhausting them in the sets to muscular fatigue during each workout over the six-week period.

DETERMINING PROPER RESISTANCE/REPETITIONS

The amount of resistance and number of repetitions to be used during strength training is a heavily debated and complicated issue. However, such debate becomes unnecessary if logic is applied to the facts. By considering the motor unit recruitment process and genetic factors, a practical basis for resistances/repetitions can be established.

The Force/Time Continuum Factor

The strength continuum concept can help to create a better understanding of the training resistance/repetition relationship in strength training. But it should not be the lone determinant of the amount of resistance or number of repetitions to prescribe. There are other factors that must also be taken into consideration.

Research suggests that the recommended minimum amount of resistance in a strength training program should be approximately 60 percent of a 1-RM (Roundtable 1985; MacDougall 1986; Fleck and Kraemer 1987). In other words, to gain at least the minimum benefits the weight in a strength training program should be significant enough to create some type of muscular tension and resultant force requirement—and roughly 60 percent of a 1-RM is generally accepted as the minimum standard. Assuming that this is plausible, a force factor of 60 percent can be established as the minimum level on the continuum. At the opposite end is the 1-RM itself or a force factor of 100 percent.

The other continuum factor is time. The number of repetitions performed can be equated to this time factor. The time factor, therefore, is the time that it takes to perform a maximum number of repetitions with a given percentage of a 1-RM. Exercising with 60 percent of a 1-RM—because it represents the lighter end of the continuum—also represents the longest potential time and highest number of repetitions on the continuum (all other factors being equal). The shortest potential time and the lowest number of repetitions is naturally the 1-RM on the opposite end.

The exact length of time it takes to perform an exercise to the point of momentary muscular fatigue with a given percentage of the 1-RM (and consequent number of repetitions achieved) is dependent upon many factors.

1. *The specific exercise.* The distance a resistance must be moved may be different from one exercise to the next. For instance, a compound exercise (e.g., an overhead press) may take longer to perform than a single-joint exercise (e.g., a bicep curl) because of the differences in range of motion (all other factors being equal).
2. *The cadence.* The speed of movement employed is also critical. One person may perform an exercise in a deliberately slow and controlled manner, while another person may move as quickly as possible. Also, one person may pause momentarily between repetitions, while another may proceed immediately to the next repetition.
3. *The amount of resistance.* Naturally, a light resistance can be moved relatively faster than a heavy resistance (all other factors being equal).
4. *Genetics.* An individual's fiber-type percentage, neurological ability, limb length, and insertion points of tendons on bones have an impact. In brief, one person may fatigue at an earlier point in time as compared to another due to his or her genetics (all other factors being equal).

Awareness of these factors makes it obvious that numerous time/repetition combinations are possible along the continuum. Regardless, the continuum concept can be best understood if an arbitrary minimum is set at the 60 percent end.

Assuming that a maximum of 15 repetitions were possible with 60 percent of a 1-RM and each repetition was performed in five seconds (relatively slow), the total time to reach fatigue in an exercise would be approximately 1:15 (one minute and 15 seconds). Assuming that a maximum of 20 repetitions were possible and each repetition was performed in two seconds (relatively fast), the elapsed time at the point of fatigue would be about 40 seconds.

The point: If a person exercises with at least 60 percent of a 1-RM—even in consideration of other factors such as the type of exercise, cadence, and genetics—the duration of the exercise from the first repetition to the point of fatigue falls within the anaerobic process. Therefore, any mention of high repetitions (i.e., 15–20) for the development of endurance must somehow be justified as endurance within the anaerobic processes. (This is not the same as cardiovascular endurance.)

The second issue relative to the continuum is the tension/force factor of motor unit recruitment. Recall the two examples that revealed the reality of lifting light and heavy resistances relative to recruitment and fatigue. The light resistance can be lifted for a longer period of time than the heavier resistance. This has to do with the initial tension caused in the muscles and the motor unit fiber-type characteristics. Figure 3.3 depicts a hypothetical comparison of light and heavy resistances, their initial tension created, and the motor unit involvement during exercise to the point of momentary muscular fatigue.

The heavier resistance activates a high percentage of motor units at the outset of the exercise due to the higher tension created and resultant demand for high force output. Due to the fiber-type characteristics within the motor units, however, the high force-producing but more fatigable Type II motor units limit the time of exercise.

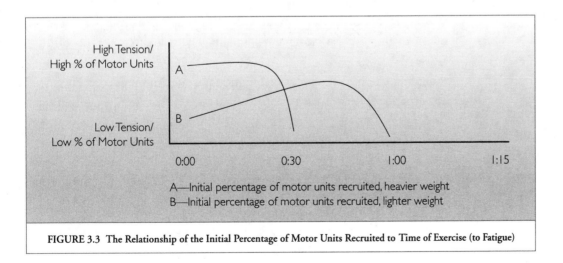

FIGURE 3.3 The Relationship of the Initial Percentage of Motor Units Recruited to Time of Exercise (to Fatigue)

The lighter resistance, relatively speaking, requires fewer initial motor units. At the outset of the exercise, it does not rely heavily upon the Type II motor units and, therefore, provides more potential working time prior to fatigue. The more enduring motor units can fuel the exercise with the Type II motor units serving as a backup source when fatigue begins to take its toll.

So, along the continuum there is the minimal tension requirement of 60 percent of a 1-RM; an initial percentage of available motor units activated depending upon the magnitude of the resistance used; and a range of repetition/time combinations that are possible depending upon many factors—all of which fall within the anaerobic process.

But the critical point here pertains to the anaerobic factor. The 60 percent of a 1-RM that is generally accepted as the minimum tension requirement is, in reality, not a light resistance. Although it is 40 percent lighter than the 1-RM, it is 60 percent more tension-producing than exercising against no resistance at all.

Analyzing this point from the latter perspective, 60 percent of a 1-RM does, therefore, create a significant amount of tension within the muscles—provided that an exercise is taken to the point of momentary muscular fatigue. As such, a great demand is placed upon the motor units activated within the anaerobic energy pathways.

Even though using 60 percent of a 1-RM involves a relatively lower initial tension (i.e., the light resistance example), a significant number of motor units—and a large percentage of muscle fibers—will be activated by continuing the exercise (fatigue/recruitment options) to the point of fatigue. The end result is an exercise performed with a high level of intensity regardless of the initial tension.

To bring all of this together at this point—and in the attempt to keep it simple—it has been shown that the optimal resistances/repetitions for strength training:

1. should allow the exercise to fall within the anaerobic energy process (from 0:00 to approximately 1:15)
2. should create a significant initial level of tension in the muscles at the outset of the exercise movement—specifically, at least 60 percent of a 1-RM
3. should be taken to the point of fatigue for a maximum overload
4. are dependent upon such factors as the type of exercise, the cadence used in performing the exercise, the person's inherent muscle fiber type and neurological ability, plus leverage factors

THE GENETIC FACTOR

To establish a practical method of prescribing appropriate resistances and repetitions, it is necessary to revisit the influence of genetics.

Fiber Type

An individual endowed with a higher percentage of Type II muscle fibers may be able to demonstrate greater strength than an individual with a lower percentage of Type II muscle fibers. Remember, Type II fibers have a higher force-generating ability than Type I fibers. On the other hand, an individual with a higher percentage of Type I fibers may be able to demonstrate a greater ability in sustaining a submaximal effort—relative to a 1-RM—than an individual with a lower percentage of Type I fibers. Note the genetic and performance characteristics in the following hypothetical examples:

Subject A
high percentage of Type I fibers
low percentage of Type II fibers
1-RM overhead-press strength of 120 pounds
80 percent of the 1-RM (96 pounds) for 13 repetitions

Subject B
average percentage of Type I fibers
average percentage of Type II fibers
1-RM overhead-press strength of 170 pounds
80 percent of the 1-RM (136 pounds) for 10 repetitions

Subject C
low percentage of Type I fibers
high percentage of Type II fibers
1-RM overhead-press strength of 205 pounds
80 percent of the 1-RM (164 pounds) for 7 repetitions

Notice that Subject A is relatively weaker compared to the other two subjects in terms of the 1-RM overhead-pressing strength. However, due to the higher percentage of Type I fibers, Subject A can perform a greater number of repetitions with a submaximal resistance—that is, 80 percent of the 1-RM. Subject C is just the opposite, with the highest 1-RM of the three subjects but a decreased ability in a submaximal effort—a result of a limited amount of Type I fibers.

Subject B represents the average person who has an average 50-50 mix of the Type I and II fibers. The resistance/repetition prescription of conventional strength training programs is based upon the abilities of the average person.

Neurological Ability

As noted earlier, many people have neglected to consider the role of neurological ability in strength training. However, this factor may have a considerable impact on the work output potential.

Neurological ability—that is, the innate ability to activate a maximal number of motor units—may be the deciding factor in a person's potential to develop muscular strength/endurance. An individual may be able to exert a great deal of strength, not only because of a higher percentage of Type II fibers but also due to the ability to activate a very large percentage of the available motor units regardless of type. In this case, the neurological ability is high. As a result, this person's submaximal ability (muscular endurance) may be lower despite having a higher percentage of Type I fibers. The following hypothetical examples should clarify any confusion:

Subject D
high percentage of Type I fibers
low percentage of Type II fibers
high neurological ability
1-RM overhead-press strength of 175 pounds
80 percent of the 1-RM (140 pounds) for 5 repetitions
75 percent of the 1-RM (131.25 pounds) for 6 repetitions
70 percent of the 1-RM (122.5 pounds) for 7 repetitions

Subject E
average percentage of Type I fibers
average percentage of Type II fibers
average neurological ability
1-RM overhead-press strength of 175 pounds
80 percent of the 1-RM (140 pounds) for 10 repetitions
75 percent of the 1-RM (131.25 pounds) for 12 repetitions
70 percent of the 1-RM (122.5 pounds) for 14 repetitions

Subject F
low percentage of Type I fibers
high percentage of Type II fibers
low neurological ability
1-RM overhead-press strength of 175 pounds
80 percent of the 1-RM (140 pounds) for 11 repetitions
75 percent of the 1-RM (131.25 pounds) for 13 repetitions
70 percent of the 1-RM (122.5 pounds) for 15 repetitions

At first glance, one might conclude that subject D—due to the higher percentage of Type I fibers and lower percentage of Type II fibers—would not be strong. However, it's quite possible that the high neurological ability permits the activation of a very large number of motor units—both Type I and Type II—during an all-out effort. Remember, the high force requires both the Type I and Type II fibers to be activated in accordance with the Size Principle of Recruitment, but in the submaximal efforts (e.g., 80 percent, 75 percent, and 70 percent) a high neurological ability means that a large number of motor units are activated and, therefore, fewer backup units are available for continued force output. This is why a relatively low number of repetitions is achieved during the submaximal exertions.

Subject F, on the other hand, is endowed with a higher percentage of Type II fibers but a low neurological ability. In an all-out effort, this low neurological ability limits the capability to activate a large number of motor units—including the Type II fibers—but it also means that more backup units are available for extending the output of force. As a result, more repetitions are possible in the submaximal efforts of Subject F as compared to Subjects D and E.

One may question the validity of this hypothetical situation and argue that the percentage of fiber type might be more significant than neurological ability. This is a legitimate point, but individuals like those described in the preceding examples do exist.

Many people are equally strong in a 1-RM but differ in terms of the number of repetitions they can perform with an identical submaximal resistance. For instance:

Subject G
1-RM overhead-press strength of 200 pounds
80 percent of the 1-RM (160 pounds) for 7 repetitions

Subject H
1-RM overhead-press strength of 200 pounds
80 percent of the 1-RM (160 pounds) for 10 repetitions

There are also those individuals who are very different in terms of 1-RM strength but who can perform the same number of repetitions with identical submaximal resistances. For example:

Subject I
1-RM overhead-press strength of 160 pounds
120 pounds (75 percent of the 1-RM) for 6 repetitions

Subject J
1-RM overhead-press strength of 150 pounds
120 pounds (80 percent of the 1-RM) for 6 repetitions

But on the average, most individuals—regardless of 1-RM strength—can perform similar repetitions with identical percentages of submaximal resistances. As an example:

Subject K
1-RM overhead-press strength of 180 pounds
75 percent of the 1-RM (135 pounds) for 10 repetitions

Subject L
1-RM overhead-press strength of 220 pounds
75 percent of the 1-RM (165 pounds) for 10 repetitions

THE NORMAL CURVE

From a statistical point of view, a large number of individuals are average in terms of fiber-type percentage and neurological ability. However, individuals with very unique genetic abilities, as described in the previous examples, exist—although they occupy opposite ends of the statistical normal curve. This distribution is depicted in Figure 3.4.

The distribution of the percentage of fiber types/neurological abilities on the normal curve shown in Figure 3.4 are hypothetical but, in reality, may be very close to this estimation. The bottom line is that force-output potential is strongly influenced by various genetic abilities. For a given percentage of a 1-RM, therefore, it is not realistic to expect that every individual can perform exactly the same number of repetitions.

FLAWS OF THE TRADITIONAL PERCENTAGE SYSTEM

It is now obvious that there are numerous possibilities for prescribing resistances/repetitions because of individual differences—especially in athletic populations. For the average person, it may be possible to establish a ballpark figure. However, there is a more practical method based on what we know so far.

The traditional method of determining repetitions for specific resistances has been based upon percentages of a 1-RM. Today, there are many different repetition tables and charts that attempt to assign an exact number of repetitions for specific percentages of a 1-RM. The established figures have some worth when one has no idea of what to prescribe. But, as shown by the previously listed genetic factors,

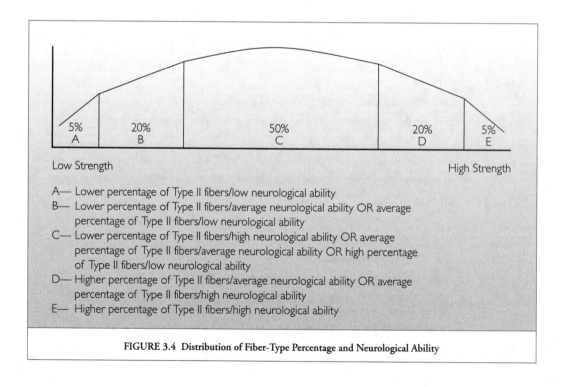

FIGURE 3.4 Distribution of Fiber-Type Percentage and Neurological Ability

relying solely upon the ability to do a specific number of repetitions with a given percentage of a 1-RM can be quite confusing and unproductive.

Studies have examined how many repetitions can be performed with a given percentage of a 1-RM. The results of this research confirm and highlight the fact that there are individual differences.

A study by Hoeger and his colleagues (1987) used 38 male subjects who had no previous experience in strength training. Each subject was tested for a 1-RM on seven different exercises and then performed a maximum number of repetitions with 40 percent, 60 percent and 80 percent of the 1-RM on separate training days.

The mean (average) number of repetitions performed (M) and standard deviation (SD) with selected percentages of a 1-RM for some of the exercises are shown in Table 3.1.

In a study by Westcott (1993), 87 subjects (49 men and 38 women) were tested for a 1-RM on a Nautilus® 10-degree chest machine. After a five-minute recovery period, each subject performed a maximum number of repetitions with 75 percent of the 1-RM. As noted in Table 3.2, the results again revealed varying abilities.

Table 3.1 Mean Number of Repetitions Performed (M) and Standard Deviation (SD) with Selected Percentages of a 1-RM (Hoeger et al. 1987)

	40% 1-RM		60% 1-RM		80% 1-RM	
	M	SD	M	SD	M	SD
Leg Press	80.1	47.9	33.9	14.2	15.2	6.5
Bench Press	34.9	8.8	19.7	4.9	9.8	3.6
Leg Curl	18.6	5.7	11.2	2.9	6.3	2.7
Lat Pulldown	41.5	16.1	19.7	6.1	9.8	3.9
Bicep Curl	24.3	7.0	15.3	4.9	7.6	3.5

CONFUSING AND UNPRODUCTIVE

Using a ballpark figure for repetitions can really cause a problem when mega-multiple sets are used. Attempting to assign a specific number of repetitions to a given percentage of a 1-RM for numerous sets can make progression a bewildering hit-and-miss endeavor. And the more sets that are performed, the worse it becomes.

Take the example of an exercise prescription that requires individuals to perform one set of exactly 10 repetitions with 75 percent of a 1-RM. Three subjects with different levels of strength achieve the following results:

Subject 1: 75 percent of a 1-RM for 8 repetitions, failed during the ninth

Subject 2: 75 percent of a 1-RM for 10 repetitions exactly, could not have performed more

Subject 3: 75 percent of a 1-RM for 10 repetitions, could have performed more

Table 3.2 Number of Repetitions Performed with 75% of a 1-RM and Number of Subjects Performing Those Repetitions (Westcott 1993)

Number of Repetitions Performed with 75% of a 1-RM	Number of Subjects Performing the Repetitions
5	2
6	3
7	4
8	10
9	9
10	16
11	11
12	10
13	10
14	4
15	3
16	1
17	2
19	1
24	1

After the completion of the exercise, it would be obvious that an adjustment should be made for Subjects 1 and 3 if the resistance was to perfectly match the 10 repetitions specified. To do exactly 10 repetitions, Subject 1 must use *less* than 75 percent of a 1-RM, while Subject 3 must use *more* than 75 percent. An adjustment can be made by simply decreasing or increasing the resistance, respectively.

Now assume that a multiple-set exercise prescription was performed by the same three subjects with the following outcomes:

	Actual Repetitions Achieved		
Prescription	Subject 1	Subject 2	Subject 3
Set 1: 75% × 10 repetitions	8	10	13
Set 2: 80% × 8 repetitions	6	8	10
Set 3: 84% × 6 repetitions	3	6	7
Set 4: 88% × 4 repetitions	2	3	5

Subject 1 was not able to achieve the prescribed number of repetitions in the first set and, consequently, the remaining three sets were well off target. Subject 2 achieved the desired number of repetitions in the first three sets but missed the last set by one repetition. Subject 3 surpassed the prescribed repetitions in all four sets. Several questions come to mind: What type of adjustment(s) in resistance should be made for each subject so that the prescribed number of repetitions is attained in the next training session? And for which set(s) should the adjustments be made? After all, which sets are the most important for the purposes of progression? Furthermore, if appropriate adjustments are made, will they allow the prescribed repetitions to be met in the next session? If not, what must be done?

It is now obvious that assigning exact repetitions for specific percentages of a 1-RM can create problems when it comes to establishing a progressive program. Constant adjustments of the resistance and/or manipulation of the percentages to establish appropriate overloads may occur so frequently that it becomes very confusing and ineffective.

EXERCISE DIFFERENCES

Another problem with using standardized percentages for specific numbers of repetitions is the differences among the exercises. In the study mentioned earlier by Hoeger and his associates (1987), the subjects managed to perform an average of 9.8 repetitions on both the bench press and lat pulldown with 80 percent of a 1-RM. However, repetitions done with 80 percent of a 1-RM on the leg curl (6.3), bicep curl (7.6), and leg press (15.2) reveal the unmistakable differences among exercises.

Personally, I have experimented in many exercises by doing as many repetitions as possible with various percentages of a 1-RM. I, too, have found that some exercises differ significantly. The problem is not with the exercises that differ by one or two repetitions but the ones that differ anywhere from four to six repetitions or more.

If the same established number of repetitions for percentages of a 1-RM were assigned to every exercise, they would be fairly accurate for some but way off the mark for others—especially for a leg press. If this is the case, some attempts at overload would be fairly accurate while others would not. And coupled with the dissimilarity between individuals, the exercise differences would create another problem: keeping track of progression. Because of this, a more accurate method must be used.

IMPLICATIONS FOR PRESCRIBING RESISTANCES/REPETITIONS

Based upon all of the information that has been presented, practical methods can be established for accurate exercise prescriptions. The ultimate goal should be to recruit and fatigue the greatest number of muscle fibers during each bout of exercise.

There are no etched-in-stone rules for exact numbers of repetitions; common sense should be the guide. The number of repetitions to perform is simply dictated by the amount of resistance (weight) that is used. Here are some general guidelines.

1. Use resistance/repetitions that allow for muscular fatigue within the anaerobic energy pathway (up to approximately 1:15 of time under tension).

2. Adopt a minimum of 60 percent of the 1-RM as a standard if percentages are used.

3. Incorporate various repetition schemes (and corresponding resistances) ranging from a higher number (e.g., 12–15) to a lower number (e.g., 3–6). This adds variety to the training program. Different repetition ranges can be used to develop a progressive plan over each training period. Finally, it accounts for individual fiber-type percentages, neurological abilities, and exercise differences. Indeed, some individuals may obtain better results with either a higher (12–15), moderate (7–10) or lower (3–6) number of repetitions.

4. Make the training productive and safe. A higher number of repetitions allows more potential time under tension with less joint stress; a lower number of repetitions allows the freedom to occasionally use slightly heavier weights that do create some time under tension but without the extreme forces that come into play when you use maximal weights.

5. Avoid using extremely heavy resistances (i.e., maximal or near maximal). If even the slightest amount of control is lost when performing an exercise, near-maximal resistances increase the risk of injury. Regardless of the lifting form, they also increase the potential dangers due to greater force being imposed upon the muscles and joints. Lastly, near-maximal resistances allow for only a few repetitions, thus reducing the quality of muscle fiber overload. Lighter (yet tension-producing) weights allow for a greater number of repetitions and, likewise, more overall fiber involvement (more time under tension).

There are three progressive resistance/repetition systems that can be used: repetition ranges, target repetitions, or a percentage-to-fatigue method.

Repetition Ranges

One of the simplest yet most effective forms of progression is the use of repetition ranges. A repetition range is a span of repetitions using the double-progression format: Increase the number of repetitions within the range with a given weight and then increase the weight when the high end of the range is achieved. Suggested formats for using repetition range are detailed in Table 3.3.

Target Repetitions

In simple terms, target repetitions are single repetitions to aim at during each set such as 6 (for a single set) or 12 and 8 (for two sets). While doing each work set,

Table 3.3 Suggested Formats for Repetition Ranges

Number of Sets per Exercise	Upper Body Exercises			Lower Body Exercises			Abs
	Low	Med	High	Low	Med	High	
1	4–6	7–9	11–13	5–7	9–11	14–16	15–20
2	5–7	9–11	11–13	6–8	11–13	14–16	10–15
	3–5	5–7	8–10	4–6	8–10	11–13	10–15
3	6–8	9–11	11–13	7–9	11–13	14–16	
	4–6	7–9	9–11	5–7	9–11	11–13	
	3–5	5–7	7–9	4–6	7–9	9–11	

it should be a challenge to obtain the prescribed target repetitions. Progression occurs by gradually increasing the weight to match the target repetitions. Suggested formats for using target repetitions are shown in Table 3.4.

Percentages to Fatigue

This is an effective progression system that can satisfy the tradition-bound coach who is unwilling to give up the percentage of 1-RM sets/repetition method. This system can also be used without actually testing for a 1-RM. The 1-RM can be estimated by using a submaximal weight for maximum repetitions. This is more practical than performing a 1-RM for all exercises, and also much safer.

Rather than use the traditional arbitrary number of repetitions for each set, percentages of 1-RM are used. However, each set is done for a maximum number of repetitions to fatigue with a given percentage (such as 76 percent or 82 percent). Not only does this ensure quality and direct overload but it eliminates the potential problems associated with predetermined repetitions and individual genetic abilities. Suggested formats for using percentages to fatigue are depicted in Table 3.5.

Table 3.4 Suggested Formats for Target Repetitions

Number of Sets per Exercise	Upper Body Exercises			Lower Body Exercises			Abs
	Low	Med	High	Low	Med	High	
1	5	8	12	6	10	15	20
2	6	10	12	7	12	15	12
	4	6	9	5	8	12	12
3	7	10	12	8	12	15	
	5	8	10	6	10	10	
	4	6	8	5	8	10	

Table 3.5 Suggested Formats for Percentages

Number of Sets per Exercise	Upper Body Exercises			Lower Body Exercises			Abs
	Low	Med	High	Low	Med	High	
1	88%	79%	70%	85%	76%	67%	NA
2	85%	76%	67%	82%	73%	64%	NA
	91%	82%	73%	88%	79%	70%	NA
3	82%	73%	64%	79%	70%	61%	
	88%	79%	70%	85%	76%	67%	
	91%	85%	79%	88%	82%	76%	

SPEED OF EXERCISE MOVEMENT

The speed at which a weight can be lifted concentrically depends upon three factors: (1) the weight itself (relatively heavy or relatively light); (2) the effort put forth (intentionally slow or intentionally fast); and (3) the muscle's level of fatigue (fresh or fatigued).

That said, keep in mind these three options for the speed of movement depending upon those factors:

Factor 1. **A light weight can be moved relatively fast when the muscles are fresh, but the momentum slows down as fatigue occurs.**

When a light weight (e.g., 60 percent of a 1-RM) is lifted relatively fast, fewer muscle fibers are initially involved because the task is a lower demand. Also, the effort to move it relatively fast creates momentum that further decreases fiber involvement. Consequently, a high number of repetitions can be performed in this manner—that is, you can lift a light weight relatively fast—until fatigue finally takes its toll on the working fibers.

Factor 2. **A light weight can also be lifted relatively slowly when the muscles are fresh, but it slows even more as fatigue occurs.**

When this same light weight is intentionally lifted relatively slowly—making it more demanding—more fibers are actually involved during each repetition as compared to Factor 1 due to reduced momentum. A lower number of repetitions (compared to Factor 1) can be performed using this intentionally slower manner until fatigue finally takes its toll on the working fibers.

Factor 3. **A heavy weight can only be lifted relatively slowly even when the muscles are fresh but it slows down as fatigue occurs.**

**(Remember, if a heavy weight can be lifted relatively fast then
it is actually a light weight.)**

When a heavy weight (e.g., 85 percent of a 1-RM) is lifted relatively slowly—the
only way it *can* be lifted—the higher demand involves more fibers initially as compared to both previous examples. Even fewer repetitions (compared to Factor 2) can
be performed due to the initial involvement of the more fatigable Type II fibers.

Now, assume the following realistic performance possibilities in the previous
factors.

1. Light weight/relatively fast–17 repetitions are done with a ballistic speed
   of movement at an average of 2.0 seconds per repetition for a total of 34
   seconds.
2. Light weight/relatively slow–10 repetitions are done with a controlled
   speed of movement at an average of 4.5 seconds per repetition for a total
   of 45 seconds.
3. Heavy weight/relatively slow–4 repetitions are done with a controlled
   speed of movement at an average of 4.5 seconds per repetition for a total
   of 18 seconds.

This leads to some very interesting conclusions.

- The 17 repetitions performed in the light weight/relatively fast example
  probably involved the same type and number of muscle fibers as the 10
  repetitions performed in the light weight/relatively slow example (force
  factor/Size Principle of Recruitment). However, the additional 7 repetitions were due to the ballistic nature of the movement (momentum = less
  fiber involvement = more fibers available for the remaining 7 repetitions).
  Therefore, nothing was gained by the ballistic emphasis other than a
  greater risk of injury. In fact, even though 7 more repetitions were performed, the total time of exercise was actually 9 seconds less.
- The 5 repetitions done in the heavy weight/relatively slow example
  required an emphasis on moving the weight with great effort (fast emphasis), but due to the intrinsic character of the weight itself, the movement
  was naturally slow.
- Slowing down the speed of movement and emphasizing the time under
  muscular tension—whether using light weights or moving heavy weights
  naturally slower—involves more muscle fibers during each repetition.
  Because momentum is reduced, this also decreases the potential for
  injury. And even though moving relatively slow, an emphasis on a controlled, explosive effort can be done with heavier weights or with lighter
  weights when fatigue naturally begins to slow the movement speed.

THE MUSCULAR STRENGTH TO MUSCULAR POWER RELATIONSHIP

Another controversial issue is the relationship between muscular strength and muscular power. Power is a measure of the rate of work performed or Force × Distance/Time (F × D/T). In athletics, it is the execution of quick and explosive—yet forceful—muscle contractions during skill performance. Strength is considered to be a display of maximum force irrespective of a time element—a maximal synchronous activation of motor units. Therefore, it is assumed that to develop power through strength training it is necessary to employ quick/explosive/fast rates of movement. At first glance, this may seem plausible. When the facts are examined more closely, however, it is flawed logic (and a dangerous practice).

It has been proven that when strength increases then power also increases (Devries 1980; Westcott 1987). Referring back to the expressions of muscle activation, the conventional descriptions of strength and power fall within the confines of the strength continuum. That is, maximal strength governs the system and power is expressed within it.

Strength/Power Example 1

Assume that an individual has a 1-RM of 400 pounds in the deadlift. Naturally, when the 400 pounds is lifted it does not move relatively fast because it is a heavy, demanding effort. Nevertheless, a maximum number of muscle fibers is activated to complete the lift. The speed of movement is relatively slow, but a larger percentage of fibers is recruited and synchronized, firing at an optimal rate to complete the demanding task. Suppose that the weight in this 1-RM lift is reduced by 50 percent to 200 pounds. If the 200 pounds is lifted with the same effort as the 1-RM (400 pounds), the weight would be lifted easier and faster. But momentum is greater, which results in lower overall muscle activation. Suppose that the 200 pounds is decreased by 50 percent to only 100 pounds. Again, the weight would move even easier and faster but with even more momentum and less overall muscle activation. Finally, suppose that the weight is reduced to that of an empty 45-pound Olympic bar. If the 45 pounds is lifted with the same effort as used when lifting the 400 pounds, the speed of movement would be very fast but the muscle activation would be at a bare minimum.

The point of this experiment is obvious: The faster the speed of movement, the less requirement there is for the muscles to perform the task. When lifting a relatively light weight fast, fewer fibers have the potential to be overloaded as compared to lifting a relatively heavy weight (a naturally slower movement but with greater fiber involvement). Heavier, slower-moving weights (proper strength training!) do, therefore, develop power via the lifter's conscious effort to recruit and synchronize fibers and emphasize explosiveness even when the lifting speed is naturally slow.

Strength/Power Example 2

Assume that the same individual with a 1-RM of 400 pounds in the deadlift can also perform a 1-RM of 250 pounds in the power clean. The person then trains for eight weeks doing deadlifts (using a slow, controlled speed and heavy weights) but no power cleans. After the eight weeks of progressive training, suppose that the 1-RM in the deadlift increased to 425 pounds. Not surprisingly, the 1-RM in the power clean should increase as well. Even though the power clean was not performed for eight weeks, the increased strength from deadlifting allows more weight to be lifted in the power clean. Does the increased 1-RM in the power clean mean that the individual has developed more power? Yes, but the increase in power resulted from getting stronger in the deadlift.

Strength/Power Example 3

An example noted by Yessis (1981) concerns the difference between strength and power using a comparison of an exercise's speed of movement. His argument is that the speed of contraction must be trained separately as—at some point—a person's strength begins to level off.

Two points should be made here.

1. At least this argument is suggesting that increasing strength does increase power.
2. If it were true that the speed of contraction had to be trained in the weight room when a strength limit was reached, it would only apply to a limited number of individuals. In terms of maximal strength, the vast majority of strength trainees are a long way from achieving their genetic potential.

A brief overview of the example given by Yessis follows.

If a subject bench pressed 200 pounds a distance of two feet in two seconds, then the power output would be 200 foot-pounds per second (200 lb × 2 ft/2 sec = 200 ft-lb/sec); if the same feat was performed in only one second, then the power output would be 400 ft-lb/sec (200 lb × 2 ft/1 sec = 400 ft-lb/sec).

It should be noted that in his article, Yessis erroneously used watts as the units in his calculations. He would have been correct if 1 watt was equal to 1 ft-lb/sec but it is equal to 44.22 ft-lb/min. So, ft-lb/sec is used here for the sake of accuracy and simplicity.

That said, here are three more points worth considering:

1. The resistance was obviously moved intentionally slower during the bench press that took two seconds to complete.
2. If the same resistance was indeed moved in half the time—that is, in one second—then it involved more momentum and less fiber activation.

3. Essentially, the strength of the subject was expressed in two different ways—both expressions falling within the confines of the existing strength level (strength continuum). Simply moving the resistance relatively fast does not mean that power is being trained.

Yessis also noted that if the subject's strength was increased so that 400 pounds could be moved a distance of two feet in two seconds, then the power output (400 ft-lb/sec) would be no different than moving 200 pounds a distance of two feet in one second.

Here are two additional points:

1. If one can move 400 pounds (a heavier resistance) a distance of two feet in two seconds, then it is clear that the same person can move 200 pounds (a lighter resistance) relatively faster.
2. If the subject's strength level was truly increased to 400 pounds, then it should be possible to lift 200 pounds even faster than one second. Assuming that 200 pounds was lifted a distance of two feet in 0.75 seconds, the power output would then be 533 ft-lb/sec—a display of 133 ft-lb/sec more power than both lifting 400 pounds a distance of two feet in two seconds and 200 pounds a distance of two feet in one second. Increasing strength, therefore, increases the expression of power.

Here is the heart of the matter: If the expression of muscular power is improved through the increase in muscular strength, then it only seems logical to implement a program that is geared toward a safe development of maximal strength. Ballistic momentum-producing methods of developing power are not necessary and significantly increase the likelihood of injury. So if an individual's strength is continually increasing, why deviate from this safer approach to power development?

THE TRUTH ABOUT THE OLYMPIC LIFTS

From a historical perspective, the Olympic lifts were incorporated in the training of athletes supposedly to develop power that could be transferred to athletic competition. The full-body, multi-joint, dynamic characteristics of the snatch, clean, jerk, and their variations are purportedly athletically related to similar movements in a wide range of sports and skills, such as jumping for a rebound, driving off the line of scrimmage, throwing a discus, and so on.

Olympic lifting (or weightlifting) is a sport in itself. Due to the nature of the sport, the lifts do require a high level of work output. Starting at zero velocity, force must be applied to the barbell to raise it as high as possible so that the lifter can drop to catch it at chest level (a clean) or at full-arm extension overhead (a snatch). In the jerk, the lower body must provide maximum force to assist in raising the bar from its resting position on the upper chest to full-arm extension overhead. Outstanding technique is a requisite for those who aspire to succeed in the sport of Olympic lifting.

Top-level Olympic lifters—those who are considered world-class competitors—are genetically gifted in terms of their body structures, leverages, and muscle quality. That is why they are at such a high level. They spend a great deal of time working on the mechanics of the lifts (skill) and, not surprisingly, they engage in strength training programs that consist of basic exercise movements such as front/back squats, presses, and so on. This is quite evident from old issues of the *Soviet Sports Review*, a periodical that is loaded with information on training for Olympic lifting. Becoming stronger is obviously important to these athletes.

The heated controversy of whether or not to use the Olympic lifts to train athletes who are not competitive weightlifters mainly pertains to the nature of the lifts. At first, the apparently explosive power demonstrated in the execution of one of the lifts may seem quite impressive. Naturally, one cannot be passive during the lift—the lifter must go all out. But—and this is a significant *but*—if one looks closely, the actual body movement isn't all that impressive. Essentially, it is a quick deadlift-type movement in an attempt to pull the bar as high as possible prior to dropping under it. More specifically, from the initial bar movement—depending upon which lift is performed—force must be applied to accelerate the bar. As force is applied, the bar accelerates, resulting in a loss of force application and a concomitant decrease in muscle activation. The bar then decelerates and the body must move quickly to catch it in the desired position. In essence, the body is moving quickly away from the intended movement of the bar. The naked eye registers the quickness of the body movement, but it is a quick movement with little or no resistance.

Some may argue that the bar is moving quickly, relatively speaking, in the latter stages of the acceleration phase—that is, when the bar passes the hips in the pull from the floor or as it passes the face during the jerk—and that this is the key benefit of the exercises. When the bar does pass the hips in the clean or snatch, the double-knee bend and scooping action of the hips, if mastered, provides further impetus for acceleration.

In the clean and the snatch, the double-knee bend and consequent scooping of the hips places the bar in a more favorable position from which to complete the pull. The slight rebending of the knees elicits a stretch reflex, which in turn increases the force that can be applied, and the bar accelerates again. So in essence, from the floor the bar accelerates, then decelerates, then accelerates again (if the knee bend and scooping are executed) and finally decelerates, which then requires the lifter to move opposite the resistance to catch the bar.

It is true that the bar is moving at its highest rate during the acceleration phases. These positions are very favorable in terms of leverage factors and this surely doesn't hinder the movements. It is also noteworthy that the Olympic lifts are unique because they require both upper- and lower-body impetus: the extension of the low back, hips, and legs, the shrugging of the shoulders, and the pulling by the arms. But remember that the initial pull on the bar along with the thrust in the double-knee bend and pulling action requires a recruitment of available motor units. However, the speed or momentum of the bar, depending on the resistance, decreases muscle activation.

Performing the Olympic lifts with light resistances allows for faster bar movement. This is obvious from the force/speed factors of muscle activation previously discussed. It is also known that light resistance requires the use of fewer motor units. It is also obvious that the opposite is true; as the resistance becomes heavier, more force is needed to move it. Therefore, the speed of movement decreases but the muscles are still exploding into the resistance, firing as hard as possible to move it.

This brings us to the crux of the matter: What do the Olympic lifts offer as a panacea to power development that slower controlled and safer exercises do not? How quickly should the bar be moving? What is the optimal speed of the bar with regard to optimal power development? Basic exercises performed with appropriate resistances also require explosiveness or rapid firing of motor units in a more controlled manner—but not with the greater potential of injury characteristic of ballistic-type movements. For example, in the ascent from the bottom position to the starting position in a barbell squat, the bar can also be accelerated. Like the Olympic lifts, this is a result of more favorable leverage. Furthermore, if a light resistance is used in the squat it can also be moved faster—but, of course, with fewer motor units required for the task. This also applies to the Olympic lifts. The same situation exists with a heavier resistance: more motor units but a slower speed of movement.

The bottom line is that the Olympic lifts may look like great power developers because unique body actions are employed and both the upper torso and the lower body are required to execute the movements, which creates more potential distance through which the bar can move, making the lifts look even more unique. But through applying the force/speed factors of muscle activation and deductive reasoning, the benefits of the Olympic lifts are really no different than the potential of basic exercises. And if the benefits lie in the stretch reflex—a natural phenomenon anyone can activate—what is its mechanism for adaptation? This has yet to be determined.

An Olympic lift becomes a strength exercise as the resistance becomes heavier. And this heavier resistance is what is needed if a maximum number of motor units are to be activated and overloaded. The movements can develop strength—and therefore power—if they are done on a regular basis, are done progressively, and create an overload. In other words, Olympic lifts can develop power if they are practiced just like any other exercise. However, by now it is obvious that they do not have to be performed to get an edge on the competition. A program might seem to lack an edge if it does not include an explosive full-body movement as a novelty exercise. But what is the real, primary goal of strength training? Is it to look impressive or to develop functional strength? Consider this point before deciding whether to implement these lifts into a program.

The fact that, compared to basic exercises, the lifts require more instruction and supervision must also be considered. Additional time and effort are required for developing the skills needed to perform the lifts properly; they are more complex than basic exercise movements. Therefore, consider whether it is practical to implement the Olympic lifts from the standpoint of time efficiency.

The other factor that must be addressed is the risk of injury. The ballistic nature and unpredictability of the Olympic lifts—is the bar going to end up being racked, dropped, or in the lifter's lap?—obviously present a risky situation. To a degree, proper instruction minimizes this problem. But again, what is the primary objective of strength training? The main focus should be to take the safest available route to build functional strength and minimize the potential for injuries in the athletic arena so that the individual can actually compete.

One more thing: An individual with unfavorable leverages—such as long legs and/or a long torso—will find it especially difficult to execute these lifts correctly and safely. What does one do in this case? If the Olympic lifts are presumed to be magical exercises, how can you justify not implementing them in an attempt to develop power in those athletes who lack desirable body proportions? Won't these athletes then be at a distinct disadvantage compared to their opponents? Good luck in explaining this to the head sport coach.

Is it realistic to believe that incorporating the Olympic lifts will result in measurable power increases? And if significant measurable power did occur, can it be certain that it wasn't a result of consistent, long-term strength increases from more controlled, less momentum-producing exercises—such as the squat, leg press, deadlift, stiff leg deadlift, upright row, and so on—combined with favorable genetics and dedicated practice of sport-specific skills? Safer methods are more practical and have been proven just as effective.

IMPLICATIONS FOR PROPER EXERCISE FORM

Knowing that muscular tension is maximized as momentum is minimized, the speed of movement during an exercise should be slower, not faster. If a relatively lighter weight is used, it should be intentionally moved slower. When fatigue begins to take its toll, the movement naturally slows down, thereby requiring the trainee to attempt to move the weight faster using a controlled, explosive effort. A relatively heavy weight naturally moves slower from the outset, which also requires the trainee to lift the weight with a controlled, explosive effort. In either case, provided that the exercise is taken to the point of momentary muscular fatigue, strength is being developed as well as power and muscular endurance.

As such, the objectives of each set of an exercise should include all of the following.

1. Involve as many muscle fibers as possible. The highest possible tension (fiber involvement) should be created, depending upon the magnitude of the resistance used. The greatest number of fibers should be recruited and synchronized during the initial repetition and continued for each repetition thereafter regardless of the weight used.

2. Perform each repetition through the greatest and safest possible ROM that is inherent to the targeted muscles. Common sense dictates that if a muscle or group of muscles act upon a joint in a certain ROM, it is necessary for the fibers to contract against a resistance through this ROM. This is important for three main reasons. First, it improves functional ability. Muscles will become functionally stronger through the exercised ROM. Second, it improves flexibility. Working a muscle or group of muscles through their greatest possible ROM at a particular joint will contribute to the functional flexibility at that joint. Finally, it involves the maximum number of fibers. The entire muscle belly will only contract fully when taken from a completely lengthened (extended) position to a completely shortened (flexed) position. Contraction through a partial ROM requires less fiber involvement, but a full ROM guarantees the involvement of more fibers.

3. Use a controlled lifting technique. For safety reasons and maximal fiber involvement, the weight should be moved in a deliberate, controlled manner. Bouncing, heaving, jerking, or moving at relatively fast speeds should be avoided because such movements create momentum that decreases the muscular tension, resulting in fewer fibers being activated and, therefore, fewer fibers being overloaded. Such movements also increase the risk of muscle and joint injury.

4. Fatigue the greatest number of fibers possible. By following the three previous rules—and then performing each set to the point of muscular fatigue—a maximal number of muscle fibers will be overloaded through a full ROM, giving the muscle(s) the stimulus to grow and adapt.

IMPACT OF NUMBER OF SETS

The number of sets necessary to improve strength is directly related to the resistance/repetition factors previously discussed. In the long run, it is the maximal involvement of muscle fibers and resultant fatigue that are the determining factors in this controversial issue.

Past studies used multiple sets and various combinations of repetitions to determine the best means to develop strength. Many different combinations of sets and repetitions proved effective. Consequently, the tradition has been to conduct strength programs with some type of multiple-set approach—usually in the range of 4–8 sets.

Multiple-set usage also has its roots in the competitive lifting arena. Weight-lifting and powerlifting—two sports that depend upon the ability to lift maximal resistances—require a lot of practice and, therefore, they use multiple sets. It is not surprising that the heavy lifting and multiple sets go hand-in-hand with strength programs aimed at enhancing athletic performance. But as an adjunct to overall development, strength training for athletes need not be performed this way.

In recent years, research has compared single-set training to multiple-set training. These studies have proved that no significant differences exist in the magnitude of strength increases between one set of an exercise and multiple sets (Westcott 1987; Carpinelli 1996). The intensity of the exercise bout—not the number of bouts—is the key element that determines the stimulus for strength gains. In other words, if a bout of an exercise is extremely demanding and involves a maximal amount of muscle tissue—thus creating an overload—only a limited number of bouts are necessary.

Strength training should also be efficient enough to allow time for other training components, such as team practices, sport-specific skill work, conditioning, and other matters that impact athletic success. Because strength training is only one piece of the performance puzzle, it stands to reason that the most time-efficient program should be sought.

The Reality of Multiple Sets

I'm not trying to discourage multiple sets. Not all individuals are capable of giving the proper effort time after time in a one-set program. Performing an additional set of an exercise—even a third set in some instances—is not going to get anyone arrested for fraudulent overuse of sets. But there is a point where enough is enough. I do, therefore, discourage mega-multiple sets. If a third set is too much, it makes little sense to perform additional sets.

Performing mega-multiple sets can create potential problems.

1. Diminishing returns. If the first set is worked hard, its effect will be felt if a second set is performed. If a third set is performed, there is no doubt that it will be quite difficult to complete—and likely not even necessary. When four or more sets are required—and each set is worked hard in succession—each succeeding set will create an unnecessary expenditure of energy, digging into recovery ability.

2. Confusion about the overload. When doing mega-multiple sets, it is confusing as to which sets are the stimulus for the overload. Knowing that performing three very demanding sets is more than enough to create an overload, assume that six work sets (not including any warm-up sets) are

scheduled for an exercise. This situation begs several questions. What is the purpose of three additional sets beyond that which is necessary to achieve an overload? Where should the three additional sets be located in the six-set sequence? How hard should the three additional sets be worked relative to their position in the sequence?

3. Confusion with progression. The more sets one performs—especially those based upon a percentage of a 1-RM scheme—the more chance he or she has of losing track of progression over a period of time. What adjustments should one make if the sets are not accurate—that is, more or fewer repetitions have been done—and how much adjustment should one make to accurately conform to the forthcoming session? Constant adjustments in the weight and percentages not only create confusion, they result in loss of quality training time.

4. Additional exercises. Besides the fact that numerous sets of a single exercise can be unproductive, many traditional programs incorporate one, two, or even three other exercises for that same body part/muscle group—each one done for multiple sets as well. Needless to say, this compounds the problem and makes the program even more unproductive.

5. An overemphasis or underemphasis of exercises. In traditional programs, some exercise movements are prioritized (with a high number of sets) and others are de-emphasized (with a low number of sets). Traditional programs usually label exercises as core (overemphasized) and supplementary (underemphasized). The supposed rationale for this is to enhance performance with presumed skill-specific exercises. Consequently, the core exercises receive more attention and the supplementary exercises receive less, thus making strength imbalances more likely.

6. Inefficient use of time. Needless to say, performing an unnecessarily high volume of sets is not time-efficient.

Something has to give in mega-multiple set schemes. When the stimulus for strength adaptation has been triggered, what purpose do extra sets—or an extra exercise—serve other than to waste time or to expend unnecessary energy? The greater the number of hard sets performed for each exercise and/or body part, the less productive each subsequent set becomes. If one, two, or even three sets are worked hard, why do more?

The Reality of Minimum Sets

The objective of proper strength training is to recruit the greatest number of muscle fibers, overload (fatigue) them, and then allow enough recovery time between training sessions for strength gains to occur. Therefore, every attempt should be made to get right to it and eliminate the unproductive work that is characteristic of many multiple-set programs. Remember, the end result is not to emulate competitive weightlifters but to develop overall functional strength.

A reduction in training volume does not necessarily mean implementing a one-set-to-fatigue-and-one-set-only approach—which usually strikes fear in the hearts of people because of the supposedly limited amount of work that is prescribed. A close look at most nontraditional high intensity training (or HIT) programs reveals that multiple sets of an exercise can be useful. Some may perform one or two different exercises for the same body part/muscle group using 1–3 sets for each exercise. But the idea is to maximally fatigue the muscle—and this can be accomplished by using a minimal number of quality sets taken to fatigue. It is important to monitor an individual's ability to tolerate this intensity. Some may need to reduce the number of sets taken to fatigue. Some may tolerate only one set.

Keep the number of sets at a minimum (1–3), get the most out of each set (perform the maximum possible number of repetitions), record the resistance used and the repetitions achieved in each set, and always attempt to progress from one session to the next. Essentially, this is a simple, efficient, and productive approach that allows for progression, accurate documentation for all exercises, and time to address all muscle groups that are important to the integrity of the entire musculoskeletal system.

Unfortunately, many people do not buy this. They believe that "more is better"—that is, performing more sets is the avenue to follow for better strength increases, particularly on the core exercises that supposedly enhance performance more than supplementary exercises do. These individuals do not fully understand the type of effort required to properly perform a set. A properly performed set to fatigue is more difficult than a set stopped prior to fatigue at a predetermined number of repetitions. It is especially difficult in those exercises that involve a great deal of muscle mass such as a deadlift and a leg press. When individuals do perform such exercises to absolute fatigue, the discomfort they experience may cause them to rationalize that it would be better to decrease the intensity of effort, stop at X number of repetitions, and perform more sets. They feel that the mental and physical demands imposed upon them are just not worth the effort.

This is actually the essence of the problem. If the intensity of effort is a key ingredient for maximum gains in strength, decreasing the intensity obviously will produce something less than maximum gains. Performing numerous sets at a lower intensity level—although less discomforting—is not the answer in terms of time efficiency, accurate progression, energy usage, and recovery.

The early Iron Game pioneers provide a lesson in strength training. Using limited resources, these individuals trained hard because this was the only way they understood. And by doing so, basic exercises were used without the complications of the set/percentage game.

The 20-rep squat routine popularized by J. C. Hise in the early part of the 1900s was very basic and productive, albeit brutally difficult. It simply called for one set of barbell squats done for 20 repetitions but with a resistance that would normally be lifted for approximately 10 repetitions. As pioneer John McCallum described it in Strossen (1989):

> "You're gonna do one set of twenty repetitions . . . and it's gonna be the hardest work you've ever done. You gotta be absolutely annihilated when you finish. If you can even think of a second set, then you're loafing. All the muscle you'll ever build depends upon how hard you work on this one set of squats."

This isn't to say that all individuals should accept the challenge of the 20-rep squat routine. However, it does show what is possible with work that is simple, limited, and demanding. If this approach to getting the most out of each set were taken, a great deal of time could be saved and invested elsewhere.

IMPLICATIONS FOR PRESCRIBING SETS

As a guideline for establishing a productive and efficient number of sets, the 8/20 and 3/3 rules are recommended. These rules apply only to total-body workouts (which are recommended), not to split-body routines (which are not recommended).

8/20 and 3/3 Rules

The 8/20 rule means that no more than 8 multi-joint exercises and 20 total sets should be performed in each workout. The 3/3 rule means that of the total number of exercises used, only 3 multi-joint exercises—one upper-body pushing movement, one upper-body pulling movement, and one lower-body movement—can be done for a maximum of 3 sets each. This will keep the workouts efficient while minimizing the risk of overtraining.

Number of Sets per Exercise

One or two sets should be done for most exercises. A third set can be used under the 3/3 rule. Because multiple pushing, pulling, and leg exercises may be used, the one- or two-set recommendation is critical due to muscle overlap, potential to overtrain, and time efficiency. Here are some examples.

- wide-grip pulldown × 3 sets
- weighted dip × 2 sets
  machine bench press × 1 set
- leg press × 2 sets
  trap bar deadlift × 1 set

Number of Sets per Workout

Using the 8/20 and 3/3 rules as a guideline, no more than 20 total sets of multi-joint exercises should be employed. Here are some examples.

- (3 exercises × 3 sets) + (3 exercises × 2 sets) = 15 total sets
- (2 exercises × 3 sets) + (5 exercises × 2 sets) + (2 exercises × 1 set) = 18 total sets
- (1 exercise × 3 sets) + (4 exercises × 2 sets) + (3 exercises × 1 set) = 14 total sets
- 8 exercises × 2 sets = 16 total sets

To prevent overtraining, using multi-joint exercises and working each set hard may require even fewer sets per workout—perhaps 9–12 total sets.

CONCLUDING COMMENTS

Although there are many different interpretations of the technical aspects of muscle contraction, this chapter examined and clarified the basic principles and their implications as they apply to strength training. The rationale behind both the fact and theory that has been discussed can benefit any individual seeking to implement a productive, safe, efficient strength training program.

For proper strength training, the bottom line is to do the following:

1. Address all major muscle structures of the body.
2. Use safe exercise technique through a full ROM.
3. Create overload by working to momentary muscular fatigue for maximum muscle-fiber recruitment.
4. Be as time efficient as possible—that is, use a minimal number of exercises, sets, and training sessions.
5. Be progressive in terms of increasing the amount of resistance and/or repetitions performed.
6. Allow enough recovery time between training sessions to permit gains in strength.

Inasmuch as muscular strength improves athletic performance, these general guidelines will help all athletes develop their maximum strength potential in preparation for competition.

A growing number of strength and fitness professionals are now beginning to align themselves with sensible interpretations of muscle contraction such as those presented in this chapter. Their programs are effective in terms of increasing muscular strength in a safe and efficient manner. They have also proven to be an integral component in the preparation of athletes for the demands of competition.

Championship teams and individual athletes at the high school, college, and professional levels have used strength training programs based upon these or very similar views.

For the sake of safety, efficiency, and productivity, there should be an all-out exodus from the traditional methods of strength training. Traditional strength training programs are usually characterized by methods that are unsafe and inefficient and frequently lead to overtraining because of excessive volume. Any athletic success using these methods is often due to highly skilled and motivated athletes who receive excellent sport coaching. In other words, the success is in spite of the strength training program not because of it.

In the future, more emphasis should be placed on the real issues of strength training, which include discussion of the following:

1. Determine the specific muscle-fiber types/neurological abilities of each athlete to individualize exercise prescriptions.

2. Determine what constitutes the minimum amount of strength training required to produce maximum gains rather than jumping on the bandwagon of tradition and arbitrarily prescribing, for example, the ubiquitous four-day split routine. Wouldn't it be desirable to discover that training only twice per week—or only once every four days—could render similar or even better results than training more frequently?

3. Reeducate sport coaches in all aspects of strength training. Coaches need to fully understand that the impact of the strength program alone—regardless of the approach—can only do so much when it comes to winning. They also need to understand that a proper strength training workout places the athlete in a depleted state and, consequently, requires adequate recovery time. This means that other program components—such as practices and conditioning activities—may need to be adjusted to reap the benefits of the strength training program.

4. Educate and then demonstrate to athletes what intense strength training actually is. Knowing that their time in the weight room can be minimized if they train with greater intensity, athletes may better appreciate hard work. Time-efficient methods that are based upon low volume and high intensity will allow them more time for other important daily commitments—in stark contrast to time-consuming methods based upon higher volume and lower intensity.

5. Motivate the athletes. Proper strength training requires commitment, focus, and effort. Some athletes simply do not like to participate in strength training because it is uncomfortable and unenjoyable. It takes time, and, frankly, some athletes are lazy. If you have athletes who are not motivated to work hard—or who totally resist your program—you have your work cut out for you. Being creative and employing different motivation techniques is an ongoing process.

Remember that the profession of strength training athletes began when someone who was highly motivated about lifting weights—either a former athlete, weightlifter, powerlifter, or bodybuilder—was employed for the purpose of getting athletes to do the same. Being a highly motivated and knowledgeable former strength trainee does not necessarily guarantee that all athletes will follow your example.

6. Once and for all, put an end to the time wasting and argued-to-death moot debates of (1) free weights versus machines and (2) the specificity of skill transfer from the weight room to the playing field. Both free weights and machines can increase muscular strength if used properly. And strength training exercises—specific skills themselves—cannot be transferred to a supposed similar movement or skill on the athletic field.

"The conventional view serves to protect us from the painful job of thinking."

John Kenneth Galbraith

REFERENCES

Bigland-Ritchie, B., F. Bellemare, and J. J. Woods. 1986. Excitation frequencies and sites of fatigue. In *Human muscle power*, ed. N. L. Jones, N. McCartney, and A. J. McComas, 197–211. Champaign, IL: Human Kinetics.

Carpinelli, R. N. 1996. Single versus multiple sets. *Hard Training Newsletter* 1: 3–5.

Devries, H. 1980. *Physiology of exercise*. 3rd ed. Dubuque, IA: W. C. Brown Publishers.

Edgerton, V. R., R. R. Roy, R. J. Gregor, and S. Rugg. 1986. Morphological basis of skeletal muscle power output. In *Human muscle power*, ed. N. L. Jones, N. McCartney, and A. J. McComas, 43–59. Champaign, IL: Human Kinetics.

Faulkner, J. A., and T. P. White. 1990. Adaptations of skeletal muscle to physical activity. In *Exercise, fitness and health*, ed. C. Bouchard, R. Shepard, T. Stephens, J. Sutton, and B. McPherson, 265–279. Champaign, IL: Human Kinetics.

Fleck, S., and W. Kraemer. 1987. *Designing resistance training programs*. Champaign, IL: Human Kinetics.

Green, H. J. 1986. Muscle power: Fibre type recruitment, metabolism and fatigue. In *Human muscle power*, ed. N. L. Jones, N. McCartney, and A. J. McComas, 65–79. Champaign, IL: Human Kinetics.

Hoeger, W. W. K., S. L. Barette, D. F. Hale, and D. R. Hopkins. 1987. Relationship between repetitions and selected percentages of one repetition maximum. *Journal of Applied Sport Science Research* 1 (1): 11–13.

MacDougall, J. D. 1986. Morphological changes in human skeletal muscle following strength training and immobilization. In *Human muscle power*, ed. N. L. Jones, N. McCartney, and A. J. McComas, 269–285. Champaign, IL: Human Kinetics.

Palmieri, G. 1983. The principles of muscle fiber recruitment applied to strength training. *National Strength and Conditioning Association Journal* 5 (5): 22–24, 63.

Perrine, J. J. 1986. The biophysics of maximal muscle power outputs: Methods and problems of measurement. In *Human muscle power*, ed. N. L. Jones, N. McCartney, and A. J. McComas, 15–22. Champaign, IL: Human Kinetics.

Roundtable. 1985. Determining factors of strength: Part I. *National Strength and Conditioning Association Journal* 7 (1): 10–19, 22–23.

Sale, D. G. 1986. Neural adaptation in strength and power training. In *Human muscle power*, ed. N. L. Jones, N. McCartney, and A. J. McComas, 289–305. Champaign, IL: Human Kinetics.

Stone, M. H., D. Wilson, R. Rozenek, and H. Newton. 1984. Anaerobic capacity: Physiological basis. *National Strength and Conditioning Association Journal* 5 (6): 40, 63–65.

Strossen, R. J. 1989. *Super squats.* Larkspur, CA: Iron Mind Enterprises.

Wescott, W. 1987. *Strength fitness.* 2nd ed. Boston: Allyn and Bacon.

———. 1993. How many repetitions? *Nautilus* 2 (3): 6–7.

Wilmore, J. H., and D. L. Costill. 1988. *Training for sport and activity: The physiological basis of the conditioning process.* 3rd ed. Dubuque, IA: W. C. Brown Publishers.

Yessis, M. 1981. A response to the reaction of Dr. Wolf to the Yessis critique of Nautilus. *National Strength and Conditioning Association Journal* 3 (2): 32–35.

Thanks to my colleagues Robert M. Otto, Ph.D., John Wygand, M. A., Richard Winett, Ph.D., and my brother Peter for their contextual and literary critique of this chapter, as well as my wife Sandee and my mom for their support and tolerance.

4

The Multiple-Set Myth

Ralph N. Carpinelli, Ed.D.
Human Performance Laboratory
Department of Health, Physical Education and Human Performance Science
Adelphi University

The *Oxford English Dictionary* defines *myth* as a "widely held belief, a misconception, or a misrepresentation of the truth." There is a myth permeating the fitness community that multiple sets of an exercise are superior to a single set for increasing muscular strength and size (hypertrophy). Accordingly, the prevalent recommendation is to perform multiple sets (at least three) of each exercise. But there is little scientific evidence and no theoretical physiological basis to suggest that a greater volume of exercise (multiple sets) elicits a greater increase in strength or hypertrophy. The absence of compelling evidence to support the multiple-set training philosophy, and the abundance of evidence suggesting that a single set of each exercise is just as effective as multiple sets, will be discussed in this chapter. This information represents an important practical application of time-efficient low-volume exercise.

The recommendation to perform multiple sets appears in strength training books; in health, fitness, and muscle magazines; and in strength training reviews and exercise physiology textbooks. However, the literature supporting the prevalent belief that multiple sets are superior to a single set is circuitous at best, and misinformative at worst, as is evidenced by the following reviews and textbooks that recommend performing multiple sets. Figure 4.1 illustrates the maze of cross-referencing that has little or no factual foundation and reveals the illusion of multiple sources of evidence. Strength training reviews by Atha (1) and Clarke (13) cited a training study by Berger (3), which is discussed in great detail in this chapter. McDonagh and Davies (49), referenced another study by Berger (4), which did not compare the number of sets (it compared different numbers of repetitions). Fleck and Kraemer (21) cited the reviews by Atha (1) and McDonagh and Davies (49). Kraemer, Fleck, and Deschenes (42) and Kraemer and Koziris (40) cited Atha (1), Clarke (13), McDonagh and Davies (49), and Fleck and Kraemer's strength training book (20), which referenced Atha (1) and McDonagh and Davies (49). Kraemer and Bush (38) cited another strength training book by Fleck and Kraemer (23). Kraemer and Baechle (37) cited Atha (1) and Clarke (13). Lillegard and Terrio (47) referenced an article by Kraemer and Fleck (39) who cited their book (20) and the reviews by Atha (1), McDonagh and Davies (49), and Clarke (13). Behm (2) cited an article by Tesch and Larsson (75), which was not a training study, and a textbook chapter on training by Tesch (76). Exercise physiology textbooks by Berger (7), Bowers and Fox (9), Kearney (34), Fox (24), Fox and Mathews (25), and Fox, Bowers and Foss (26), cited Berger's training study (3). Enoka (19) referenced the book by Fleck and Kraemer (20), reviews by Atha (1), McDonagh and Davies (49), and Sale and McDougall (63), which did not discuss the number of sets. Wilmore (83) cited Clarke (14), who cited Berger's study (3). Wilmore and Costill (84) and Plowman and Smith (55) cited the book by Fleck and Kraemer (20). Fleck and Kraemer (23) cited the reviews of Atha (1) and McDonagh and Davies (49), as well as three strength training studies that did not support the superiority of multiple sets. Powers and Howley (58) cited Berger's study (3), Berger's textbook (7), and a book by Stone and O'Bryant (71), which cited Berger (5) and Clarke (13). Brooks, Fahey, and White (10), DeVries and Housh (18), Fleck and Kraemer (22), Guyton (28), Howley and Franks (30), Knuttgen (35), Lamb (44), McArdle, Katch and Katch (48), Noble (53), Schmidtbleicher (64), Shaver (65), Shepard (66), Snyder (68), Tesch (76), Wathen (79), and Zatsiorsky (86) had no references to support their recommendations to perform multiple sets.

With the exception of Berger (3), there was no training study reported in any of the aforementioned strength training reviews (1, 2, 13, 21, 37, 38, 39, 40, 42, 47, 49) or textbooks (7, 9, 10, 18, 19, 20, 22, 23, 24, 25, 26, 28, 30, 34, 35, 44, 48, 53, 55, 58, 64, 65, 66, 68, 71, 76, 79, 83, 84, 86) that would support the claim that multiple sets are superior to a single set for increasing muscular strength and hypertrophy.

Many of the studies that are cited in this chapter have extraneous variables such as different numbers of repetitions, amount of resistance, specific muscle groups, exercise equipment, and types of muscle actions within a single investigation. An extraneous variable is anything other than the independent variable (e.g., the number of sets) that may influence the outcome of an investigation (e.g., muscular strength and hypertrophy). To validate a training study, the investigator needs to control, or at least seriously consider, the extraneous variables. However, the purpose of this chapter is to present an objective account of all the published strength training studies that reported the results of training with single or multiple sets. For a comprehensive review of the methodology and results of all the studies in this chapter, please refer to a review article by Carpinelli and Otto enti-

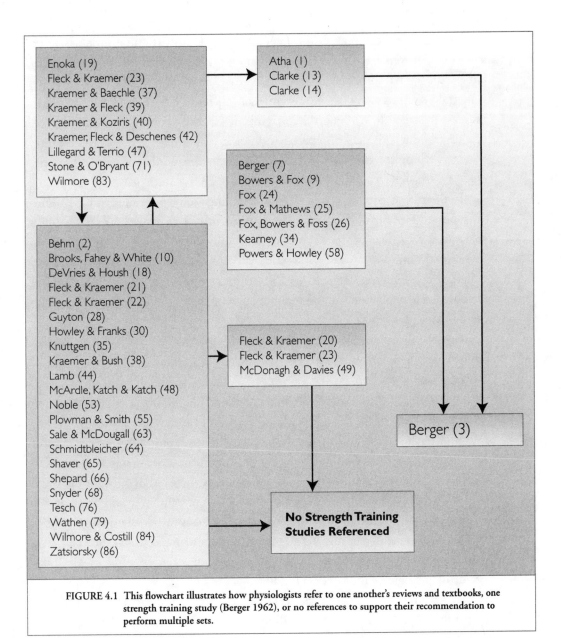

FIGURE 4.1 This flowchart illustrates how physiologists refer to one another's reviews and textbooks, one strength training study (Berger 1962), or no references to support their recommendation to perform multiple sets.

tled "Strength Training: Single Versus Multiple Sets" in *Sports Medicine* 26 (2): 73–84, 1998.

The word *significant*, which is used many times in this chapter, implies that a statistical procedure was used by the researchers to determine whether or not there was a change in some variable, such as the one-repetition maximum (1-RM) strength, and whether the change was due to the training protocol or to chance. The possibility of chance (a random event) influencing the results is real, and statistical analyses can help identify how often chance may influence the results. Most researchers use the *P<.05 level of significance*, which means that the probability of the results occurring by chance is less than 5 percent; that is, more than 95 percent of the time the results are due to the specific training protocol. This level of significance applies to differences in pre- to post-training variables as well as to comparisons between different training protocols. For example, two different protocols may produce significant increases in 1-RM strength, such as 15 percent and 20 percent, and show no significant difference between protocols for the increase in strength. Although the magnitude of change may be greater as a result of one training protocol compared to another, the difference may not be great enough to indicate that one protocol is superior to the other. That is, the difference is probably accidental (random fluctuations), not statistically significant.

In the most frequently cited strength training study, published in 1962, Berger (3) reported that nine groups of males (approximately 20 in each group) exercised three times a week for 12 weeks. In addition to their regular weight-lifting program, which was not described in the report, participants performed different combinations of sets and repetitions (sets × repetitions) in the free-weight bench-press exercise. All of the groups showed significant increases in 1-RM bench press (Table 4.1).

Berger (3) reported that the maximal rate of strength development resulted from three sets of six repetitions (3 × 6). The 3 × 6 protocol did produce the greatest increase in 1-RM bench press. However, a comparison of the individual groups, who performed similar numbers of repetitions (2, 6, or 10), shows that the increase in strength for the 3 × 6 group was significantly greater than for the 2 × 6 group, but not significantly greater than for the 1 × 6 group. The 3 × 2 group had a significantly greater increase in strength than the 2 × 2 group, but it was not significantly greater than the 1 × 2 group. Nor was there any significant difference in 1-RM between the following groups: 1 × 6 and 2 × 6, 1 × 2 and 2 × 2, 1 × 10 and 2 × 10, 1 × 10 and 3 × 10, 2 × 10 and 3 × 10. Seven out of the nine possible comparisons (groups performing the same number of repetitions) showed no statistically significant difference in the magnitude of strength gains as a result of performing single or multiple sets (Table 4.2).

Berger (3) also compared the results of training with one, two, or three sets by combining the nine groups according to the number of sets performed in training. Training with either one set or two sets produced similar improvements in strength (22.3 percent and 22.0 percent, respectively), while training with three sets elicited an increase of 25.5 percent (Table 4.3). The difference between training with one set and three sets was 3.2 percent (1.8 kg) at the end of 12 weeks of training in apparently healthy, previously untrained, college-age men (pre-training 1-RM = 56.6 kg). Berger concluded: "Thus, training with three sets increased

Table 4.1 Increase in 1-RM Bench Press (Berger 1962)								
Group	**1 × 2**	**1 × 6**	**1 × 10**	**2 × 2**	**2 × 6**	**2 × 10**	**3 × 2**	**3 × 6**	**3 × 10**
%	20.0	25.5	21.6	17.3	22.9	25.1	23.5	29.6	23.0
kg	11.3	14.5	12.2	9.3	12.9	14.2	13.3	16.7	13.0

Table 4.2 Comparison of Groups Performing a Similar Number of Repetitions (Berger 1962)

Groups	
3 × 6 and 2 × 6	SD
3 × 6 and 1 × 6	NSD
2 × 6 and 1 × 6	NSD
3 × 2 and 2 × 2	SD
3 × 2 and 1 × 2	NSD
2 × 2 and 1 × 2	NSD
3 × 10 and 2 × 10	NSD
3 × 10 and 1 × 10	NSD
2 × 10 and 1 × 10	NSD

NSD: No statistically significant difference between groups
SD: Statistically significant difference between groups at .05 level

strength significantly more than training with one or two sets, and training with one or two sets produced essentially similar improvement." However, Berger also stated that "the improvement rates were practically the same during the last three weeks of training." In fact, the rate of improvement from weeks 9 to 12 for the combined groups was 4.0 percent for the one-set group and 3.4 percent for the three-set group. Similarly, the rate was 4.8 percent for the 1 × 6 group and 4.0 percent for the 3 × 6 group.

If three sets of six repetitions were superior to other training protocols, subsequent studies should have replicated those results, and they have not.

A follow-up study by Berger (5) failed to support his conclusion that three sets of six repetitions (3 × 6) was the best training protocol. Three groups trained three times a week for nine weeks performing either a 6 × 2, 3 × 6, or 3 × 10 protocol in the bench-press exercise. All groups showed significant increases in 1-RM bench press (16.9 percent, 21.3 percent and 20.0 percent, respectively), with no significant difference among the groups. That is, the 3 × 6 protocol was not superior to the 3 × 10 protocol. In Berger's previous investigation (3), he reported that the 3 × 6 protocol showed significantly greater increases in 1-RM bench press than the 3 × 10 protocol. Berger (5) concluded: "Further research is needed to determine the optimum combination of sets and repetitions per set to perform for the

Table 4.3 Percent Increase in 1-RM Bench Press When the Nine Groups Were Combined into One-, Two-, and Three-Set Groups (Berger 1962)

One Set	Two Sets	Three Sets
22.3%	22.0%	25.5%*

* Increase for three sets was significantly greater than either one set or two sets.

greatest improvement of strength." Regrettably, Berger did not publish additional strength training studies.

Ten years later, in his book *Conditioning for Men* (6), Berger recommended performing three to five sets of each exercise for optimal strength, and in his *Introduction to Weight Training* (8), he recommended performing five to nine sets of each exercise. In his textbook *Applied Exercise Physiology* (7), published 20 years after his original training study, Berger claimed that for maximizing strength, three sets were more effective than fewer sets. The only reference that Berger cited was his first training study (3).

The only other study to support multiple-set training was by Kraemer and colleagues (43). They compared single and multiple sets of seven free-weight exercises performed three times a week for 14 weeks. The groups had significant increases in 1-RM squat. The multiple-set groups showed significantly greater increases in 1-RM squat than the single-set group. There was no significant change in body mass or body composition in any group. No data were reported for the changes in 1-RM strength or amount of resistance for the other six exercises, which were all excluded from the results. Another study by Kraemer and colleagues (41) compared single-set and multiple-set groups who trained for nine months. However, no absolute values or percent increases in strength were reported, nor any statistically significant differences in strength between the two training groups for any of the exercises at any of the 1-RM evaluations, which were performed at 0, 4, 6, and 9 months. Because the absence of data and statistical analyses leaves the report open to different interpretations, no legitimate conclusions can be drawn from this study. The two aforementioned studies (3, 43) constitute the only evidence suggesting that multiple sets may be superior to a single set for increasing muscular strength in two exercises: free-weight bench press and squat.

Thirteen studies (11, 15, 27, 31, 36, 51, 52, 57, 60, 61, 62, 77, 81) reported the results of training with either one set or two sets of each exercise. All the studies showed significant increases in strength. No study reported any significant difference in the increase in muscular strength or hypertrophy as a result of training with either one set or two sets. (See Figure 4.2.)

Seventeen studies (16, 17, 29, 32, 33, 45, 46, 50, 56, 59, 67, 70, 73, 74, 78, 80, 82) compared the effects of a single set versus three sets. All the studies reported significant increases in strength. No study showed any significant difference in the increase in muscular strength or hypertrophy as a result of training with either one set or three sets. (See Figure 4.3.)

Different studies compared one set, two sets, and three sets (72), one, two, and four sets (54), two sets and three sets (69), three, four, and five sets (85), and five sets and fifteen sets (12). All these studies reported significant increases in strength with *all* of the training protocols. However, none of these studies showed any significant difference between groups when comparing increases in muscular strength or hypertrophy. A greater number of sets was *not* shown to be better than one set.

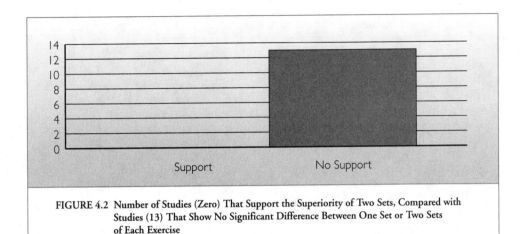

FIGURE 4.2 Number of Studies (Zero) That Support the Superiority of Two Sets, Compared with Studies (13) That Show No Significant Difference Between One Set or Two Sets of Each Exercise

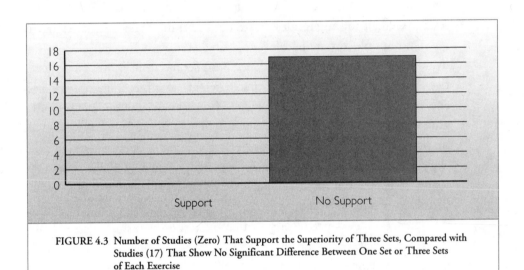

FIGURE 4.3 Number of Studies (Zero) That Support the Superiority of Three Sets, Compared with Studies (17) That Show No Significant Difference Between One Set or Three Sets of Each Exercise

It may be inferred that because most research showed no significant difference in strength gains or muscle hypertrophy between one set and two sets (11, 15, 27, 31, 36, 51, 52, 57, 60, 61, 62, 77, 81); one set and three sets (16, 17, 29, 32, 33, 45, 46, 50, 56, 59, 67, 70, 73, 74, 78, 80, 82); two sets and three sets (69); one, two, and three sets (72); one, two, and four sets (54); three, four, and five sets (85); and five sets or 15 sets (12), then no significant difference in the magnitude of strength gains or muscle hypertrophy should be expected as a result of training with one set or multiple sets, up to 15 sets. Figure 4.4 shows that only two strength training studies support the superiority of multiple sets compared with 35 studies that show no significant difference in the increases in strength as a result of training with a single set or with multiple sets. Most of the research, in fact 95 percent of the strength training studies, showed no difference between single- and multiple-set strength training.

This perusal of strength training research raises the question of whether one training study by Berger (3) that reported on one exercise (the bench press), and

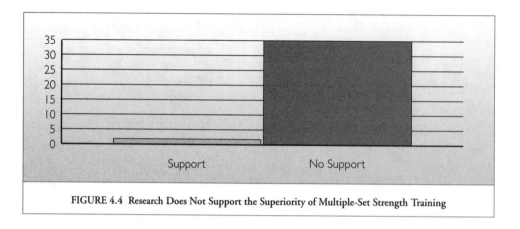

FIGURE 4.4 Research Does Not Support the Superiority of Multiple-Set Strength Training

one other study by Kraemer (43) that reported on one exercise (the squat) should set a precedent for an eternity of strength training. The preponderance of *opinion* that multiple sets are better than a single set of each exercise is not supported by the consensus of scientific evidence. One set has been shown to be just as effective as multiple sets—and more time efficient—for increasing muscular strength and hypertrophy in males and females of various ages, for a variety of muscle groups using diversified exercise devices. That is, there is insufficient evidence to support the prevalent belief that a greater volume of exercise (multiple sets) will elicit superior muscular strength or hypertrophy than will the minimal volume (one set). People can achieve similar results in less time, and with less work and a decreased potential for injury.

There is no evidence to suggest that the response to single versus multiple sets in trained athletes would differ from the response from untrained people. Nor is there any evidence that a single set of each exercise would be less productive than multiple sets for people in the general population, or in special populations such as the elderly, or cardiovascular or orthopedic patients who will not, or perhaps should not, perform each exercise to the point of muscular fatigue.

In addition to the increases in muscular strength and lean body mass, there are other potential health benefits to resistance exercise training, such as increased bone mineral density, increased connective tissue strength (ligaments and tendons), enhanced functional capacity (sports performance, stair-climbing power, walking speed, etc.), decreased body fat, decreased gastrointestinal transit time, lower resting blood pressure, lower heart rate and blood pressure responses to specific activities, increased metabolic rate, and enhanced psychological effects. There is no evidence that multiple sets are superior to a single set of each exercise in attaining these benefits.

Although it is often purported that multiple sets are required to properly warm up the muscles, there is no evidence to suggest that exercise specificity in warm-up is superior to a proper total-body warm-up for producing increases in strength. If a low range of repetitions, such as three to five, is desired for training, or if a competitive powerlifter or Olympic weightlifter is attempting a 1-RM, then one warm-up set with a lighter resistance may be appropriate.

From a psychological perspective, when a person anticipates the performance of multiple sets, the sets are commonly performed at a submaximal intensity. With only one opportunity (one set) to perform a specific exercise, there is a greater need to focus on each repetition and to perform that set at a higher intensity. This should result in a greater stimulus to the neuromuscular system. There is a lack of scientific evidence to suggest that the resulting stimulus ought to be applied multiple times.

In every aspect of applied physiology, science first requires that a protocol must be shown to be safe and effective; then a dose-response ratio is established. The rule is to prescribe the smallest dose that will elicit the desired response, with minimal adverse effects. The preponderance of scientific research reports that one set (minimal dose) elicits the desired response (muscular strength and hypertrophy), so why perform three, five, or a larger number of sets of each exercise with the false notion that more is better? If this approach were applied to prescription medication, the results could be disastrous. Fitness enthusiasts and recreational athletes should attempt to attain the benefits of resistance exercise training by administering the minimal dose of exercise (that is, the minimal dose required to achieve the desired response), not the most tolerable dose.

The Size Principle of Recruitment states that muscle fibers are recruited from the smaller fibers to the larger fibers, and that recruitment through the spectrum of muscle fibers is primarily dependent on the intensity of exercise; that is, how difficult the exercise is, not how much exercise is performed. There is no physiological concept that would suggest that a larger volume of exercise elicits greater increases in strength or hypertrophy. The goal should be to *stimulate* physiological adaptation, such as increased muscle size and strength, not to increase the number of sets that can be *tolerated*.

Science places the burden of proof on the claimant. If the claim is that multiple-set strength training is superior to single-set training, it should be supported by a preponderance of evidence from peer-reviewed scientific literature. At this time, it is not. Dedicated trainees and well-intentioned trainers and coaches who are concerned about the safest and most efficient way to increase muscular strength and hypertrophy are bombarded with a plethora of misinformation, most of it based on variations of training routines performed and promoted by genetically gifted, often drug-induced athletes. Meaningful scientific research, such as the strength training studies cited in this chapter, is conducted primarily with drug-free participants who have average genetic potential for increasing muscular size and strength, and who represent the vast majority of the exercising population. Guidelines for training should be based on the results of these studies.

Scientific research proceeds by the systematic performance of experiments and the carefully controlled collection of data that will either support, or fail to support, a specific hypothesis (an unproved theory). People who believe in myths use the adage: *The absence of evidence is not evidence of absence.* However, in science this line of reasoning is inadmissible. When a hypothesis is formulated, and the research fails to support that hypothesis, *that absence of evidence is evidence of absence.* If the hypothesis is that multiple sets of an exercise are more productive than a single set and the preponderance of research fails to support that hypothesis, that absence of evidence is evidence that there is most likely no significant difference in the increase in muscular strength or hypertrophy as a result of performing single or multiple sets.

Regardless of how strongly one believes in a myth, or how often a myth is repeated or convoluted, it is still a myth. The widely held belief that multiple sets are superior to a single set is still a myth.

REFERENCES

1. Atha, J. 1981. Strengthening muscle. *Exercise and Sport Science Reviews* 9, ed. D. I. Miller, 1–73. Philadelphia, PA: Franklin Institute.

2. Behm, D. G. 1995. Neuromuscular implications and applications of resistance training. *Journal of Strength and Conditioning Research* 9 (4): 264–274.

3. Berger, R. A. 1962. Effect of varied weight training programs on strength. *Research Quarterly* 33 (2): 168–181.

4. ———. 1962. Optimum repetitions for the development of strength. *Research Quarterly* 33 (3): 334–338.

5. ———. 1963. Comparative effects of three weight training programs. *Research Quarterly* 34 (3): 396–398.

6. ———. 1973. *Conditioning for men.* Boston, MA: Allyn and Bacon, Inc., 36.

7. ———. 1982. *Applied exercise physiology.* Philadelphia, PA: Lea & Febiger, 42.

8. ———. 1984. *Introduction to weight training.* Englewood Cliffs, NJ: Prentice-Hall, Inc., 79, 126, 132, 133, 135, 137, 168.

9. Bowers, R. W., and E. L. Fox. 1992. *Sports physiology.* 3rd ed. Dubuqe, IA: W. C. Brown Publishing, 151–152.

10. Brooks, G. A., T. D. Fahey, and T. P. White. 1996. *Exercise physiology: Human bioenergetics and its applications.* 2nd ed. Mountain View, CA: Mayfield Publishing, 390.

11. Capen, E. K. 1956. Study of four programs of heavy resistance exercise for development of muscular strength. *Research Quarterly* 27 (2): 132–142.

12. Ciriello, V. M., W. L. Holden, and W. J. Evans. 1982. The effects of two isokinetic training regimens on muscle strength and fiber composition. In *Biochemistry of exercise* 13, ed. H. G. Knuttgen, J. A. Vogel and J. Poortmans, 787–793. Champaign, IL: Human Kinetics Publishing, Inc.

13. Clarke, D. H. 1973. Adaptations in strength and muscular endurance resulting from exercise. In *Exercise and sport science reviews* 1, ed. J. H. Wilmore, 73–102. New York: Academic Press.

14. Clarke, H. H. 1974. Development of muscular strength and endurance. *Physical Fitness Research Digest*, President's Council on Physical Fitness and Sports. Washington, DC: U.S. Government Printing Office (January).

15. Coleman, A. E. 1977. Nautilus vs. Universal Gym strength training in adult males. *American Corrective Therapy Journal* 31 (4): 103–107.

16. De Hoyos, D. V., T. Abe, L. Garzarella, C. Hass, M. Nordman, and M. L. Pollock. 1998. Effects of 6 months of high- or low-volume resistance training on muscular strength and endurance. *Medicine and Science in Sports and Exercise.* Supplement 30 (5): S165.

17. De Hoyos, D. V., D. Herring, L. Garzarella, G. Werber, W. F. Brechue, and M. L. Pollock. 1997. Effect of strength training volume on the development of strength and power in adolescent tennis players. *Medicine and Science in Sports and Exercise.* Supplement 29 (5): S164.

18. DeVries, H. A., and T. J. Housh. 1994. *Physiology of exercise for physical education, athletics, and exercise science.* 5th ed. Dubuque, IA: Brown & Benchmark Publishing, 441–442.

19. Enoka, R. M. 1994. *Neuromechanical basis of kinesiology.* 2nd ed. Champaign, IL: Human Kinetics, 313.

20. Fleck, S. J., and W. J. Kraemer. 1987. *Designing resistance training programs.* Champaign, IL: Human Kinetics, 57–58.

21. ———. 1998. Resistance training: Basic principles (part 1 of 4). *Physician and Sportsmedicine* 16 (3): 160–171.

22. ———. 1996. *Periodization breakthrough!* Ronkonkoma, NY: Advanced Research Press, Inc., 36–37.

23. ———. 1997. *Designing resistance training programs.* 2nd ed. Champaign, IL: Human Kinetics, 19, 93, 94, 119, 233, 236, 240.

24. Fox, E. L. 1984. *Sports physiology.* 2nd ed. New York, NY: CBS College Publishing, 130–131.

25. Fox, E. L., and D. K. Mathews. 1981. *The physiological basis of physical education and athletics.* 3rd ed. Philadelphia, PA: Saunders College Publishing, 156.

26. Fox, E. L., R. W. Bowers, and M. L. Foss. 1993. *The physiological basis for exercise and sport.* 5th ed. Madison, WI: Brown & Benchmark Publishing, 175–176.

27. Graves, J. E., B. L. Holmes, S. H. Leggett, D. M. Carpenter, and M. L. Pollock. 1991. Single versus multiple set dynamic and isometric lumbar extension training. Eleventh international congress of the world confederation for physical therapy. Proceedings Book III. (July 28–August 2): 1340–1342.

28. Guyton, A. C. 1991. *Textbook of medical physiology.* 8th ed. Chapter 84: Sports physiology. Philadelphia, PA: W. B. Saunders Co., 940–950.

29. Hass, C. J., L. Garzarella, D. V. De Hoyos, and M. L. Pollock. 1998. Effects of training volume on strength and endurance in experienced resistance-trained adults. *Medicine and Science in Sports and Exercise.* Supplement 30 (5): S115.

30. Howley, E. T., and B. D. Franks. 1986. *Health fitness instructor's handbook.* Champaign, IL: Human Kinetics, 103.

31. Hurley, B. F., R. A. Redmond, R. E. Pratley, M. S. Treuth, M. A. Rogers, and A. P. Goldberg. 1995. Effects of strength training on muscle hypertrophy and muscle cell distribution in older men. *International Journal of Sports Medicine* 16 (6): 378–384.

32. Jacobson, B. H. 1986. A comparison of two progressive weight training techniques on knee extensor strength. *Athletic Training* 21 (4): 315–318, 390.

33. Jesse, C., D. McGee, J. Gibson, and M. Stone. 1988. A comparison of Nautilus and free-weight training. *Journal of Applied Sports Science Research* 2 (3): 59.

34. Kearney, J. T. 1980. Resistance training: Development of muscular strength and endurance. In *Toward an understanding of human performance*, 2nd ed, ed. E. J. Burke, 45–51. Ithaca, NY: Mouvement Publishing.

35. Knuttgen, H. G. 1976. Development of muscular strength and endurance. In *Neuromuscular mechanisms for therapeutic and conditioning exercise*, ed. H. G. Knuttgen, 107. Baltimore, MD: University Park Press.

36. Koffler, K. H., A. Menkes, R. A. Redmond, W. E. Whitehead, R. E. Pratley, and B. F. Hurley. 1992. Strength training accelerates gastrointestinal transit in middle-aged and older men. *Medicine and Science in Sports and Exercise* 24 (2): 415–419.

37. Kraemer, W. J., and T. R. Baechle. 1989. Development of a strength training program. In *Sports medicine*, 2nd ed, ed. A. J. Ryan, and F. L. Allman, Jr., 120. San Diego, CA: Academic Press, Inc.

38. Kraemer, W. J., and J. A. Bush. 1998. Factors affecting the acute neuromuscular responses to resistance exercise. In *ACSM's resource manual for guidelines for exercise testing and prescription*, 3rd ed, ed. J. L. Roitman et al., 169. Baltimore, MD: Williams & Wilkins.

39. Kraemer, W. J., and S. J. Fleck. 1988. Resistance training: exercise prescription (part 4 of 4). *Physician and Sportsmedicine* 16 (6): 69–81.

40. Kraemer, W. J., and L. P. Koziris. 1992. Muscle strength training: Techniques and considerations. *Physical Therapy Practice* 2 (1): 63.

41. Kraemer, W. J., R. V. Newton, J. Bush, J. Volek, N. T. Triplett, and L. P. Koziris. 1995. Varied multiple set resistance training programs produce greater gains than single set program. *Medicine and Science in Sports and Exercise* 7 (5): S195.

42. Kraemer, W. J., S. J. Fleck, and M. Deschenes. 1988. A review: Factors in exercise prescription of resistance training. *National Strength and Conditioning Association Journal* 10 (5): 36–41.

43. Kramer, J. B., M. H. Stone, H. S. O'Bryant, M. S. Conley, R. L. Johnson, D. C. Nieman, D. R. Honeycutt, and T. P. Hoke. 1997. Effects of single vs. multiple sets of weight training: Impact of volume, intensity, and variation. *Journal of Strength and Conditioning Research* 11 (3): 143–147.

44. Lamb, D. R. 1984. *Physiology of exercise: Responses and adaptations.* 2nd ed. New York, NY: MacMillan Publishing, 276–277.

45. Larshus, J. L., W. K. Werner, and J. R. Moore. 1997. Effects of multiple exercise training on the development of triceps strength. *Research Quarterly for Exercise and Sport.* Supplement (March): A33–A34.

46. Leighton, J. R., D. Holmes, J. Benson, B. Wooten, and R. Schmerer. 1967. A study on the effectiveness of ten different methods of progressive resistance exercise on the development of strength, flexibility, girth, and bodyweight. *Journal of the Association for Physical and Mental Rehabilitation* 21 (3): 78–81.

47. Lillegard, W. A., and J. D. Terrio. 1994. Appropriate strength training. *Medical Clinics of North America* 78 (2): 457–477.

48. McArdle, W. D., F. I. Katch, and V. L. Katch. 1996. *Exercise physiology: Energy, nutrition, and human performance.* 4th ed. Baltimore, MD: Williams & Wilkins, 427.

49. McDonagh, M. N., and C. M. Davies. 1984. Adaptive response of mammalian skeletal muscle to exercise with high loads. *European Journal of Applied Physiology* 52: 139–155.

50. Messier, S. P., and M. E. Dill. 1985. Alterations in strength and maximal oxygen uptake consequent to Nautilus circuit weight training. *Research Quarterly for Exercise and Sport* 56 (4): 345–351.

51. Miller, J. P., R. E. Pratley, A. P. Goldberg, P. Gordon, M. Rubin, M. S. Treuth, A. S. Ryan, and B. F. Hurley. 1994. Strength training increases insulin action in healthy 50- to 65-yr-old men. *Journal of Applied Physiology* 77 (3): 1122–1127.

52. Nicklas, B. J., A. J. Ryan, M. Treuth, S. M. Harman, M. R. Blackman, B. F. Hurley, and M. A. Rogers. 1995. Testosterone, growth hormone and IGF-1 responses to acute and chronic resistive exercise in men aged 55–70 years. *International Journal of Sports Medicine* 16 (7): 445–450.

53. Noble, B. J. 1986. *Physiology of exercise and sport.* St. Louis, MO: Times Mirror/Mosby College Publishing, 306.

54. Ostrowski, K. J., G. J. Wilson, R. Weatherby, P. W. Murphy, and A. D. Lyttle. 1997. The effect of weight training volume on hormonal output and muscular size and function. *Journal of Strength and Conditioning Research* 11 (3): 148–154.

55. Plowman, S. A., and D. L. Smith. 1997. *Exercise physiology for health, fitness, and performance.* Boston, MA: Allyn and Bacon, 473.

56. Pollock, M. L., T. Abe, D. V. De Hoyos, L. Garzarella, C. J. Hass, and G. Werber. 1998. Muscular hypertrophy responses to 6 months of high- or low-volume resistance training. *Medicine and Science in Sports and Exercise.* Supplement 30 (5): S116.

57. Pollock, M. L., J. E. Graves, M. M. Bamman, S. H. Leggett, D. M. Carpenter, C. Carr, J. Cirulli, J. Matkozich, and M. Fulton. 1993. Frequency and volume of resistance training: Effect on cervical extension strength. *Archives of Physical and Medical Rehabilitation* 74: 1080–1086.

58. Powers, S. K., and E. T. Howley. 1997. *Exercise physiology: Theory and application to fitness and performance.* 3rd ed. Dubuque, IA: Brown & Benchmark Publishing, 399.

59. Reid, C. M., R. A. Yeater, and I. H. Ullrich. 1987. Weight training and strength, cardiorespiratory functioning and body composition. *British Journal of Sports Medicine* 21 (1): 40–44.

60. Rubin, M. A., J. P. Miller, A. S. Ryan, M. S. Treuth, K. Y. Patterson, R. E. Pratley, B. F. Hurley, C. Veillon, P. B. Moser-Veillon, and R. A. Anderson. 1998. Acute and chronic

resistive exercise increase urinary chromium excretion in men as measured with an enriched chromium stable isotope. *Journal of Nutrition* 128: 73–78.

61. Ryan, A. S., R. E. Pratley, D. Elahi, and A. P. Goldberg. 1995. Resistive training increases fat-free mass and maintains RMR despite weight loss in postmenopausal women. *Journal of Applied Physiology* 79 (3): 818–823.

62. Ryan, A. S., M. S. Treuth, M. A. Rubin, J. P. Miller, B. J. Nicklas, D. M. Landis, R. E. Pratley, C. R. Libanati, C. M. Gundberg, and B. F. Hurley. 1994. Effects of strength training on bone mineral density: Hormonal and bone turnover relationships. *Journal of Applied Physiology* 77 (4): 1678–1684.

63. Sale, D., and D. MacDougall. 1981. Specificity in strength training: A review for the coach and athlete. *Canadian Journal of Applied Sports Science* 6 (2): 87–92.

64. Schmidtbleicher, D. 1992. Training for power events. Chapter 18. In *Strength and power in sport*, ed. P. V. Komi, 387. London: Blackwell Scientific Publishing.

65. Shaver, L. G. 1981. *Essentials of exercise physiology.* Minneapolis, MN: Burgess Publishing, 262.

66. Shepard, R. J. 1985. *Physiology and biochemistry of exercise.* New York, NY: Praeger Publishing, 389.

67. Silvester, L. J., C. Stiggins, C. McGown, and G. R. Bryce. 1982. The effect of variable resistance and free-weight training programs on strength and vertical jump. *National Strength and Conditioning Association Journal* 3 (6): 30–33.

68. Snyder, A. C. 1998. *Exercise, nutrition, and health.* Carmel, IN: Cooper Publishing, 198–201.

69. Stadler, L. V., Jr., N. B. Stubbs, and M. D. Vokovich. 1997. A comparison of a 2-day and 3-day per week resistance training program on strength gains in older adults. *Medicine and Science in Sports and Exercise.* Supplement 20 (5): S254.

70. Starkey, D. B., M. L. Pollock, Y. Ishida, M. A. Welsch, W. F. Brechue, J. E. Graves, and M. J. Feigenbaum. 1996. Effect of resistance training volume on strength and muscle thickness. *Medicine and Science in Sports and Exercise* 28 (10): 1311–1320.

71. Stone, M. H., and H. S. O'Bryant. 1986. *Weight training: A scientific approach.* Minneapolis, MN: Burgess Publishing, 200.

72. Stone, W. J., and S. P. Coulter. 1994. Strength/endurance effects from three resistance training protocols with women. *Journal of Strength and Conditioning Research* 8 (4): 231–234.

73. Stowers, T., J. McMillan, D. Scala, V. Davis, D. Wilson, and M. Stone. 1983. The short-term effects of three different strength-power training methods. *National Strength and Conditioning Association Journal* 5 (3): 24–27.

74. Terbizan, D. J., and R. L. Bartels. 1985. The effect of set-repetition combinations on strength gain in females age 18–35. *Medicine and Science in Sports and Exercise.* Supplement 17 (2): 267.

75. Tesch, P. A., and L. Larsson. 1982. Muscle hypertrophy in bodybuilders. *European Journal of Applied Physiology* 49: 301–306.

76. Tesch, P. A. 1992. Training for bodybuilding. Chapter 17. In *Strength and power in sport*, ed. P. V. Komi, 377–378. London: Blackwell Scientific Publishing.

77. Treuth, M. S., A. S. Ryan, R. E. Pratley, M. A. Rubin, J. P. Miller, B. J. Nicklas, J. Sorkin, S. M. Harman, A. P. Goldberg, and B. F. Hurley. 1994. Effects of strength training on total and regional body composition in older men. *Journal of Applied Physiology* 77 (2): 614–620.

78. Vincent, K., D. De Hoyos, L. Garzarella, C. Hass, M. Nordman, and M. Pollock. 1998. Relationship between indices of knee extension strength before and after training. *Medicine and Science in Sports and Exercise.* Supplement 30 (5): S163.

79. Wathen, D. 1994. Periodization: Concepts and applications. In *Essentials of strength training and conditioning*, ed. T. R. Baechle, 459–472. Champaign, IL: Human Kinetics.

80. Welsch, M. A., W. F. Brechue, M. L. Pollock, D. B. Starkey, and J. E. Graves. 1994. Effect of reduced training volume on bilateral isometric knee flexion/extension torque. *Medicine and Science in Sports and Exercise.* Supplement 26 (5): S189.

81. Westcott, W. L. 1986. 4 key factors in building a strength program. *Scholastic Coach* 55: 104–105, 123.

82. Westcott, W. L., K. Greenberger, and D. Milius. 1989. Strength training research: Sets and repetitions. *Scholastic Coach* 58: 98–100.

83. Wilmore, J. H. 1982. *Training for sport and activity: The physiological basis of the conditioning process.* 2nd ed. Boston, MA: Allyn and Bacon, Inc., 80.

84. Wilmore, J. H., and D. L. Costill. 1994. *Physiology of sport and exercise.* Champaign, IL: Human Kinetics, 82.

85. Withers, R. T. 1970. Effect of varied weight-training loads on the strength of university freshmen. *Research Quarterly* 41 (1): 110–114.

86. Zatsiorsky, V. M. 1995. *Science and practice of strength training.* Champaign, IL: Human Kinetics, 209.

This chapter is dedicated to my family. To my wife and children whose absolute love, support, and immeasurable patience make the job possible. And to my parents who instilled the importance of perspective and the need for education and who are always there unconditionally.

5

In Search of the Perfect Program

Chip Harrison, M.S.
Head Strength and Conditioning Coach
Penn State University
University Park, Pennsylvania

It seems as though the quest for the perfect strength training program has taken on almost mythical proportions. From the competitive athlete to the fitness fanatic to the weekend warrior, people are seeking the ideal routine. In some ways this is good. People are more aware of and educated about the intrinsic benefits of strength training. And, in general, people are more critical of what constitutes reasonable information. The downside of the situation is that a market has been created for health clubs, equipment manufacturers, and fitness gurus to capitalize on the public's demand for appropriate direction. The process of capitalizing on this demand has caused a marketing blitz that depends on specific identity and the differentiation of one approach from another. This has led to the dissemination of superior equipment and training philosophies as irrefutable fact rather than the personal preferences they actually represent. Instead of pursuing the destination (in this case, the perfect routine), we would be better advised to look at the journey. The true journey lies in finding programming variables that make sense along with training choices that are productive. The perfect program will undoubtedly vary from one individual to another and is even likely to vary for the same individual at different times in his or her life. So the desire to find a single perfect program is not only a waste of time, it may in fact be futile. Likewise, those who would have you believe that they have discovered the perfect program are being misleading.

There are, however, common elements of well-designed programs that are consistent regardless of the age, ability, and training status of an individual. These elements transcend manufacturer loyalties, modality choices, and personal biases. This chapter will identify and delineate these elements and provide a basis for the selection of exercises and equipment that addresses the personal needs of the trainee.

It is important to remember that in this era of high-tech equipment, infomercials, and fitness televangelists, the basics of resistance training have not changed. As a matter of fact, the more we learn through research and greater numbers of participants, the more solidified these basics become.

For the fitness professional, the task of designing a strength training program is as much an art as it is a science. The almost miraculous adaptability of human physiology makes the process of designing a program relatively simple. The truth is, a lot of things work. The downside of this phenomenon is that even poorly designed programs may elicit some desired responses. The process then becomes self-perpetuating: If it works then it must be right. Unfortunately, the fact that a program elicits improvement in some of the desired areas may represent improvement in spite of the program rather than because of it. Continuing such a program may only subject the trainee to a submaximal training response. However, devotion to and execution of a poorly designed program may also lead to acute injury and/or long-term disability.

It is because of the tendency of the body to indiscriminately adapt when exposed to a stress that programming is so important. Making sure that the long-term adaptations are desirable and that no physical damage is being done during the training process separates a simple stress from a well-designed program.

TRAINING ELEMENTS

The following are four key elements of a well-designed program. This section will address each of them in turn.

The Repetition

Despite some claims to the contrary, it appears that the most beneficial repetition includes a concentric (or positive) phase in which the weight is raised and an eccentric (or negative) phase in which the weight is lowered. In simpler terms, the best repetition includes a raising and lowering of a resistance.

Can strength improvements occur when only raising (and not lowering) a weight? In some cases yes, but generally there will not be as much improvement as there would have been if the weight were lowered as well.

Can strength improvements occur when only lowering (and not raising) a weight? Again, yes, but this technique increases the potential of placing too much stress on the muscular and connective tissues, thereby increasing the possibility of injury and/or overtraining.

Are there times when concentric-only or eccentric-only exercises might be programmed into a routine for specific rehabilitation or variety reasons? Certainly. However, it is unlikely that these training styles would represent the most productive choices for long-term training.

Can strength improvements occur from isometric training (i.e., tension development without joint movement)? Yes. Isometric training can create dramatic strength improvements. However, the improvements are reasonably specific to the angle of contraction and would not represent a time-efficient training choice in most circumstances.

The Resistance

As mentioned previously, the body adapts relatively indiscriminately to stresses placed upon it. Therefore, the resistance could be almost anything—from the most intricately machined stainless steel barbell, computer-controlled electromagnet, or powder-coated, belt-driven, variable-resistance, selectorized machine to a simple hay bale, sandbag, orange crate, or human partner. Any resistance of sufficient magnitude can represent a training stimulus. It does not matter whether the resistance is supplied from an external or internal source. It does not matter if the resistance comes from traditional strength training modalities or from something less traditional. The key is to use a resistance that demands the development of tension within a muscle or group of muscles that is greater than typical demands (i.e., an overload). This demand for tension development beyond typical demands constitutes a training stimulus. It is this stimulus that requires the body to adapt and thereby deliver a training response. This training response is commonly referred to as a *training effect* and usually constitutes the desired outcome.

Some tools provide better means of applying resistance than others. Typical strength training modalities (such as barbells, dumbbells, machines, and so on) have been developed to systematically apply resistance to specific muscles or muscle groups. Most have been designed to apply resistance of varying degrees while making it possible for incremental changes in load. Varying loads and changing loading patterns in small increments provides the opportunity for a wide variety of users to take advantage of these modalities. The absence of varying loads and inability to adjust the load incrementally represents major shortcomings of less traditional sources of resistance (such as hay bales and orange crates).

Each of the previously outlined modalities has inherent advantages and disadvantages. These specific advantages and disadvantages will be explored later in this chapter. When designing an appropriate strength training program, it is enough to recognize that these differences exist and thereby represent considerations.

Is it possible to elicit improvements in strength without traditional equipment? Absolutely. The problem comes in trying to systematically change the load as strength improves so that it continues to provide an appropriate training stimulus.

Are traditional modalities superior to other modalities for developing strength? In the sense that most of these modalities have been specifically developed for the job of systematically applying resistance to the muscles/muscle groups trained, yes. However, since muscles are incapable of discriminating one source of tension from another, any object (or technique) that applies an appropriate resistance to the musculature could stimulate a training response.

Total-Body Training

All well-conceived programs are designed to address the specific needs of the individual trainee. And while these needs are likely to vary from individual to individual, there will be many more similarities than there are differences. As such, it is unlikely that there would be any reason a specific muscle group or body area would be left untrained. The benefits of training any one muscle group are the same as those for any other. Since the body is a package in its entirety, any area not trained to its immediate potential could represent a liability regardless of the activity. Therefore, all the major muscle groups of the body should be trained. Specific orthopedic or medical concerns might necessitate avoiding a particular exercise or the modification of training technique. However, it is unlikely that this would include a complete abstention from the training of a particular muscle group or body area. Therefore, it would be difficult to justify a partial-body approach to programming. Even if sport or activity demands might appear to indicate the need to train only one area of the body (i.e., upper body or lower body), the benefits of a total-body approach for overall development and general fitness are clear. Likewise, the ramifications of training one muscle/muscle group or one body area could be severe.

Balance

Like total-body training, the need to provide a balanced training program is paramount. Not only is it advantageous to provide some level of training for the entire musculature, it is critical that this training balances the development on both sides of a joint. Since a muscle can only contract (it can not lengthen with force), each joint generally has at least two muscles/muscle groups that facilitate movement around that joint. These muscles, along with the connective tissue surrounding the joint, maintain the integrity (stability) of the joint. Under ideal circumstances, the muscles used to move in one direction and those used to move in the opposite direction are in balance. This is not to imply that an equal amount of weight can be lifted during opposing exercises. There are a variety of biomechanical reasons why one might be able to demonstrate more strength (i.e., lift more weight) in one direction than would be possible in the other. It simply means that an adequate amount of tension can be developed on both sides of a joint so that the joint functions properly and is not prone to misalignment or slipping. In reality, the muscles on one side of a joint are often stronger than those on the other side. This occurs because of the types of activities a person participates in, the physical demands of a career, or simply the ravages of gravity. If the imbalance is slight, there may be no noticeable problem. If the imbalance is severe, however, there can be significant problems in mobility, range of motion, or joint integrity. Many acute and long-term orthopedic problems can be linked (at least in part) to muscular imbalances around a joint. While proper stretching and strengthening can often diminish or even eliminate these imbalances, careless programming can easily add to the problem.

It is imperative to follow a balanced training approach. Not only balance between the upper and lower body, but also to the right and left sides of the body. It may seem obvious, but most people are dominant on one side of their body. This generally means that a greater number of physical tasks are performed with one arm or leg. Over time, this predisposition to exercise one side of the body more than the other (during daily living) can lead to increased development and the potential for postural problems. An equally important consideration relates to promoting balance between pushing and pulling (flexion and extension) movements. Many programs (both athletic and recreational) stress pushing movements (such as the bench press, overhead press, squat, leg extension and so on) far more than pulling movements (such as the row, lat pulldown, leg curl, and others). Most justify this practice by pointing to athletic competition and sport movements that appear to require more pushing than pulling. While the observation may be valid in the field of competition, the idea that there is no need for a proportional increase in the strength of the muscles that oppose those muscle groups and add to the integrity of the joint is ludicrous. If for no other reason than to balance the acquisition of strength in one direction, the training of antagonistic muscle groups is important. In actuality, these antagonistic muscles are often subject to as much or more stress in the process of slowing down a limb or counteracting a movement than the muscles that initiated the movement. Knowing this, would it ever make sense to systematically program less work for these muscles?

THAT'S IT?

If there are only four key elements to consider when developing a strength training program, what's all the hype about? The truth is that even in this day and age of increased awareness, participation, and research base, many people (including fitness professionals) continue to hang on to preconceived notions of what is appropriate and necessary. The bottom line is that any program that combines appropriate loading and dynamic training can potentially deliver a desired training effect. The real art to programming is combining other elements in such a way as to ensure the desired training effect and deliver results as rapidly as possible.

FIVE CHECKPOINTS

The following guidelines have been noted for many years in strength training books, research protocols, and course curriculums to delineate appropriate training protocol. While it is possible to elicit a training response without following these guidelines, there are a number of safety and efficacy concerns.

1. *Train using a full range of motion (ROM) for each exercise.* Since strength improvements are specific to the joint angles exposed to the stress, dynamic exercise represents the most productive means of improving strength throughout a muscle's ROM. Likewise, shortening a repetition at either the mid- or endpoint of an exercise diminishes the total amount of work being done and can compromise flexibility around the exercised joints. For the competitive athlete, improving strength throughout a muscle's ROM is a wise choice in terms of injury prevention and performance enhancement. The same holds true for the fitness enthusiast who is interested in improving overall strength for daily activity.

2. *Eliminate fast, jerky movements while raising the weight.* One common misconception about strength training is that lifting the heaviest weight possible will produce the greatest gains. While there is a need to develop sufficient tension within a muscle to elicit a training response, it does not hold that lifting the heaviest weight possible provides the greatest tension. In actuality, lifting a very heavy weight by incorporating a great deal of momentum into the lift will usually lead to a decrease in tension development in certain ranges of the movement. Sufficient momentum can allow a weight to be carried through some of the movement with little or no muscular tension. Too much momentum will actually cause a weight to be thrown rather than lifted. This throwing virtually ensures that muscular tension throughout the ROM will be submaximal. And while it is possible to lift additional weight by imparting additional momentum to the movement, it does not result in better muscular training.

Another by-product of momentum is extreme (impulse) forces being transferred to the muscular and connective tissues during the acceleration and deceleration phases of the lift. It is possible for these forces to exceed the structural integrity of the tissues, resulting in acute or long-term injury to the muscles and/or connective tissues. Proponents of such training techniques often claim that lifting faster produces quicker muscles or improves power production. Programming that incorporates this type of training is often referred to as *sport specific*. This is an especially appealing claim to the competitive athlete who knows that improved power could lead to improved sports performance. The problem with this claim is that it ignores the basic principles of neurophysiology and the specificity of muscle-fiber recruitment. The fact is that every physical movement results from a very specific neurological message sent from the brain to the motor units (muscle fibers) necessary to execute the movement. The message is unique to the parameters of the demand. In simple terms, this means that any change in movement demand (i.e., a change in speed, load, angle, ROM, and so on) requires a completely different neurological message to be sent from the brain to the motor units. Thus, any movement (no matter how similar) that differs from an actual movement (i.e., a sports movement) trains a separate and unique muscle-fiber recruitment pattern. Therefore, any claims that sports movements can be trained and improved in the weight room and then transferred to a competitive situation are false.

3. *Emphasize the lowering of the weight.* Many who train with weights are specifically concerned with the raising phase of an exercise. Often, they give little consideration to the lowering phase of the exercise. It is important to remember that the same muscles used to lift the weight are also used to lower the weight. By ignoring the lowering phase, these trainees are ignoring half of the exercise and, ultimately, half of the workout. Likewise, since we are physiologically able to lower more weight than we can raise, the workout is further compromised by not emphasizing this phase.

Research indicates that the eccentric (or lowering) phase of an exercise may actually be more important for improving strength and increasing muscular size (hypertrophy) than the concentric (or raising) phase. Since nearly everyone involved in a strength training program has a desire to improve overall strength and/or body composition to some degree, this becomes an especially important consideration. Any notion that the eccentric portion of a lift merely represents a means of getting in position to lift the weight again clearly underestimates the value of the eccentric contraction.

4. *Reach momentary muscular failure/fatigue in the prescribed number of repetitions.* Momentary muscular failure/fatigue can be defined as "the point at which a repetition of an exercise can no longer be completed in proper form." This means that all the available motor units have been recruited and fatigued to the point where they are no longer able to generate enough muscular tension to overcome the current resistance and complete another repetition. It does *not* mean that the entire muscle has been completely fatigued and is no longer able to contract. It simply represents an objective concluding point of an exercise with a given resistance. As a matter of fact, it would be possible to do additional repetitions if the resistance was to be sufficiently decreased, a spotter was used to help in the completion of a repetition, or the training form was compromised—the latter is a method that is not encouraged. These training practices are sometimes used to lengthen a set and increase the amount of time the muscles spend under tension. However, they represent modifications to the initial parameters of the exercise and should be considered separately.

While it is possible to make improvements in strength without training to the point of momentary failure/fatigue, these improvements generally would not be as significant as if failure/fatigue had been reached. Such improvements represent a submaximal stimulus to the muscle or muscle groups involved. (This doesn't mean that there is no value in training if failure/fatigue is not achieved. For years, hundreds of strength athletes have developed incredible strength, won medals, and set records by following a percentage-style loading pattern while rarely if ever having trained to failure/fatigue.) This strength-building process is just made easier by following the more objective training guidelines outlined here.

To make consistent training progress, the principle of progressive overload must be followed. Simply put, this principle states that a muscle or muscle group must be exposed to progressively heavier loads to stimulate a training response. If this does not occur, the muscle will eventually cease the adaptation response (i.e., it will stop getting stronger). The only way to know for sure how many repetitions can be done with a given weight is to do as many as possible. If the repetitions completed fall within the guidelines of the established goal, the weight chosen is appropriate. If, however, the repetitions completed exceed or fall short of the established goal, then the weight should be adjusted so that it continues to supply the desired stimulus. If there is no objective measure of how many repetitions are possible with a given weight (i.e., point of momentary failure/fatigue), it becomes difficult to determine whether the training load is appropriate and at what point it should be increased to maintain the desired stimulus.

5. *Train under supervision and/or with a partner.* In this case, supervision can take the form of a recording sheet or workout diary that describes in detail the results of a workout. Complete and proper recording of workout data constitutes the only means of objectively choosing exercise loads, establishing training volumes and evaluating progress. As stated earlier, individual variability is a given. Therefore, a single-minded approach to programming will usually fall short of the desired goals if applied to a large number of trainees. Each individual will have specific adaptation responses to a given stress. In other words, the same program will probably have a different effect on different individuals. The best programs are those that can be modified to suit the goals of a variety of individuals. The only means of identifying which variables need to be modified is to have consistent records of the workouts done and the responses delivered.

Supervision can (and should) also take the form of a workout partner or spotter. A partner provides added safety while training. Partners can provide immediate feedback on training form and lend a hand in case a spot is needed. A partner can also provide a means of increasing the intensity of an exercise by allowing the trainee to complete repetitions he or she otherwise would have missed. By assisting in the completion of the concentric phase or stripping weight from the apparatus, additional repetitions can be safely completed and additional stress placed on the exercising muscle or muscle group. Other techniques can be incorporated into a training routine to increase training demand safely and effectively when a partner is available. A partner can also provide motivation and encouragement to the trainee. This is especially important for long-term commitment and consistency. The process of training has an inherent element of redundancy and repetition. Those who train with a partner generally stay committed longer and are more consistent in their workouts.

As stated previously, it is possible to achieve results from strength training without following these guidelines. However, the guidelines provide a cornerstone from which to build an effective training regimen; they provide a means of objectively evaluating progress and identifying areas for modification.

Any resistance of sufficient magnitude can represent a training stimulus—even when the resistance is supplied by a human partner. (photo by Matt Brzycki)

MODALITIES

When designing a strength training program, there are an ever-expanding number of modalities (equipment choices) available. Each of these modalities has advantages and disadvantages. Variables like safety, ease of use, flexibility, anatomical fit, and orthopedic limitations all enter into the equation when selecting an appropriate exercise modality. In general, incorporating a variety of modalities provides a more complete training stimulus than using a single modality. Over time, it will usually be necessary (as well as advantageous) to use different modalities in your programming. By balancing the strengths and weaknesses of any given modality with those of another, it is possible to get the best of all worlds.

One of the most common (and egregious) misconceptions surrounding strength training is that the use of free-weight equipment is somehow superior to all other training modalities and therefore represents the only acceptable equipment choice. While free-weight equipment offers variety and a number of training advantages, it also has several critical limitations—the most obvious being the fact that it is inherently more dangerous than most other modalities. The simple fact that a weight can be dropped, bumped, or impacted on a trainee represents a liability. Admittedly, this liability can become almost inconsequential for most people with time and practice. However, it is difficult to argue that one isn't more likely to drop a dumbbell on their head than they are a Nautilus® machine. Another notable limitation is the fact that free weights have no mechanical ability to change the direction from which the resistance is supplied. In other words, since gravity always works in the same direction (straight down), free-weight equipment always applies resistance in a vertical, straight-line fashion. With some exercises, this straight-line resistance represents a reasonable and proper direction for the application of resistance. However, there are a number of exercises that are simply too difficult, too dangerous, or downright improper to execute with free-weight equipment.

Another misconception surrounding the use of free weights is that it is inherently better than the use of machines (or other modalities) for increasing muscular size. Many believe free weights produce increases in muscular size (bulk) while machines produce a toning effect. The reality is that since a muscle is incapable of distinguishing one source of load from another, an appropriate resistance (from any source) can provide the training stimulus necessary to stimulate improvements in either muscular hypertrophy or muscular endurance. The ability of any muscle/muscle group to increase in size and/or endurance is dependent upon individual genetic, training, and programming variables, not the choice of modality.

The point is that while free-weight equipment represents one exceptional tool in the arsenal of strength training modalities, it is neither the only tool nor the best tool available in all circumstances (contrary to what some would have you believe). The truth is, training would be more difficult, less complete, and dramatically less variable if the only tool available were free weights. The best programs will incorporate a variety of training modalities in such a way as to maximize the advantages and minimize the limitations of the chosen modalities. For your convenience, the advantages and disadvantages of various types of modalities are shown in Figure 5.1.

DESIGNING A PROGRAM

Two of the most important considerations in designing a program are repetition ranges and set schemes.

Repetition Ranges

Strength and endurance are inversely related and exist on a continuum. The heavier the load, the greater the strength requirement to execute any given repetition and the fewer the total number of repetitions possible; the lighter the load, the smaller the strength requirement to execute any given repetition and the greater

Figure 5.1 Advantages and Disadvantages of Various Types of Modalities

Modality	Advantages	Disadvantages
Free Weights: Barbells	• Many exercises possible • Many angles of execution possible • Allows varied grip widths • Well suited for multi-joint exercises • Utilizes many muscles/muscle groups at once • Significantly utilizes stabilizing muscles/muscle groups • Accommodates users of various size • Relatively inexpensive • Available in most facilities	• More dangerous due to balance/technique requirement • Requires additional time to master technique • More conservative loading required • Nonvariable resistance throughout range of motion • Bar limits range of motion • Applies vertical, straight-line resistance • Large space requirement • Difficult to isolate individual muscles/muscle groups • Usually requires weight adjustment of at least 5 pounds • Plate-loaded, more difficult to manipulate • Not well suited to single-arm exercises • Generally requires gripping of bar; not well suited to hand injuries
Free Weights: Dumbbells	• (See Free Weights: Barbell/Advantages) • Allows varied paths of resistance • Suited to single- and multi-joint exercises • Significantly utilizes stabilizing muscles/muscle groups	• (See Free Weights: Barbells/Disadvantages) • Usually requires weight adjustment of at least 5 pounds/dumbbell
Machines: Selectorized	• Relatively safe due to decreased balance and technique requirements • Direct resistance • Many manufacturers utilize variable-resistance loading • Generally allows smaller increments of weight adjustment • Allows more aggressive loading • Only requires enough space to accommodate various stations • User friendly for novice trainees • Can be safely modified to accommodate limited ranges of motion • Allows easy weight changes • Well suited to no-hand workouts • Available in most facilities	• Can only do exercises for which there are machines • Relatively expensive • Fixed path of resistance • Fixed angle of execution • Does not accommodate very large or very small users well • Some equipment is less adjustable to individual limb/torso dimensions • Generally does not allow varying grip widths • May not accommodate iso-lateral movements

Figure 5.1 Advantages and Disadvantages of Various Types of Modalities (continued)

Modality	Advantages	Disadvantages
Machines: Plate-loaded	• (See Machines: Selectorized/Advantages) • Moderately expensive • Some manufacturers accommodate extensive iso-lateral training	• (See Machines: Selectorized/Disadvantages) • Not available in many facilities
Machines: Pneumatic	• (See Machines: Selectorized/Advantages) • Allows easy weight changes	• (See Machines: Selectorized/Disadvantages) • May not accommodate iso-lateral movements • Some manufacturers utilize concentric-only loading • Not available in many facilities
Machines: Electrostatic	• (See Machines: Selectorized/Advantages) • Some equipment can provide additional eccentric load • Allows easy weight changes	• (See Machines: Selectorized/Disadvantages) • Not available in many facilities
No Equipment: Body Weight	• No expense • Can train large numbers at one time • Can train in virtually any location	• Difficult to vary resistance • Does not allow for additional loading beyond body weight • Limited number of exercises possible • Not well suited for isolation exercises
No Equipment: Flex-Cord	• (See No equipment: Body weight/Advantages) • Minimal expense • Very easy to change resistance • Wide variety of exercises possible	• (See No equipment: Body weight/ Disadvantages) • Difficult to quantify resistance
No Equipment: Manual Resistance	• (See No equipment: Body weight/Advantages) • Can utilize maximal concentric and eccentric loading	• (See No equipment: Body weight/ Disadvantages) • Difficult to quantify resistance • Knowledgeable spotter required • Cannot train alone

the total number of repetitions possible. In the first example, a great deal of strength and a relatively small amount of endurance are required; in the second example, a relatively small amount of strength and a significantly greater level of endurance are required. This may seem ridiculously simple but it forms the cornerstone of strength versus endurance training. As mentioned previously, it is necessary to provide a stimulus to the body to cause a training response. This

Research has shown repeatedly that it takes only one properly performed set to stimulate improvements in strength. (photo courtesy of Bob Whelan)

stimulus (or overload) can take a variety of forms. Increased load, increased repetitions, increased sets of exercise, decreased recovery time, or combinations of the four can represent sufficient training stimuli to elicit an effect. The key is to make sure that the stimulus facilitates the desired response. If the desire is a significant increase in strength, it makes little sense to train with light loads for many repetitions. Likewise, if the desire is for increased muscular endurance, it makes little sense to train with heavy loads for very few repetitions. What follows is a general guideline for repetition ranges and training responses. It is important to remember that individuals vary in their response to training and that there is likely to be some overlap between individuals and individual muscle groups.

1–5 repetitions: Highly technical in nature; high strength requirement, minimal endurance requirement; primarily used by those competing in strength contests.

6–10 repetitions: High strength requirement, low to moderate endurance requirement.

11–15 repetitions: Moderate strength requirement, moderate endurance requirement.

16–20 repetitions: Low strength requirement, high endurance requirement.

More than 20 repetitions: Very low strength requirement, high endurance requirement; generally used for rehabilitation and training the postural muscles.

Using these repetition guidelines, it is possible to target specific muscles or muscle groups for the desired training response. It is important to remember that muscular strength is likely to increase through endurance training. It will, however, increase at a significantly slower rate than if a more aggressive strength-producing protocol were followed. Therefore, it is important to choose repetition ranges that will facilitate the desired training effect in a reasonable time frame.

Set Schemes

Another programming variable is workout volume. Volume is usually defined as *the amount of weight lifted multiplied by the number of repetitions done multiplied by the number of sets executed.* For the sake of this discussion, we will consider volume merely as the number of sets executed. Most programs utilize a multiple-set scheme. In other words, each exercise is performed for a series of sets (generally ranging from one to four). A high-volume program is one that incorporates a number of sets for each exercise. Many consider this high-volume approach a necessity for strength gains. In reality, research has demonstrated repeatedly that it only takes one properly performed set to stimulate improvements in strength. And while there may be some benefit to performing multiple sets of a given exercise (especially if the set is done with submaximal intensity) it is clearly not a necessity. Most multi-set programs also incorporate a series of exercises for the same muscle or muscle group. In essence, this means that 10, 12, or even more sets (for the same muscle group) are used to stimulate muscular gains. This requires a great deal of time in the weight room and also necessitates a significant time demand for proper recovery. If it is possible to achieve virtually the same results from a program that requires less than one-third the time demand, why waste the time?

In an effort to further minimize the potential benefit of a multi-set approach, a combination of three or four exercises for the same muscle group can be done. This allows for different joint angles to be trained, resulting in a more complete activation of the musculature. In reality, this type of approach is more appropriate for the overall developmental goals of the athlete and nonathlete alike. By combining several different movement patterns with one or two intense sets of exercise (totaling three to four per muscle group) for each of the major muscle groups of the body, a significant training stimulus can be applied to the exercising muscles without exceeding the body's recovery ability. In this way, systematic demands can be placed on the entire musculature and consistent gains can be achieved.

PUTTING IT ALL TOGETHER

Once the basic decisions have been made regarding exercise selection and modality choice, it is simply a matter of combining exercises in such a way as to train the desired muscle groups. There are a number of ways to combine exercises depending upon the desired training effect. Some prefer to alternate pushing and pulling movements. One advantage of this method is additional recovery time for the muscles not being trained by a specific exercise. Another advantage is the fact that exercising antagonistic muscle groups facilitates recovery of the opposing muscles by speeding the removal of metabolic by-products and a more complete relaxation of the muscles through neural inhibition. This sometimes means that additional weight can be used on an exercise, thus improving the training effect. Other programs choose to group exercises for specific muscle groups rather than separating them with antagonistic movements. One advantage of this type of training is the development of local muscular endurance. This trains the ability of a muscle or muscle group to continue contractions for longer periods of time and in the presence of higher levels of metabolic by-products. In situations where higher levels of endurance are required, this may prove to be a desirable effect. Still other programs will separate movement patterns or specific muscle groups into separate workouts. This method allows for additional concentration on specific movements or muscle groups. In general, this method requires additional workouts but may decrease the time commitment needed for any one workout. All of these program designs can represent reasonable choices for improving strength as long as they follow the guidelines previously outlined.

A well-designed program will train all the major muscles of the body. This includes exercises for the hips, legs, upper body, arms, and midsection. In general, exercises should be selected that require movement around all the major body joints. This procedure may be modified in cases where injury exists or where the development of strength may be medically contraindicated. Obviously, it is possible to individualize the exercise selection so that more or less emphasis is placed upon specific muscles or muscle groups. However, it is unlikely that a well-designed program would ever completely neglect a specific body area or muscle group.

Choosing specific exercises is a matter of personal choice and equipment availability. A combination of compound (or multi-joint) and isolation (or single-joint) movements usually provides the necessary stimulus to promote strength development throughout a muscle's ROM. While it is certainly possible to train exclusively with either compound or isolation exercises, a combination of these movement patterns allows different joint angles to be exposed to the training load and will provide for a greater stimulus area and more complete training. By utilizing a combination of movement patterns, different repetition ranges, and a variety of modalities, an almost endless supply of workouts becomes available. Each has inherent, specific strengths and weaknesses that combine to produce a unique training stimulus. By continually modifying these programming variables, it is possible to consistently stimulate gains and avoid the pitfalls of repetition and boredom.

In an effort to continually challenge the muscular system and provide a progressive overload to stimulate gains, it will be advantageous to vary the stimulus. These variations can take a number of different forms. Simply changing an exercise may provide the needed variety for a routine. Other variations, such as changing modality, exercise order, or repetition goals, can be systematically manipulated (individually or in combination) to provide the necessary stimulus to continue improving.

SAMPLE PROGRAMS

Several possible strength training programs are outlined in Figure 5.2. All of the guidelines delineated in this chapter have been utilized in the designs. While any of these program designs would represent a reasonable choice for training, I've purposely kept them general. Taking any program from a book or magazine and adopting it as *the* program without first analyzing the exercise selection, modalities, and loading patterns to see if they coincide with individual goals, abilities, and orthopedic concerns would be shortsighted. Use these program designs as general guidelines for an individualized program that addresses your specific needs.

Note that the program designs in Figure 5.2 do not delineate specific repetition ranges. Since the loading pattern depends upon the specific training effect desired, this variable is best established by individual goals. In addition, the exercise selections in the program designs in Figure 5.2 are by no means exclusive. Additional exercises for the neck, hips, rotator cuff, and forearms may be appropriate and necessary. Modifications in sequence, angle of application, and grip should provide additional variety and individualization.

THE "PERFECT" PROGRAM

To summarize, while many approaches can yield positive results, some methods are safer and more effective than others. Take advantage of the available resources, train hard, keep good records, and listen to your body. Perfection is in the eye of the beholder and the perfect strength training program is the one that allows you the most effective pursuit of your physical goals.

I would like to acknowledge and extend my sincere appreciation to Matt Brzycki for the opportunity to participate in this project. I would also like to thank Penn State associate athletic director W. Herbert Schmidt for his support, guidance, and willingness to allow me to pursue excellence in my job. I would also like to express my gratitude to the instructors (especially those associated with the physiology program) whose direction and time investment will always be appreciated. Finally, I would like to thank those individuals with whom I have worked over the years (especially Mark Verratti and Brad Andress) for the contributions they have provided to the job, and, most importantly, for their friendship.

Figure 5.2 Sample Strength-Training Program Design

Push/Pull	Body Part	Prefatigue
Leg Press	Overhead Press	Leg Extension
Leg Curl	Front Raise	Leg Curl
Leg Extension	Side Lateral Raise	Leg Press
Leg Curl	Underhand Lat Pulldown	Chest Fly
Calf Raise	Pullover	Bench Press
Bench Press	Seated Row	Pullover
Seated Row	Incline Press	Underhand Lat Pulldown
Overhead Press	Pec Dec	Seated Row
Underhand Lat Pulldown	Preacher Curl	Side Lateral Raise
Chest Fly	Tricep Pushdown	Overhead Press
Pullover	Lunge	Bicep Curl
Side Lateral Raise	Seated Leg Curl	Tricep Extension
Bicep Curl	Leg Extension	Abdominal Crunch
Tricep Extension	Seated Calf Raise	Back Extension
Abdominal Crunch	Abdominal Crunch	
Back Extension	Back Extension	

All Compound	4-Day Split	4-Day Split
Leg Press	(Mon./Thurs.: Upper Body)	(Mon./Thurs.: Upper-Body Push)
Lunge	Bench Press	Incline Press
Upright Row	Seated Row	Pec Dec
Overhead Press	Overhead Press	Overhead Press
Overhand Lat Pulldown	Underhand Lat Pulldown	Front Raise
Seated Row	Chest Fly	Side Lateral Raise
Underhand Lat Pulldown	Pullover	Tricep Pushdown
Incline Press	Side Lateral Raise	Back Extension
Dip	Bicep Curl	
Preacher Curl (isolation)	Tricep Extension	(Tues./Fri.: Upper-Body Pull and Legs)
Tricep Pushdown (isolation)		
Abdominal Crunch (isolation)	(Tues./Fri.: Lower Body)	Underhand Lat Pulldown
Back Extension (isolation)	Leg Press	Pullover
	Leg Curl	Seated Row
	Leg Extension	Preacher Curl
	Leg Curl	Leg Press
	Calf Raise	Leg Curl
	Hip Adduction	Leg Extension
	Hip Abduction	Leg Curl
	Abdominal Crunch	Calf Raise
	Back Extension	Abdominal Crunch

6

High Intensity Training: What It Is

Ken E. Leistner, D.C., M.S.
Oceanside, New York

The long history of strength training has moments of genius, incidents of scandal, and, since its inception, plenty of individuals who tout themselves as experts and attempt to make a living from an unsuspecting public. To this day, many of the trends established in the late 1800s and at the turn of the century continue. What is lost in all of the rhetoric surrounding weight training, strength enhancement, and the development of useful, functional muscle tissue is that resistance training, when properly performed and done consistently over time, offers all that its many proponents ceaselessly espouse.

THE EARLY YEARS

In the early 1900s, an organized body of training information was presented to the interested public, mostly as a result of the popularity of the many strongmen and strength performers who toured Europe and the United States at that time. Each strongman had his own unique approach to training, foreshadowing the current marketplace where each individual needs to establish an identifying characteristic to his or her training methods to attract the buying public. This marketing angle makes for a confusing array of courses, booklets, and pamphlets. However, there was an underlying common theme: limited amounts of work. The availability of equipment allowed for only basic movements utilizing barbells, dumbbells, and other variously shaped pieces of metal and pipe. This was not necessarily a negative; many men became much stronger and muscularly larger as a result of their diligent training.

Through the 1930s and 1940s, the United States suffered through a depression and a world war. Training time, available materials, and the perception of the public did not encourage the pursuit of weight training or competitive lifting as a leisure activity. Those who could and did train regularly stood out; they were often seen as freaks. While perhaps admired at work for their ability to lift heavier objects than coworkers, weight training was still viewed as an underground activity.

At the end of World War II, veterans returned to enjoy the leisure time denied to them during combat. California became a siren song for many. The first popular bodybuilding community sprang up. While there were always small pockets of lifting enthusiasts scattered throughout the United States, the New York City area and California became havens for those seeking others with the same interests: a devotion to either lifting heavy weights or building the body beautiful.

York, Pennsylvania, became the epicenter of Olympic-style weightlifting due to the efforts of Bob Hoffman and the York® Barbell Company. Lines were clearly drawn and kept very much in place through the 1950s and into the early 1960s. Simply put, if you were interested in Olympic-style weightlifting, you traveled to or lived in the York area and followed the training procedures established there; if you were interested in bodybuilding, you went to New York City or California where the training procedures were quite different from those used at the York Barbell Club. By the mid-1960s, three trends served to further separate those who lifted weights. The first was the rise of odd-lift contests, which eventually metamorphosized into the sport of powerlifting. What began as contests of strength, utilizing typical training exercises such as the squat, bench press, curl, and deadlift, grew quickly. The first official national championship was held in 1965, following the success of the first United States tournament in 1964. Hoffman and the Olympic lifting powers fought hard to prevent the growth of powerlifting, at least in the beginning. While Hoffman actually provided a great deal of support once he saw the tide moving against him, he always lamented the loss of so many potential Olympic lifters to a sport that, in his estimation, required little or no athletic ability.

Weight-training procedures as a means to improve performance in specific sports, especially track and field and football, was another late-1950s and early-1960s trend. It injected new interest in weight training and provided a separate category of trainee. While the occasional star like football's Stan Jones and shot-putter Dallas Long lifted weights, excelled as a result of their weight training, and extolled the virtues of resistance exercise at every turn, organized training programs for athletes were practically nonexistent. But slowly, open-minded coaches began to realize that weight training would not make their athletes muscle-bound, tight, or slow. On an almost monthly basis, *Strength & Health* magazine featured colleges and high schools that turned out All-State, All-America, and All-World athletes as a result of their weightlifting activities. By the early 1970s, almost every major college had a semblance of a weightroom and Boyd Epley's appointment as the nation's first strength coach at the University of Nebraska propelled the acceptance of weight training as a legitimate tool for athletic enhancement. Epley followed the lead of Alvin Roy who was professional football's first strength coach, working in an official capacity with the San Diego Chargers in 1963.

Olympic-style weightlifting continued to decline in popularity. Bodybuilding, on the other hand, grew more popular, despite its reputation as a haven for deviants, narcissists, and those without the athletic ability to compete in powerlifting, Olympic lifting, or some other sport. In the late 1950s, full-scale battles erupted. Some involved various publications and legal suits. Popular bodybuilders began to endorse various nutritional products. Advertising opportunities were waged between a number of individuals in the industry. At stake was an ever-increasing amount of money being spent on leisure-time activities that either directly or peripherally involved weights, weight training, and/or nutritional supplements. In short, the age of commercialism had reached the world of weight training. Many people took this as an opportunity to hurtle full speed ahead to find ways to garner as much of that money as possible. The factionalism of those days established varying interests, perspectives, and goals related to weight training. These trends continue to create divisiveness and negativity in the field today. The only losers have been those who feed off the excercise industry solely for the purpose of making money while only contributing false promises and confusion.

THE START OF A NEW ERA

In 1970, the field of strength training entered a new era thanks to Arthur Jones, a brilliant, sarcastic, ambitious, and ultimately wealthy man who foresaw the future in weight training much more clearly than anyone who had come before him. He had a lifelong interest in strength training and, in fact, had been one of the bodybuilding enthusiasts that made up the early Northern California training scene. He had often trained at Ed Yarick's gym with future legends Steve Reeves, Jack Dellinger, and Clancy Ross. Jones was an inventor of sorts, having developed a camera-mounting system that allowed him to photograph animals romping across the plains of Africa while taking the wobble out of the picture. He also spent many years developing a machine that would allow a person to work the major muscle structures of the upper body while eliminating the use of the arms during the movement. Jones eventually found his way to a small Florida hamlet called Lake Helen and began production of his unique exercise machine. The finished model may have resembled something that should have been harvesting wheat, but its effectiveness was undeniable. The first plate-loaded Nautilus® Pullover Torso Machine, in conjunction with a number of other functional exercise movements, caused a stir at the 1970 Senior National Weightlifting Championships and

Mr. America Contest, where they were initially displayed. It was the beginning of a change in the entire industry.

Arthur Jones built many more machines based upon the biomechanics of the human body. Nautilus® Sports/Medical Industries became the first company to mass market nothing but exercise machines to a national audience. Other companies, such as Paramount® and Marcy, made multi-station exercise machines and primarily sold them to West Coast markets. Nautilus® became the ground breaker. Its impact brought exercise and exercise equipment into the public consciousness.

In addition to his machines, Jones advanced a training philosophy that required the trainee to perform a very limited amount of very hard and intense work. This harkened back to an earlier era where men trained hard on a few basic movements. Jones was quick to state that his revolutionary machines provided basic training exercises that more readily and accurately conformed to the biomechanics of the human body but were, nonetheless, basic training exercises that worked the major muscular structures. His training theories, admittedly not originated by him, were deemed efficient and effective. Ultimately, Jones had one of the best packaged programs for those who wished to train in a cogent and intelligent fashion.

Predictably, there was a backlash. Jones threatened not only the status quo in the industry but the industry itself. Publishers of the popular muscle-building publications shrieked their disbelief in his machines and his training methods. However, the popularity and acceptance of his equipment was immediate. No longer having a tangible target to attack, these long-established manufacturers, supplement producers, and publishers went after Jones's training ideas. Jones's philosophy was easier to attack, for how many trainees wanted to face the prospect of training "as hard as possible" in each and every workout? Of course, those who did produced excellent results because the admonition to "train hard and intensely" was coupled and tempered with the need to train relatively infrequently. This system limited not only the frequency of training but the actual number of exercises done in each workout. People could train hard and intensely if they limited both the volume of work in any specific training session and the actual number of training sessions per week or per month. This was considered a radical departure in an era where the effectiveness of a workout was still measured not by its result-producing abilities but by the volume of the work done.

There should have been nothing radical about a training program that asked the trainee to do each exercise in proper form, train as hard as possible, and then take enough time to recover so that the next workout could be as effective and result-producing as possible. However, when seen within the context of being combined with exercise machinery, it posed a real threat to the economic security of everyone else in the business. Anything remotely related to Nautilus® was seen as a negative by those with a stake in the fitness business—and there were many.

So for most, high intensity training became synonymous with the training done on Nautilus® equipment. It became equivalent to doing one set of an exercise and one set only. It simply required the trainee to do each repetition of an exercise raising the weight to the completed or contracted position within a specified number of seconds and then lowering it within a specified number of seconds. The truth about high intensity training was lost, especially to those who had made a decision to defend any other professional position in the field of training. In truth, much of this stemmed from the animosity Jones created between himself and one of his employees, Dr. Ellington Darden. Jones was abrasive. Those who worked for him, including myself, and spent any amount of time in his presence understood that he was eccentric. He was completely focused upon whatever he was involved with at a particular moment. He tolerated fools poorly and was quick-witted and outspoken—and damn the consequences. At a lecture he delivered at Duke University, he began by telling an auditorium filled with medical doctors and related personnel that they were essentially idiots and knew little or nothing about exercise and exercise science, and if they did know anything about the topic it was much less than what he knew. And the start of that speech was the nicest and gentlest part!

PROPER TRAINING

Dr. Darden was "anointed" by Jones as his messenger. Dr. Darden had writing ability and became the Nautilus® spokesperson through his many books on the subject of training, nutrition, and the use of the company's equipment. Many of his books were written while in the employ of either Nautilus® or Jones, but even those books written afterward carried the Nautilus® theme: brief, productive training done for one set of a specified number of repetitions on machines specifically designed to stimulate growth in a certain muscle or muscle group. While Dr. Darden's work, much like Jones's, referred to barbells and dumbbells as effective tools of strength training and bodybuilding, the message was clear that in their opinion the various Nautilus® machines were far superior for the specific task at hand.

Dr. Darden too often engendered animosity by a smugness borne of the knowledge that his was the correct stance on training. At a strength training clinic in Cincinnati in the mid-1980s, the directors of the training programs of many YMCAs throughout the country were in attendance. They were there specifically to hear from guest speakers who had some relationship to high intensity training which had, through the years, come to be known simply as HIT. Kim Wood, the long-time strength coach of the Cincinnati Bengals, the general manager and managing partner of Nautilus® Midwest (the distributors of Nautilus® equipment in seven midwestern states), and eventual manager of Hammer Strength®

Corporation, was one of the lecturers. It should be pointed out that Mr. Wood was also instrumental in the design of many Nautilus® and Hammer Strength® machines and was an employee of Arthur Jones in the first few years of the company's existence. In short, Kim Wood knew and continues to know strength training and muscular development as well if not better than anyone in the country. At the time, his Bengals had one of the lowest injury rates in the NFL and had been both conference champions and Super Bowl participants. Other strength coaches envied his record and his ability to produce results.

At this particular seminar/clinic, Wood trained Bengal linebacker Reggie Williams. Mr. Williams had graduated from Dartmouth University after three years of study. He was a team captain with the Bengals and an All-Pro player. He had been awarded the NFL Man-of-the-Year title. As an intelligent and serious student of the game of football, he was interested only in the most effective and safest way to prepare his body for the rigors of professional football. He had complete confidence in Kim Wood and the two had managed to produce a very effective training regimen that was typical of HIT programs: The repetitions were done so that tension was produced in the muscle being worked; the exercise form was such that the muscle purported to be targeted by the exercise was, in fact, the primary mover in the exercise during each repetition; each repetition was done so

Reggie Williams of the Cincinnati Bengals was interested only in the most effective and safest way to prepare his body for the rigors of football. (photo by Kathy Leistner)

that the involved musculature was brought through the greatest possible safe range of motion while under tension; each set of each exercise was done until no further repetitions could be completed in proper form; the workout was paced so that the trainee moved from one exercise to the next with minimal rest; and the workout itself was extremely demanding and challenging, leaving the trainee (in this case, Mr. Williams) completely spent by its conclusion.

At the same seminar, I was also a featured speaker and trained my son Kevin Tolbert. Like Reggie Williams, Kevin was a superb athlete and football player who had a longstanding history of training very hard. The attendees were spellbound by the workouts performed by both men. They both displayed tremendous strength, using a great deal of weight on both the barbell and machine exercises. They both trained with great intensity and concentration. They both allowed their respective trainers to push them to their momentary limits. When Kevin had completed his workout, a general discussion and exchange of ideas was initiated. Dr. Darden immediately stood up and declared that he had not "witnessed one properly performed repetition" by either athlete. After more discussion, Dr. Darden made the admission that he did not believe that either athlete had trained properly because they had not trained the way he thought they should train. In other words, in his opinion, there was only one proper way to train, and he was the sole arbiter. If an individual did not follow his previously published list of training guidelines to the letter, then that individual had not trained properly. That there might be more than one exacting standard never dawned on Dr. Darden.

I had been personally trained on many occasions by Arthur Jones. I was one of the individuals Jones used to demonstrate both Nautilus® machines and proper training procedure at the Nautilus® manufacturing facility in Lake Helen. Arthur's instructions were simple: "You will train as hard as is humanly possible in good form." "Good form" meant that one would maintain a safe body alignment while exercising so as to avoid injury to an uninvolved body part. It meant that each repetition would be raised and lowered in a manner that would not cause injury to the involved part. While Arthur wanted every repetition controlled, he did not request that a specific number of seconds be used either to raise or to lower the resistance. In fact, when no further repetitions could be completed in good form, we were asked to complete one or two more by cheating (using extraneous body movement). Rather than stopping when another repetition could not be completed in "good form," we would move the resistance until it could not be moved, to the point where the barbell or machine arm would not budge from the starting position. Yet, Dr. Darden had the audacity to state that if the exercise wasn't done his way it wasn't being done properly. Darden's arrogance—combined with Jones's attitude that it was not his job to explain his actions or thoughts to those who did not fully understand him, his machines, or his training theories—made for many enemies in the field and further confused the exact definition of HIT.

WHAT HIT IS

HIT is a philosophy of training and not a specifically defined set of dictums that delineate a training methodology. The philosophy utilizes basic principles that allow for safe and productive training. These principles do not limit the practitioner to a narrow view of the equipment used or the number of sets done in any one workout. In short, HIT is an effective training procedure suitable for the most advanced and well-trained athlete or the mere beginner.

HIT is brief by necessity. If one accepts that the most efficient way to stimulate muscle-tissue growth and increases in strength is to train hard, ideally to the extent of one's momentary ability, common sense dictates that the training in any one session must be brief. It has often been stated that one can train long or one can train hard but one cannot train long and hard, at least not consistently without risking injury, illness, or psychological negativity toward the training. Training "hard" or "with maximal intensity" refers to the completion of each set of exercise utilizing all of one's concentration and effort. The set is completed when one can no longer do another repetition properly or safely. If one actually can train that hard within the workout from one exercise to the next, he or she obviously will have to limit the amount of work to adequately recover for the next workout. To date, no legitimate studies have implicated the ultimate results of training with the volume of work done within any one workout.

HIT cannot be done frequently. Training as hard as possible does not allow a person to train a large number of times within any one week or month. The trend in athletics, as it seems to be in many areas of the popular culture, is to assume that more is better. Business executives and football coaches are praised for their willingness and ability to work ungodly hours each day. We revere the athlete who adopts a spartan training regime that requires massive amounts of work. I believe that this concept allows many to justify their inability to achieve similar goals. They believe that only those blessed with outstanding abilities and an inordinate amount of time for training can succeed. But in reality training very hard requires time for rest and recovery.

Efficiency is a key component of HIT. Even those with differing training philosophies recognize and agree that what are termed "basic" exercises—multijoint movements that engage a relatively large amount of muscle tissue during the performance of a repetition or set of the specific exercise—are more efficient for stimulating gains in muscular size and strength when compared to isolation exercises, which work perhaps one muscle or one specific portion of a muscle group. These basic multi-joint movements are also relatively more demanding upon the physiological systems of the body than isolation exercises. Again, common sense dictates that an all-out set of squats, done until one cannot rise from the bottom position of the movement, done for as many repetitions as possible with a particular amount of weight, will be more difficult and thus more intense, and be more demanding and stimulating to the overall physiology of the body than any other

During HIT, each set is completed when one can no longer do another repetition properly or safely. (photo by Kathy Leistner)

set, including an all-out set of leg extensions. Doing these basic multi-joint exercises as the basis of the program allows one to work the major muscular structures of the body with a minimal number of exercises. If one is seeking to maximize training intensity while limiting training volume, this is the most efficient and effective way.

Most properly designed exercise machines are merely a redesigned barbell that allows for more efficient and/or safer exercise performance. It is true that some machines offer a physiological and/or biomechanical advantage compared to standard barbells or dumbbells, but a machine is neither inherently advantageous nor disadvantageous. A particular individual's bodily leverages and emotional predisposition may dictate the use of one or the other, but a cogent training philosophy allows the use of whatever effective and safe training modality is available at the time. HIT is not the use of a machine or particular grouping of machines and, in fact, may not involve an exercise machine at all if a barbell or dumbbells are preferred or exclusively available.

"HIT," to quote a statement I made many years ago, "is going all out, not almost all out; it is taking each set to one's absolute limit, not almost to the limit; it is using whatever piece of equipment that's available, not just a machine or group of machines; it is not the words of two or three men, but a commitment to work as hard as possible while in the gym or weight room . . . without socializing, resting excessively between sets, or falling prey to the 'this isn't going to work so I'll copy the star' attitude." HIT is hard but it is effective. It is hard but it should be safe relative to other methods of training. It is demanding but rewarding. It can, if used properly, be the necessary vehicle to alter one's physical strength, muscular size, and level of confidence both in and out of the athletic arena.

This chapter is dedicated to Mike Mentzer, Arthur Jones, and the memory of Ayn Rand for their influence on my scientific and objective approach to anaerobic exercise.

7

High Intensity Versus High Volume

Brian D. Johnston
President and Founder
International Association of Resistance Trainers
North Bay, Ontario, Canada

Everything existent has but one truth unto itself, an identity it cannot contradict, which can be neither ignored by man's conceptual faculty nor escaped if man is to exist and prosper within reality. Identity is an irreducible primary, an axiomatic concept that is a fundamental of epistemology (the study, nature, and acquisition of knowledge) and metaphysics (the study of existence). As a rational animal, man has a unique identity, as does an apple, a tree, celestial bodies, and everything within the universe.

Anaerobic exercise (strength training), likewise, is a specific concept within reality that has a specific identity and, therefore, has an exact meaning or definition. If it did not, the term *anaerobic exercise* could not be properly integrated with other abstractions or concepts and therefore could not exist per se. The exorbitant perceptions of what constitutes anaerobic exercise are so varied among the so-called experts that the term has become a nebulous approximation to the extent that the average individual is perplexed in securing its proper meaning. Accordingly, anaerobic exercise must be grounded on noncontradictory principles.

Anaerobic exercise is characterized as being high in intensity/effort and brief in duration (with frequency adhering to individual tolerance to stress for systemic recovery and overcompensation of muscle tissue). Deviation from these two elements alters the basic nature of anaerobic exercise such that it no longer exists as true anaerobic exercise. Although the approach to strength training can vary in application (number of repetitions, repetition speed, and time under load—all within limited reason), the anaerobic discipline must still hold true to its identifying principles for optimal meaningful progress.

Currently, the only valid qua theory of anaerobic exercise that upholds these principles has been discovered and established by Mike Mentzer. His is known as the Heavy Duty Theory. A valid theory cannot consist of unwarranted assumptions; instead, it must logically (noncontradictively) unite a maximum number of facts so that it can assimilate new facts in the future without damage to its own structure. The significance of integrating anaerobic exercise theory vis-à-vis Heavy Duty becomes more apparent when contrasting various strength training methodologies. The high-volume, multiple-set approach to strength training is an incongruous, nontheoretical, random, disconnected, contradictory set of ideas and cannot act as a guide for successful action. Essentially, the Heavy Duty Theory (high intensity training in its most precise form) states that to a certain degree, any amount of exercise stress represents a negative factor in that any exercise at all causes an inroad into the body's recovery ability. Therefore, it must be cautiously regulated; if there is an inroad into recovery ability, that much of the body's resources must be used to compensate for the merely exhaustive effects of the exercise (i.e., overcome the inroad), leaving that much less of the body's limited reserve of resources for growth. Accordingly, for optimal progress exercise must be prescribed in an exact dose–response relationship in accordance with each individual's tolerance to stress.

To increase muscle strength and size, one's existing anaerobic functional ability must be challenged continually via an increase in weight and/or repetitions. Heavy Duty Theory indicates that this can only be accomplished as long as overtraining is nonexistent, by taking each working set to a point of momentary muscular fatigue—regardless of the number of repetitions—thereby resulting in the eventual generation of 100 percent effort. Effort of a lesser degree will not challenge current functional ability and may, at best, only maintain current strength levels.

There must be adequate recovery time between training sessions to provide for replenishment of fuel resources, compensation, and eventually overcompensation in the form of new muscle-tissue growth. Although stress has a localized effect on the trained body part in question, it also has a general effect on the entire body. Consequently, recovery time between sessions for unrelated body parts is just as important as recovery time between sessions for the same body parts. Training again before the body has had sufficient time to compensate and overcompensate will hamper training progress and result in generalized fatigue.

Although the above may appear quite evident upon review, high volume, orthodoxy collectivists are eager to refute Heavy Duty, charging that there is more than one valid approach to strength training. The reason they are adamant in their position is because Heavy Duty Theory exposes the frailty of high-volume application (gross overtraining [overuse atrophy] due to excessive volume and frequency). Yet, when these experts are pushed to delineate their own theories of anaerobic exercise, silence ensues—blank out!

Mike Mentzer has repeatedly and logically elucidated the basis of Heavy Duty Theory as outlined previously. His standard of proof of the validity of his theory far surpasses that of any other strength training authority.

Moreover, suggesting there is no single theory or approach to anaerobic exercise raises the premise that there cannot be any known truths and that man must continue his subjective, arbitrary quest for whatever may work in accord with his wishes and desires. Whereas one expert suggests 3 sets of 3 exercises, another recommends that 10 repetitions of 10 sets is best, and yet another indicates that training each body part twice weekly in a light-heavy alternation is vastly superior. Each believes the competence of his own formula, but all succumb to theoretical abandonment since individual provisions can only be discovered by way of a valid theory—a guide for successful action. To properly apply training derivatives (i.e., repetitions, sets/volume, and frequency), a theory must initially be reasoned then followed, which high volume training and periodization fail to do and cannot do.

In essence, the two principal genera of strength training can be reduced to: (1) high intensity training (HIT)—extreme effort while incorporating only one work set per exercise with minimum work sets per body part per workout (what exactly "minimum" means remains subjective among trainees) and (2) high volume training (HVT)—moderate to extreme intensity/effort while incorporating multiple work sets (2+) per exercise per body part per workout. These lax abstractions further accommodate the more explicit ideologies and perceptions of the fitness industry. For instance, some advocates of HIT avoid direct sets for smaller body parts to justify for any crossover effect (e.g., biceps stimulation during lat pulldowns). Others include up to three sets per body part of different exercises. Doing so may or may not be too voluminous but volume is relatively diminutive when contrasted to typical HVT methodologies (e.g., 10+ sets per body part). The high volume Weider approach to bodybuilding recommends an ambiguous 3–5 sets of 3–5 exercises per muscle group, whereas periodization fluctuates the intensity, volume, and frequency from one "season" to another depending upon specific training goals such as strength, power, mass, or endurance. (Varying seasonal training is ludicrous and will be addressed later.) Although perception of what constitutes purposeful strength training application is a source of chaotic diversity even among colleagues of similar methodologies, the argumentative and theoretical discrepancy between HIT and HVT remains obvious.

The purpose of this chapter is to address:

1. the physiological effects of both HIT and HVT
2. how HVT proponents perceive HIT and the myths underlying their beliefs
3. the basis for which HVT should be considered and the myths underlying these beliefs
4. the inadequacies and biases of research in the field of strength testing research

PHYSIOLOGICAL EFFECTS OF HIT AND HVT

HIT has distinct attributes via a cause-and-effect relationship. Increases in phosphogenic concentration and glycolytic substrates (both energy-yielding components of anaerobic exercise) and increases in anaerobic enzyme activity are most notable. Consequently, there is also a gradual abatement of aerobic-oxidative enzymes with long-term implementation of HIT. Moreover, and primarily due to longer recovery intervals than those of HVT, HIT has been linked to enhanced immunogenicity. These factors are reflective of the SAID principle (specific adaptations to imposed demands), wherein the physiological mechanism optimizes and adapts to a particular stressor for survival. Conversely, training that encompasses less than maximum effort or repetitive bouts of activity on a highly frequent basis increases aerobic-oxidative enzymes and mitochondrial proliferation to, likewise, adapt to a particular physiological environment—that being endurance.

Although HVT approaches can incorporate very intense effort interspersed throughout total work volume, there is a disproportionate inclusion of lower-intensity valueless effort. In effect, HVT becomes a psychologically dependent provocation of how much one can endure to prove merit as an iron warrior; hence, there is a focus on total work volume rather than quality and effort. As a result, there is also a proclivity for fast-twitch fibers to atrophy due to overuse stimulation. Fast-twitch fibers have a specific identity or nature affiliated with very intense but brief, infrequent work. They can tolerate neither the strain of high load time under tension (set duration) nor high volume and frequency.

Physiologically, strength training is an unnatural event, forcing adaptation to a greater apex of functional capacity and ability for survival. When subjected to stress—whether it be exercise, extreme cold, or emotional and psychological anxiety—specific events transpire as discovered by the father of modern stress research, Hans Selye, including:

1. enlargement of the adrenal cortex
2. atrophy of the thymus, spleen, lymph nodes, and all other lymphatic structures of the body (including a large reduction in eosinophil cells [a type of white blood cell])
3. ulcers in the lining of the stomach

Therefore, although working the biceps may have a localized effect on the myofibrillar architecture within the biceps, there is also a generalized—endocrinological—systemic effect on the entire body. Performing 15 sets for the biceps means performing 15 sets for the body. This is empirically evident the day after an intense thigh workout when the trainee feels reluctant to exercise the upper back, chest, or some other muscle group due to an overall feeling of general fatigue.

To compare the cumulative, depleting effect of a high-intensity modality to that of a high-volume approach, consider the following: 1 set per body part × 7 body parts × 52 occasions per year (i.e., once every 7 days) × 25 years = 9,100 bouts of stress. Conversely, 10 sets per body part x 7 body parts × 73 occasions per year (i.e., once every 5 days) × 25 years = 127,750 bouts of stress. This equates to 14 times the magnitude of stress as that incurred by the sample HIT approach. If, for the sake of argument, HIT produces no better strength gains than a lower-intensity high-volume periodization approach, it would appear logical to implement a HIT approach, thereby exposing long-term systemic wear and tear on the body to a more tolerable degree.

MYTHS OF HIT

This section examines many of the misconceptions held by HVT advocates. These have not been fabricated but were, in fact, extracted from various authoritative sources.

Perception: "It is impossible to knock off the entire motor unit pool of Type I, Type IIa, and Type IIb fibers from performing only one set."

First, what is meant by *knock off*? It can be presumed that the term refers to the eventual firing and exhaustion of all motor neurons thereby fatiguing all muscle fibers within said muscle group. Notwithstanding, it is implausible to knock off all motor units (and likewise fibers), even by means of multiple sets. First, not all myofibrils exert force to the same magnitude throughout the length of a sarcolemma; only as a muscle loses its mechanical efficiency—due to the force deviating from a straight line—wherein it increases its girth at the point of full contraction will those myofibrils toward the center of the muscle belly be called upon to work. (See Figure 7.1.) This is basic mechanical physics of which few experts are even aware. As a result, if an exercise does not afford adequate resistive force at a particular juncture—including the point of full contraction, e.g., bicep curls—then specific myofibrils will not fully work/fatigue at that juncture (one of the limitations of most free-weight exercises). Second, such a degenerative/exhaustive process, if it were possible, would painfully yield total incapacitation of the muscle group for several days (accompanied by a reduction in potential functional capacity for several weeks). Atrophy of the fast-twitch fibers would correspondingly eventuate since endeavoring to "knock off" all motor units would demand outrageous volume.

How many sets, then, are warranted to knock off all motor units? And, if "all motor units" was an exaggeration of proposition, how many must be knocked off to bring about profits in strength? Most HVT proponents insinuate that 10 or more sets appear to be the requisite number as reflected by their training protocols. But

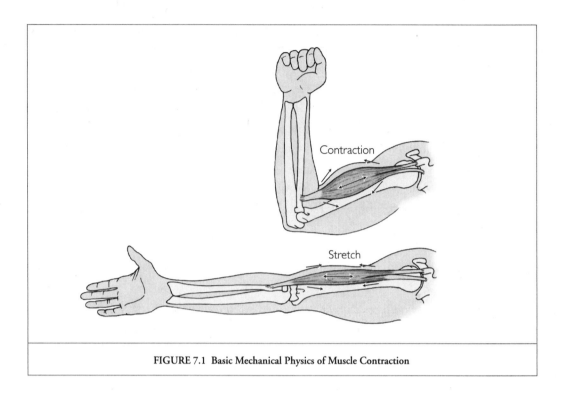

FIGURE 7.1 Basic Mechanical Physics of Muscle Contraction

how was that conclusion reached, and which is it exactly: 10, 11, 15, 18, 20 sets or more? To arbitrarily suggest 10, 15, or 20 sets is fatuous since performing more sets than necessary becomes an act of redundancy and only serves to make greater inroads into recovery ability.

Strength training can be defined as the use of progressive resistance methods to increase the ability to exert or resist force, hence the Overload Principle. Constantly challenging current strength/force capacity—by either using more weight for the same number of repetitions or performing more repetitions with the same weight (within reason and without attempting to optimize endurance)—will increase strength accordingly. This task cannot be achieved other than by training to momentary muscular failure or fatigue. Effort, even one repetition short of muscular fatigue, can not challenge a muscle's capacity and so will not act as a catalyst for initiating the growth-mechanism response. Conversely, by implementing 100 percent intensity of effort—even within a solitary set of exercise and by exceeding past lifting accomplishments—hypertrophy becomes highly probable as long as adequate recovery has transpired and nutritional requirements are met. Intensity is the governing factor in anaerobic progression—and in aerobic progression, for that matter—not volume consisting of multiple sets per exercise. Indeed, HVT proponents understand the need for intensity since they typically push the final set of an exercise. Yet, they do not fully grasp the concept; instead they opt to define intensity as the amount of weight lifted or the amount of work performed in a given period of time. Rather, intensity is the percentage of possible momentary muscular effort exerted.

Perception: "HIT may be good in theory but not in practice."

How can a theory be good yet its actions flawed? If a theory is not true to its corresponding actions, it no longer is a valid theory. The practice of specific, conscionable actions is the result of a theory.

Perception: "HIT proponents are dogmatic."

Dogma, as Ayn Rand stated, refers to "a set of beliefs accepted on faith; that is, without rational justification or against rational evidence. A dogma is a matter of blind faith." If actions do not follow an established theory, they are left to pursue gut hunches, blind faith, and subjectiveness. Hence, the actions become random and arbitrary. Since no high-volume, periodization proponent has ever established a theory based on a set of noncontradictory principles, unlike Heavy Duty, it is the HVT proponents who are dogmatic.

Perception: "Considering the warm-up sets that high intensity trainees implement, it really is the same thing as HVT. They're still performing 2–3 sets per exercise or more."

It certainly isn't written in stone that HIT cannot implement warm-up sets to facilitate a more efficient workout. In fact, to use a progressively heavier weight to reflect the Overload Principle, it is often necessary to increase body-core temperature and psychological preparedness prior to the work set(s). However, progressing a warm-up beyond the requisite generates additional stress and fatigue, diminishing total muscle force output. Hence—and this is the most crucial distinction between HIT and HVT—as with the workout, the warm-up must essentially be kept to the minimum, thereby making the least amount of inroads into functional capacity.

For instance, if 100 pounds × 10 repetitions is your work set (taken to the point of momentary muscular fatigue), an ideal warm-up may consist of: 50 pounds × 3 repetitions, followed by 75 pounds × 1–2 repetitions, followed by the work set. The function of the initial two sets is to prepare both mind and body for intense work, yet not fatigue or challenge functional capacity. Considering the extremely low effort one would expend on the initial two sets, they cannot be labeled work sets nor do they contribute to any consequential degree to the total volume, à la HVT.

For those concerned about the risk of injury following such a brief warm-up, bear in mind that by implementing slow, continuous, nonballistic movement—as suggested by HIT practice—the risk of injury remains relatively nonexistent. Injury occurs when forces exceed the integrity of soft tissues or negate complete tissue remodeling due to overuse—that is, when there is too much volume and too much frequency. Both factors can arise under explosive, ballistic, plyometric HVT practices, and even under exorbitant warm-up rituals.

A well-known periodizationalist advocates an extravagant warm-up prescription of 5 sets of an exercise using the same weight for the same number of repetitions (e.g., 5 sets × 5 repetitions × 300 pounds) and working to muscular fatigue on the fifth set only. He believes that you must "own" the weight before making subsequent workout increases—thus the need for replication.

First, if the trainee were to complete the requisite number of repetitions with a given weight in the initial work set, would he or she, at that time, not "own" it? If not, who would? Was the completion of that initial set a hallucination in the mind of the trainee? Second, the degree of energy squandered on the initial 4 sets of 5 repetitions renders the person incapable of using a possibly greater weight than that eventually used on the fifth and final set. Perhaps 320 pounds could have been used for 5 repetitions if only a minimal warm-up was performed, rather than repeating a task that was already within the trainee's ability. After all, you do not observe sprinters running the 100-meter dash four times with slightly less than maximum effort. Doing so would tax their physical ability to run a meaningful race later. Rather, sprinters jog lightly on the spot and walk about to increase blood circulation then perform mild stretching for the ankles and knees. At all times, the preparatory effort remains minimal yet essential.

Perception: "Compare the number of champions using HVT to that of HIT. Obviously, HVT is more productive."

Champion bodybuilders and strength athletes are elites within the population, outliers with respect to physical potential for building strength and muscle mass. They are on the far end of a normal bell curve. Moreover, these individuals often use nightmarish quantities of drugs. They represent an infinitesimal segment of the population and are not a representation of the average resistance trainee. Hence, such a statement commits the fallacy of hasty generalization, basing the presumption on instances that do not constitute a fair sample. It also commits the fallacy of false cause since these champion athletes are the result of their genetics and drugs, not of their workout practices; most likely they would have succeeded regardless of the method of training.

It is interesting to note that periodizationalists boast of their clients' progress. They claim to train NFL, NHL, and NBA athletes with great success; they are top coaches or trainers to the champions. Again, star athletes are not typical. Nor have I known any average trainee who has made meaningful progress on a high volume or periodization approach, excepting rookies who suffer from underuse atrophy and who often progress on nearly any program despite its inefficacy. The only trainer that I have known to provide and submit legitimate client testimonials is Mike Mentzer. He has posted regularly on his website (www.mikementzer.com) and in the *Heavy Duty Bulletin* (now called *Exercise Protocol*) the names, addresses, e-mail, and telephone numbers of average individuals who have made remarkable gains utilizing HIT.

An objective indication of what training method works would require a copious random sample of experienced resistance trainees—they must be experienced since nearly all beginners make initial progress on any program—then measure their progress over a one-year span using a reliable body-composition analysis system to determine ratio differences of fat versus lean body tissue. Accurate strength-increase measurements would also be useful but must be conducted on specialized equipment to account for impact forces, stored-energy torque, gravity, and internal muscular friction—such as that offered only by MedX®, Incorporated. (Strength testing will be addressed later.)

Perception: "Although some champions have used HIT, many have returned to an HVT approach."

The personal reasons for returning to a less effective method of training vis-à-vis high volume, are various. Some champions have done so as a result of peer pressure—a testament to tribalism, not individualism. They commit a breach of integrity: they know what is right, then proceed through rationalization to defy the truth that HIT is the only logical approach.

Other champions can see a more easily traveled road through mindless, low-intensity pumping and anabolic steroids. Conversely, HIT is irrefutably hard work, requiring utmost focus, determination, and motivation for optimal success. Notwithstanding, HIT can be tolerated by anyone—including the elderly—with clear, objective goals and determination. It is not reserved for a special breed of individual.

Another explanation for shifting from HIT to HVT may be downright ignorance in comprehending the vital connotations in regulating intensity, volume, and frequency. Years ago, upon obtaining Mike Mentzer's Heavy Duty Arms course, I enthusiastically integrated the suggestions within my routine, performing one set of rest-pause curls for biceps together with a pre-exhaust set for triceps once weekly. Considering my previous training practices of 10 sets for each muscle group, this was truly low volume. After four workouts, I increased my upper-arm size by one half inch. Upon witnessing the speedy results, I rationalized that two sets twice weekly would be better. The result was flagrant overtraining, overuse atrophy, and a loss of my one-half-inch gain. I thusly concluded that Heavy Duty did not work, so I reinstated HVT in my quest for progress. Rather than realizing that as I became larger and stronger I would require more recovery time—as Mentzer clearly indicated—I substituted his advice with the current-day orthodoxy: "Be persistent and you will triumph" and the infamous "More is better."

Perception: "HIT is hard on the joints and tendons."

It may be presumed that such a notion stems from the nomenclature Heavy Duty. Perhaps some people believe that the weight (force) must be heavy. This is not necessarily so since "heavy" relates primarily to the percentage of a trainee's one-repetition maximum (1-RM). Modern HIT is a low-force activity associated with a resistance that typically can be employed for 45–90 seconds while moving under maximum control.

What *is* hard on the joints and tendons are both impact forces and excessively frequent training. In the first instance, maximum control eliminates dangerous impact forces. In the second instance, training too frequently—as with HVT and periodization—does not allow for adequate tendon remodeling. (See Figure 7.2.) Tissues proceed through a period of transient weakness as they adapt to exercise and their mechanical strength diminishes at some point during remodeling. This situation is reflective of both muscle and tendon although it is slower for tendons due to a poorer blood supply. Hence, a sequence follows of degradation, compensation, then overcompensation. By not affording adequate time for necessary adaptive responses, these changes cannot take place regardless of the training protocol—whether high or low volume, or high or low intensity. However, brief, infrequent HIT not only provides the stimulus to initiate a growth-mechanism response, but ample recovery time for desirable changes to evolve as well.

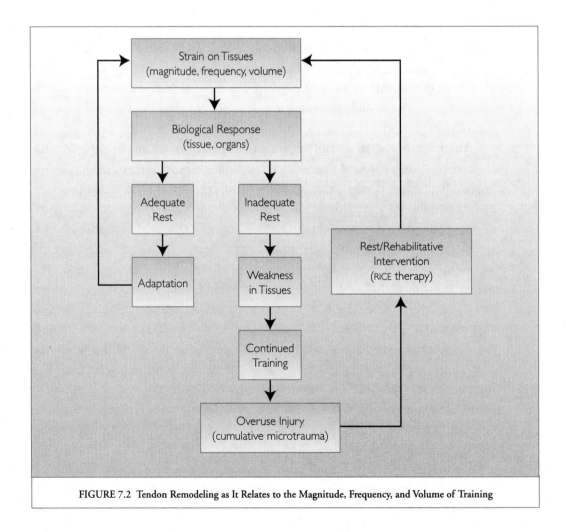

FIGURE 7.2 **Tendon Remodeling as It Relates to the Magnitude, Frequency, and Volume of Training**

Perception: "HIT has some value, but it is short-lived."

If a particular method of strength training has value, why would it be short-lived or why would it cease to be of value? As Ayn Rand stated, "Value presupposes a standard, a purpose and the necessity of action in the face of an alternative. Where there are no alternatives, no values are possible." If HIT has value, it must possess that value in the face of an alternative that does *not* have that particular value; the only diametrical alternative is HVT. Since the value of HIT (anaerobic exercise) is optimum strength development and muscle growth, HVT must not hold this particular value, thereby making HVT valueless in the realm of anaerobic exercise. Moreover, as previously defined, a theory—such as Heavy Duty—is a set of abstract principles purporting to be either a correct description of reality or a set of guidelines for successful action. Repression of further improvement, while using HIT, merely postulates that the theory's principles were not correctly heeded, which in turn suggests that the trainee neglected to properly regulate intensity, volume, and frequency as he or she grew larger and as demands (weight) increased.

Perception: "The only reason HIT initially works is that previous over-training conditions are supervened by additional rest time and briefer training sessions."

If reducing volume and frequency result in strength and muscle-mass increases—the desired commodities—what purpose lies in subsequently increasing volume and frequency through HVT or periodization? Why leave an effective program for one that is less effective? Why fix what isn't broken? It is impossible to justly and logically answer any of these questions. Moreover, what caused the previous over-training conditions? Could it have been HVT? In accordance with the Heavy Duty Theory, any stress (volume and frequency) over and above the minimum required to initiate a response contributes to overtraining, as superfluous work only serves to make greater inroads into recovery ability. In effect, a training regimen consisting of unnecessary volume and frequency can be classified as HVT which, upon reflection, even holds true for some purported high-intensity programs with an illogical infrastructure. Moreover, and to provide a more lucid identification, any program that instills work above the minimum required should be dubbed needless volume training.

Perception: "I've tried HIT, but it didn't work for me."

The reasons behind this claim are numerous but can be generalized into three categories. First, most HVT trainees perform exercise utilizing reckless lifting technique including ballistics and explosiveness. If this were not so, it would be impossible to perform the volume these individuals enthusiastically incorporate. Such shoddy technique is quite evident when viewing the various Weider and bodybuilding videos available on the market.

To illustrate, I previously trained a potentially muscular woman who, at the time, performed 3–5 exercises for 3 sets each per muscle group. She trained each muscle group once every 5 days. I drafted a routine consisting of only 1–2 sets per muscle group (training each group once weekly at most). Three weeks into the program, she felt discouraged due to nonexistent strength and muscle gains. Upon closely observing her form, I realized that she was not stimulating her muscles through controlled tension but, rather, jerking the weights about ferociously. When she reduced the velocity and instilled various isolation techniques, she felt literally debilitated within a few sets—much to her stupefaction and delectation. Thereafter, she produced the best gains of her life in a matter of two months. Since there is a distinction between quality and quantity, the two cannot coexist—at least within physical work—just as capitalism and communism or logic and mysticism cannot coexist.

Second, high intensity effort requires high motivation for meaningful progress. It is not an easy approach to training nor can everyone cope with the assiduous and requisite psychological and physical challenges. If a trainee is not mentally there at all times, he or she should not anticipate optimal physical progress. However, such is required when training within an anaerobic environment where the goal is to determine not your stamina but, rather, the level of intensity you can generate.

Third, those new to HIT who have trained with high volume beforehand are often overtrained—which has resulted in fast-twitch fiber overuse atrophy. Even a drastic reduction in volume and frequency will not prove advantageous. Once in an overtrained predicament, a total layoff is the only logical prescription for returning the body to a nonexhaustive, responsive state. Unless this condition is absolute, no method of strength training can be productive, including HIT.

WHY PERIODIZATION/HVT?

Premise: "It is necessary to work muscles from multiple angles to stimulate development and strength throughout the entire strength curve."

Regarding hypertrophy, muscles contract progressively from points of origin to insertion. You cannot, for instance, develop the outer pectorals separate from the inner pectorals nor the lower biceps from the upper biceps.

Although it can be argued that many free-weight exercises tax only one-third of the strength curve—hypothetically necessitating additional exercise inclusion—a viable solution would be to incorporate variable resistance machines such as Nautilus® and MedX®. These machines render fairly consistent effort throughout the entire range of motion by making work more demanding as full contraction eventuates, muscular efficiency decreases, and progressively more myofibrils participate. However, even variable resistance is not the most crucial factor in acquiring strength; it merely makes the application of exercise more meaningful. Rather, it is the effort generated that determines results. The deadlift, squat, chin-up, and bar dip remain some of the most exhaustive and productive exercises, yet they only tax the strength curve through a portion of their range. Including additional exercise to work the stretch, midrange, and contraction points of a muscle's range of motion only serves to make greater inroads into functional and recovery ability, thereby increasing the likelihood of overtraining.

It is true that being strong in the squat does not make you correspondingly strong in the leg press or lunge since neurological adaptation among exercises differs. However, there are dozens of movements for each body part, which raises the questions: Which exercises do you include? How many exercises do you include? How often do you implement or change the various exercises? Many periodization authorities clearly understand that being strong in one movement does not make one correspondingly strong in another (include a variety of exercises to affect the strength curve at all angles), yet they cannot grasp this connection within sport-specific biomechanics (i.e., throwing a ball, tackling in football, rowing a boat). Sport-specific skills must be practiced to properly and optimally demonstrate strength within the sport. Resistance training merely serves to increase strength generally—thereby bettering force output in sporting activities. Many coaches are nevertheless inclined to prescribe power cleans, snatches, and jumping plyometrics supposedly to increase an athlete's overall explosiveness. If this method were viable, world-class Olympic lifters would, likewise, be world-class rowers, football players, hockey players, and so on.

Premise: "You require variety in your training, which means altering training specifics (i.e., strength, power, mass, endurance) and speed (i.e., slow, moderate, fast/explosive). This can only be accomplished through periodization methods."

Although HIT can incorporate perpetual variety (exercise selection, order of exercises, repetition ranges, intensity variables), it is adaptation to a stimulus (exercise stress) that produces results. However, since the objective of strength training is to constantly increase demands (as in the Overload Principle), adaptation remains in flux even when implementing the same exercises, repetition speed, and repetition range over a long term. Variety merely helps a person maintain motivation and thus ward off boredom. Variety through diverse training modalities is utterly groundless, contradicting basic mechanical physics.

Strength can be defined as "the force generated by a muscle or muscle group." Power is equal to force times distance divided by time. Although strength can exist without demonstrating power (i.e., isometrics), power cannot exist without demonstrating strength. Likewise, speed of muscular contraction is dependent on force; the greater the force, the faster the movement. To illustrate, simply attempt to run faster without generating more force. Speed beyond maximum capacity can only increase by acquiring stronger, greater force-producing muscles via strength training (although skill of the movement can likewise increase speed to a modest degree). It is amusing to note that periodizationalists agree that slow movement contributes to greater muscle tension and is, therefore, more applicable to strength training. Then, erroneously, they indicate that fast, explosive movement correlates to increasing power and speed as if these entities are divorced from the concept of strength. Not even Olympic lifters are judged on the explosiveness or speed of their muscles. Rather, they are judged by how much weight they can lift, how strong they are, and how much force they can generate.

To increase muscle mass, you must consistently train with heavier weights. This will subsequently make you stronger. Obviously, a larger cross-sectional area of a muscle (via hypertrophy) results in greater force production or strength.

Endurance is, likewise, associated with strength. For example, if you can perform 6 repetitions with 70 pounds, your 1-RM might be 100 pounds (depending on fiber type and exhaustibility of the working muscles). By increasing your endurance to the point where you can perform 6 repetitions with 80 pounds, your strength (1-RM) will, in like manner, increase. Consequently, as your 1-RM increases so will your endurance capacity for a given number of repetitions.

These examples illustrate basic mechanical physics—laws of nature that must be obeyed even if periodizationalists wish to ignore them.

Premise: "Periodization implements active rest, which allows for continued exposure to stress while recuperating. This is known as loading and unloading by alternating light and heavy weight loads from one workout to the next. The result is no loss of neurological conditioning and constant stimulus for regular progress."

This is where confusion lies, in the premise that lighter weight loads (even if carried to the point of muscular fatigue) are low intensity as opposed to the high intensity, heavier weight loads. Regardless of semantics, effort is effort. Exercise in any capacity, whether implementing light or heavy weight loads, physically results in localized and generalized stress to the body. To adapt and grow stronger, the body must follow a sequence of steps: energy replenishment, compensation, then overcompensation. If the first and second steps are intervened via continuous assaults of localized stress (even of varying weight loads), the general effect on the entire system negates the possibility of overcompensation, thus halting further progress. The result is stagnation or, most likely, overtraining. Active rest is an oxymoron. Recovery and activity cannot coexist since each has a particular identity and subsist as separate entities.

Neurological conditioning is not lost over the course of weeks, let alone months. This is particularly true of anaerobic capacity, which has a much longer deconditioning and detraining period than aerobic capacity. Such is evident with high intensity trainees who only perform specific exercise movements every 2–3 weeks yet continue to prosper. Moreover, it is not uncommon for a trainee to exclude an exercise for several months only to resume where he or she left off. The skills of the squat, for example, are not lost from a brief period of neglect (i.e., while performing leg presses) and cannot be analogous to the technical discipline and cultivation of brain surgery. Exercise movements are natural movements in consonance with human biomechanical tendencies, neither demanding years of training experience to acquire nor days to relinquish neurological adaptation. A world-class Olympic lifter once stated that after 15 years of training, he was not content with his lifting technique. What a discouraging predicament; one might suppose that he was suffering from a progressive neuromuscular disease.

Premise: "Due to years of conditioning, advanced trainees can and should perform more sets than beginners."

Beginning trainees are characterized as having disuse atrophy of the fast-twitch fibers from lack of previous intense neuromuscular stimulation. Therefore, beginners are more apt to flourish under conditions of higher volume, at least initially, until they eventually adapt to anaerobic conditions. In effect, before the onslaught of strength training, most individuals possess greater endurance properties as suggested by the SAID principle and as reflected through their previous standard of low intensity activity. Confusion then arises when progress stagnates or regresses. Trainees are often unable to conceptualize why their program is no longer effective since, up to that point, it produced results. They then rationalize—rather than logically adhere to the principles of anaerobic exercise science—that more exercise must be the solution. As a result, trainees often convince themselves to walk farther off the beaten path of reason.

Stress physiology adamantly states that as an organism (bodybuilder) becomes larger and stronger, the *demands* of stress—not the *duration* of stress—must, too, increase, thereby altering homeostasis and anaerobic adaptation (i.e., greater strength and muscle mass). Antithetically, recovery ability remains virtually unchanged, being dependent on the reactionary time constraints of endocrine and soft-tissue remodeling limitations. Analogously, consuming more protein or vitamins than the body can assimilate and utilize is not beneficial but results in auxiliary systemic strain. Unlike values, ethics, and money, the idiom "more is better" cannot be practiced within the discipline of meaningful exercise.

THE ROLE OF STRENGTH TESTING RESEARCH

The influence of studies has become the establishing factor in determining modern strength training protocol. HVT proponents quote research supporting multiple sets per exercise while ignoring any evidence that suggests that one set is just as effective, if not more so. Conversely, HIT proponents opt to embrace any shred of evidence that supports their objective. However, there are a number of obstacles that must be accounted for to separate useful test results from those presenting flawed, observational conclusions.

1. *Suitable test subjects.* The benefit of selecting rank beginners is that all subjects are on equal ground with no previous training experience. However, as implied previously, beginners are subjected to disuse atrophy and can progress initially on a slightly higher volume of training than is necessary. Multiple sets provide additional neurological adaptation time to acquire the technical lifting skills of the prescribed exercises, implying that multiple sets may be superior. As a result, it is preferred that all testing subjects have at least six months of training experience followed by a four-week layoff prior to the study to eliminate any possible degree of overtraining.

The selection of subjects must be a fairly large random sample—perhaps 50 or more rather than the typical 20—to account for the wide spectrum of genetic differences. It would then be imperative to test subjects for their tolerance to stress (fiber type), placing each subject in an appropriate category of fast-twitch, mixed-fiber, or slow-twitch. In this respect, each individual's potential, within his or her group, is more uniform regardless of high or low volume testing procedures. It also negates the skewing of data that can arise when comparing the results of genetically superior subjects. The University of Florida has established a gold standard of comparable testing of twins and triplets, which increases the concluding data's accuracy. Their studies, incidentally, confirm that one set is just as efficacious, if not more so, as multiple sets and that one weekly session, if not less, is just as efficacious as multiple weekly sessions.

2. *Training approach.* It is standard that high intensity models are afforded one set per exercise yet most HVT subjects usually perform three sets per body part. Initial questions arise: Why three sets? Is there something magical about this number? Does it simply coincide with the influential religious connotations of the Father, Son, and Holy Spirit? Of pyramid power? The notion that good things happen in threes? Similarly, the number 7 has mystical significance in our society, but 7 sets per exercise, even for HVT, appears to be too extensive. Rarely do you read of studies incorporating two or four sets of an exercise. It would then be necessary for researchers, who attest that multiple sets are superior, to determine how and why three sets alter physiological attributes better than any other quantity. What phenomenon occurs on that third set? Studies conducted to determine the superiority of single or multiple sets should, therefore, create further subdivisions of one, two, three, and four sets per exercise to determine their effects. Comparing one set to three sets leaves a hole, questioning the possible value of two or four sets. Moreover, since multiple sets (three) are so effective, why not four sets? If "more is better"—that is, three is better than one—why not four, five, or six sets? What physiological factor establishes the cutoff point for multiple-set effectiveness?

3. *Number and type of exercises.* To eliminate inferior results of subsequent exercises due to exhaustion, the number of exercises should be limited. The type of exercise is a crucial factor. Although the subject may have a large percentage of fast-twitch fibers in the biceps, he or she may have a large percentage of slow-twitch fibers in the upper back—which would significantly alter the strength results in an exercise such as the lat pulldown. Such a proposition clearly indicates that few isolation exercises—perhaps only one—should form the basis of testing protocol to eliminate any misinformation, namely outside influences of neighboring muscle groups due to fiber type. Currently, this can only be accomplished with the muscles of the knee joint and those of the lumbar spine, thoracic spine, and cervical spine. This leads to the fourth point.

4. *Method of measuring strength increases.* To date, only the testing machines manufactured by MedX®, Incorporated, account for the following essential properties:

- Tolerance to stress. As indicated, each person's tolerance to stress is reflective of fiber type and therefore subjects must be addressed on an individual basis. If one subject has a high percentage of fast-twitch fibers or recovers slowly and is put into a group that trains twice weekly, he or she will overtrain and lower the results of the entire group. Therefore, the results are misleading. MedX® equipment provides data on pre- and post-exercise testing to determine fatigability rate of a tested muscle. Likewise, an exact amount of exercise (volume and frequency) can be prescribed to avoid overtraining. Nearly all studies on strength ignore the crucial repercussions of individual recovery ability.

- Total isolation of the muscle. If the muscle is not completely isolated via a single-joint movement—with the remainder of possibly influential body parts restrained—it is impossible to determine the degree of work performed by the tested muscle. For example, during leg presses the working muscles include the gluteals, hamstrings, and quadriceps (and, to a lesser extent, the lower back, abdominals, and calves). There is no way to accurately conclude the exact magnitude of work performed by any one muscle and its acquisition of strength by the study's end. Test results are further compromised in light of each working muscle's tolerance to stress. Although the foregoing may appear logical, many strength studies utilize multi-joint exercises and, therefore, the results are worthless.

- Nonmuscular torque. The measure of stored energy (stretched and compressed tissue) and the effects of gravity on the working limbs (body parts must be counterbalanced if there is a vertical component of movement) must be eliminated and considered in the final results. If not, the data will be misleading.

- Isometric testing. Dynamic testing implies internal muscular friction, thereby underestimating the results (concentric) or overestimating the

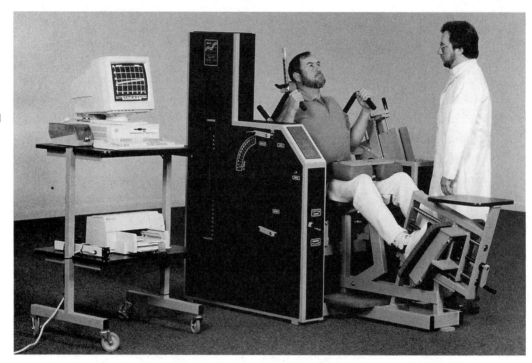

To date, only the testing machines manufactured by MedX®, Inc., account for tolerance to stress, total isolation of the muscle, nonmuscular torque, isometric testing, and exact positioning. (photo courtesy of MedX®, Inc.)

results (eccentric). Only isometric testing eliminates muscular friction, thereby providing meaningful data. Moreover, dynamic testing also produces impact forces with varying degrees of force throughout the strength curve as a muscle decreases or increases efficiency. Consequently, computer readings often suggest greater than actual strength levels since it is impossible to determine how much force was produced by muscular contraction and the extent of impact measurement. Isometric tests must be conducted approximately every 12 degrees of the muscle's range of motion since force output varies with muscle length and positioning. If testing is not isometric, the data are misleading.

- Exact positioning. Within each of the isometric tests, the exact positioning must be determined throughout the joint's permissible range of motion. Even a slight alteration in joint position changes torque output due to lever length and muscular efficiency. If exact positioning cannot be determined, one subject may be considered—erroneously or not—to be stronger than another subject at the same perceivable position.

5. *Body composition testing.* It is essential to determine the ratio of fat-to-lean-muscle content of each test subject before and at the conclusion of the study. Since muscle hypertrophy has a strong correlation to strength levels, this factor should be deemed a significant element in the final results. The only valid methods of measuring lean- and fat-tissue composition of which I am aware include hydrostatic (underwater) weighing, DEXA (dual energy x-ray absorptiometry) and the bioelectrical impedance system manufactured by Bio/Analogics.

The meager results encountered by most studies lasting up to 12 weeks is validation that many researchers know relatively little about anaerobic exercise science, i.e., the regulation of intensity, volume, and frequency. The typical strength gain among subjects ranges from 12 to 25 percent, even among beginning trainees! When the University of Florida on more than one occasion produced strength increases in excess of 400 percent over a 12-week period while utilizing an HIT protocol with beginners, those studies were ignored as being too unbelievable. The West Point study, as well, demonstrated incredible results but with experienced trainees on an HIT protocol. Although the Cooper Institute independently measured and recorded the data for the West Point study, people refused to believe the extraordinary anaerobic and aerobic achievements.

Some biased authorities purposely misinterpret data or conduct fraudulent studies in the attempt to prove their own convictions. Besides utilizing improper testing equipment, the self-interests of some researchers have guided their subjectiveness to the point of gross irrationality. One study had a periodization group perform hang cleans along with many other multi-joint exercises, whereas a high intensity group did not perform the hang clean and used a higher percentage of single-joint exercises. The method of testing strength consisted of the hang clean! Obviously, due to strength and skill acquisition of said specific movement, the periodization group performed best.

In another study, a researcher wanted to prove that HIT leads to overtraining. The subjects performed 10 sets of their 1-RM of an exercise movement at least twice per week. This regimen would never be suggested as a valid HIT model, nor would it ever be implemented by any HIT proponent. Not even powerlifters—who occasionally perform single-rep sets—would attempt such an extreme. Without investing the time and money, any logical-thinking individual could deduce that the preposterously copious bouts of intense effort would, in fact, result in overtraining.

In summary, few studies on strength training have much validity because they implement tools that were not designed for their intended purpose. You cannot measure speed with a toaster, and neither can you measure strength without the proper tool. Read and implement strength training studies with caution and reservation.

8

Improving Muscular Strength

Shaun Brown, M.S.
Strength and Conditioning Coach
Boston Celtics
Boston, Massachusetts

The primary purpose of a strength training program for athletes is to decrease injury potential; its secondary purpose is to increase performance potential. Make no mistake about it—strength training is primarily a mechanism to prevent injury. Increasing the strength of the muscles, bones, and connective tissue will reduce the likelihood that athletes will incur an injury while playing. And improving their functional strength is an important step toward realizing their potential as athletes.

Scientific research has yet to prove that any one method of strength training consistently produces greater results than another. In truth, the only thing that studies have shown is that many different programs can produce favorable results. Normally, anecdotal reports are not accepted as convincing information. In this case, however, a tremendous amount of anecdotal evidence also indicates that many diverse protocols can yield favorable results. The bottom line is that a number of different programs can be effective. The task is to find the program that works best in the given situation.

Unless athletes are also competitive weightlifters or bodybuilders, there's no need for them to exercise that way. A safe, efficient, productive, comprehensive, and practical strength workout can be performed with virtually any type of equipment by incorporating the concepts laid out in this chapter.

The primary purpose of a strength training program for athletes is to decrease injury potential; its secondary purpose is to increase performance potential.
(photo by Steve Lipofsky)

INTENSITY

There is a level of intensity (or effort) below which little or no gains in strength can occur. This threshold is suggested in the literature by the Overload Principle. Basically, this principle states that in order to increase the strength of a muscle, it must be stressed—or overloaded—with a workload that is beyond its present capacity. The extent to which this occurs then becomes a function of your inherited characteristics such as the length of your muscle bellies, your predominant muscle-fiber type, your neurological efficiency, and so on.

The harder you train, the better your response will be. As such, you should train with a very high level of intensity. In the weight room, a high level of intensity is characterized by performing each exercise to the point of concentric muscular fatigue or failure—when you have exhausted your muscles to the extent that you literally cannot raise the weight for any additional repetitions. Failure to reach a desirable level of intensity—or muscular fatigue—will result in little or no improvement in strength.

After reaching concentric muscular fatigue, you can increase the intensity even further by performing 3–5 additional post-fatigue repetitions. These post-fatigue repetitions may be either negatives or regressions and will allow you to overload your muscles in a safe, efficient manner.

Negatives (also called *forced repetitions*) are accomplished by having a training partner raise the weight while the lifter resists the movement during the lowering (or eccentric) phase; regressions (also called *breakdowns* or *burnouts*) are done by having the lifter (or the training partner) quickly reduce the starting weight by about 25–30 percent. The lifter then does 3–5 post-fatigue repetitions with the lighter resistance.

PROGRESSION

Suppose that today you do a set of leg curls for 10 repetitions with 100 pounds and a month from now you are still doing 10 repetitions with 100 pounds. It's not likely that you have gotten any stronger. On the other hand, what if you were able to do 11 repetitions with 120 pounds a month later? In this case, you would be able to perform 10 percent more repetitions with 20 percent more weight.

The fact of the matter is that for you to increase your muscular strength, your muscles must be stressed with a workload that is increased steadily and systematically throughout the course of your strength training program. Therefore, every time you work out you should attempt to increase either the weight you use or the repetitions you perform in relation to your previous workout.

If you reach concentric muscular fatigue within your prescribed repetition range, you should repeat the weight for your next workout and attempt to improve upon the number of repetitions. If you attain the maximum number of prescribed repetitions, you should increase the resistance for your next workout. Your muscles will respond better if the increases in resistance are 5 percent or less. Remember, however, that the resistance must always be challenging.

You should not be concerned with what you can lift relative to someone else. However, you should be concerned with what you can lift relative to your previous performance.

SETS

There is an overwhelming amount of evidence—both scientific and anecdotal—showing that one set of an exercise performed with a high level of intensity can produce essentially the same results as two or three sets. It is clear that one set of an exercise performed to the point of muscular fatigue is all that is required for increasing strength. A brief, follow-up "set" of post-fatigue repetitions can be done immediately after reaching exhaustion to further fatigue the muscles. Multiple sets are relatively inefficient in terms of time and, therefore, are undesirable. Also keep in mind that performing too many sets will increase the risk of an overuse injury. The most efficient program is one that produces the maximum possible results in the least amount of time.

REPETITIONS

In general, concentric muscular fatigue should be reached within about 15–20 repetitions for exercises involving the hips/gluteals, 10–15 repetitions for the legs, and 8–12 repetitions for the upper torso.

If concentric muscular fatigue occurs before the lower level of the repetition range is reached, the weight is too heavy and should be reduced for the next workout. If the upper level of the repetition range is exceeded before muscular exhaustion is experienced, the weight is too light and should be increased for the next workout by 5 percent or less.

It should be noted that attempting a one-repetition maximum or performing low-repetition movements—that is, fewer than about 3–4 repetitions—significantly increases the risk of injury. Likewise, if an activity exceeds the recommended number of repetitions, it becomes a test of aerobic endurance rather than muscular strength.

TECHNIQUE

A quality program begins with a quality repetition. A quality repetition consists of raising the weight to the midrange position, pausing briefly, and then returning the weight to the starting/stretched position. The weight should be raised and lowered in a deliberate, controlled manner. By emphasizing a controlled speed of movement, each repetition becomes more efficient and each set becomes more productive. A repetition should be at least 4–6 seconds in length.

A quality repetition is done throughout the greatest possible range of motion that safety allows—from a position of full stretch to a position of full muscular contraction and back to a position of full stretch. Exercising throughout a full range of motion allows you to maintain (or perhaps increase) your flexibility, which can reduce your potential for injury in certain situations. Furthermore, it ensures that you are exercising your entire muscle, not just a portion of it.

DURATION

More isn't necessarily better when it comes to strength training. If you are training with a high level of intensity, you literally can not exercise for a long period of time.

Generally speaking, you should be able to complete a productive workout in less than one hour. Under normal circumstances, if you are spending much more than an hour in the weight room, then you are probably not training with a desirable level of intensity.

By emphasizing a controlled speed of movement, each repetition becomes more efficient and each set becomes more productive. (photo by Steve Lipofsky)

VOLUME

A comprehensive strength training program can consist of as few as 14 exercises during each workout. The focal point for most of these exercises should be the major muscle groups—that is, your hips/gluteals, legs, and upper torso. Include one exercise each for your hips/gluteals, hamstrings, quadriceps, calves/dorsi flexors, biceps, triceps, abdominals, and lower back. Since the shoulder joint allows movement at many different angles, you should select two exercises for your chest, upper back (or lats), and shoulders.

If you participate in a combative sport—such as wrestling, judo, boxing, or football—you should perform 2–4 neck exercises to strengthen your cervical area as a safeguard against injury. Similarly, if you are involved in a sport or activity that requires grip strength—such as baseball, softball, golf, tennis, or wrestling—you should do one forearm exercise to strengthen your wrists, hands, and fingers.

SEQUENCE

Whenever possible, exercise your hips/gluteals first followed by your upper legs (hamstrings and quadriceps), lower legs (calves or dorsi flexors), upper torso (chest, upper back, and shoulders), upper arms (biceps and triceps), abdominals, and, finally, your lower back.

If you are performing neck exercises, include them in the beginning of your routine while you are still fresh mentally and physically. If you wait until the end of your workout to do your neck exercises, you won't be as enthusiastic or as aggressive. You should perform your forearm exercises after training your upper arms.

It is important not to exercise your upper or lower arms before exercising your upper torso. Multi-joint movements done for your upper body require the use of your arms to assist the movement. If you fatigue your arms first, the workload placed upon the muscles of your upper torso will be limited. Likewise, avoid training your legs—especially your hamstrings and quadriceps—before performing an exercise for your hips/gluteals, such as the leg press.

FREQUENCY

Believe it or not, your muscles do not get stronger during your workout—your muscles get stronger during recovery from your workout. When you lift weights, your muscle tissue is broken down and the recovery process allows them the opportunity to rebuild. There are individual variations in recovery ability. However, a period of about 48–72 hours is usually necessary for muscle tissue to recover sufficiently from a strength workout. A period of at least 48 hours is also required to replenish depleted carbohydrate stores.

Some research has indicated that a muscle will begin to lose strength if it isn't exercised within about 96 hours of its previous workout. That's why it's important for an athlete to continue strength training even while in-season or while competing. However, the frequency of workouts will need to be reduced to twice a week—or even once a week—due to the increased activity level of practices and games.

RECORDS

The importance of accurate record keeping cannot be overemphasized. Records are a log of what you accomplish during each and every exercise of each and every strength session. In a sense, a workout card is a history of your activities in the weight room.

A workout card can be an extremely valuable tool for monitoring your progress and making your workouts more meaningful. It can also be used to identify exercises where you have reached a plateau. In the unfortunate event of an injury, you can gauge the effectiveness of the rehabilitative process if you have a record of your pre-injury strength levels.

REFERENCES

Brown, S. 1994. Strength training principles. *Coaching Women's Basketball* 8 (special issue): 12–14.

Brzycki, M., and S. Brown. 1993. *Conditioning for basketball.* Indianapolis, IN: Masters Press.

To my lovely wife, Wendy, who has endured countless lonely days and nights while I pursued my dreams.

9

The Dose-Response Relationship of Exercise

M. Doug McGuff, M.D.
President
Ultimate Exercise, Inc.
Seneca, South Carolina

In the spring of 1997, I came across some old notes from medical school detailing the development stages used by researchers and pharmaceutical companies when working on a new drug. In these notes I had written that a drug was a stimulus that acted on the body (or a body system) that produced a sought-after physiological response. The notes then detailed how one would determine optimum dose concentration, amount, and frequency. The notes concluded with the final stage of research, which determines the maximum dose that will produce additional response and the point at which toxicity begins. I marveled at how this had never been done in the field of strength training; how, instead, it seemed to be a grab bag of personal experience, testimonials, and, at times, outright fraud. Shortly after this, I read a quote from Vert Mooney, M.D., in Mike Mentzer's column (*All Natural Muscular Development*, March 1997). Dr. Mooney made the eloquent statement that "Modern medical care should have the same precision and reproducibility in exercise programs that is expected in a dosage of prescribed medicine." Exercise is a powerful therapeutic modality that should go through the same rigorous process of determining an optimum dose amount and frequency that is used by researchers when they invent a new drug. Such a process should be able to produce a prescription for exercise that would be appropriate for the majority of the population. The same process can also be used to adjust dosage and frequency for subjects that have unusually weak or strong tolerances to the exercise stimulus.

Let us explore how we could apply this process to exercise. First we must recognize that the human body is an organism, and this organism is able to make adaptive responses to various stimuli. Once identified, such responses should be reproducible across the vast majority of the population of that given organism. A drug is a stimulus that will act upon an organism; then, under the correct circumstances, the organism produces a response. Likewise, exercise is a stimulus that acts upon the organism. It is the organism that produces the response under the correct circumstances.

When one is researching a drug (or exercise), the basic equation is as detailed below:

$$Stimulus \rightarrow Organism \rightarrow Response$$

With regard to the stimulus, the basic issues to be identified are the concentration of the drug and the dosage of the drug. Analogous issues in exercise would be the intensity of the exercise and the amount of exercise performed per session. With regard to response, our researchers would wait to record the desired response and note at what point in time this response occurs. The amount of time it takes the response to occur is what dictates an optimum dosing schedule. When designing a therapeutic drug, the key is to optimize the concentration so that minimum dosing is required to produce maximum response. Likewise in strength training, the goal is to optimize intensity so that minimum exercise duration and frequency are required to produce a maximum response.

While this may seem complicated, it is actually quite a simple process as long as you control all the known variables and systematically manipulate the unknown variables. I will go through these variables individually and show you how to control and manipulate them. To expedite this process, we need to rely on the work of other respected peers in this field to establish good starting points so that we won't have to do everything by complete trial and error.

Since the desired response is produced by the organism and that response takes time, this is the first variable we should identify. If we are not allowing adequate time for this response while we are testing other variables, we will never get a response, and we will be left wondering what is wrong. My data collected on subjects at my training facility showed a slight response after 48–72 hours of recovery, adequate at about 4 days and very good for most at 7 days. In my opinion, somewhere between 5 and 7 days of recovery is a good starting point. (In retrospect, I can now say that working out more frequently than once a week will constitute overtraining for about 95 percent of the population.) There are several other variables that must be held constant.

The first of these variables is intensity (analogous to dose concentration). Since our capability with regard to intensity changes on a moment-by-moment basis, the only accurate recording of intensity that we can measure is 0 percent or 100 percent; anything else would be guesswork. (To give credit where it is due, Arthur Jones was the first exercise theorist to recognize this fact.) Therefore, we must standardize 100 percent intensity, that is, we will train to momentary muscular failure or fatigue.

The next variable that we must hold constant is the dosage. In drug research, one generally starts with the lowest dosage expected to produce some response. This is done to guard against toxicity, which could interfere with the organism's response. In my empiric experience training clients, I feel that the average subject has much less tolerance for exercise than previously thought. (The writings of Mike Mentzer predate my experience and shaped my thinking on the subject. I feel that he should be credited with pioneering ultrabrief workouts that optimize exercise dosage relative to recovery ability.) If exercise tolerance for the human population was charted, it would likely form a bell curve distribution. I feel that until recently, we have been operating way too far to the right on the graph (that is, recommending way too much exercise for the average trainee). This natural mistake has occurred because of a statistical concept known as selection bias. People tend to become interested in strength training when they show at least some above-average potential for it and part of this potential is above-average exercise tolerance. Also, people naturally tend to mistake the stimulus (the actual exercise) as the entity that causes growth. As a result, even great minds such as Arthur Jones have decreased volume relative to this grossly inflated baseline rather than what is actually required. In general, I recommend for our experiment no more than 3–5 compound exercises. A good 3-set routine would be leg press, lat pulldown, and chest press. For 5 sets, a compound row and overhead press could be added. Do not vary the workout or your record keeping will be meaningless. Do not fret over the lack of variety. Variety is not necessary for progress. These movements track muscle and joint function, which does not change over time. If the intensity of your work is adequate, this will stimulate all the muscular structures of your body.

The next issues we must tackle are interrelated. We must standardize the way we administer the dose, and we must have an accurate means of recording the response of the organism. The units of a drug dose might be milligrams; the unit of our dose is the repetition. We must standardize our unit so that we maximize the efficiency (intensity) of our dose. Just as we want to eliminate any impurities from our drug, we should eliminate any impurities from our exercise. Such impurities include anything that will allow the muscle to escape from being under continuous load. This would include heaving, jabbing, or throwing the weight. Indeed, we want to eliminate even the smallest amount of momentum so we can know that every second of every repetition represents muscular loading. For measurement purposes, our unit must be exactly reproducible. In drug research, a milligram is a milligram—all the time, every time. In our research a repetition should be a repetition—all the time, every time. At Ultimate Exercise (my one-on-one training facility), we use SuperSlow® repetitions that are done by raising the weight in 10 seconds and lowering the weight in 10 seconds. (Note: We use a 10-second negative rather than a 5-second negative because our equipment has been retrofitted for the SuperSlow® protocol. This allows us to ensure the purity of the exercise and the precision of our basic unit of record keeping.)

Finally, we need to know what to monitor to accurately quantify the response produced by the organism. Ultimately, most people's desired response is bigger muscles and this is what they would like to measure. Unfortunately, this is a fairly gross change and the units of measure (fractions of inches) are too large to allow us to make the fine adjustments of optimizing volume and frequency. Also, empiric evidence shows that muscle growth can be delayed and sporadic. What we need is a reliable marker for muscle growth. Fortunately, such a marker has been found. We know that a muscle's strength is directly related to its cross-sectional area. In a given individual, if a muscle becomes stronger it will also become larger; or if a muscle is noted to have become larger, we will find that it is stronger. It has also been empirically noted that the strength gain always seems to precede the size gain. A subject may gain strength for many consecutive workouts without any change in measurement; but then, in delayed fashion, the size gain will suddenly occur. While size gains may be sporadic and unpredictable, they are always preceded by a gain in strength. Such gains in strength reliably can be found in our workout record, provided that the routine is standardized and not varied and provided that our units of performance recording are strictly standardized.

Now that we have identified the salient variables, here is a six-step prescription that I feel is a good starting point for almost any subject.

1. Rest completely from exercise for 14 days (or longer).
2. Select a generic routine of 3–5 compound exercises (that is, multi-joint movements).
3. Perform each exercise in a high-intensity fashion, going to complete muscular fatigue and attempting continued movement for 10 seconds after fatigue. Allow little or no rest between exercises.
4. Use the SuperSlow® protocol. This will keep the muscle under continuous load and will standardize your repetitions so that your record keeping is precise.
5. Begin by allowing seven days of rest between each workout. Keep accurate records. If the recovery period is adequate, you should note improvement on every set of every workout.
6. If you are not seeing strength gains on every set of every workout, systematically insert an extra rest day until you do. Do not get intimidated if the rest period gets pushed out to 10 days or more. This is where most trainees break down in the experiment. But trust me on this. You have probably tried some ridiculous things in the past; why not muster the courage to try the one thing that may bring the results you so passionately desire?

If you follow these six steps, you should be able to produce a rate of improvement that will literally shock you. I have one client who doubled his strength on all five movements in six weeks in a total elapsed training time of 92 minutes. This client lamented about all the time that he had wasted by training longer than 92 minutes four mornings a week for years with no visible results. Once you have established this training pattern, don't expect to hold it forever. Continued progress is a dynamic process that must pay heed to another pharmacological concept: the narrow therapeutic window.

The term *narrow therapeutic window* is used in the study of pharmacodynamics (how a drug works in the body). The body is an efficient homeostatic organism, which is very resistant to change and very protective of the status quo. To encourage a desired physiological change, a fairly severe stimulus is required; this is true whether the stimulus is a drug or an exercise. The problem with most drugs is that there is a narrow window between the amount of stimulation that produces the desired response and the amount of stimulation that produces a toxic effect. Generally, the more effective a drug is at producing a stimulus, the more narrow the space between a therapeutic and toxic dosage. As you become stronger, you will become capable of delivering a more severe stimulus and a more severe stimulus will be required to encourage further strength adaptations. Therefore, as you become stronger the gap between the minimum therapeutic dose and toxic dose of exercise becomes narrower and narrower; overtraining is a constant threat. Another critical observation is that the therapeutic effect always plateaus so that pushing the dose higher only produces toxicity and never produces additional therapeutic effect. There is no benefit to risking toxicity. Once you cross the threshold from a therapeutic level of stimulus into the toxic range, the organism does not produce any more of the desired response, and usually the desired response is prevented by the toxic effect. For instance, the pain-relieving effects of ibuprofen max out at about 400 milligrams. As dosages go higher, there is no more pain relief, but you may burn a hole in your stomach lining. With acetaminophen (Tylenol®), you can take the required dose every 4–6 hours. However, if you take it more frequently you will end up on the liver transplant waiting list. The same relationship exists with your training, but in that case your increased strength causes the dose concentration to become higher at each encounter thus increasing the risk of toxicity. The only choice is to decrease the dose amount and frequency to compensate for this fact. The reason most trainees fail to show continued improvement is that they don't make such adjustments. Most avoid the adjustments because they fear decompensation during an increased rest period.

One of the biggest obstacles that I have to overcome in more advanced subjects is the fear that their strength gains will decompensate in a relatively short time. Somewhere Arthur Jones heard that decompensation occurs in 96 hours. He then wrote it, everyone else repeated it, and it became unquestioned gospel that even Arthur himself could not undo years later. I spent seven solid hours in the medical library at the University of Texas Health Science Center at San Antonio performing an extensive literature search trying to find a study supporting this contention. I could not find a single source that even addressed this issue much less proved it. Simple logic and personal experience have brought me to the conclusion that this rule of decompensation after 96 hours is simply not correct.

Please refer to the following diagram for the next discussion. Consider time as a continuum flowing from left to right:

Stimulus ➡ Organism ➡ 7 days ➡ Response ➡ ?? days ➡
Decompensation

As you refer to this diagram, consider what an expensive metabolic process your desired response is going to be. Remember, you are focused on building muscle but your body is making global metabolic adaptations. It is upregulating its metabolic efficiency by synthesizing more enzymes to make all of metabolism more capable. Such improvements include aerobic metabolism, anaerobic metabolism, gluconeogenesis, glycogen breakdown and transport, changes on the hemoglobin molecule, alterations in angiotensin converting enzyme, neovascularization, blood-buffering agents, and new muscle growth. All of this new synthesis is extremely metabolically expensive. This is why your body will not invest in these changes unless a severe stimulus is applied and the organism is left undisturbed afterward to make these changes. By the time you have made the response, your body has made a huge investment. Your body does not make big investments in anything it plans to hold on to for only a short time.

Refer to the previous diagram again. By the time you have made your response, you have made a huge metabolic investment. The day after the response occurs is simply the earliest time at which the organism is capable of dealing with another stimulus—not the *best* time, just the *earliest* time. The best time might be several days later but no one knows because no one has yet to explore this time frame. With regard to decompensation, we must acknowledge that nobody honestly knows when this begins. My own theory is that it does not begin for a very long time. I know of cases where my clients have dropped out of training for six weeks and returned with equal or greater strength. As you refer to the previous diagram, I want you to think about this question: Why would a highly evolved organism spend seven days making a huge metabolic investment only to allow that investment to deteriorate over an equal (or lesser) period of time? What metabolic or economic sense would this make? This would be like spending a year building a house that you would expect to crumble to the ground within a year of its completion. If the human organism were this metabolically inefficient, we never would have survived as a species.

Once you understand the concept that an adaptive response takes time and that early decompensation makes no metabolic sense, you will see that periodization of training makes no sense whatsoever. For instance, realize that the term *active rest* is an oxymoron. What your body needs between intense workouts is not a submaximal workout or active rest; what it needs is rest. Period. The concept of periodization does not address any real physiological needs; instead, it is designed to address a person's psychological needs. Training activity is a very positive experience that diverts our attention from our daily problems and, as such, can become a psychologically addictive activity. As a result, many subjects become very uncomfortable when I try to get them to train infrequently. They almost invariably slip in extra exercise. But proper training should be a logical process of stimulating a desired physiological change.

An example from my medical practice will highlight my point. If I have a patient with a medical problem that is purely physical in nature, I will prescribe the simplest, most direct treatment available. If you have strep throat, I will give you a single penicillin injection. If you have high blood pressure, a once-daily pill is in order. If, on the other hand, you are suffering from something that has a large psychosomatic component to it, then I will make the treatment plan complex. I will prescribe one pill to be taken every eight hours on an empty stomach and another to be taken every six hours with food. I will give you specific dietary and sleep guidelines. All this activity and focus acts to divert your attention from the psychological problems that are contributing to your symptoms and miraculously, you get better. Realize that periodization is designed to satisfy a neurotic addiction to exercise rather than the requirements of productive exercise. It is a method of trying to deal within the constraints of overtraining rather than to eliminate overtraining to begin with. What you desire to produce are physical results, thus you should maximize the physical aspects of training and get your psychological needs fulfilled elsewhere.

Even when I get my clients to understand all that I have been discussing, I am frequently confronted with the following question: "If what you say is true, why have these other training methods produced so many bodybuilding/strength champions?" Again, the answer is selection bias. People with above-average potential for bodybuilding and strength sports are easy to recognize; they are usually amazingly muscular before they even touch a weight. These people are naturally drawn to strength sports, and when they are exposed to any form of training they grow muscle quickly. These people select themselves out as bodybuilders/strength athletes and pursue this activity because it is easy for them to do well at it. Naturally, they assume that their results are due to their superior effort or training technique when the truth is that they would have grown if you had thrown tomatoes at them. The test of a training technique's efficacy is not how it performs on a genetic freak but how well it performs on those of average or below-average potential. High intensity training (HIT) wins hands down every time. In short, it is a natural mistake to seek advice from those with superior physiques, even though their physiques may have been produced in spite of, rather than because of, their training techniques. Remember, 99 percent of people die in bed; but that doesn't mean we should assume beds are killing people.

Having explained with clarity and logic the reasons for the superiority of the HIT approach, I know that the vast majority of those who read this chapter will not apply my advice. Why? I am not sure, but I have a theory that may encourage a few more people to give it a try. Throughout my career in emergency medicine, I have been amazed at the human capacity for self-delusion; we are the only animal in nature that can lie to ourselves. We do it so well that the majority of people are totally unaware of what motivates their actions. Most people do not act to achieve consciously named goals; rather, they act to placate subconscious psychological value conflicts. If this sounds cynical, so be it—I am convinced it is true—even in myself. Such self-delusion might explain why HIT often is rejected by those with great genetic potential as well as those with average-to-below-average potential.

Most genetically gifted individuals, even if they understand the logic of HIT, will reject it for reasons they can't name. Why? If you are gifted in any endeavor, you will tend to make it a vocation or at least devote a large part of your time to it. As such, this will make up a large part of your identity. In most such endeavors, large time requirements are necessary to actualize one's potential. Paradoxically, in bodybuilding/strength training it actually is a requirement for a small amount of time to be spent training to produce results. For those who feel that they have the potential to justify devoting their lives to bodybuilding or strength sports, learning that best results will be produced with little time commitment can be psychologically devastating. Such people are now left with a huge void to fill. Rather than using this time for more meaningful and challenging endeavors, most of these people choose to ignore the facts. Instead, they will look to their own superior physiques and use their perceived results to justify hours spent in the gym, fortunes spent on supplements, and entire weekends spent preparing and freezing meals for the next week.

As for those who are less genetically gifted, most behave with equal irrationality. Even if they understand the salient concepts, most will reject them without giving them a trial. Why? They recognize that if this does improve their

The training environment at Ultimate Exercise, Inc. (photo courtesy of M. Doug McGuff, M.D.)

results and rate of progress, it may also end up pointing out the limits of their potential. Many prefer the hype of empty promises to facts because it allows them to hold on to their fantasies. Many commercial interests in the bodybuilding field deeply understand this phenomenon and are getting rich from it. There are multitudes of horse-and-buggy bodybuilders who are rejecting the automobile and airplane because they know it won't carry them to the moon.

If you are like most bodybuilding enthusiasts, you are probably dissatisfied with your current rate of progress. If so, what is this doctor's prescription for you? First, realize that you are probably nowhere near your muscular potential; but also realize that if you had truly great potential, you would already be massive beyond belief no matter how you trained. If you are reading this chapter, it is most likely that you will never have a physique like those pictured in the muscle magazines. Once you have done the considerable soul-searching to put your goals in proper perspective, then you are ready for action. First, take a break from training for at least 14 days. Next, resume training using only 3–5 exercises and train every seventh day. If results are not quickly obvious, insert an extra rest day until you begin to see results. (At Ultimate Exercise, we find every seventh day to be average.) Finally, have the courage to refrain from training until you are recovered; the only thing you will regret is the time you wasted by training more frequently.

This chapter is dedicated to my coauthors, Jessica, Liza, Dan, and Kristi, who have helped me stay motivated and focused and to be that much better.

10

Blueprint for Motivation: Theory and Applications for Exercise Training

Richard A. Winett, Ph.D., Jessica A. Whiteley, B.S., Liza Rovniak, B.S., Daniel I. Galper, M.S., and Kristi D. Graves, M.A.
Center for Research in Health Behavior
Department of Psychology
Virginia Polytechnic Institute and State University
Blacksburg, Virginia

Athletes, coaches, and strength and fitness enthusiasts at all levels of proficiency and achievement are constantly searching for concepts and strategies to increase motivation. Even with the most favorable genetics and the optimal training program, motivational factors are critical for maximizing and sustaining performance attainments. For the less-than-gifted athlete (that is, the vast majority of athletes and exercisers), motivation may mean the difference between achieving very little and achieving highly satisfying and credible outcomes. Such outcomes for some particularly committed individuals eventually may even rival outcomes attained by more genetically gifted athletes. For a person seeking some minimal strength and fitness benefits from training, motivation will often determine if, in fact, any health benefits are achieved. While everyone agrees on the importance of motivation, until recently there has been disagreement about exactly what it is, not to mention how to harness it to improve both short- and long-term strength, muscle mass, and fitness outcomes.

WHAT IS MOTIVATION?

For psychologists and the general public, the understanding, study, and application of motivation has been hampered in two major ways. First, motivation is often conceptualized as an overriding dispositional trait and a single entity. In other words, you are a highly motivated individual or you are not. This conception is unfortunate. It assumes that motivation is relatively fixed and therefore any attempt to alter one's motivation is largely futile. This is obviously the most extreme version of this conception, but it is not unusual. Hiring people based on motivation for jobs or sports teams is an indication of how motivation can be viewed as a fixed entity.

Contemporary psychology (and frankly common sense) does not support the existence of such broad dispositions that effectively operate across different behaviors and situations. Motivation, as will be discussed in this chapter, is much more specific to individuals and their circumstances. For example, I may display a great deal of persistent behavior in my pursuit of athletic goals and show little of the same behavior in my pursuit of everyday career and job goals. My interests, efforts, and skills are simply directed to one but not the other set of activities.

Second, motivation is also often thought to have only one major determinant. This leads to the idea that if one factor can be focused on and unleashed then new and perhaps spectacular performance levels will follow. The quest for this kind of magic bullet permeates much of athletic training as well as other endeavors. Athletes, coaches, and exercisers search for that one magic supplement to dramatically alter their metabolism, that one optimal routine to sculpt their physique, and the one powerful psychological strategy that will be the ultimate key to motivation. However, motivation for athletic and exercise training is determined by the interaction of multiple factors.

Motivation can be defined as *the interaction of cognitive, affective, behavioral, and social processes contributing to purposeful, often goal-directed behavior.* Rather than being determined by a single entity, motivation involves an interlocking web of processes. To increase motivation for a given person and set of circumstances, we need a guiding theoretical framework to delineate and assess the key processes involved in heightening motivation and channeling purposeful behavior. A careful assessment of these processes generally points toward the optimal path for intervention given a specific set of circumstances.

The major goals of this chapter involve the delineation of a theoretical framework for conceptualizing motivation, the description of key components and variables, and specific assessment information needed to pinpoint problems in motivation. The chapter provides both the conceptualization and methodology for assessing specific determinants of motivation and, where indicated, modifying key determinants.

Some processes involved in motivation may be more central and important than others, but all motivational processes operate in a dynamic context where their effects are dependent upon their relationship with other factors. This means that processes involved in motivation, as with other goals, are interdependent. It also means that particular outcomes depend on reciprocal influence. This concept is at the heart of understanding motivation and will be discussed and illustrated in detail later. But, it is an important and easy-to-understand concept that illustrates the inadequacy of fixed- or single-entity approaches. For example, as our beliefs (self-efficacy beliefs) increase concerning our ability to do certain kinds of workouts for strength and muscle gain, it is likely we will train harder (behavioral performance) and see tangible results (outcomes). Achieving tangible outcomes through appropriately planned workouts will feed back and fuel our performance and our self-efficacy beliefs, which in turn will enhance how we approach future training sessions and outcomes.

As this simple but important example shows, beliefs, behaviors, and outcomes reciprocally influence each other. We are always concerned with feedback's influence on a number of related variables, as is the case with any process leading to a goal.

SOCIAL COGNITIVE THEORY

A theoretical framework capturing the critical multiple determinants of behavior is social cognitive theory (SCT), an integrative approach developed by Dr. Albert Bandura of Stanford University in the late 1960s. As with any useful theory, SCT has evolved considerably over the years. Today it is the dominant paradigm in psychology (Bandura 1997). Most contemporary behavior-change programs are based on SCT. It has proven remarkably adaptable to a wide variety of behaviors and human concerns.

The term *social cognitive* suggests the primary focus of the theory. SCT is concerned with the interplay of social and environmental influences with cognitive factors such as beliefs and various self-regulatory skills (discussed later) and their mutual effects on behavior. When we point toward social cognitive determinants of behavior, we are referring to social and cognitive factors that fit within the SCT framework and have been shown to have important impacts on behavior.

We would like to reiterate that because motivation has multiple determinants, we need to assess multiple determinants and decide where it is best to intervene to enhance motivation. Some motivational problems may be attributable to faulty knowledge about training, some to diminished efficacy beliefs or to inappropriate goals, and still others to incorrect implementation strategies. Indeed, critical determinants and problems for each person can change over time. Once again there is no magic-bullet approach to motivation. Rather, the key is understanding and assessing the multiple social cognitive determinants and then designing an intervention consistent with the assessment. Thus, while the concepts and principles of SCT apply to everyone, assessments are used to develop interventions that are more idiographic and targeted to specific problems.

Figure 10.1 illustrates the key SCT determinants and processes involved in optimizing performance and subsequent outcomes. Our specific examples will always refer to exercise training, but the set of variables and processes are germane to all kinds of behaviors and performance attainments. Thus, the variables and processes are applicable to enhancing the performance of the beginning trainer as well as

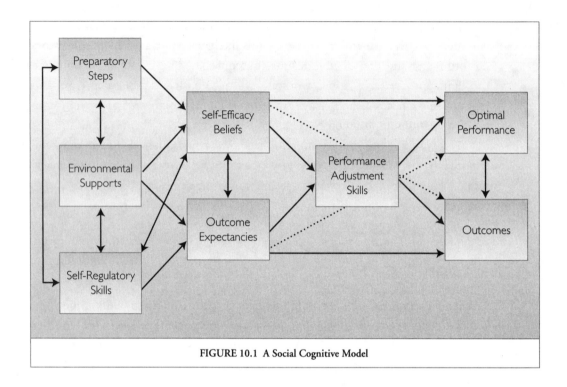

FIGURE 10.1 A Social Cognitive Model

the experienced and even gifted trainer. But more generally, the variables and processes can be used to understand and modify anything from an individual's private behavior to a group's very public behavior. As the examples are developed for training, you are encouraged to think of the same determinants and processes as they apply to other behaviors.

Human agency is the critical philosophical idea underlying SCT. People are perceived as acting intentionally to produce specific outcomes and personal self-efficacy beliefs about specific courses of action are the most critical determinants of whether or not specific courses of action are indeed undertaken. While we can discuss determinants of behavior from the SCT perspective, people are not robotlike creatures stirred into action by environmental events. People perceive their environments differently. They act in unique ways to modify those environments. Here again is an example of reciprocal influence so central to the basic understanding of behavior.

The first point to notice in Figure 10.1 is that determinants and processes are generally linked by bidirectional arrows. These arrows represent reciprocal influence, the feedback process described previously. Another important point, as we will see, for enhancing performance is attending to and maximizing reciprocal influence. As we have suggested above, a good example of reciprocal influence is increasing self-efficacy to create discernible performance increases, which, in turn, will increase self-efficacy and hence, further enhance performance. Envision this process as a spiraling effect.

For each subsection of the chapter, there is a figure that delineates key terms and then provides questions or points that can be used to evaluate the multiple determinants and processes of motivation.

PREPARATORY STEPS

Let us begin the review of the key SCT determinants and processes with preparatory steps. (See Figure 10.2). These are steps that should be in place prior to undertaking a specific endeavor, and they facilitate specific processes and behaviors. This is not a formal SCT label but one that we have devised. The preparatory steps may seem to apply mostly to beginners but it will be apparent that these steps apply to anyone not completely satisfied with performance and outcomes. Where performance or outcomes are not satisfactory, we recommend as a starting point the assessment of preparatory steps.

The first preparatory step is knowledge acquisition about proper training. This includes selecting training activities that fit personal goals, understanding principles of training (e.g., stress and recovery, specificity of training), knowing how to perform different training functions (e.g., an effective repetition), and implementing this knowledge in the form of routines. As simple and basic as this step is, it is one that is often missed. Many people, at varying levels of experience, are quite clueless. Without knowledge, the probability of training correctly, much less altering a training problem, is not very high. Often the wrong approach will be taken to solve a problem. For example, many people still mistakenly believe that the way to become more defined (i.e., lose body fat) is to use lighter weights for higher repetitions and do countless hours of lower-intensity aerobic training. Such an approach will likely lead to some minimal fat loss but with a substantial loss of strength and muscle mass. Or, take the case of sticking points in training, an almost inevitable phenomenon. With sparse or incorrect information, many people in the face of sticking points will increase the volume and/or frequency of their training. Knowledge of training principles indicates that the exact opposite tactic is often what it takes since many sticking points are attributable to overtraining.

While knowledge can come through words, there are better ways both to convey information and to develop and modify behaviors. Modeling involves live or video demonstrations of specific behaviors, such as the proper way to perform the squat exercise, the speed of movement, and the appropriate degree of intensity. Modeling is an important way to convey information and standards of performance and to change behavior. However, guided-mastery experiences are even better for conveying information and changing behavior. As the term suggests, guided-mastery experiences involve first the demonstration of a behavior, followed by hands-on guidance with feedback and additional practice. It is best done as a step-by-step process.

Preparatory Steps
Preparatory steps refer to a number of cognitive and behavioral prerequisites for effective training and exercise

Knowledge
- Principles of training such as the relationship of frequency, duration, and intensity of training
- Basic principles of overload and specificity of training
- Understanding and recognizing signs of overtraining
- Principles of progress and how to rectify overtraining
- Basic principles of metabolism

Applying Knowledge
- Understanding how to do specific exercise movements
- Using modeling and guided-mastery experiences to learn proper technique

Goal Setting
- Choosing goals that are challenging, hard but reachable, and specific
- Choosing goals that are realistic based on present condition and expectations for improvement
- Arranging a series of proximal goals leading to distal goals

Matching
- Choosing training programs that match goals
- Choosing training goals that match lifestyle and personal preferences

Implementation
- Understanding how principles, goals, performance, and personal preferences are exemplified in training routines

Social Support
- Enlisting the help and feedback of other valued people for exercise training

Questions
- Define frequency, duration, and intensity of training.
- List four signs of overtraining.
- What training factor has been most associated with improvement in strength and cardiovascular fitness?
- Describe how you perform a repetition in your resistance training program, i.e., speed of movement.

Questions
- Do you understand the proper technique? If not, do you have someone to show you?

Questions
- What is your plan for progressing in your resistance training program?
- You have not shown any progress in your training in the last three weeks. Name two strategies you will use to alter your present routine.
- Define as specifically as possible your short- and long-term training and exercise goals.

Questions
- Does your training plan match your goals?
- Do your goals fit with your lifestyle and personal preferences?

Questions
- Briefly describe your plan to reach your short- and long-term goals.
- How does your present routine match your goals?
- Describe why your current training and exercise program best fits your lifestyle. Explain why you enjoy doing activities.

Questions
- Who do you talk to about your training and exercise?
- How important and how encouraging are these people to you?

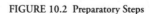

FIGURE 10.2 Preparatory Steps

166

Think of how you learned to drive and you will understand how well-guided mastery works. You weren't just shown (modeling) how to drive and hopefully did not learn to drive through trial and error. Rather, a patient parent or instructor showed you each small step, let you try, provided corrective feedback, and then let you try again. You didn't move beyond the simple steps (e.g., driving in an empty parking lot) until you showed mastery. Then you were ready for the next, somewhat harder step (e.g., driving in your neighborhood), again preceded by modeling and practice with feedback.

Many people do not attain satisfactory results from their training and become unmotivated to continue in their efforts simply because they have not learned or experienced effective training. For example, the most common mistake that trainers see is that most people throw a resistance rather than move it with muscle power (and without momentum). Consequently, they derive little benefit from their weight training while greatly increasing the chance of injury. Corrective guided-mastery experiences can help.

By way of further illustration, the lead author of this chapter has recounted how one of his friends, an exercise scientist, gave him a hands-on experience with slower controlled repetitions. It was a profound learning experience because even after decades of training, he had really never seen, much less performed, very slow, controlled repetitions. In fact, he had become frustrated and somewhat unmotivated in his training because of an inability to lift heavier and heavier weights. He had also experienced a series of minor injuries and chronic joint pain. After that guided-mastery experience, he was able to apply this new training methodology while training alone. He recorded strength and muscle gains with no injuries and no joint inflammation. Merely talking about slower controlled repetitions, or even just viewing a demonstration of such training, would not have been as effective in producing permanent behavior change and excellent performance and outcomes as was the guided-mastery experience.

Other preparatory steps are also important. Goal setting and goal attainment are critical processes that will be discussed at length later. In the preparatory steps we are focusing on defining a person's goals. A person primarily interested in appearance, for example, may not care about fluctuations in training performance but may be greatly concerned by some barely noticeable accumulation of body fat. Likewise, a person focused on performance may not care about seemingly unrelated body-composition change, and a person most concerned with health may become disturbed with a weight gain resulting from an addition of some muscle. The point is that without clear goals, it is not possible to set the stage for proper performance and outcome appraisals.

Under preparatory steps, we have also included matching. The basic notion of matching is that goals, and the approach undertaken to pursue specific goals, should match a person's personal preference and lifestyle. For example, there are quite a number of ways (different modalities, settings, and routines) to improve cardiovascular fitness. Some people may prefer to improve their fitness while communing with nature while others may prefer very brief, very intense indoor training with the accompaniment of blaring music. In the end, as long as an approach can offer some progression, improvement will be evident. But of course there can be no improvement if a person does not stick to a routine because they find it aversive and inconvenient.

A final preparatory step involves enlisting social supports. In the most general sense, this means organizing support from others to help optimize training. It can include such diverse factors as rearranging family meals to fit training schedules, to working with a training partner, to simply hearing words of encouragement from people we value. Social support acknowledges we are social beings living in a social world and not merely individuals strictly going it alone.

Many training programs succeed or fail because of attention or inattention to preparatory steps. However, as suggested by this discussion, at any point in a training career preparatory steps can be assessed and altered. For example, after decades of training, this chapter's lead author was able to achieve new personal records by grasping and applying the principle of the downward regulation of volume and frequency of training. He virtually eliminated his chronic joint inflammation, a constant companion of many exercise enthusiasts, through the use of lower-volume routines featuring a much slower repetition cadence. These examples illustrate the acquisition of new knowledge and the implementation of this knowledge to alter performance and achieve specific outcomes.

ENVIRONMENTAL SUPPORTS

Environmental supports are also important for optimizing training. When an environment is not well matched to individuals' styles and preferences, does not fit their goals, or is simply not conducive to maximizing their personal outcomes, effective training becomes difficult. (See Figure 10.3.)

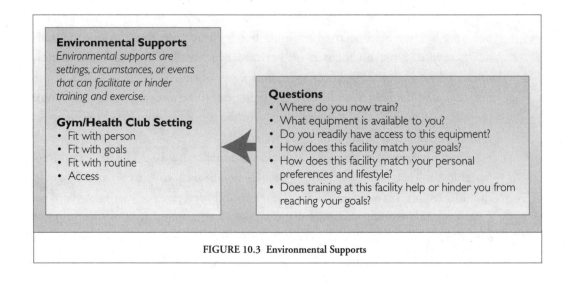

Environmental Supports
Environmental supports are settings, circumstances, or events that can facilitate or hinder training and exercise.

Gym/Health Club Setting
• Fit with person
• Fit with goals
• Fit with routine
• Access

Questions
• Where do you now train?
• What equipment is available to you?
• Do you readily have access to this equipment?
• How does this facility match your goals?
• How does this facility match your personal preferences and lifestyle?
• Does training at this facility help or hinder you from reaching your goals?

FIGURE 10.3 Environmental Supports

However obvious this point may appear, it deserves attention. For example, a person interested in high intensity training (HIT), as described in this book and other publications, often requires a special kind of environment, although not necessarily a fancy or expensive one. A gym crowded with all the latest equipment but with people who basically talk and hang out on the equipment will not be conducive to optimal training. A more basic gym with a group of serious trainers may provide a better degree of training.

Certain training that is very precise is difficult to do in many commercial gyms. For example, effective SuperSlow® training may require not only access to particular kinds of equipment but also a relatively quiet setting.

However, while such no-nonsense gyms may be ideal for some, others may find this kind of environment austere and not conducive to their goals. For some people, training provides an important social interaction and reinforcement component that no-nonsense settings may lack. Additionally, as more older people exercise and train, a typical commercial gym may be bewildering and intimidating. Thus, we are suggesting that an important motivational consideration to assess is the match, or nonmatch, of personal preferences, goals, and environments.

SELF-REGULATORY SKILLS

This section will focus on goal setting as a primary self-regulatory skill but we also want to describe the other important self-regulatory skills listed in Figure 10.4.

Self-regulatory skills allow purposeful goal-directed behavior to be planned, monitored, self-corrected, reinforced, and maintained even in the absence of substantial environmental supports. Thus, the ability to envision and plan specific courses of action is important as is the ability to monitor key behaviors contributing to performance and preferred outcomes. An overlooked skill in athletic performance is the ability to use problem-solving strategies (e.g., generating alternative solutions, within an appropriate knowledge base, delineating the cost and benefits of each, prioritizing solutions, and trying out a solution) when difficulties invariably crop up. Other important self-regulatory skills involve appraising performance and outcomes based on the correspondence of performance and outcomes to personal standards and goals and applying self-incentives when certain performances and outcomes are attained. Obviously, these skills, which are ones that people can learn, go far beyond merely putting numbers into a training diary. Indeed, without self-regulatory skills, people would respond passively to their environments; they would not display human agency. Therefore, any assessment of motivation should include a look at a complete array of self-regulatory skills.

Interestingly, some people may apply a number of self-regulatory skills in one domain (e.g., work) but do not apply those skills to their exercise training. In this case, enhancing motivation may involve not so much teaching of basic self-regulatory skills but rather practice in transposing them to a new domain.

Self-Regulatory Skills

Self-regulatory skills are individual behaviors that allow purposeful goal-directed behavior to be planned, self-corrected, reinforced, and maintained even in the absence of substantial environmental supports.

Monitoring Target Behaviors
- Systematic record keeping is important.

Questions
- How do you keep track of your exercise behaviors?
- What do these records tell you about your performance?

Goal Setting
- Distal goals are your long-term goals.
- Proximal goals are short-term goals.
- Maintain important goal qualities: salient, specific, hard, challenging, reachable, in a series or in steps.
- Feedback is necessary for goal setting to be effective.
- See beyond limited goals.

Questions
- What are your long-term goals?
- How important is achieving these goals for you?
- What are your short-term goals?
- How do you know if you are achieving your short-term goals?
- Do your goals meet the qualities of those on the left?
- If not, what could you do to change them?
- What will you do when you achieve your short-term goals?

Questions
- If you are not meeting you goals, see Problem Solving below.
- If you are meeting your goals, what are your new goals?

Appraising Performance and Outcomes
- It is important to assess your performance and outcomes.

Questions
- What do you do when it is apparent you are not reaching a training goal?
- What has worked in the past?
- What are the alternatives?
- List the costs and benefits of the alternatives.
- What is your plan?

Problem Solving
- It may be necessary to problem solve when you are not meeting your goals.

Self-Incentives
- Providing rewards for yourself can help maintain motivation.

Questions
- Do you reward yourself?
- If so, how do you reward yourself when you perform well or reach a goal?
- If not, think about what you find rewarding and implement these rewards.

Personal Standards
- Keep in mind the expectations you have for yourself are related to your performance.

Questions
- How would you describe your personal standards for a successful/effective exercise session?
- Do you use your personal standards to evaluate your exercise sessions?
- Are your personal standards realistic?

FIGURE 10.4 Self-Regulatory Skills

In the discussion of preparatory steps, we mentioned the importance of understanding and choosing specific goals. Goal setting is a critical self-regulatory skill. But improving performance through goal setting is more involved (and far more effective) than simply picking some amorphous ("get stronger") or ultimate goal ("bench press 300 pounds"). A series of goals leading toward a well-defined concrete goal is required. The more immediate goals are called *proximal goals* and the longer-term goals are called *distal goals*.

Proximal goals should be carefully planned to comprise a logical series. For physical performance hard, challenging, but reachable goals are most effective. Goals should be clearly stated in behavioral terms that are attainable. For example, "having a great workout" is a vague goal, but "increasing certain exercises by certain amounts" is a concrete attainable goal (e.g., increasing performance in a weight training movement by one repetition per workout). Likewise, "reducing a diet by a prescribed number of calories and curtailing the consumption of particular high-fat foods" are concrete obtainable goals while "losing weight" is not as well defined. The process of assessing and clarifying goals is important not only for regulating performance but for properly choosing and appraising actual outcomes.

Besides the specific qualities we have noted, goals also should be directly tied to the kinds of performance and outcomes that are valued by a given individual. For example, not every individual is very focused on performance indicators such as resistance lifted or the exact time of a particular run. Rather, the personal value of the workout may revolve around the positive effect achieved from engagement in the specific activity. Being fully engaged in the workout may be an important personal standard. Achieving such positive feelings can be a powerful stimulus for continuing workouts. For such individuals, even the attainment of reasonable and even exceptional performance will not satisfy their goals if positive effect and engagement are not present. A string of such workouts could lead to termination of training even when there is tangible evidence of physical improvement. Thus, we urge coaches and trainers to consider a range of goals and personal standards as vital. This seems particularly important as exercise training becomes less the province of gifted athletes and dedicated fanatics. Creative coaches and trainers need to design programs that can produce favorable physical outcomes within a context suitable to the goals of given individuals.

Because the literature on goal setting indicates that rather tightly restricted goals, once attained or narrowly missed, can result in depression, anxiety, and listless behaviors (Bandura 1997), it also seems particularly critical to delineate a series or hierarchy of goals having some vision beyond a narrow set of conceived goals. Specific challenging and limited goals may generate a great deal of focused behavior in the short run but long-term behavioral engagement in training and exercise may require a somewhat wider view.

Many athletes and fitness enthusiasts understand the importance of goal setting, but what many do not realize is that setting goals without a system of performance tracking and feedback is not an effective way to improve behavior.

Likewise, feedback in the absence of defined goals is worthless. What is needed are a few simple ways to track performance in relation to proximal and distal goals. For an athlete oriented toward strength, for example, the tracking can mean keeping accurate records of sets, repetitions, resistance, and repetition cadence; time for sets; duration of the entire workout; and attendant factors that may have affected performance. With defined goals and a principled program, feedback provided by a training log can fuel attainment of future goals.

Feedback and goal setting are not sufficient in and of themselves, however. As we have discussed, other self-regulatory skills are required. Individuals need to know how to appraise performance and outcomes, and how to solve problems and make changes in training and other salient lifestyle factors to further optimize performance and concomitant outcomes. Record keeping aids this process, but a person needs a set of principles to understand training and what to do if and when some proximal goals are not reached or are reached at very high costs (e.g., physical exhaustion). Thus, performance appraisal must be done within the context of knowledge. A lack of progress should, for example, lead a person to review what he or she knows about overtraining. Knowledge about overtraining would then suggest several courses of action. Given the circumstances and training history, a person would weigh the relative merits of each course of action and then implement a plan that would try out one method (e.g., reduced frequency of training) to remedy the problem. Optimizing performance has to begin with knowledge that then becomes the basis and context for enacting self-regulatory skills such as problem solving.

Performance appraisal is also linked, as we have suggested, to monitoring performance and assessing performance in relationship to goals and personal standards. Meeting goals and personal standards can lead to self-incentives, including self-praise, feelings of accomplishment and joy, and more tangible reinforcers. The role of personal standards in motivation and the evaluation of performance, as we have also suggested, is often overlooked. For instance, a weight training goal may be reached within a workout, but a personal standard for a workout (e.g., extreme focused attention) may not have been met, which renders the workout disappointing. Articulating personal standards can help an individual both design more effective training strategies and better understand his or her personal responses to training.

SELF-EFFICACY AND OUTCOME EXPECTANCIES

Self-efficacy beliefs and outcome expectancies, described in Figures 10.5 and 10.6, are the beliefs that are most associated with changing and maintaining specific behaviors. Self-efficacy is the belief in one's ability to organize and execute different types of requisite performances (such as intensive training) under somewhat different circumstances (e.g., different routines, different degrees of stress in one's life, and different gym conditions) and to the degree necessary to produce certain attainments (e.g., complete a workout that will increase your strength and muscle). It is not a global trait such as self-esteem that has little value in explaining how to optimize performance and does not predict performance. Self-efficacy for training is more specific to training. It can entail a belief in one's ability to do a number of different movements in a few different routines over some time period with the appropriate degree of intensity and the correct form. Such training appears to be necessary to produce a gain in strength and muscle. Equally important in gaining strength and muscle is the belief in one's ability to perform specific training behaviors.

Several dimensions of self-efficacy are important. Self-efficacy refers to our belief in performing the behaviors to produce certain attainments but not directly to the outcomes such attainments may themselves produce. Thus, we can have strong self-efficacy beliefs in our ability to train in a way to produce a strength increase, but whether such a strength increase brings valued outcomes such as the admiration of peers is another matter. Notice also that self-efficacy is not so specific that it is limited, say, to one repetition on one day (although self-efficacy for producing a personal record on one lift can be this specific). There also is some sense of continuity across time. It is not merely doing the behavior (the instrumental act) once, but performing in certain ways over time that is important. This is a somewhat different sense of self-efficacy from earlier versions of SCT. It is a more inclusive and more useful definition; of all the factors discussed in the SCT framework, self-efficacy is the most predictive of behavior. Therefore, it is critical not only to assess self-efficacy for specific behaviors and performances, but also to understand how to increase self-efficacy.

Before providing a discussion about methods to enhance self-efficacy, it is important to note again that people's self-efficacy may differ from one training activity to another. Few experienced trainers, for example, would suggest low self-efficacy for properly performing high-intensity arm work sufficient to produce gains. Yet many may have lower self-efficacy ratings for producing gains in the lower body with squats and deadlifts. These lower-body exercises are much more taxing than arm exercises. Thus it becomes necessary to have separate self-efficacy assessments pertinent to the different exercises.

While self-efficacy can be modestly increased through persuasive information and modeling (demonstrations), it is best increased through performance feedback. It is behavior that best influences self-efficacy and enhanced self-efficacy that in turn enhances behavior. This is why well-planned principled training sessions, proper selection of proximal goals, some initial guided-mastery experiences, and performance appraisals are so critical. Successfully reaching valued specific goals fuels self-efficacy, and heightened self-efficacy fuels the quest for new behavioral levels (i.e., reciprocal influence).

In the reciprocal influence process between self-efficacy and behavior, how we interpret our accomplishments is also critical. For instance, goals may be achieved through such extraordinary efforts that self-efficacy may be decreased. In this case

Self-Efficacy Beliefs

Self-efficacy is the belief in one's ability to organize and execute different types of requisite performances (behaviors such as intensive training) under somewhat different circumstances (e.g., different routines, different degrees of stress in one's life, different gym conditions), and to the degree necessary to produce certain attainments (e.g., complete a workout capable of increasing strength and muscle).

Enhancing Self-Efficacy
- Modeling
- Guided mastery experiences
- Performance feedback

Reciprocity
- Increase self-efficacy
- Increase behavior
- Increase self-efficacy

Specificity
- Specific behaviors
- Specific circumstances

Continuity of Beliefs and Behaviors over Time and Conditions

Context
- Costs versus benefits of behavior and performance

Answer the questions below using the following scale:

1 2 3 4 5 6 7 8 9 10
Not at All   Most
Confident   Confident

Questions
- How confident are you that you can adhere to your current diet to reduce your body fat?
- How confident are you that you can consistently train your lower body with sufficient intensity in squats and deadlifts to increase the strength and muscle size in your thighs and lower back?
- How confident are you that you can train your upper body with sufficient intensity with such movements as presses, rows, and pulldowns to increase the strength and muscle size in your chest, shoulders, upper back, and arms?
- How confident are you that you can increase the resistance or repetitions on each movement in your routine every workout?
- How confident are you that you can consistently train with enough intensity in your cardiovascular workouts so that you can increase your performance and fitness?

➡ If you answered above a 7 on any of these questions, you are fairly confident in your abilities in this area.
➡ If you answered below a 5 for the above questions, you may want to look to see which items you had particularly low scores on. Then, try to figure out why you are less confident in these areas.
➡ Think about other areas of training that are important to you and assess your level of confidence in these areas.

FIGURE 10.5 Self-Efficacy Beliefs

it will be difficult to accomplish the same feats again, let alone surpass them. Goal attainment may be too easy, which can enhance self-efficacy but in a distorted way. The skillful athlete, exerciser, and coach set up a series of challenging but reachable goals and know how to leave some challenges for next time.

Indeed, self-efficacy is likely to decrease if an endurance or strength feat was accomplished through a "near-death" workout experience. After all, there seems to be only one way to surpass a near-death experience, and it is a sure way to terminate an athletic and exercise career. This chapter's lead author recalls how he has learned to just slightly exceed what he accomplished in the previous training session, rather than striving for heroic efforts that beg the question of what will be the encore. The seminal learning experience involved a 20-set whole-body HIT routine that always concluded with 20 repetitions in the stiff-leg deadlift. After collapsing for 25 minutes following one such workout, he realized that a better

Outcome Expectancies
Outcome expectancies refer to the self-evaluative, physical, and social outcomes a person expects to derive from performing the target behaviors in specific ways. Meaningful outcome expectancies are specific to each person.

Benefits to Costs for Achieving Specific Outcomes

Self-Evaluative Outcome Expectancies
- Expected self-appraisals of worth

Physical Outcome Expectancies
- Expected physical benefits

Social Outcome Expectancies
- Expected social benefits

Answer the questions below using the following scale:

1 2 3 4 5 6 7 8 9 10
Very   Very
Unlikely   Likely

Questions
- If I reach my exercise goals in a particular workout, I will feel a great sense of accomplishment. (Self-evaluative)
- If I can stick to my exercise program for three months, I will have more self-respect. (Self-evaluative)
- Consistently following my resistance-training workout plan for two months will result in noticeable increases in strength and muscle. (Physical)
- Consistently following my cardiovascular workout plan for two months will result in noticeable differences in my cardiovascular fitness. (Physical)
- If I become noticeably stronger and more muscular, my friends will be impressed. (Social)
- If I can lose noticeable body fat, I will be more attractive to others. (Social)

➡ Which of the above gave you your highest scores? You may find that self-evaluative, physical, and social outcome expectancies may or may not be of equal importance to you.

FIGURE 10.6 Outcome Expectancies

training strategy involved making consistent and systematic progressions and just slightly exceeding prior efforts. The encore problem was solved because self-efficacy to surpass the previous workout was high and such beliefs were invariably reinforced by the performance attainments of the next workout.

People who achieve success in any kind of endeavor not only typically do the kind of planning suggested by the prior scenario, but also have what Dr. Bandura has called a "resilient sense of self-efficacy." Such a sense does not come from badgering or persuasion from others (as some well-known coaches seem to believe) but rather from experiences in analyzing deficiencies in failed performances, modifying goals or behaviors in some clear way, trying again, and eventually reaching a goal. Such experiences are priceless. They explain how behaviors we value as particular signs of motivation and persistence are developed and maintained. Thus, failure at some points is inevitable. What is important is that a backlog of past experiences in overcoming failure can build a resilient sense of self-efficacy that is necessary to continue on a more productive path. Assessing self-efficacy for specific exercise behaviors is central to an overall assessment of motivation, as is an understanding of what an individual has done before in the face of failure in similar situations.

Outcome expectancies, as shown in Figure 10.6, include self-evaluative, physical, and social outcomes that we expect to derive from performing the target behaviors in particular ways. Outcome goals are generally not about the performance itself but what we expect to derive from the performance, such as self-satisfaction, recognition, awards, personal records, or apparent health benefits.

For each dimension of our outcome expectations, we can consider a kind of benefits-to-cost analysis. For example, do I feel an appreciable sense of accomplishment (self-evaluative) after reaching goals in a workout? Is this personal evaluation important to me? Likewise, how do I evaluate myself when I fail to reach designated goals? For physical outcome expectancies, are the strength and muscle gains worth the great physical effort that is consistently required to obtain them? Social outcome expectancies generally relate to the balance of positive-to-negative feedback from others that may be achieved if certain outcomes are produced. For instance, an individual may value being perceived as strong or very attractive among peers. Great strength may, in fact, be achieved, but the training producing great strength may be discontinued if that individual finds that few peers are interested in such extraordinary strength. Outcome expectancies are different for each of us. They have different personal value benefits to costs and ramifications.

While self-efficacy relates to beliefs in one's ability to do behaviors in certain ways, outcome expectancy has to do with the value and anticipated benefits of the outcome for a particular individual. Thus, a person may appear demotivated for training not because self-efficacy has diminished but rather because the goals and outcomes of training, or a type of training, are no longer valued. Moreover, expected outcomes, the actual benefits, may not materialize. For example, and as noted previously, a person may develop an outstanding physique but discover that no one particularly cares about that attribute. Thus, assessments and regular reviews of goals and expected outcomes are important for understanding motivation and channeling effort.

PERFORMANCE ADJUSTMENT SKILLS

Where self-regulatory skills refer more to cognitive processes involved in maintaining behavior, performance adjustment skills (Figure 10.7) refer to actually instituting proper behaviors to enhance performance. Thus, understanding how rapid speeds of movement produce injury and distort progress in resistance training is worthless if explosive repetitions are still used. Likewise, understanding that HIT requires recovery time and that lack of progress may indicate too little recovery time is also worthless unless it engenders a decrease in training frequency. Knowing the importance of hard, challenging goals is one thing. Operationalizing such steps in a training program and adjusting goals over time based on performance is another. Appreciating how a training environment helps or hinders performance is important, but modifying or changing to another training setting may be what is required to continue to progress and reach personal goals.

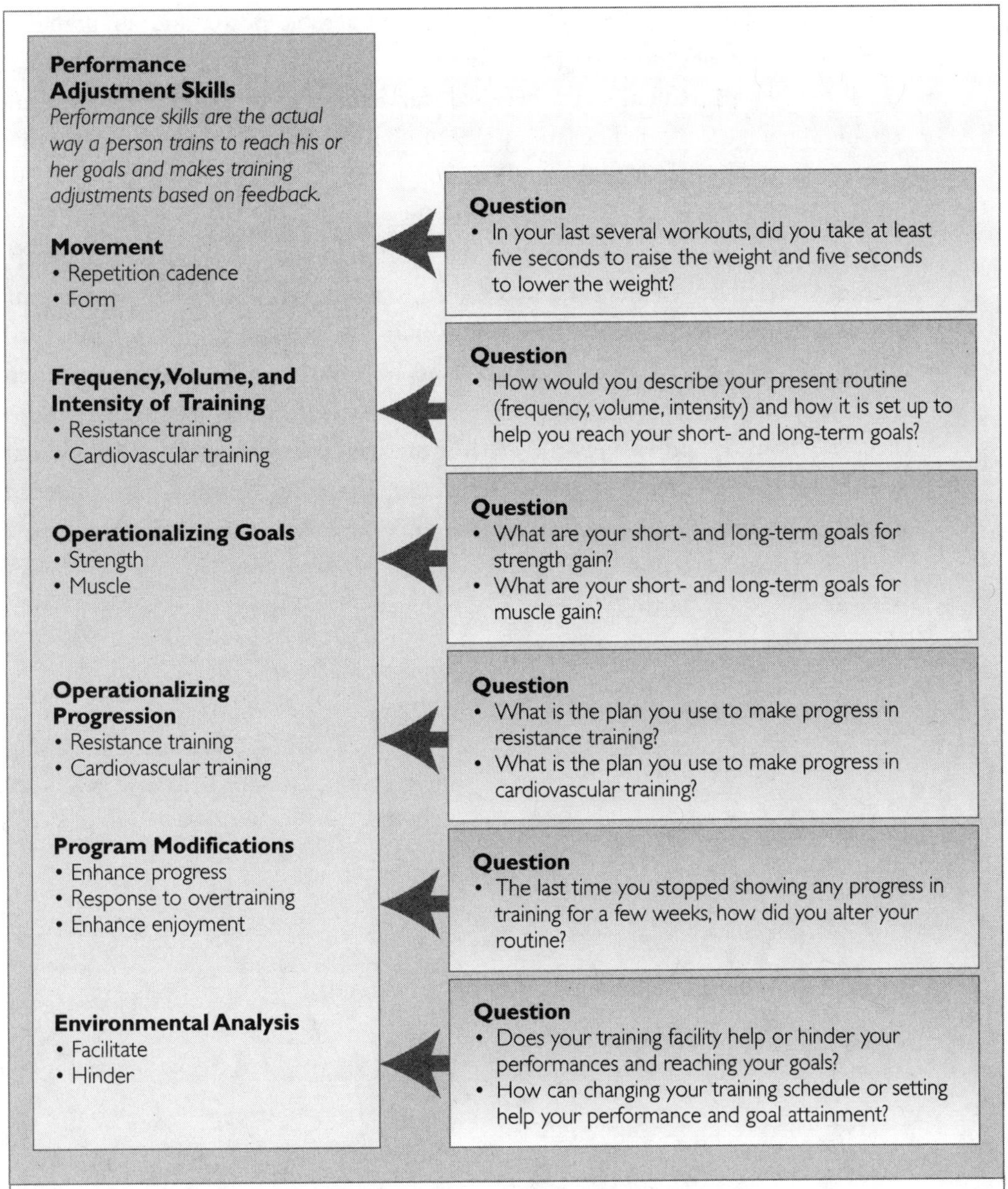

Performance Adjustment Skills

Performance skills are the actual way a person trains to reach his or her goals and makes training adjustments based on feedback.

Movement
- Repetition cadence
- Form

Question
- In your last several workouts, did you take at least five seconds to raise the weight and five seconds to lower the weight?

Frequency, Volume, and Intensity of Training
- Resistance training
- Cardiovascular training

Question
- How would you describe your present routine (frequency, volume, intensity) and how it is set up to help you reach your short- and long-term goals?

Operationalizing Goals
- Strength
- Muscle

Question
- What are your short- and long-term goals for strength gain?
- What are your short- and long-term goals for muscle gain?

Operationalizing Progression
- Resistance training
- Cardiovascular training

Question
- What is the plan you use to make progress in resistance training?
- What is the plan you use to make progress in cardiovascular training?

Program Modifications
- Enhance progress
- Response to overtraining
- Enhance enjoyment

Question
- The last time you stopped showing any progress in training for a few weeks, how did you alter your routine?

Environmental Analysis
- Facilitate
- Hinder

Question
- Does your training facility help or hinder your performances and reaching your goals?
- How can changing your training schedule or setting help your performance and goal attainment?

FIGURE 10.7 Performance Adjustment Skills

Both self-regulatory and performance adjustment skills are necessary for ensuring optimal performance. Assessing past actions to modify impasses seems to be important for understanding adaptability and the continued ability to perform at a high level.

OPTIMAL PERFORMANCE AND OUTCOMES

Optimal performance can be defined as demonstrating strength, power, and endurance in resistance-training workouts (primarily using repetitions and resistance in key movements as indicators) and aerobic power and endurance in cardiovascular workouts (using work per unit of time and duration as indicators), consistent with proximal goals, personal standards, and the training context and setting (see Figure 10.8). The latter point of consistency with goals, standards, and context is important because people define optimal performance in a number of personal ways. Thus, as discussed previously, a person may reach a specific training performance in a workout but the workout may be judged unsuccessful because certain key elements such as a keen focus and concentration were lacking.

In addition, and quite importantly, as noted before and shown in Figure 10.1, actually doing what is judged by all accounts to be an optimal performance is generally not the major goal (although it can be where in a real sense the means become the ends and vice versa). What is critical is producing actual valued outcomes—self-evaluative, physical, or social (see Figure 10.9). Thus, performance is usually a vehicle for producing valued outcomes. Achieving desired outcomes fuels the entire enterprise.

Optimal Performance
Optimal performance is the demonstration of strength, power, and endurance in resistance-training workouts and aerobic power and endurance in cardiovascular workouts consistent with proximal goals, personal standards, and the training context and setting.

Strength
- Repetitions and resistance used in key exercise movements +

Power
- Work accomplished in the workout per unit of time +
- Workout pace +

Endurance
- Duration of the training session

Aerobic Power
- Work per unit of time + +
- Heart rate and other markers

Focus and Engagement
- Concentration
- Effect

+ = used as indicant
+ + = distance/time, caloric expenditure/time

Questions
- Delineate specific levels of optimal performance in resistance training that are consistent with your personal standards and goals.
- How often are you able to obtain such levels of optimal performance?
- Delineate specific levels of optimal performance in cardiovascular training that are consistent with your personal standards and goals.
- How often are you able to obtain such levels of optimal performance?
- How must workouts be performed to meet your standards?
- What kind of focus, engagement, and effect are required for your optimal performance?

FIGURE 10.8 Optimal Performance

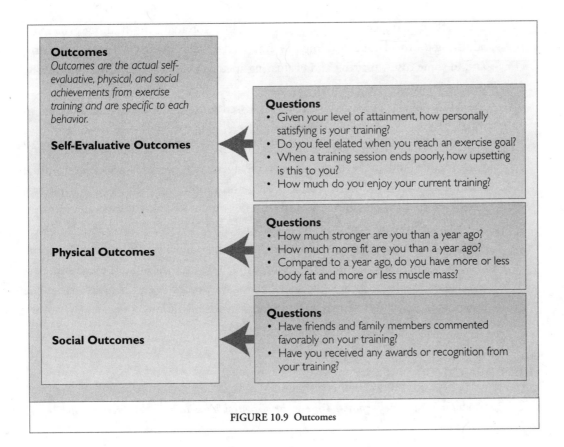

Outcomes

Outcomes are the actual self-evaluative, physical, and social achievements from exercise training and are specific to each behavior.

Self-Evaluative Outcomes

Questions
- Given your level of attainment, how personally satisfying is your training?
- Do you feel elated when you reach an exercise goal?
- When a training session ends poorly, how upsetting is this to you?
- How much do you enjoy your current training?

Physical Outcomes

Questions
- How much stronger are you than a year ago?
- How much more fit are you than a year ago?
- Compared to a year ago, do you have more or less body fat and more or less muscle mass?

Social Outcomes

Questions
- Have friends and family members commented favorably on your training?
- Have you received any awards or recognition from your training?

FIGURE 10.9 Outcomes

As noted, a dilemma for many hard-training athletes and exercise enthusiasts is that while self-efficacy is very high, outcomes are greatly valued, and performance is absolutely optimal, the expected outcomes do not accrue. For example, winning an athletic contest may only bring a small trophy and no recognition from others. Earlier assessments of achievable outcomes were probably faulty. The world doesn't necessarily deliver accolades for winning a race or game—at least not most of the time. Or, particular fitness goals are achieved such as running two consecutive seven-minute miles but a relatively high percentage of body fat is still evident. These examples suggest outcome expectancies and actual outcomes achieved need to be assessed, if only to note the rationality of the outcomes and probability of success. A lack of motivation to continue an endeavor can indicate that there is a discrepancy between outcome expectancies, performance attainments, and actual outcomes.

One example of failure to obtain actual outcomes is germane to middle-aged and older athletes. Training performance may be optimal and outcomes highly valued but hormonal and other physical changes diminish the hoped-for outcomes. An expected race time isn't reached. A high degree of strength and muscularity previously achievable now becomes elusive. Failure to achieve valued outcomes in the face of seemingly optimal performance should not lead to despair but to analysis of all processes related to outcomes. A resilient sense of self-efficacy does not mean simply trying again or trying harder with the same thing. Rather, a resilient sense of self-efficacy involves having a sufficient backlog of successful experiences with self-regulatory skills for analyzing training principles, adjusting protocols, reevaluating proximal and distal goals and personal standards, and in some cases, making and evaluating specific changes and further modifying distal goals and valued outcomes.

Thus, all the processes we have discussed within SCT are highly dynamic in much the same way that motivation often seems to ebb and flow. Effective coaches and individual exercisers recognize the dynamic nature of training and performance and make the necessary changes. SCT provides a rich conceptual framework for periodically both assessing and modifying the diverse but interrelated factors that contribute to motivation.

Successful long-term training and achievement in any endeavor requiring persistence and motivation depend upon these reciprocally influencing processes. Understanding how to assess the complex web of motivation and exercising personal agency to modify specific social cognitive processes can help us master the dynamic complexities of maintaining long-term motivation.

REFERENCE

Bandura, A. 1997. *Self-efficacy: The exercise of control.* New York: W. H. Freeman and Company.

To my parents, Garr and Pat Bradley, and to my coaches.

The Repetition

Michael Bradley, M.A.
Assistant Strength and Conditioning Coach
Stanford University
Palo Alto, California

Perhaps the most difficult thing for many fitness enthusiasts to understand and accept is that strength training is actually quite simple. Conflicting information—both commercial and interpersonal—often leaves people confused. The fact is, individuals will obtain at least some results from any type of exercise that involves progressive resistance and allows adequate recovery. However, the potential to train in different ways has forced strength and fitness enthusiasts to swim through a murky sea of confusing rhetoric that is based largely upon anecdotal evidence, past experiences, sometimes bogus research publications, Eastern European training "secrets," media hype, and/or the current strength training program at Big Time U.

Strength training can be a mysterious venture. There's no shortage of self-proclaimed experts who are willing to peddle their advice to the masses. Magical formulas, catchy buzzwords, opinionated organizations, and biased certification tests all contribute to make proper exercise appear as something to which only the chosen few have learned the secret. In truth, exercise is so fundamental that the average person probably knows more than he or she suspects. Too often, common sense is disregarded in favor of advice from the experts. Consequently, many people do not understand the immediate consequence of strength training. They spend valuable time dreaming up unnecessarily complicated schemes and routines that are designed to develop nonexistent muscular properties such as "basic strength," "speed strength," "endurance strength," and "explosive strength." Let's set the record straight once and for all. Despite all the hype, the chemical composition of muscle fibers cannot be changed by varying the sets, repetitions, and/or speed of exercise movement. It is important to understand that strength, power, and short-term muscular endurance are different expressions of the same thing, not separable training entities. A muscle is just a tension-creating machine. If you improve one muscular function, then you improve all three. A muscle simply adapts and grows stronger.

This chapter will demonstrate how training can be simple and practical yet effective. As with any art or science, however, there are many subtleties that are difficult to articulate and can only be learned by participating in and supervising workouts.

If you are looking for the answer to your strength training dilemmas, you need only look at the way you train. Do you work hard? Do you train consistently? If you are a competitive athlete, do you train during the season? Is your training closely supervised? Can you perform basic exercises? Can you do a repetition properly? Before evaluating programs, set-and-repetition schemes, the exercise of the month, or the latest Eastern Bloc training secrets, make sure you are doing the fundamentals properly. The most basic part of productive strength training is the properly performed repetition. Because of the high level of concentration it requires, the repetition is also the most difficult aspect of training to execute correctly.

While the exact stimulus for increasing the size and strength of a muscle is uncertain, it is obvious that a muscle must experience something. Most likely, the stimulus is related to the intensity of the muscle contraction, the time under tension, and the amount of fatigue or inroading into fresh muscular strength. A clear understanding of these points will serve to simplify evaluation of different exercises, equipment, and training schemes. The best methods produce the highest levels of effort, muscle contraction, and constant tension in the safest manner possible.

The speed of movement while lifting weights is one of the most controversial subjects in strength training. While there are proponents on each end of the slow-to-fast spectrum, careful observation of athletes training in weight rooms rarely mirrors the protocols that are espoused by their coaches when they speak at clinics and write their training manuals. The fast lifters are not really moving the weight all that fast—at least compared to the speeds seen on the athletic fields—and the slow lifters rarely lift at the prescribed speed (e.g., "up in two seconds, down in four seconds"). At Stanford University, our description of a properly performed repetition is based upon muscle function and simple physics. It is more defined than many and less defined than some. More importantly, we can coach the repetition and get several hundred athletes to apply it correctly, which is how repetitions are taught to athletes at Stanford University.

FIVE COACHING POINTS

The purpose of a properly performed repetition is to have the muscle produce tension, which, when repeated for a short period of time, will increase the intensity of muscular contraction and create a desirable level of muscular fatigue. To do this in the most efficient way possible, it is important to follow five coaching points for a properly performed repetition.

1. *Minimize momentum.* If you move the weight too quickly, it will increase in speed to the point of actually traveling on its own. The increase in momentum will reduce the load on the muscle, making the exercise easier throughout most of the range of motion (ROM)—and more dangerous at the end when the weight must come to a stop. Momentum means that the muscle experiences a lighter weight than what is actually on the bar. In all likelihood, there is an optimum speed at which a weight should be lifted, but no one knows what that speed is. So we teach our athletes to lift the weight at a speed that

If the weight can be moved fast, it is not heavy enough to stimulate gains in strength and power. (photo by Matt Brzycki)

forces the muscle to do as much of the work as possible. There should not be any point in the ROM where momentum has taken over and the weight feels light or nonexistent. There will be times when you won't need to move the weight with maximum effort. At the beginning of the set, you should not push as hard as possible. As the set continues, however, you should perform the repetitions with increasing effort until the end of the set when the effort is maximal and the speed of movement is very slow or nonexistent. As the exercise continues, the muscle gradually fatigues to the point where the force-generating capability is not much greater than the weight that it must overcome. Then you can push with as much effort as possible, but the weight will move slowly because of muscle fatigue and the concomitant decrease in strength. According to the Size Principle of Recruitment, it is the *intent* to raise the weight quickly that is the key to developing explosive power, not that the weight itself actually moves fast. In fact, if the weight can be moved fast, it is not heavy enough to stimulate maximum gains in strength and power. To lift a weight fast would be to throw it; and throwing weights will not do much to increase strength.

2. *Pause briefly in the position of full muscle contraction.* Once raised, the weight should be held momentarily in the position where the muscles are most fully contracted. This brief pause serves three purposes. First, it helps to minimize momentum. Second, because you can hold statically more weight than you can raise concentrically, it demonstrates that the weight was lifted—not thrown—into position. Third, it is believed that the maximum amount of muscle fibers can only be activated in the fully contracted position. If this position is not emphasized, momentum will cause the weight to swing into and out of the only position where the greatest part of the muscle can be stimulated.

3. *Emphasize the lowering phase of the repetition.* Lowering the weight involves the same muscles as raising the weight. Because a fresh muscle can lower approximately 40 percent more than it can raise, the nervous system will recruit fewer muscle fibers unless more weight is added during the lowering phase—which is not always practical—or more time is taken to lower the weight. Due to gravity, if a weight is dropped it will accelerate to the ground. We teach our athletes to prevent acceleration of the weight in the lowering phase. If the weight is accelerating, then the force of gravity is a greater factor than the force of the muscle. Just as throwing a weight is an inefficient and dangerous way to train, dropping weights will do nothing to develop muscular size and strength.

Using the leg extension as an example, the weight should be raised slowly and smoothly at a speed whereby the quadriceps are loaded throughout the full ROM. In the midrange position—where the legs are fully extended—the person should pause for a second. If the weight stack floats, recoils, bounces, or travels on its own prior to the momentary pause, then the weight was lifted too quickly. After pausing briefly in the midrange position, the individual should slowly release the tension from the muscle—that is, exert less muscular torque—until the weight begins to lower at a constant velocity. If the velocity begins to increase while the weight is being lowered, then the weight is being lowered too fast. When in doubt, raise and lower the weight slower, not faster.

4. *Be conscious of body position and leverage.* These two factors are important considerations for exercising the muscles in a safe and efficient manner. Leverage can be used to make an exercise much easier. For instance, arching the back during some free-weight exercises—such as the bench press, seated press, front raise, and bicep curl—improves leverage, thereby enabling a person to lift more weight. Because more weight is used doesn't mean that the lifter is stronger—it only appears that the lifter is stronger. Simply lifting more weight with little or no regard as to how it is lifted may be fine for the ego but it doesn't necessarily translate into stronger muscles. Remember, with enough leverage you can even move the earth.

On many machines the weight used can be very dependent upon leverage. On a leg press, for example, placing the seat a few inches closer to or farther from the foot pedals will decrease or increase leverage, thereby causing the lifter to use much less or much more weight. Therefore it is important to use the same seat position consistently during every workout. Pay attention to the body's position while performing all exercises; make sure you're getting the most out of your workout.

Since the goal of exercise is to load the muscles and produce high-effort muscular contractions, exercise should be as difficult as possible. This means that you should use the leverage or body position that allows for the greatest ROM within the realm of safety and comfort. Many individuals are unaware of their body when they lift weights. They squirm, twist, and use spastic motions while trying to obtain another repetition. They adjust their body positions and/or seat heights (on machines) to give themselves better leverage. All of these adjustments make the repetition easier, but the sudden changes in force when shifting body positions make the exercise more dangerous.

5. *Provide constant muscular tension.* The final coaching point pertains to muscular tension and is a subtlety that separates skillful trainees from beginners. When performing an exercise, the muscle should be forced to work through a full ROM by producing constant tension. Too often, trainees permit their concentration to lapse as the exercise becomes uncomfortable and they seek relief by resting partway through the repetition or by bouncing the plates off the unused portion of the weight stack. Recall the earlier example of the leg extension. When unskilled trainees begin to lower the weight and the lever arm approaches the lower half of the ROM, they will sometimes unload the quadriceps and allow the weight to accelerate. Then, using this increased momentum they will bounce the plates off the weight stack in order to get the weight moving again. To maintain constant muscular tension, the trainee should lower the weight slowly and smoothly and then turn around the weight in the same fashion.

Pumping up a balloon is an excellent analogy to help understand the need for maintaining constant muscular tension. Suppose you attempt to inflate the balloon—trying to increase the pressure (or tension) to a maximal level—while at the same time someone else lets a little air leak out. Is this the most efficient way to increase the tension in the balloon? Of course not. You may get the job done but in a much less effective manner than you would by doing it while maintaining constant tension. The same is true when training the muscular system. You may get the job done but in a much less efficient manner than you would by doing it the right way. In practice, this does not mean that you can

During the performance of a set, constant muscular tension should be produced for as long as possible. (photo courtesy of Richard Winett)

never take the load off the muscles being worked. It does mean, though, that during the performance of a set, constant muscular tension should be produced for as long as possible. Once you cannot do any additional perfect repetitions, it may be necessary to take a breath or two before you can continue. In exercises that involve large muscle structures—such as the leg press—you may have to take *several* breaths before continuing the movement. You can still count and record such repetitions as long as the pit stop does not become excessive.

REPETITION REPLICATION

The first repetition of a set is the most important. The goal is to block out all distractions and perform the repetition perfectly. The weight should be raised smoothly followed by a brief pause in the midrange position and then lowered slowly to a full stretch. After performing the first repetition, the second repetition becomes the most important and should be done in the very same manner as the first repetition. The goal is to replicate perfect repetitions. If a set of repetitions was videotaped, there should be no detectable differences in the repetitions when the tape is played back. At Stanford we teach our athletes that when they know how to do something right, they should do it every single time by force of will.

Just as you will not take off a play or a possession in a game, you should not take off a repetition in the weight room. Our training technique gives us a window into the current mental abilities of our athletes. When the exercise gets hard, do they panic and throw the weight? When the exercise becomes uncomfortable, do they lose concentration and let gravity pull the weight down? Rep replication ties together the three major fundamentals of our strength training program: effort, technique, and mental toughness.

PURPOSEFUL TRAINING

Keep in mind that the purpose of a properly performed repetition is to develop a level of strength that you do not presently have—it is *not* to demonstrate a level of strength that you wish you had. There are many exercises that have been touted as being great for training athletes but that violate all three checkpoints of a properly performed repetition. These include power cleans, snatches, push presses, and a host of other Olympic-lift variations. These movements rely heavily upon momentum, leverage, flawless technique, little constant tension produced by the involved muscles, no constant load on the muscles, and no lowering portion of the exercise. Is this really a productive way of training? I say no.

Most of us are result-oriented. Some believe that the purpose of strength training is simply to make the weights go up and down. Others believe that the purpose of a strength program is to create a person who can bench press a certain amount of weight and who can then have his or her name on a record board. But muscles do not care if the weights go up or down, or even if there are any weights at all. Muscles only care about how hard they are being forced to work. And it all starts with the properly performed repetition.

REFERENCE

Riley, D. 1998. *Redskin conditioning manual.* Ashburn, VA: Washington Redskins.

I would like to dedicate this chapter to my wife, Susie; my son, Mitchell; and my daughter, Madison; and to thank them for all of their love and support. I would also like to thank Aaron Hillmann, Heather Mason, and Mike Vorkapich for their input and loyalty.

12

Overcoming the Strength Plateau

Mickey Marotti, M.S., M.A., C.S.C.S.
Head Strength and Conditioning Coordinator
University of Notre Dame
Notre Dame, Indiana

Some of the most frequent questions that a strength coach, personal trainer, or fitness specialist will be asked are "My bench press has been stuck—how can I increase it?" or "Is there anything I can do differently to promote strength gains at a faster rate?" or "I'm tired of the same old workout—what else can I do?" These and similar questions are commonly asked in weight rooms and gyms around the United States.

There are many techniques you can use to alter your workouts and stave off plateaus. These techniques can be manipulated to fit into every workout or training approach. If you have reached a strength stalemate in your workout and a decrease in motivation is evident, it's time to assess the entire situation. Numerous influences from outside the weight room can have a negative effect on training, such as improper nutrition, inadequate recovery, loss of interest or enthusiasm, emotional or social distress, injury, and sickness. An increase in a job or school workload, greater participation in running or conditioning workouts, absence from training, and overtraining may also have a detrimental impact on your workouts. Any of these—or other outside circumstances—could be reasons for a plateau in strength.

The adjustments I'll discuss in this chapter need only be performed for a short time. However, some adjustments may turn into permanent changes for you. The following is a suggested agenda that will help reduce the dreaded standstill of strength.

VARY THE TRAINING DAYS

Some workout regimens call for three days of strength training per week. This protocol often consists of a total-body workout on all three days. A different type of workout regimen is a split routine. Three total-body workouts per week could be changed to a three-day split, for instance, in which the first day of training could target the upper body, the second day the lower body, and the third day the entire body. (Note that this three-day split would actually reduce the volume of training since each muscle is trained twice a week instead of three times.) Changing the training days or the frequency of training is a good practice to compensate for staleness. As with all changes, the idea is to force the body to adapt to different stimuli. From a psychological standpoint, changing from three total-body workouts per week to a three-day split routine can also help you become better-prepared to lift. Mentally, one can focus on the specifics of a brief, intense workout involving a limited number of muscle groups.

The same holds true if training is done using a four-day split routine in which there are two upper-body workouts and two lower-body workouts per week. Altering the frequency of the workout days can alleviate some of the monotony. Remember, too, that switching from a three-day to a four-day program can be beneficial as long as the volume of training doesn't exceed your recovery ability.

MODIFY WORKOUT SPECIFICS

The order of exercise is a very important component of strength progression. However, always performing the same exercises in the same sequence can ultimately affect the productivity of workouts. Some people enjoy doing the same workout over and over again for long periods of time but their strength may eventually plateau. The body learns to adapt to stresses that are placed upon it. Hence, changing workouts is a great way of giving the body a whole new wardrobe of stimuli.

In typical programs, exercises for the large muscle groups are performed first, followed by those for the smaller muscle groups; some programs have the core exercises, or the power exercises, at the beginning of the workout. However, your own preferences can dictate your sequence.

One method of change is to utilize exercises for the smaller muscle groups or single-joint movements immediately prior to exercises for the larger muscle groups or multi-joint movements. For example, instead of doing a bench press first followed by a bent-arm fly, pre-exhaust the chest with the bent-arm fly followed by the bench press. With this method, obviously the resistance will not be as heavy in the bench press when the chest is pre-fatigued with the bent-arm fly. However, put your ego aside and remember that the end result—namely muscle fatigue—is what counts. Some programs call for performing a squat or leg press first followed by another multi-joint exercise for the lower body. Again, you can change the order of execution based upon your preferences. You will be surprised at how effective it is to pre-exhaust your hips with a single-joint exercise and then blast them with a multi-joint exercise. Try this technique for a few weeks, then go back to your regular routine. You probably will see some improvement in all of your exercises.

Other programs call for a push-pull sequence where one executes a pushing movement (such as an incline press) immediately followed by a pulling movement (such as a lat pulldown) or vice versa. You can change the traditional push-pull routine so that you perform all of the pushing movements (in any order) and then all of the pulling movements. Again, do not be concerned with the decrease in weight on some exercises. Rather, look at the big picture. Once you go back to your original routine, you will notice the positive adaptation from changing the order of exercises.

CHANGE THE EQUIPMENT

Varying the type of equipment can also be a great manipulation technique. There are several different kinds of possibilities.

Free Weights and Machines

If your routine calls for all free-weight exercises, try incorporating some plate-loaded or selectorized machines. Machines can be great substitutes for any free-weight exercise. Since numerous machines change the resistance throughout the range of motion (ROM) during an exercise, this could ultimately provide a different stimulus to the muscles. Here's how: The resistance used in free-weight exercises is limited to the weakest point in your ROM—the point where your biomechanical leverage is the worst. Exercises done with proper technique cannot override this sticking point, so the resistance will be limited. On the other hand, many machines have overcome this obstacle by varying the resistance to approximate the changes in your leverage. The same idea applies if your program consists only of machines. In that case, use some barbell or dumbbell exercises in your routine. Since muscles respond to different stimuli, it is important to provide variety.

Sandbag Training

A good nontraditional type of activity is sandbag training. The sandbags can vary in weight from 20 to 200 pounds. You can make one yourself or purchase one from a manufacturer. Sandbag exercises require a great deal of grip strength and, therefore, will give an exercise a whole new twist. Many upper-body movements can be performed using sandbags, ranging from a simple bicep curl to a military or shoulder press. In fact, most exercises that are performed with a barbell or dumbbells can be performed with one or two sandbags. For example, two smaller sandbags can be substituted for dumbbells in a shoulder press.

Squats, lunges, step-ups, and deadlifts are great sandbag exercises for the lower body. These movements are done by first bear hugging a sandbag and then performing the desired movement.

A popular exercise among the football and wrestling populations is neck flexion. To do this movement, lie on your back on a bench and place a sandbag on your forehead. (The weight of the sandbag will depend upon your neck strength.) Then pump out a set of the exercise while holding the sandbag in place with your hands.

Thick Bars

The use of thick bars or other unorthodox bars can also provide variation in the workout. Thick (or fat) bars can range from 2 to 3 inches in diameter. Many exercises can be done with the thick bar by simply substituting this tool for a standard Olympic barbell. The bench press, military press, and standing bicep curl are great movements into which the thick bar can be incorporated.

The use of thick bars or other unorthodox bars can provide variation in the workout. (photo courtesy of Bob Whelan)

Manual Resistance

Manual resistance (MR) is another excellent alternative to more conventional forms of training. In MR, a spotter or training partner provides the workload. Any exercise done with a barbell or dumbbells can be done with MR. Besides providing variety in a routine, MR has several other advantages. For one thing, it requires little or no equipment and can be done anywhere. MR has a few pitfalls, however. For instance, an experienced spotter is needed to perform the exercises properly and there is no way to quantify or qualify the resistance.

One of the best applications of MR is as a post-exhaustion activity. After completing a machine or a barbell exercise, the lifter is immediately taken through an MR exercise until muscular fatigue. For example, suppose a lifter executes a concluding work set of 5–8 repetitions on the bench press with the last repetition being almost impossible to complete. Immediately, the lifter is taken through an MR bent-arm fly exercise to a further state of exhaustion. Towels, sticks, pipes, and chains also can be used during MR. The lifter would hold onto one of these implements and—with a partner providing the resistance—perform an exercise that normally would be done by gripping a barbell or dumbbell, such as an upright row.

Body-Weight Exercises

Unfortunately, the use of body-weight exercises nowadays is rare. Simple exercises involving the weight of one's body—such as dips, chin-ups, pull-ups, push-ups, and the ever-popular wall sit—are great options for providing an extra zap of intensity when trying to fight through the sticking points of training. A great example is performing the final work set of 8–10 repetitions of barbell squats or leg presses where there wasn't enough strength left to get another repetition. After completing the last repetition, the lifter would lean up against the nearest wall (concrete of course) with a flat back and knees bent at a ninety-degree angle (i.e., with the upper legs parallel to the ground) and hold this wall-sit position for as long as possible. If the lifter was especially tough and motivated, a number of 45-pound plates could be added to his or her lap for further resistance. The goal is to maintain this static position for a prescribed amount of time or until overcome by exhaustion or mental anguish—whichever comes first.

SWITCH THE GRIP/STANCE

Changing the hand or foot placement can also be a good technique to use for variety. An example of this would be to vary your hand position from a wide grip to a close grip when performing a chin-up or pull-up exercise. This seemingly minor variation drastically alters the exercise. You can also widen or tighten the grip during barbell exercises. For instance, you could do a close-grip bench press rather than a wide-grip bench press. In fact, any pushing movement for the upper body done with barbells could be slightly altered by changing the hand position. In addition, a high-bar squat (where the bar sits high up on the trapezius) can be performed instead of a low-bar or power-position squat.

Repositioning the body during ground-based activities can also be a positive stimulus to the muscles. The ROM can be altered by narrowing the stance during a barbell squat or by changing the grip placement or body position while performing a free-weight, machine, or manual-resistance exercise.

Making any of these alterations will affect the plane of movement and the angle of push or pull, essentially changing the exercise. Ultimately, these exercises will provide a new stimulus for the muscle.

VARY THE VOLUME (SETS/REPETITIONS)

Another training variable that easily can be manipulated for the purpose of avoiding the detestable strength plateau is the volume of sets/repetitions. One of the most controversial areas of strength training is the question of which set/rep scheme works best. Some common questions are:

- If I want to get toned, don't I need to do high repetitions?
- If I want to bulk up, how heavy should I go?
- How many sets should I do if I want to increase my bench press?
- Isn't periodization the best program for me?

All of these questions—or variations of them—have been asked on a daily basis for years in most gyms or strength facilities. Remember, every situation is different. But every set/rep scheme can be productive as long as it is designed to be progressive and provide an overload. Progression can be attained by using more resistance for the same number of repetitions or by using the same resistance while increasing the repetitions. A successful strength program not only needs to be progressive in terms of intensity, but the muscles also need to be overloaded on a consistent basis.

A productive program also needs to be systematic. Some programs call for a classical model of periodization. Other programs use a basic three sets of 8 or 10 repetitions or a periodized repetition scheme. Still others call for a low number of sets done with very intense effort. Each of these protocols can be effective. The volume of training depends upon each situation or personal preference. Some people like to train for a long period of time. Some do not have time. Your volume of training should fit your own circumstances and inclinations provided that it doesn't surpass your recovery ability.

If a strength plateau has occurred, try changing the set/rep scheme. There are a few popular options.

20-Rep Sets

An excellent change is to use a high-repetition protocol such as a 20-rep set. This protocol works particularly well with squats and leg presses. Prior to the 20-rep effort, perform 2–3 relatively easy warm-up sets working up to the desired weight. To perform a 20-rep set, use a weight with which you can do 3 × 10 (i.e., three sets of 10 repetitions, where the tenth repetition of the third set is very difficult to complete. Attempt to perform a work set of 20 repetitions with this weight without setting it down while taking big breaths between repetitions. If your mental readiness is high, the training environment is ripe, and the motivation of your training partner or spotter is maximal, do not be surprised if you can do a single 20-rep set with a weight that you can do 3 × 10. This technique can truly help avoid a plateau. Use the 20-rep scheme for 4–6 weeks, increasing the resistance progressively on the work set, and then switch back to your old scheme. No doubt, you will notice improvements in strength.

5 × 50 Scheme

Pick five multi-joint exercises that involve different muscle groups. Warm up to a weight with which you reach muscular fatigue between 10 and 15 repetitions. After the first work set with this weight, take 2 minutes of rest. Then, do another work set using the same weight and attempt to perform as many repetitions as possible. Keep doing this until you achieve a total of 50 repetitions. Use the same procedure with each of the other four exercises.

Heavy 3 × 5

Warm up to a weight that you can perform 5 repetitions with a maximal effort (i.e., to muscular fatigue). After this first work set, take 2–3 minutes of rest. Then, attempt the same weight for another work set of 5 repetitions. After a 2–3 minute rest, try a third work set of 5 repetitions. If you cannot achieve 5 repetitions on the second or third work set, repeat the weight in your next workout. Once you have achieved 3 × 5 with the same weight, increase the resistance by about 5 percent or less for your next workout.

Multiple Work-Set Training

This training technique offers challenging goals. The work sets are performed with intense exertion to promote strength gains. Three different repetition protocols are shown along with a brief explanation of how they are executed. These repetition schemes are ideal for multi-joint exercises such as the squat, leg press, deadlift, and bench press. With all of these protocols, use the same weight during all three sets for the prescribed number of repetitions and rest no more than two minutes between sets. Finally, once you can complete three work sets for the prescribed number of repetitions, you should increase the resistance by about 5 percent or less.

> Example 1: Start with a weight that is about 65 percent of your estimated one-repetition maximum (1-RM) and perform three work sets of 15, 10, and 5–10 repetitions.

Example 2: Use a weight that is roughly 70 percent of your estimated 1-RM and do three work sets of 12, 8, and 4–8 repetitions.

Example 3: Begin with a weight that is approximately 75 percent of your estimated 1-RM and do three work sets of 10, 7, and 4–7 repetitions.

Remember, the set/rep scheme you choose is not as important as your intensity of effort. It is a good idea to shock your system periodically with a new set/rep protocol. For this technique to be most effective, the change must be distinct. Going from a 3 × 8 to a 3 × 10 scheme really is not enough of a difference. If you're a low-rep (4–7), multiple-set enthusiast, switch to a moderate-rep (8–15) or high-rep (15–20), single-set protocol; if you usually use a high-rep or moderate-rep scheme, change to a low-rep scheme and give it your best shot. There is no wrong way or only way. Be open-minded in designing a program. Your body will adapt to a stimulus as long as it offers a progressive overload. Change the stimulus and you'll promote gains in strength.

ADVANCED TECHNIQUES

There are a number of advanced techniques that can also be used to overcome the strength plateau. Although these strategies are beneficial, they should be used sparingly and changed on a regular basis. These techniques can place a demand on the body that can help increase strength. However, you can also overtrain if you overuse these techniques.

Negative Training

The two phases of a repetition are the concentric (or raising) portion and the eccentric (or lowering) portion. Negative training emphasizes the eccentric phase of a repetition. There are two main applications of negative training. One is the use of post-exhaustion negatives at the end of a hard work set. At the completion of the last groveling repetition that you can perform on your own, immediately do the concentric portion of another repetition with assistance from a partner/spotter and then emphasize the eccentric portion of the exercise by lowering the weight in at least 3–5 seconds. After reaching muscular fatigue, perform 2–3 repetitions of these negatives.

The other popular application of negative training is negative-only exercise. For an entire set beginning with the first repetition, one or more spotters assist the lifter in raising the weight while the lifter concentrates on lowering the weight. Since eccentric strength is greater than concentric strength, the lifter should use a heavier weight than he or she can normally handle—perhaps as much as 30–40 percent more. If you can leg press 300 pounds, for example, then you could probably use about 390–420 pounds for a set performed in a negative-only fashion. In this application, the eccentric portion of the repetition should take about 6–8 seconds to complete.

Forced Repetitions

Forced repetitions are done after the lifter reaches muscular fatigue and can no longer perform another repetition properly. At that point, the spotter assists with the exercise by helping the lifter with 3–5 additional post-fatigue repetitions. These are similar to negatives except that with forced repetitions, the spotter gives the lifter just enough assistance to raise the weight and applies additional resistance as the weight is being lowered. This technique is great for increasing the intensity of effort. For this technique to be effective, the spotter must make sure that the lifter works extremely hard during both the concentric and eccentric phases of the exercise.

Breakdown Sets or Burn-Outs

A breakdown set is done immediately after reaching muscular fatigue. At the end of an intense set, the weight is decreased by 20–30 percent and another set is performed as soon as possible. This breakdown can be done 2 or 3 times. For example, if a lifter squats 400 pounds for 10 repetitions, the lifter would rack the bar, decrease the weight to about 280–320 pounds and promptly perform another set. If a second breakdown set is desired, the weight would be quickly reduced to about 195–225 pounds.

Speed of Movement

Many people have different beliefs when it comes to the speed of movement of a repetition. One approach is to perform repetitions in a slow, controlled manner with the greatest emphasis put on the negative phase of the exercise. Another is SuperSlow® training where the repetitions are also done in a slow, controlled manner but the greatest emphasis is placed on the concentric or lifting portion of the exercise. Yet another approach is to perform repetitions in a ballistic manner, stressing high speeds of movement.

Adjusting the speed of movement to a little faster or slower than usual could be a great change. Just be sure to do all the repetitions with good form/technique, and don't let momentum be a factor in the efficiency or safety of the exercise. In particular, slowing the speed of movement can be just what the doctor ordered. Remember, the intensity of effort is increased as the speed of movement is decreased. By slowing the speed of the bar or lifting tool, you are ultimately asking the muscles to work harder; greater recruitment of muscle fibers is needed to move a resistance slowly.

Length of Workouts

The length of a workout is another variable that can be manipulated. Workout length is often determined by the type of training one is doing. If powerlifting or Olympic lifting is the emphasis, then the length of the workout is probably maximal due to the number of skill sets; if a basic strength training program is incorporated, the length of the workout is probably minimal. Therefore, you may have to decrease or increase the length of your workouts depending upon the goal of the training.

If a lifter is on the verge of overtraining, then it is extremely important to reduce the length of the workout. More is not always better. One needs to recuperate during heavy training. Don't forget, rest is just as important as strength training—but make sure that the work comes first.

Rest and Recovery

As in all types of physical training, successful strength training is usually dictated by effort, consistency, diet, and rest. You need energy to train with a high degree of effort; it is as important as the task at hand. If an individual wants to obtain maximum gains in strength, then the diet must be adequate to elicit the desired results. Likewise, if the body is not properly rested it will have a difficult time producing and sustaining the high level of intensity necessary for optimal results. The main two aspects of the recovery and rebuilding process are diet and rest. Food helps the body heal from intense training; rest helps the body recover physically as well as mentally. Mental rest is a very important variable. The main factor in the equation is to perform hard consistent work first, then rest and recover next.

Rest Between Sets/Exercise

Manipulation of the rest interval between sets/exercises can change the entire makeup of a workout. Changing the amount of rest alters the intensity of each exercise. When you increase the amount of rest time between sets, you can probably handle a little more weight; if you take less rest, then you cannot handle as much weight but the intensity is increased. A good rule of thumb is to take as much rest as needed to perform each exercise with a maximum effort but not so much rest as to take away from the overall intensity of the workout. The rest interval between exercises should only be long enough to get a drink, adjust the weight, and take a deep breath before getting after the set. Manipulation of the rest time can add variety without changing the exercises.

MAKE IT FUN

Avoiding the strength plateau is a learned art. Coaches, trainers, and enthusiasts should recognize the warning signs of a plateau, then adapt by adding variety to

As in all types of physical training, successful strength training is usually dictated by effort, consistency, diet, and rest. (photo by Kathy Leistner)

withstand and overcome it. Try to use as many techniques as possible to manipulate the different training variables. When staleness or plateaus occur, examine your training regimen and modify one or two variables. Change is a warranted aspect of strength training. After a few weeks of a new workout and changed regimen, return to your old workout. There is a good chance that you are going to see great results and notice a difference in your strength. Variety is the part of setting up strength training programs that is enjoyable. Adding a new wrinkle into your workouts is like getting a new toy when you were a kid. It is as much fun as that.

My chapter is dedicated to Bob Hoffman, John Grimek, and Peary Rader.

13

Balanced Training

Bob Whelan, M.S., M.S., C.S.C.S.
Strength Coach/Owner
Whelan Strength Training
Washington, D.C.

Many individuals may be training hard but they aren't necessarily training smart. This is especially true of those who don't properly balance their training program with an equal amount of pushing and pulling movements and an emphasis on total-body development. For example, some people get obsessed with certain ego lifts—such as the bench press—which usually results in a disproportionate physical development. So, they might be able to bench press the world (a pushing movement) but they can't do a single chin-up (a pulling movement). This imbalance is actually more serious than people realize; it is the cause of many injuries. (To avoid confusion, it is important to note that all muscles pull when they contract; however, muscle contractions cause joints to extend and flex, which produces movements that can be described as either pushing or pulling. The chest, anterior deltoid, and triceps are involved during pushing movements. The upper back (or lats), posterior deltoid, and biceps are used during pulling movements.)

The bench press and other ego lifts are important exercises but they are no more important than any other major movement. Equal attention to both pushing and pulling movements is necessary to provide a proper balance of muscular development and physical strength. In fact, a ratio weighted more heavily to the often underworked pulling exercises is sometimes needed temporarily to equalize those muscles with muscles that produce pushing movements. This is especially necessary if the muscles involved in pulling movements have been neglected for a lengthy period of time.

Equal attention to both pushing and pulling movements is necessary to provide a proper balance of muscular development and physical strength.

(photo by Kevin Fowler)

A REAL-LIFE APPLICATION

Here is an excellent example that illustrates imbalanced training: I once had a gentleman named Bill visit my facility for a consultation and a workout. (His name has been changed to protect his privacy.) At the time, Bill was 29 years old, 5′ 10″, and about 190 pounds. When he came to see me, he had been lifting weights for about seven years. Bill stated that his best bench press was about 315 pounds and his best squat was just a bit more than that. (As a side note, he did not deadlift regularly.)

During his first workout with me, Bill worked very intensely. However, I couldn't help but notice that he had a severe imbalance of strength between his upper torso and lower body. The ratio of pushing and pulling strength for his upper body was also out of whack. For instance, he could perform eight repetitions with 225 pounds on the barbell bench press but had a difficult time using a relatively light weight of 150 pounds on the Hammer Strength® Iso Row; he could do eight repetitions with 170 pounds on the barbell shoulder press but used a comparatively easy weight of about 120 pounds on the Hammer Strength® Lat Pulldown and could not chin himself with his body weight more than three times. To remedy this situation, Bill needed more emphasis on his overall lower-body strength as well as on the pulling movements for his upper body. This would help him begin to balance his muscular strength and physical development.

It was obvious that Bill had spent a large portion of his time in the weight room lying on his back doing bench presses. He had good muscular development in his chest and anterior deltoids but had far less development in his hips, legs, upper back, and posterior deltoids. It was all a matter of observation: During his previous workouts, Bill didn't emphasize his hips and legs or pulling exercises for his upper torso. For some reason, he thought that movements for those areas were relatively unimportant. As long as his bench press and his shoulder press were increasing, Bill was satisfied. (He was also concerned with his bicep curl.) His ego was not attached to exercising his lower body in the same way as it was for his upper body; nor was his ego attached to pulling movements for his upper body in the same way as it was to pushing movements. These exercises had second-class status; Bill would just go through the motions when doing them, fitting them into his workouts whenever he could. After our initial session, Bill realized that he had been consistently training hard for the past seven years—but he'd only been working about half his muscles. He demonstrated that he could train intensely when he put his mind to it; he just needed to change his approach and do it for his entire body.

ACHIEVING BALANCE

For optimal gains in muscular size and strength, start the workout with exercises for the hips and the legs as these movements involve the greatest amount of muscle mass and are the most physically demanding. Nothing calls attention to an imbalanced training program more quickly than seeing someone with a huge upper body coupled with an underdeveloped—or, in some cases, undeveloped—lower body. Unfortunately, you can find examples of this in practically any gym throughout the world. Multi-joint (or compound) movements for the lower body—such as the squat, leg press, and deadlift—are the foundation of a balanced program and should be a top priority.

It is also important to balance the pushing and pulling movements of the upper torso. Many strength and fitness professionals design strength training programs that do not take this into consideration. While it is better to do less than more, it is best to do the right number of exercises so that the program is balanced.

Many coaches (myself included) put a high value on a few basic exercises. The problem is that some individuals overlook several other exercises that are equally important. Quite often, the design of their programs shows poor balance between pushing and pulling movements—usually not enough pulling movements. I have read many articles where the authors have gone to great lengths to describe in detail pushing movements for the upper body. They then casually state something to the effect that you should "throw in a rowing movement to round out the program." Unfortunately, that's the extent of pulling movements for many people.

Horizontal and Vertical Movements

Most pushing and pulling movements for the upper torso can be categorized as either horizontal or vertical. In this sense, the terms *horizontal* and *vertical* don't necessarily refer to the movements' relationship to the ground. Rather, the terms describe the movement of the hands in relation to the upper torso. For instance, both a barbell bench press, where the lifter is lying down, and a Hammer Strength® Chest Press, where the lifter is sitting upright, are examples of horizontal pushing movements.

As noted previously, some exercises—such as the bench press—are directly connected to the ego. There's nothing wrong with this as long as the exercise isn't done to an extreme. A bench press is an important exercise. As a horizontal pushing movement, however, it is not any more significant than an exercise such as a seated row, Hammer Strength® Iso Row, or any other horizontal pulling movement. Likewise, a shoulder press is an important exercise. But as a vertical pushing movement, it is no more important than a chin-up, Hammer Strength® Lat Pulldown, or any other vertical pulling movement.

A good rule of thumb is not to be preoccupied with any one particular exercise. You should strive for balanced strength and muscular development. This should not be seen as condemning the use of the bench press or any other ego lift, as they also are important.

I recently had a phone conversation with my friend, Dan Riley. Dan is the strength and conditioning coach of the Washington Redskins and one of the most respected people in the strength and fitness profession. He advocates programs that maintain a balance of pushing and pulling movements. My approach to pushing and pulling movements is quite similar to Dan's except that he prescribes exercises that involve more planes of movement (i.e., horizontal and vertical) for the simple reason that he has access to many more machines in a much larger facility.

Basically, I use the following simple guideline for a balanced upper-body program: a horizontal push, a horizontal pull, a vertical push, and a vertical pull. For the lower body, I recently began alternating between the squat, deadlift,

A pushing movement (such as a tricep extension) should be balanced with a pulling movement (such as a bicep curl).
(photo courtesy of Bob Whelan)

and Hammer Strength® Leg Press. In effect, each of these exercises is done about once every 10 or 11 days. (Some people may need a longer recovery time for their spinal erector muscles and, therefore, may only deadlift twice per month.)

Some movements can be classified as either a push or a pull but are not easily matched with a movement that does the opposite function. For example, a pullover and a shoulder shrug can be categorized as pulling movements but they have no real pushing counterparts.

Remember, too, that the core of a program should consist of multi-joint exercises. Single-joint (or isolation) exercises—such as a leg extension, leg curl, tricep extension, and bicep curl—can certainly be added to the infrastructure of a program, but they are not substitutes for multi-joint movements that involve large amounts of muscle mass.

Some trainees (especially those who do multiple sets) can eventually overtrain from using too much volume if they perform pushing and pulling movements for the upper body in the horizontal and vertical planes in the same workout. In this case, these individuals should alternate the vertical and horizontal pushing and pulling movements and do each of them once per week. For instance, horizontal pushing and pulling movements could be done on Mondays and vertical pushing and pulling movements on Thursdays.

There are a variety of common exercises that can be used to fit the bill, so no one need get bored or lose enthusiasm. Some examples are:

- vertical pushing movements: shoulder press with a barbell, dumbbells, machines (selectorized and plate-loading), and manual resistance
- vertical pulling movements: chin-up, pull-up and lat pulldown with machines (selectorized and plate-loading)
- horizontal pushing movements: bench press with a barbell, dumbbells, and machines (selectorized and plate-loading); manual resistance push-ups; incline press with a barbell, dumbbells, and machines (selectorized and plate-loading)
- horizontal pulling movements: seated row with machines (selectorized and plate-loading); bent-over row with dumbbells

INJURY PREVENTION

A balance between pushing and pulling is also important to prevent injuries. Many injuries are caused by muscular imbalance. There is a strong relationship between joint injuries and the balanced development of the musculature that surrounds that joint. Just like a car that pulls to one side when it is out of alignment, your muscles will pull a joint to one side if the strength of one side is out of alignment with the other. Many shoulder, knee, and other joint problems are a direct result of this imbalance.

BALANCE AND PERIODIZATION

Periodization is a subject of great disagreement in the strength training field. The traditional periodization model is quite complicated, inflexible, and often imbalanced. An unsophisticated application of periodization is simply to change the planned program or the macro version by implementing variety every few months, or as needed, while still following the same general principles of balanced training that I have described.

Personally, I am not an advocate of the traditional and theoretical model of periodization with different phases that supposedly emphasize hypertrophy, strength, power, and endurance. In my opinion, this model is illogical. To me, periodization is simply changing the program to promote a mental as well as a physiological boost. I believe that if you are going to train, you should do so with an all-out intense effort. Hypertrophy and strength go hand in hand, not in separate phases. If you exercise your entire body twice per week, then you should get plenty of recovery. Of course, coaches would still need to make adjustments for their athletes in terms of volume, frequency, and intensity (and other factors) depending upon whether they are in-season or off-season. This is not periodization, just common sense.

Exercises, repetition ranges, equipment, and so forth can be changed to work the body from different angles while maintaining a balanced approach. A change in repetition ranges can also be good for the joints. I prefer to train with higher repetitions for several months and then switch to lower repetitions for a while. I enjoy the change. If you are training to demonstrate strength, or your athletic performance requires that you train a specific energy system, however, then changing the repetition ranges too much probably isn't a good option.

GET BALANCED!

When designing your program, always start with the core foundation of the lower body first, followed by a balance of pushing and pulling movements for the upper body. Stick to these principles when periodizing or making changes to your workouts every few months or as needed. Consider muscle groups and general planes of motion when designing your program and don't get addicted to certain exercises. Your balanced body will thank you for it.

This chapter is dedicated from John to his wife, Kelly, and their two sons, Jake and Logan; Jeremy dedicates this chapter to his family for all their support.

14

Training the Injured Athlete

John Thomas, B.S.
Head Strength and Conditioning Coach (Football)
Penn State University
University Park, Pennsylvania

Jeremy Scott, M.Ed.
Assistant Strength and Conditioning Coach (Football)
Penn State University
University Park, Pennsylvania

The two primary purposes of strength training should be injury prevention and the enhancement of performance potential. Although it is inevitable that injuries will occur on the athletic fields, the likelihood of those injuries can be decreased with proper strength training. Once an injury occurs, an athlete should be evaluated and treated by qualified sports-medical personnel such as physicians, athletic trainers, and so on. Normally, the sports-medicine staff will classify the injury as traumatic or nontraumatic. Once the severity of the injury has been determined, the strength staff—along with the athletic trainers—will decide on what changes should be made in the athlete's training to prevent further setbacks from the injury.

The approach to rehabilitative strength training should be an aggressive one. It is important that all of your athletes—both injured and healthy—train with a maximum level of intensity. If too much time passes by without strength training, muscles will begin to lose size and strength. For this reason it is recommended that injured athletes begin training—however limited the training may be—as soon as possible following the injury. Some traumatic injuries will not permit any training of the injured area. In this situation, intense training should continue for the unaffected parts of the body. For less severe or nontraumatic injuries, training of the injured area can often continue with modifications. Therefore, the severity of the injury—and to some extent, the mental toughness of the athlete—will determine the initial changes and progression back to full recovery.

ADJUSTMENTS TO THE ROUTINE

There are several different options or adjustments that can be made to the basic lifting routine so an injured athlete can continue training.

Exercise Uninjured Body Parts

For the most severe or traumatic injuries, an athlete will only be able to train the unaffected body parts. For example, a dislocation of the right shoulder involving immobilization of that arm is a traumatic injury that limits the training to the uninjured body parts. In this instance, the athlete can certainly continue to train the lower body and midsection. It is also important to exercise the unaffected limb of the torso (in this case, the left arm) if possible. Some research has shown that training one side of your body will also affect the other side. This is called *indirect transfer* or *cross transfer*. Figure 14.1 details a sample of a basic in-season routine with adjustments made for one-limb training due to a dislocated right shoulder.

Changes in the lower-body movements need only be made if a particular exercise places pressure on an injured limb. As an example, an athlete should not

Basic Routine	Adjusted Routine
Neck Flexion	Neck Flexion (MR only)
Neck Extension	Neck Extension (MR only)
Shoulder Shrug	Shoulder Shrug (left arm, DB)
Upright Row	Upright Row (left arm, MR)
Bench Press	Iso-Lateral Bench Press (left arm)
Row	Iso-Lateral Row (left arm)
Shoulder Press	Iso-Lateral Seated Press (left arm)
Pulldown/Pullover	Iso-Lateral Pulldown (left arm)
Lateral Raise	Lateral Raise (left arm, MR)
Incline Press	Iso-Lateral Incline Press (left arm)
Leg Extension	Leg Extension
Leg Curl	Leg Curl
Leg Press or Squat	Leg Press
Hip Adduction	Hip Adduction (MR)
Hip Abduction	Hip Abduction (MR)
Calf Raise	Seated Calf Raise
Midsection	Midsection (MR)
Back Extension	Back Extension (MR)
Bicep Curl	Bicep Curl (left arm)
Tricep Extension	Tricep Extension (left arm)

Notes: DB = dumbbell; MR = manual resistance

FIGURE 14.1 Sample of a Basic In-Season Routine with Adjustments Made for One-Limb Training Due to a Dislocated Right Shoulder

do a barbell squat or any squatting motion that puts a load on an injured shoulder. In this situation, a seated leg press can be used. If a leg press is not available, ball squats or manual resistance squats are other options.

Ball squats can be done by placing a a 65-centimeter Swiss ball between the athlete's lower back and a firm wall. The feet are placed shoulder-width apart or a bit wider (depending upon the athlete's flexibility) and slightly in front of the body. To do this exercise, slowly lower the hips to the point where the upper legs are parallel to the ground or slightly lower. Pause in this (midrange) position and then slowly return to the starting position. The heels should remain in contact with the ground and the lower legs should stay perpendicular to the ground throughout the exercise. This eliminates pressure on the knees and keeps the athlete from leaning forward, thereby maintaining the shoulders and hips in a straight line.

It is important to note that the starting position for ball squats is with the legs fully extended. Therefore, the first part of the repetition is in the negative—or eccentric—phase. Many different speeds of movement and repetition ranges can be used for ball squats. Here are three examples:

- 10/5/10: 10-second negative, 5-second pause in the midrange position, 10-second positive; 3–6 repetitions
- 5/5/5: 5-second negative, 5-second pause in the midrange position, 5-second positive; 5–10 repetitions
- 8/1/4: 8-second negative, 1-second pause in the midrange position, 4-second positive; 6–12 repetitions

Use Different Equipment

Having a wide variety of equipment will give you more options to make adjustments for training an injured athlete. There are a number of equipment manufacturers—such as Hammer Strength® and Nautilus®—that have developed machines with independent movement arms, a function that allows trainees to do iso-lateral work safely. Essentially, the independent movement arms create an independent workload—each side of the body is forced to work independently of the other without the threat of losing balance or attaining an awkward position from favoring one side. If machines are unavailable, training with dumbbells or manual resistance is another option for iso-lateral training. In this situation, all or most of the exercises should be done with manual resistance until the athlete feels comfortable training with one dumbbell at a time instead of two.

In the event of traumatic injury to the lower body—such as any knee injury that requires surgery—the same guidelines can be followed for iso-lateral training. Alterations may also be needed for the torso so that the athlete can train the lower body in a comfortable manner.

PROGRESSING TO FULL RECOVERY

For traumatic injuries, the following routines can be part of the progression back to full recovery.

SuperSlow® Training

For a less traumatic injury—such as tendinitis—SuperSlow® training should be the first option. This would also be the next step in progression for a more severe injury once the medical staff has cleared an athlete to begin training the injured limb.

The greatest benefit of SuperSlow® training for exercising an injured area is that the slower speed of movement eliminates momentum, which decreases the amount of stress placed upon the joint. Because of the slower speed of movement, a lighter-than-normal weight is used, which will eliminate even more stress on the joint.

The standard speed of movement for the SuperSlow® protocol is 10/5—that is, a 10-second count for the concentric (or raising) phase of the lift and a 5-second count for the eccentric (or lowering) phase. Incorporating a slight pause at the beginning and midrange of each repetition will further eliminate momentum. Due to the shorter range of motion for some exercises, the speed of movement may change from 10/5 to 5/5. Examples of exercises with very short ranges of motion are a shoulder shrug and a calf raise.

To maintain the same time under tension—or time of muscular loading—the repetition ranges should be adjusted when using slower-than-usual speeds of movement. A base repetition range of 8–12 with a 2/4 speed of movement means that the muscles are loaded for between 48 and 72 seconds. Decreasing the repetition range to 3–5 with a 10/5 speed of movement means that the muscles are loaded for between 45 and 75 seconds—roughly the same amount of time under tension as 8–12 repetitions with a 2/4 speed.

If available, a wide variety of equipment can be used for bilateral training in a SuperSlow® manner. However, an athlete training in this fashion for the first time should use as many machines as possible. This process will give the athlete a chance to become comfortable with the routine—both mentally and physically—before using barbells or dumbbells. Figure 14.2 details sample routines for the upper torso performed in a SuperSlow® fashion.

Iso-Lateral Training

The final step in recovery before returning to regular lifting is iso-lateral training. Once the injured limb can be exercised through a full, pain-free range of motion (ROM), it's time to begin doing regular repetitions. However, an athlete should start with a reduced weight for the injured limb. When he or she is able to exercise both limbs with the same weight and achieve the same number of repetitions, a normal routine can be used again.

Torso Iso-Lateral Training	Torso Bilateral Training
Neck Flexion (MR only)	Neck Flexion (MR only)
Neck Extension (MR only)	Neck Extension (MR only)
Shoulder Shrug (right arm, DB, 5/5)	Shoulder Shrug (5/5)
Upright Row (MR only)	Upright Row (MR only)
Iso-Lateral Bench (right arm, 10/5)	Bench Press (10/5)
Iso-Lateral Row (right arm, 10/5)	Row (10/5)
Iso-Lateral Seated Press (right arm, 10/5)	Shoulder Press (10/5)
Iso-Lateral Pulldown (right arm, 10/5)	Pulldown (10/5)
Lateral Raise (right arm, 10/5)	Lateral Raise (10/5)
Iso-Lateral Incline Press (right arm, 10/5)	Incline Press (10/5)

(The left side is trained the same as the previous workout.)

Notes: DB = dumbbell; MR = manual resistance; 5/5 = 5-second concentric, 5-second eccentric; 10/5 = 10-second concentric, 5-second eccentric

FIGURE 14.2 Sample Routines Involving SuperSlow® Training for the Upper Torso

No-Hands Workout

Another benefit of having access to many types of equipment is that there are more options for training an athlete who is unable to hold onto a bar or dumbbell. With the proper equipment, it's possible to train the torso muscles involved

In the event of an injury, it is important to exercise the unaffected limb through iso-lateral or one-limb training. (photo by Matt Brzycki)

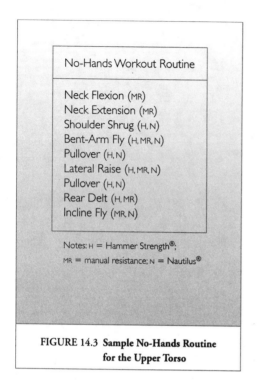

No-Hands Workout Routine

Neck Flexion (MR)
Neck Extension (MR)
Shoulder Shrug (H, N)
Bent-Arm Fly (H, MR, N)
Pullover (H, N)
Lateral Raise (H, MR, N)
Pullover (H, N)
Rear Delt (H, MR)
Incline Fly (MR, N)

Notes: H = Hammer Strength®;
MR = manual resistance; N = Nautilus®

FIGURE 14.3 **Sample No-Hands Routine
for the Upper Torso**

in pushing movements (i.e., the chest, shoulders, and triceps) along with the pulling movements (i.e., the upper back and biceps) without having to use the hands for gripping. With the right equipment combined with manual resistance exercises, it is even possible to train an athlete with a cast on the hand or lower arm. Figure 14.3 is an example of a no-hands routine for the upper torso. (The sample routine in Figure 14.3 can also be used if an athlete has a hyperextended elbow, provided that all of the exercises can be done without pain.)

Other Options

These are just a few examples of how workouts can be altered to continue the training of injured athletes. Some other adjustments for minor injuries include changing the grip, the angle of the exercise, or the entire exercise. For some minor injuries, changing just one exercise in an athlete's routine might be sufficient.

READY TO PLAY!

While training the injured athlete, there are some important points to remember. First and most important is staying in constant communication with the medical professional involved in the athlete's rehabilitation. The second point involves communicating with the athlete. Both the athlete and sport coach need to know that there is a difference between muscular pain and joint pain. Muscle pain is an indication that high-intensity work is being done and the muscle is being fatigued; joint pain during exercise usually means that there is a structural problem. Some athletes and coaches proclaim that you have to work through the pain. If the athlete is feeling localized joint pain, it is probably causing more damage, which would be detrimental to the rehabilitation process. Because there are so many different body types and physiques, not every exercise or piece of equipment will be suitable for every athlete. When athletes say that they are not comfortable doing an exercise, this could result from either a physical or structural problem or, in some instances, a lack of mental toughness. However, to achieve more productive workouts, a good approach is to change the exercise instead of forcing the athlete to train on an exercise or modality that is uncomfortable.

When staying within the guidelines mentioned previously, it is important to keep the injured athlete physically and mentally involved with his or her team or sport. This will enhance that athlete's ability to prepare and train as hard as possible.

This chapter is dedicated to my son, Rocco Anthony; my brother, Anthony; and Christina Cavallo for making my life a more positive experience.

15

Fiber Types and Repetition Ranges

Rocco Castellano, B.S., C.P.F.T.
Owner
Rocco's Complete Fitness Systems
Covington, Kentucky

Most people begin exercising or strength training by jumping into a program headfirst without properly educating themselves beforehand. This often results in a poor response and, unfortunately, sometimes injury. The only way you can train yourself effectively is by educating yourself correctly.

One of the most critical elements in improving the size and strength of muscles is directly related to your muscle fibers and their properties. Your muscle-fiber types dictate your potential for improving your muscular size and strength. And using appropriate repetition ranges that are suited to your muscle fiber type can greatly improve your potential for increasing size and strength.

Before discussing how training your muscle fibers with suitable repetition ranges can maximize your potential, it is important to understand the differences among the various fiber types.

FIBER TYPES

Since the late 1960s, physiological investigations have helped us to understand skeletal muscle function and muscle fiber types. Through biopsy, enzyme histochemistry, and various physiological studies, it is now known that fiber types differ in their contractile speed, myosin ATPase enzyme characteristics, and metabolic enzyme profile. From these differences, three main types of muscle fibers have been documented.

Using appropriate repetition ranges that are suited to your muscle-fiber type can greatly improve your potential for increasing size and strength. (photo by Steve Lipofsky)

There are several ways of classifying muscle-fiber types. One of the more popular ways is to refer to the three muscle-fiber types as red or slow twitch (ST), pink or intermediate FT fibers (FT), and white or fast twitch (FT). Researchers also designate the ST fibers as Type I, intermediate FT fibers as Type IIa, and FT fibers as Type IIb.

Slow-Twitch Muscle Fibers

ST muscle fibers are red—like the dark meat of a turkey—and very thin. The presence of slow-acting myosin ATPases at each myosin head is the cause for its designation as slow twitch. Due to the slow step in the production of adenosine triphosphate (ATP), ST fibers contract much slower than the other muscle-fiber types. The red color comes from many oxygen-carrying molecules called myoglobin, which have a distinct red color. Myoglobin molecules bring oxygen into the muscle cell and increase the rate of its distribution within the muscle cell.

ST fibers have substantial amounts of mitochondria—an energy provider for cellular activity—and an extensive network of blood vessels. This, coupled with a strong presence of myoglobin, makes the ST fibers highly aerobic and heavily dependent upon oxygen. As such, ST fibers are generally referred to as oxidative. Because no fatiguing by-products are formed in the presence of oxygen, ST fibers don't exhaust very easily. In other words, they are extremely fatigue-resistant.

Although ST fibers have great endurance, they do not produce a large amount of force due to their small diameter. ST fibers are thought of as muscle fibers that allow for superior performance in endurance-type activities such as long-distance running and swimming. An individual with a high percentage of ST muscle fibers may happen to have excellent hand–eye coordination, balance, agility, and other important qualities that are required for success in athletics. However, someone with a high percentage of ST fibers would probably be a poor candidate as a running back on a football team, where success is highly dependent upon speed, power, and explosiveness.

Fast-Twitch Muscle Fibers

FT muscle fibers are very pale in color—like the white meat of a turkey. The white color is a direct result of the low amounts of myoglobin. For this reason, FT fibers cannot rely upon oxygen when making ATP. As a result, FT fibers are dubbed anaerobic and depend almost entirely upon the breakdown of glucose as a source of energy. Glucose is a simple sugar that is stored as glycogen in the liver and muscles. Because FT fibers stockpile large amounts of glycogen, they are sometimes referred to as *glycolytic*.

As the name suggests, FT fibers contract very quickly. In fact, the fiber's speed of tension developing and shortening is three to five times faster than that of its ST counterpart. The speed is primarily due to the ability of the myosin ATPases to break down ATP very quickly, causing a fast contraction cycle. The incomplete breakdown of glycogen generates large quantities of a substance known as *lactic acid*. The buildup of lactic acid usually causes the fibers to tire quickly and become inactive. Although FT fibers can only stay active for short periods of time, the size of the fibers allows them to produce large amounts of force when innervated. (FT fibers are almost twice the size of ST fibers.) This force is demonstrated when a sprinter drives out of the starting blocks and accelerates down the track.

Intermediate Fast-Twitch Fibers

Intermediate FT muscle fibers appear pink in color. These muscle fibers possess characteristics of both FT and ST fibers. Like FT fibers, they possess fast-acting myosin ATPases and can contract very quickly. Despite the fast speed of contraction, intermediate FT fibers have large amounts of myoglobin and a large network of blood vessels. This allows the fibers to take advantage of available oxygen for the resynthesis of ATP and permits them to be more resistant to fatigue. They are larger than ST fibers but smaller than FT fibers. Because of their size, they can contract powerfully but not as powerfully as FT fibers. Intermediate FT fibers are found in all muscles and serve an intermediate function during the sequential recruitment of fibers.

PERFORMANCE AND FIBER TYPE

It is important to understand that skeletal muscle fibers can greatly influence athletic performance. Individuals have a combination of all three fiber types within their musculature and the ratio of the fibers predisposes them to certain performance characteristics. Although all muscles contain a mixture of fibers, some contain a greater distribution of one type of fiber depending upon their function. For example, your postural muscles—such as the abdominals and the erector spinae muscles of the lower back—tend to be more ST because they are constantly used to keep you erect. On the other hand, the muscles surrounding your eyes are predominantly FT due to their ability—and necessity—to move and react quickly.

Contrary to popular belief, your amount of FT and ST fibers is not a result of your training. Your fiber-type mixture is a genetic factor that is predetermined before birth and is not subject to change. These inherited ratios of muscle fibers are part of what makes athletics so interesting. They help establish the sports and activities in which a person will be most competitive. An athlete who possesses a large amount of ST muscle fibers probably would not be a good bet to qualify for the Olympics as a high jumper; likewise, an athlete who has predominantly FT fibers should not expect to become a highly competitive cross-country runner.

What about your performance in the weight room and your response from weight training activities? The technical term for an increase in muscle size is *hypertrophy*. Both FT and ST muscle fibers have the potential for muscular growth. However, FT fibers have a much greater capacity for this than do ST fibers. Consequently, individuals who possess a high percentage of FT fibers have a much better chance to make significant improvements in muscular size (everything else being equal). As mentioned earlier, FT fibers have a greater potential than ST fibers for producing force. This means that a person with a predominance of FT fibers has a greater capacity for increasing muscular strength (everything else being equal).

Your muscular endurance is also based upon your inherited fiber-type ratio. A person who possesses a high proportion of ST fibers will have a greater potential to exhibit a higher level of muscular endurance than someone who possesses a high proportion of FT fibers (again, everything else being equal). So, it's not likely that you would see an athlete with a high percentage of FT fibers cycling in the Tour de France.

WHAT'S YOUR FIBER TYPE?

Most individuals probably don't know their proportion of FT fibers to ST fibers. One method that has attempted to determine fiber type is a muscle biopsy. In a muscle biopsy, a needle is inserted into a muscle and a small plug of tissue is removed. The tissue sample is eventually examined under a microscope and a fiber-type percentage is estimated. Though not as popular as they once were, muscle biopsies are sometimes done at sports-medical facilities or universities that conduct research in the biological or exercise sciences. For the majority of the population, however, the procedure isn't accessible or practical. Nor is it without some degree of pain. Also, the accuracy of such testing has been questioned. Indeed, is it possible for a scientist to take an accurate microscopic count of muscle fibers? Moreover, in estimating a ratio of FT to ST muscle fibers, how are the intermediate fibers perceived and are those fibers counted as FT or ST? There are several alternatives to muscle biopsy for estimating your muscle fiber types that are more convenient, more practical, and certainly less painful.

Muscular Endurance Test

One way that you may be able to predict your dominant fiber type is to test your muscular endurance. Compared to a muscle biopsy, this evaluation is somewhat less technical and less scientific, but it is nevertheless reasonably accurate. Because most tests of muscular endurance require a potentially dangerous one-repetition maximum (1-RM), they should be approached with great caution. You should test for a 1-RM with some type of machine (selectorized or plate-loaded) rather than with free weights. For added safety, you should perform the 1-RM—and the muscular endurance test—with a controlled speed of movement. I also suggest that you do the 1-RM with single-joint movements, not multi-joint movements. There are two reasons for this. First, single-joint movements present less risk during the performance of a 1-RM. Second, single-joint movements tend to isolate one muscle, making it easier to evaluate endurance. When using a multi-joint movement, it's impossible to determine the contributions of several different muscles during the muscular endurance test. One final point: You should perform the 1-RM and the endurance test without any supportive gear—such as wrist straps or weightlifting belts—as these items could distort your results.

Suppose that you determined your 1-RM on the leg extension to be 150 pounds. To test your muscular endurance, you can use 80 percent of your 1-RM or, in this case, 120 pounds. If you can do more than about 15 repetitions with 120 pounds before you fatigue, you can assume that your quadriceps are composed primarily of ST fibers—the more repetitions you do, the higher the number of ST fibers. If you fatigue before you do about 10 repetitions, it's likely that your quadriceps have a high percentage of FT fibers—the fewer repetitions you do, the higher the number of FT fibers. If you fatigue somewhere between about 10 and 15 repetitions, you probably have about a 50/50 split of FT and ST fibers. In other words, you don't have a predominant fiber type in your quadriceps. In an endurance test for the muscles of the upper body, doing more than about 12 repetitions with 80 percent of your 1-RM probably means that you have a high percentage of ST fibers; fewer than about 8 repetitions most likely indicates a high number of FT fibers. A normal mix would be indicated if you do about 8–12 repetitions. Because the distribution of fiber types can vary from muscle to muscle, an endurance test would have to be performed for each major muscle group. As such, you might choose to do this test with a leg extension (quadriceps), leg curl (hamstrings), calf raise (calves), bent-arm fly or a pec dec (pectorals), pullover (upper back or lats), lateral raise (middle deltoid), bicep curl (biceps), and tricep extension (triceps).

Other Options

There are several other ways to evaluate your muscle-fiber type. They have more to do with common sense than common science. One way to make a logical estimation of your fiber-type mixture is to examine your performance characteristics. If you seem to do well in sports or activities that require muscular endurance, you probably possess predominantly ST muscle fibers; if you do well in sports or activities that require speed, strength, and/or power, the odds are that you have predominantly FT muscle fibers.

Another way to evaluate your muscle-fiber type is by inspecting your general physical appearance. Recall that FT muscle fibers have a greater capacity for hypertrophy than do ST muscles fibers. Consequently, if you have a well-developed physique you probably have predominantly FT muscle fibers; on the other hand, if you have slight muscular development it's likely that you have a higher percentage of ST muscle fibers (assuming, of course, that the low muscle development isn't a result of inactivity).

REPETITION RANGES

Once you have a general idea of your muscle-fiber type, you can customize your repetition ranges to achieve your body's natural potential. Many highly successful bodybuilders have a predominant amount of FT muscle fibers. This means that they exhaust their muscles with a relatively low number of repetitions—that is, within a short period of time—and this was believed to be the only way to train everyone interested in improving his or her strength. Magazines and books are filled with workouts that promote this belief. For years, many individuals with a high percentage of ST muscle fibers have been strength training with relatively low repetition ranges—such as 6–8—without experiencing much success.

A study by Dons and his colleagues (1979) showed that a group who trained at 50 percent of their 1-RM increased their muscular endurance and a group who trained at 80 percent of their 1-RM made significant increases in their muscular size and strength. Understand, this is not necessarily considered to be endurance training because individuals with a large number of ST fibers are already predisposed to higher levels of muscular endurance. The point is that those who have predominantly ST muscle fibers can use a relatively high percentage of their 1-RM and per-

form a large number of repetitions and make significant
gains in strength. (It should
be noted that in the previously mentioned study, the
group who trained with 80
percent of their 1-RM had
an increase in muscular
strength of 42.3 percent
while the group who trained
with 50 percent of their 1-RM
not only had an improve-
ment in muscular endurance
but also had an impressive
improvement in muscular
strength of 23.9 percent.)

Counting repetitions
has been a mainstay of
strength training for
decades. However, the time
that the muscles are loaded
within a set is actually more

Performing higher
or lower repeti-
tions will only help
to improve your
response to
strength training
based upon your
already established
predominant
muscle-fiber type.

(photo by Matt Brzycki)

important than the number of repetitions. You must exercise your muscles for a
certain amount of time at a high level of intensity to maximize increases in their
size and strength. The optimal time frames for people with an average mix of fiber
types are about 90–120 seconds for the hips/gluteals, 60–90 seconds for the legs,
and 40–70 seconds for the upper torso. (The muscles of the lower body need to
be trained longer because of their greater size and work capacity.) Someone who
has a high percentage of ST fibers should train for a slightly longer duration. For
instance, more appropriate time frames might be about 120–180 seconds for the
hips/gluteals, 90–120 for the legs, and 60–90 for the upper torso. Someone who
has a high percentage of FT fibers should exercise for a slightly shorter duration.
For example, better-suited time frames might be about 60–90 seconds for the
hips/gluteals, 50–70 seconds for the legs, and 40–50 seconds for the upper torso.

In a study by Westcott (1987), sprinters trained with low repetitions, mid-
dle-distance runners with medium repetitions, and long-distance runners with
high repetitions. The study revealed excellent and equal strength gains in all
three groups. (Remember that successful sprinters likely inherit a high percentage of FT fibers and successful distance runners likely inherit a high percentage
of ST fibers.)

It is usually not practical to perform sets for a precise period of time.
Generally, you would need access to a metronome or someone to monitor you

with a stopwatch. Being that it is much easier to count repetitions, you can use these optimal time frames to formulate your individualized repetition ranges.

When training at a higher intensity, each repetition you perform should be around 6 seconds in length: about 2 seconds when raising the weight, and about 4 seconds when lowering it. If you were to divide 6 seconds into the time frames that were previously suggested you would obtain roughly the following repetition ranges:

- Normal fiber-type mix: 15–20 repetitions for the hips/gluteals, 10–15 for the legs, and 6–12 for the upper torso.
- ST dominant: 20–30 repetitions for hips/gluteals, 15–20 for the legs, and 10–15 for the upper torso.
- FT dominant: 10–15 repetitions for the hips/gluteals, 8–12 for the legs, and 6–8 for the upper torso.

Remember, these repetition ranges are based upon 6-second repetitions. Furthermore, they are not set in stone. Due to the diversity of genetics, each individual has a unique blend of muscle fibers. A person with an exceptionally high percentage of either FT or ST fibers may need even shorter or longer repetition ranges to maximize the response.

One final note about muscle-fiber types: There is no evidence or research pertaining to humans that hyperplasia—that is, an increase in the number of muscle fibers—is possible. Nor does the conversion of muscle fibers from one type to another appear to be possible. Performing higher or lower repetitions will only help to improve your response to strength training based upon your already established predominant muscle-fiber type.

REFERENCES

Brzycki, M. 1997. *A practical approach to strength training.* 3rd ed. Indianapolis, IN: Masters Press.

———. 1998. Fiber types and repetition ranges. *Wrestling USA* 3 (10): 9–10, 12.

DeLorme, T. L. 1945. Restoration of muscle power by heavy resistance exercise. *Journal of Bone and Joint Surgery* 27: 645–667.

Dons B., K. Bollerup, F. Bonde-Petersen, and S. Hancke. 1979. The effect of weight-lifting exercise related to muscle fiber composition and muscle cross-sectional area in humans. *European Journal of Applied Physiology* 40: 95–106.

Enoka, R. M. 1988. *Neuromechanical basis of kinesiology.* Champaign, IL: Human Kinetics.

McArdle, W. D., F. I. Katch, and V. L. Katch. 1996. *Exercise physiology: Energy, nutrition and human performance.* 4th ed. Philadelphia, PA: Lea & Febiger.

Westcott, W. L. 1987. Individualized strength training for girl high school runners. *Scholastic Coach* 57 (December): 71–72.

This chapter is dedicated to my parents for teaching me the value of hard work.

16

Free Weights Versus Machines

Sam Gannelli
Strength and Conditioning Coordinator
San Diego Padres Baseball Club
San Diego, California

In the ongoing debate over training tools, much has been written and said about the superiority of free weights over machines and vice versa. It's your decision as to whether one is superior to the other. There are, however, some issues and misconceptions about both modalities that you must understand.

SAFETY

The first thing to consider is how safe the piece of equipment is for you or your athletes. What good are machines or free weights if someone gets injured while using them? Should a long-legged 32-year-old athlete with a history of low-back and knee problems exercise his hips and legs by performing barbell squats? Or would this particular individual be better off using a seated leg press machine, which reduces the stress in his lower back and knees?

We must accept the fact that each person is different. Some people believe that the only way to get bigger and stronger hips and legs is to do barbell squats. Others—myself included—disagree. Please realize that there is more than one way to do almost anything. Your hips and legs can get bigger and stronger using a machine, free weights, manual resistance, or running stadium steps for an hour—as long as you give an all-out intense effort every single time you train—*and* as long as the workload is progressive. Push your car around the block three times a week and see if your hips and legs don't get bigger and stronger.

Never lose sight of the fact that the number-one reason why athletes should lift weights is to prevent injury. It would be contradictory, therefore, to have your athletes use equipment—or to do an exercise—that may lead to immediate injury or predispose them to future injury. It is important to examine each athlete's medical history and determine the safest way to train the desired muscle group. Just because the facility you're in at the time doesn't have your favorite piece of equipment, don't assume you are unable to train effectively. Understand that there is always a safe way to train no matter where you are. Maybe it's not what you would prefer to use but if it's the only safe alternative available, then it's a productive training tool.

Sometimes you or your athletes must train alone. When this is the case, it is easier—and often safer—to use machines. It is more difficult to train by yourself with free weights since certain movements require a spotter as a safeguard against injury. This is especially true if the person is performing each set to momentary muscle fatigue. When training alone, use machines; you are less likely to get injured when you reach the point of muscle fatigue—when you try but are unable to complete another repetition.

COST

Unfortunately, not everyone has an unlimited budget. If you are selecting equipment for a weight room, you have to take into account not only what will fit into the available space but also what you can afford. In general, free weights are less expensive than most machines. However, free weights can become costly if you purchase other amenities such as racks, dumbbell sets, heavy-duty rubber flooring, and so on. Selectorized machines already have weight stacks. When purchasing plate-loaded machines, however, one must take into consideration the added cost of purchasing weight plates as well as the machine itself.

Whatever you can afford or have access to—be it a two-dollar towel for manual-resistance exercises or a $2,000 piece of equipment—will be just fine as long as you are working out intensely, consistently, and progressively. At the University at Buffalo, our weight room was 85 percent free weights and our players got stronger; here in San Diego, our weight room is 85 percent machines and our players get stronger. Don't fall into the trap of thinking it's the equipment that you are using that determines productive results. Rather, it's how you use the equipment.

Some strength and fitness professionals feel that there is a danger of a person accidentally dropping a weight onto his or her foot while loading the machine. So they would rather avoid plate-loaded machines altogether. Others believe that by having their weightrooms equipped entirely with selectorized machines, individuals will be more likely to come in and work out. Still others feel that a greater level of muscle fatigue can be achieved with a machine rather than a comparable free-weight exercise—such as the leg press versus the barbell squat—because a machine can vary the resistance to match the changes in your biomechanical leverage while a barbell cannot.

Each person is different. You should use equipment because it is what works best for you, not because someone else told you to. If you don't like machines, don't use them; if you don't like free weights, don't use them. It's that simple. Choosing equipment need not be a scientific or complicated process. Remember this: If you're not training on a regular basis with a progressive overload and giving an all-out effort during each workout, it really doesn't matter what you're using because you won't obtain optimal results.

VARIETY

Whether you are training with weights for a major competition such as the World Series or you simply want to look and feel better, you should try to incorporate some variety in your program. In this case, variety means changing the training tool. By using the same piece of equipment every single workout, it is more likely that you will hit a plateau. Incorporating both free weights and machines into your training routine will help keep your workouts from getting monotonous. Instead of performing your bicep curls with dumbbells every session, switch to a seated bicep curl machine one workout and a barbell the next.

MISCONCEPTIONS

Unfortunately, there are several misconceptions about free weights and machines. First, muscles don't have eyes. So, the notion—promoted by many—that free weights are used to get bigger and stronger while machines are used for toning defies logic. When you exercise, your body has no idea what the source of the resistance is on the muscles. Your muscles simply know that they have to get stronger to adapt to the workload being placed on them. You must force your body to change. Your body does not adapt simply because you worked out on the latest and greatest machine on the market. This misconception is a result of the fact that when people started lifting weights years ago, the only tool available was free weights. Again, there is more than one way to do just about anything. A highly conditioned athlete can do a manual-resistance workout with no equipment other than a towel and end up crawling for the door afterward *if* he or she gives an all-out effort on every single repetition of each exercise. Effort, not equipment, is the key to getting stronger.

Certain exercises such as the power clean are not specific to any sport and, therefore, will not automatically make you a better athlete—unless, of course, you are a competitive weightlifter. In a weight-room setting, *sport specificity* is a term dreamed up by someone unable to understand the real purpose of lifting

There is nothing you can do in the weight room—be it with barbells, dumbbells, or machines—that will transfer directly to the athletic arena regardless of the sport. (photo by Matt Brzycki)

weights. Lifting weights is done to prevent injury by strengthening the muscles, ligaments, and tendons. There is nothing that you can do in the weight room—be it with barbells, dumbbells, or machines—that will transfer directly to the athletic arena regardless of the sport. You improve on the athletic field by repetitively practicing sport-specific movements that are actually done in competition. Free weights and machines are tools to get your muscles, ligaments, and tendons as strong as possible. Great athletes are not successful because they use free weights or because they use machines. They are successful because of what they accomplish on the field of competition.

THE RIGHT CHOICE

Productive workouts are all about effort. You only get out of it what you put into it. You may have access to the greatest workout facility in the world with state-of-the-art machines, free weights, or whatever equipment makes you happy. But if you are not training as hard as you can and on a consistent basis, then that's what the problem is—it has nothing to do with the equipment.

Remember that both free weights and machines are merely training tools. A knowledgeable strength and fitness professional still has to develop and implement the program. An athlete still has to perform the exercises. Realize that safety should be the first and foremost concern. Never lose sight of why you work out: to reduce your risk of injury. As long as you are comfortable with the training tool you are using—be it free weights, machines, or both—then it is the right choice for you.

17

Tools of the Trade

Tony Alexander, C.M.E.S.
WorkSTEPS® Coordinator
Physical Therapy Sports Rehab
The Club at Woodbridge
Woodbridge, New Jersey

A variety of tools and ideas can be used to make a workout routine more successful. There are endless items that can fall into this category, but the ones I deal with in this chapter are those that are readily accessible and easily attainable by anyone.

THE WORKOUT CARD

A very useful, often overlooked tool is the workout card. Some of the reasons given for not using a card are "it's too cumbersome" and the ever-popular "I keep all of that information in my head." Carrying around a clipboard, workout card, and pencil while training can be a bit cumbersome but when the card is used correctly, it can be extremely worthwhile in a number of different ways. First, it provides you with up-to-the-minute data on the progress you are making. It also provides you with a series of short-term goals that can enable you to achieve the physical perfection you seek. Additionally, a card may act as your motivator when working without a training partner. Whatever your goal is—whether it be weight loss, weight gain, or rehabilitation of an injured body part—a workout card is an invaluable tool.

One of the things that you should keep track of is your body weight. You should only weigh yourself once per week (at the same time of day). This is because your body weight may fluctuate naturally from day to day as a result of water retention. You should also record the date of your workout along with several performance measures including the amount of weight that you lifted in each exercise, the number of repetitions that you completed in each exercise (without assistance and in good form), and the order in which you performed the exercises.

Your cardiovascular or cardio performances should also be documented. One component to record is your level of intensity. Most cardio machines provide some type of readout of your intensity level whether it be oxygen consumption, metabolic equivalent (MET) level, or caloric expenditure. However, some cardio activities—such as running or cycling outdoors—are more difficult to monitor in terms of intensity. You should also chart the distance that you traveled (if that information is provided or known), the amount of time it took to complete that distance, and the number of calories you used (which will vary from machine to machine and/or from exercise to exercise). Progression in cardio activities may be achieved by completing the same distance in a shorter amount of time; covering a greater distance in the same amount of time; or completing a greater distance in a shorter amount of time.

SADDLE PLATES AND SMALL-INCREMENT PLATES

A saddle plate is a small portable weight that can be placed atop the weight stack of a selectorized machine. The most common types of saddle plates in weight rooms are the half plates that accompany many Cybex® selectorized machines. On most Cybex® machines, each plate of the weight stack is 12.5 pounds (the half plates weigh 6.25 pounds). Nautilus® saddle plates are also common. A typical plate on a Nautilus® selectorized machine weighs 10 pounds. Saddle plates for this equipment come in three different pound increments: 2.5, 5, and 7.5. Unfortunately, the company no longer manufactures 1.25-pound saddle plates. Some selectorized machines have a unique compound weight stack that enables you to make small progressions in 1-, 2-, or 2.5-pound increments without using saddle plates. If saddle plates aren't available, you can take a lighter weight plate and pin it to the weight stack.

Obviously, lighter weight plates that are 1.25, 2.5, and 5 pounds can be loaded on barbells and plate-loaded machines. If lighter plates aren't available, however, some known weight can be attached to the bar—for example, a small ankle weight.

Magnetic weights of 1.25 and 2.5 pounds are also available. These can be attached to free weights or to the weight stacks of selectorized machines. While these magnetic weights can be somewhat expensive, they are well worth the cost.

Whichever option you choose, any one of these tools can be useful in realizing your goals. More often than not, these tools are not used to their fullest potential. Some people may ask, "Why are you using those baby weights?" The truth of the matter is that if you are training at a higher intensity level—meaning that you are attempting to reach momentary muscle fatigue—*any* increase in weight will make the exercise more challenging in a subsequent workout. However, a smaller increase provides you with a smoother and more attainable means of systematic progression. It also minimizes the likelihood of reaching a plateau—which sometimes results from making a larger increase of five pounds or more.

Here is an example of how progression is attained. Suppose that you successfully performed 12 repetitions in a set of bicep curls, with 12 being the maximum number of repetitions that you want to attain before increasing the weight. The next time you do this exercise in the same sequence, you should add 1.25 or 2.5 pounds to the machine or barbell and attempt to perform as many repetitions as possible. Should you fall short of your 12-repetition goal, repeat the same weight during your next exercise sessions until you reach your target of 12. It is this subtle increase that will give you the ability to achieve your fullest physical potential and to avoid the pitfalls of reaching a plateau.

WRIST STRAPS

Wrist straps are usually made out of a nylon-and-cotton blend. They are about 12–14 inches long and about 1 inch wide. Wrist straps are used to assist in holding onto a bar or a dumbbell when performing multi-joint pulling movements for the upper torso such as chin-ups, lat pulldowns, seated rows, bent-over rows, and upright rows. Wrist straps are also helpful during deadlifts and shoulder shrugs.

Straps should not be used as a replacement for doing various exercises to strengthen the forearms, wrists, hands, and fingers—such as wrist flexion/extension, pronation/supination, and pinch gripping. However, straps are certainly beneficial in exercises that are meant to address larger muscle groups. Here's why: Your body has many different muscles, some large and some small. In multi-joint pulling movements, the larger muscles of the upper back—namely the latissimus dorsi or, simply, the lats—cannot be properly fatigued because of the smaller muscles used in gripping. These smaller muscles will fatigue much sooner than the larger muscles. Utilization of wrist straps will assist the gripping muscles, thereby enabling you to fatigue your upper-back muscles. One particular order of exercises vividly demonstrates this point. In a sequence that emphasizes the biceps, a set of curls is performed to muscle fatigue. This is followed quickly by a set of chin-ups. You can imagine the tremendous demands that are placed upon the gripping muscles during the chinning movement. Hence, the straps allow the lifter to work the desired areas by preventing the smaller muscles from fatiguing too quickly. There are only a few other instances where wrist straps may be warranted; however, these rare cases merely serve as positive arguments for the use of this particular tool.

THE TRAP BAR

The trap bar is a unique and valuable training tool in that it can be used for several productive exercises. If you are not familiar with this piece of equipment, it is a bar with a diamond-shaped opening and handles positioned on both sides of the opening that run parallel to each other. Like other bars, plates are loaded on the ends as the resistance.

As the name suggests, one of the exercises that can be performed with a trap bar is a shoulder shrug, which involves the trapezius muscle. To assume the starting position for this exercise, step inside the diamond-shaped opening, spread your feet about shoulder-width apart, squat down, grasp the handles, and stand up. To do this movement, keep your arms straight, raise your shoulders as high as possible toward your ears, pause briefly in this position, and then lower the weight slowly to the starting position.

Another productive exercise that can be done with a trap bar is a hack squat or deadlift, which addresses the hips, quadriceps, hamstrings, and lower back. To assume the starting position, step inside the diamond-shaped opening, spread your feet slightly wider than shoulder-width apart, squat down, and grab the han-

As the name suggests, one of the exercises that can be performed with a trap bar is a shoulder shrug, which involves the trapezius muscle.

(photo by Kim Piche)

dles. Your hips should be low, your chest out, and your back flat—that is, not rounded. To do this exercise, simply stand up, pause briefly without locking your knees and then return the weight slowly to the starting position. Two key points: First, lift the weight with a combined effort of your hips, legs, and lower back. Second, don't bounce the weight off the floor between repetitions.

Though it is not often done with a trap bar, a final exercise that can be performed is an overhead press, which works the anterior deltoid and the triceps. In assuming the starting position, it is helpful to use a trap bar rack that allows the lifter to grasp the bar at shoulder height while in the seated position. Otherwise, two spotters can hand the lifter the bar. To do this movement, simply press the bar directly overhead, pause briefly (without locking the elbows), and then lower the weight back to the starting position.

With proper instruction, the trap bar is a uniquely versatile and effective training tool.

THE MENTAL CONCEPT

In training, the so-called mind game is an often overlooked tool. Preparing yourself mentally to perform well on any particular activity is a key to your success. Your mind has a tremendous effect upon your overall performance. You need to pay attention to several things. First of all, it is important to focus on simply doing the workout. Many people have a very difficult time motivating themselves to just get going. Setting reasonable goals is crucial. One way to crush yourself mentally is to set goals that are too high. Set attainable goals. Push yourself during every exercise that you have to perform in a particular workout session. Here's where the workout card comes into play. If you reached your goal in the previous workout, try not to settle for repeating the same performance. Your primary goal is to do better than your previous workout. If you have given it your best effort and do not reach your goal, don't give up; simply try to attain it the next time.

Under the circumstances, you are going to be the best judge of your efforts. Personal trainers can be very good at keeping your goals and enthusiasm at their optimal levels. If a personal trainer is not an option for you, the next best thing is to find a reliable and motivated workout partner.

Other components that will require your mental focus during each set are the speed of movement, the range of motion, and—in the event a training partner is not available—counting the actual number of repetitions you complete.

Counting repetitions during an exercise can be a little nerve-racking. For example, suppose that you have just completed 6 repetitions and your muscles are burning, yet your goal is to get to 12. How do you continue to perform the exercise? Some people may count down from 12 to trick themselves into working through the pain; others may skip every other number as a distraction. As long as you complete the task, any way will do.

It is important to breathe properly while exercising. Exhale when raising the weight and inhale when lowering it. (photo by Matt Brzycki)

Breathing while doing the exercises is yet another very important aspect of the mind game. At the beginning of most exercises, it is usually not difficult to breathe. As your intensity of effort increases, however, your breathing will become more labored. It is at this point that you really need to focus upon what you're doing. What happens during this time is that while you're exerting effort to lift the weight, your heart is rushing oxygen-laden blood to the involved muscles. If you restrict your oxygen intake during this time by holding your breath, your heart will receive signals from the brain to pump more blood and will be under tremendous stress—which, in a worst-case scenario, could result in a loss of consciousness. It is very important to breathe properly while exercising. Proper breathing means that during the positive portion of the movement—when exerting force to raise the weight—you exhale to relieve the buildup of internal pressure. Then during the negative portion of the movement—when lowering the weight—you inhale to obtain oxygen. This is especially critical as the exercise becomes increasingly difficult to perform, thus resulting in the need and demand for greater oxygen. Remember, breathe in a relaxed manner until the need for more oxygen becomes apparent. Then, exhale during the exertion phase of the exercise.

VARIETY

A final tool to consider is variety, which may be necessary to keep yourself motivated. Over time, routines get stale. In fact, boredom is a major reason why people drop out of their workout regimens. Periodically, you should change your exercises to work the muscle groups in different ways. When you do make a change in your exercises, it is important to stay with the change for a little while to chart some type of progress. Changing your routine too often can result in confusing and inaccurate data, which could ultimately lead to a loss of motivation.

I want to thank Dr. Steve McCaw, associate professor at Illinois State University, for his editing of this chapter. Steve served as the chair for my master's thesis and his assistance in both academic and outside interests has paved the way for many of my achievements.

18

Avoiding Injury to the Lower Back

Jeff Friday, M.S.
Strength and Conditioning Coach
Baltimore Ravens
Baltimore, Maryland

The purpose of any strength training program for athletes is twofold: (1) to reduce the risk of athletic-related injury and (2) to enhance the ability to play the sport (Peterson 1982). Unfortunately, the first goal often is not met, which leads to increased potential for injury in the weight room. Instead of protecting the athlete, the implementation of strength training programs often causes injuries, especially to the lower back. The purpose of this chapter is to identify specific hazards in the weight room so you can minimize or eliminate unnecessary risk to the lower back. The hazards include lifting a maximum amount of weight for one repetition, doing exercises at a fast speed of movement, and performing exercises that are potentially dangerous to the lower back.

A BRIEF HISTORY

Before discussing specific dangers, a quick history of strength training for athletes is in order. The mid-nineteenth century saw the appearance and rise of professional strongmen (Riley 1979). Exhibitions of strength later evolved into two main types of weightlifting competitions: Olympic-style weightlifting and powerlifting. Organizations were created to regulate and govern the various feats of strength at competitions. The first national championship in Olympic-style weightlifting took place in 1928; powerlifting was not organized on a national level until 1965. Nowadays, Olympic-style weightlifting includes the snatch and the clean and jerk; powerlifting involves the squat, bench press, and deadlift (Garhammer 1984). The purpose of both sports is to lift a maximum amount of weight one time or, in other words, to perform a one-repetition maximum (1-RM). Though not a contest of strength, a related sport is bodybuilding, which became popular during the 1970s. The goal of bodybuilding is to build muscle mass and decrease body fat while developing body symmetry.

The term *weightlifting* should not be confused with weight training. *Weight training* (used interchangeably with *strength training*) is an all-encompassing term. Weight training is a conditioning technique using various modalities—such as free weights or machines—to increase muscular strength for sports participation or fitness enhancement. Athletes' main interest is in their particular sport; however, weight training becomes a focus during certain periods of the year. The hazards occur when the aforementioned competitive lifting philosophies are incorporated into weight training programs.

Regardless of whether an athlete is weightlifting or weight training, for a muscle to get stronger, the Overload Principle must be followed (Lamb 1984). This principle states that the training program should provide an overload (i.e., an appropriate stress) to the musculature. Not only must an overload be supplied but the loads must also be progressively increased to keep pace with new advances in strength. The overload must be great enough for an adaptive response by the muscle. In general, this can be safely accomplished by performing no fewer than about six repetitions of an exercise. By systematically increasing the weight or repetitions an athlete performs from workout to workout, muscle growth will occur and the athlete will get stronger.

During the 1960s, strength training for athletes became an accepted practice. Lacking knowledge of how to implement a strength training program, sport coaches turned to those who had experience in strength training: competitive weightlifters and bodybuilders (Riley 1979). The contest lifts thus became common strength training exercises and were used in the conditioning programs of sports other than competitive weightlifting. Training programs not only contained the competitive exercises themselves but also subdivisions or parts of the complete lifts (e.g., power cleans and push jerks), as well as assistance or supplemental exercises directed at improving the competitive lifts. Besides including the same exercises, the resistance and repetition schemes of competitive lifting were also incorporated. The focal point of the training programs was to gain strength by increasing the athletes' 1-RMs on the competitive or subdivision lifts, and programs included periodic 1-RM testing of the athletes to measure their strength gains.

Programs incorporating some or all of the competitive lifting philosophies are prevalent in the strength and conditioning programs of many high school, college, and professional teams today (Dunn et al. 1983; Stiggins 1992; Ebben and Blackard 1997; Goss 1998). Although athletes do have success with such programs and can get stronger, the hand-me-down information does not necessarily meet the goals of every athlete (Riley 1979).

Many programs require athletes to spend hours and hours in the weight room carrying out the training protocol. Athletes devote much of their time to practicing the skill of lifting with heavy loads; for example, using the pyramid system adopted from competitive lifting. This system incorporates the performance of a set of 3–5 repetitions with a light resistance and adding weight to the bar for each succeeding set of 3–5 repetitions until only one repetition can be performed (Fleck and Kraemer 1987). There are other factors that reveal why the needs of the athlete often are not met. Requiring the lifter to perform potentially dangerous exercises with near maximum weights on selected exercises is an invitation to injury. These are time and risk factors that competitive weightlifters assume as part of their sport. Athletes who are not competitive lifters, however, should not have to spend long hours in the weight room or perform exercises that have a high risk of injury.

RELEVANT STUDIES

A review of the literature concerning competitive lifting will illuminate the risks of implementing these lifting philosophies into strength training programs for athletes other than competitive weightlifters. In a study of adolescent powerlifters by Brown and Kimball (1983), the subjects were relatively inexperienced with about 17 months of lifting background. The researchers found powerlifting potentially injurious to the lower back, knees, shoulders, and elbows. Of the 98 injuries reported, 50 percent occurred in the low-back region.

Experienced or elite powerlifters suffer from low-back injuries as well. Quinney and colleagues (1997) found that the low-back and shoulder regions had the highest occurrence and level of pain associated with powerlifting.

The potential for injury is not limited to the short term. The effects of a competitive weightlifting program can remain with an athlete for life. Granhed and Morelli (1988) reported that 46 percent of retired heavyweight lifters aged 40–61 years had residual physical problems that were caused by their former athletic activities. The areas with the highest frequency of problems were the lower back, knees, and shoulders. Although the incidence of low-back pain did not differ from a control group, a significant decrease in disc height was found among the lifters.

In a study of weight training injuries in secondary school football players, Risser, Risser, and Preston (1990) found that the most common site of injuries was the lower back. All of the athletes who injured their lower backs were performing one or more of the following lifts: the power clean, clean and jerk, squat, and deadlift. The authors pointed out that the greater use of these exercises may explain the larger proportion of low-back injuries in high school athletes (60 percent of injuries) compared with junior high school athletes (14.3 percent).

Despite studies quantifying competitive lifting injuries, a weight training program may be a contributing cause of chronic injuries observed in sports. The majority of weight training-related injuries appear gradually as a cumulative trauma over time; therefore athletes are unable to determine the exact point when the symptoms began. The injury may appear in an athletic event and be diagnosed as an athletically related injury. Thus, it is hard to decipher whether it was the sport or the training program that caused an injury to an athlete.

WHY THE LOWER BACK?

The spinal column is the vertical supporting structure linking the upper and lower body. Because of this role, it is exposed to a great deal of stress. The spinal column itself is unstable and relies on support from surrounding musculature and ligaments. The abdominals (rectus and transverse) and obliques (external and internal) make up the anterior muscle groups while the erector spinae group is located posterior to the spine. Ligaments provide flexibility and strength along the length of the spinal column.

The lumbar spinal column is composed of five individual bony segments or vertebrae (the singular form is vertebra). (See Figure 18.1.) The lumbar vertebrae are relatively large in size compared to the rest of the spinal vertebrae. The increased size reflects the strength of the vertebrae. The joints between the vertebrae contain intervertebral discs, which consist of a fibrous ring and a jellylike nucleus that is 70–90 percent water. Because of the high water content, the pressure within the disc is spread evenly on all sides. The discs are designed to accommodate movement, weight bearing, and shock by being strong yet deformable (Gargan and Fairbank 1996).

Most low-back injuries occur between the fifth lumbar and the first sacral (L5–S1) vertebrae (Alexander 1985). The L5–S1 region is the axis of movement for flexion and extension of the spine. The curvature of the spine in this area makes it

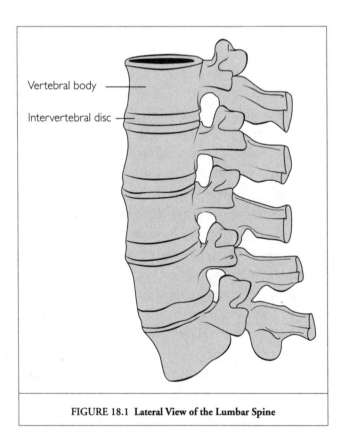

Vertebral body

Intervertebral disc

FIGURE 18.1 **Lateral View of the Lumbar Spine**

susceptible to both compressive and shearing forces. (Compressive forces run perpendicular to the intervertebral discs and press the spine together; shearing forces run horizontal to the intervertebral discs.) These forces can be large in magnitude, and injuries to the intervertebral discs, ligaments, and muscle can result from the great amount of stress.

The mechanical strength of the intervertebral discs during a vertical load is adequate; it is not inferior to the strength of the adjoining vertebra (Zatsiorsky 1995). However, once the upper half of the body leans forward (i.e., the trunk angle is that of flexion), there is considerable shear stress placed on the discs. The intervertebral joints (including the discs) are best able to withstand compression, not shear. An upper-body lean has a tendency to occur in exercises where the weight is placed either directly on the shoulders or indirectly through the arms. With an upper-body forward lean, the erector spinae muscle group attempts to stabilize the trunk against the load, causing flexion. Because of the mechanics of the trunk, the counterbalancing force by the muscles often exceeds the weight being lifted. This imposes a large stress on the intervertebral discs.

A common spinal injury in the lumbar area that results from weightlifting is called *spondylolysis*. Spondylolysis is a fracture of the lumbar vertebrae—most commonly the fifth lumbar vertebra—resulting from repetitive high loads imposed on the spine. Spondylolisthesis—which commonly accompanies spondylolysis—is a forward slippage of one vertebra over another. Spondylolisthesis typically occurs between the fifth lumbar vertebra and the sacrum.

As is the case with any exercise where the athlete is lifting a weight from the floor or supporting a weight on the shoulders, not only is a forward-lean position dangerous but a rounded back while in a bent-knee position increases the chance of spinal injury. The rounded-back position allows uneven pressure from both compression and shear forces acting on the intervertebral discs. The large amount of force thus falls on a small unit of disc surface and may result in an injury.

Weightlifting exercises such as the clean and jerk, snatch, squat, and deadlift are potentially dangerous to an athlete because of the heavy loads combined with the tendency to use a forward-lean position, thereby creating high compressive and shear forces in the lumbar region of the lower back.

TECHNIQUE FACTORS

Technique is an important element when performing any lift. Deviation from the correct movement pattern may cause undue stress on the spinal discs, ligaments, and musculature resulting in injury. Even if technique is efficient, inherent risks in the execution of the exercises themselves may result in an injury.

Weightlifting: The Clean and Jerk and the Snatch

The clean and jerk is a movement consisting of two main phases. In the clean phase, the athlete pulls the bar from the floor to the shoulders; the jerk phase consists of moving the weight from the shoulders to an overhead position. The snatch involves pulling the bar from the floor to an overhead position in one motion. Subdivisions of these lifts occur in partial movements such as the power clean and push press.

Success in the clean and jerk and the snatch is dependent upon proper technique. It is so important that beginning competitive lifters spend two-thirds of their training time on technique (Bates 1976). To be successful at weightlifting, the weight must be moved with great speed. Even if technique is efficient, the high speed combined with the heavy load makes these lifts potentially dangerous to the lower back.

When performing weightlifting movements, compressive and shear forces are typically highest early in the lifts—specifically when the lift is one-fifth of the way through. This is usually the point where the athlete is accelerating the bar from the floor and the trunk angle is flexed (Hall 1985). Increases in compressive and shear forces in the lumbar area are observed when the lifting speed is increased (Hall 1985; Buseck et al. 1988).

Another area of concern when performing the clean and jerk or snatch is the second part of the pull off the floor, or what is typically referred to as the *scoop*. This is the point where the bar has been lifted from the floor to an area between the midthighs and crotch. Prior to this point, the lower back has been in a fixed inclined position (about 30° for the snatch and 45° for the clean) from the ground and the lifting has been done with the hips and legs. During the scoop sequence, the hips move forward and down. During the next and final part of the pull, the lifter extends the body to the maximum, bringing the hips forward and up while rotating the shoulders backward and up (Baker). Forward movement of the hips throws the lower back into a hyperextended position creating enormous shearing stresses on the lumbar spine (Jesse 1977). Ballistic hyperextension movements can also lead to tissue damage. The lower back is again hyperextended at the completion of the lift when the lifter holds the weight in the overhead position.

Powerlifting: The Deadlift and Squat

The deadlift exercise involves raising the barbell from the floor to a standing position by straightening the knees and spine. Studies of skilled and unskilled lifters competing in championship meets have identified a difference in technique (Brown and Kaveh 1985).

During the lift-off in the deadlift, the skilled lifter assumes a less-flexed trunk position. The more-flexed trunk position of unskilled lifters leaves them more susceptible to compressive and shearing forces in their lumbar area. Unskilled lifters also take less time than skilled lifters from the point of lift-off to passing the knees. The increased speed may add to the compressive and shear forces acting on the lumbar region. (Many athletes participating in other sports who incorporate these exercises in a weight training program would be considered novice or intermediate subjects, possibly amplifying the technique differences.)

The squat involves holding a weighted bar behind the neck on the shoulders and squatting down to a point where the thighs are parallel to the ground, then returning to the standing position. During the lowering (or descent) phase of the movement, a less-skilled lifter maintains a higher downward bar velocity and greater trunk flexion than a skilled lifter (McLaughlin, Dillman, and Lardner 1977). To counteract the increased downward speed of the bar, the unskilled lifter exhibits a bounce in the final position of the lowering phase. The bounce actually occurs between the lowering phase and the raising (or ascent) phase of the lift. Bouncing out of the bottom position increases the shear forces across the lumbar discs (Fortin 1996).

In the bottom position of the squat, the less-skilled lifter moves the hips and bar horizontally backward more than the higher skilled lifter (McLaughlin, Dillman, and Lardner 1977). In competition, this position is usually where the top level of the thighs is below parallel with the platform. During the raising phase of the lift, the unskilled lifters—who are already at a greater trunk flexion than the higher skilled—lean forward even more than during the descent phase. Both the increased speeds of the bar and the greater trunk lean occurring in this lift increase compressive and shear forces in the lumbar area. (See Figure 18.2.)

These studies reiterate that when performing the deadlift and squat with heavy loads for low repetitions, any variation in technique or lifting speed may result in undue stress to the musculature and connective tissue, thereby increasing the opportunity for injury.

RECOMMENDATIONS

1. *Strengthen the musculature surrounding the spine.* Because the muscles around the spinal column provide support and compensate for high forces, it is important to strengthen the abdominals, obliques, and erector spinae. Exercises should be selected that involve the greatest possible range of motion (ROM) for these muscles.

The lumbar muscles are responsible for two major functions: to help maintain an upright position and to help control the descent of the vertebral column in forward flexion and raise it back to normal (Twomey, Taylor, and Flynn 1995). These functions should be the focus of any strength training exercises for the lumbar muscles. Many lifting exercises are carried out with the lower back in a fixed position, thus strengthening the musculature isometrically. However, the lower back should be strengthened through a full ROM. To strengthen the lower back (erector spinae) properly, Pollock and his associates (1989) believe

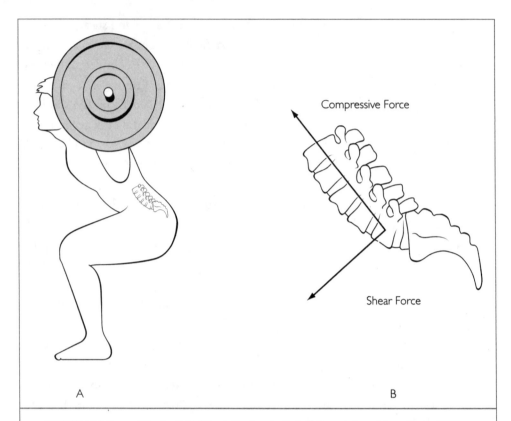

FIGURE 18.2 **Forces Affecting Spinal Loads During the Barbell Squat (adapted from Fortin 1996).** "A" depicts the angle of the lumbar and sacral spine in the forward-lean position; "B" shows how compressive forces (which run perpendicular) and shearing forces (which run horizontal to the intervertebral disks) concentrate on the L5-S1 vertebrae.

that the pelvis must be stabilized to avoid involvement of the hamstring and gluteal muscle groups, which otherwise perform most of the movement.

2. *Avoid maximum single repetitions.* Only competitive lifters should attempt a 1-RM. A 1-RM is a method to measure strength, but successful performance of a 1-RM is an acquired skill and takes much practice to develop the correct neurological firing pattern of the muscles. Athletes have no reason to demonstrate strength in this way. Training in this fashion may also invite injury by exposing the muscles, tendons, and connective tissue to high forces caused by improper technique.

An athlete should use the heaviest weights possible for a moderate number of repetitions. When doing sets of low repetitions, a breakdown in technique is amplified and is much more likely to result in an injury. Training for strength using low force/moderate repetitions (about 6 repetitions and higher) will minimize the loads in the lumbar area. Strength gains can safely be accomplished by performing repetitions in this range. If an athlete needs to test strength, performing an all-out intense effort of more than about 6 repetitions of an exercise and

Only competitive weightlifters should attempt a one-repetition maximum. (photo by Kim Piche)

duplicating or improving upon that performance in a subsequent workout is a much safer alternative.

3. *Substitute a leg press exercise when necessary.* The deadlift and squat are exercises that develop the hips, quadriceps, hamstrings, and, to a lesser extent, the abdominals and low-back muscle groups. These exercises, however, are not the only way to strengthen those muscles, especially when there is a possibility of inconsistent technique. A study by Hay and his colleagues (1983) showed that trunk lean is directly attributable to the amount of weight being lifted. When performing the squat, trunk flexion inceases as the load increases. Greater trunk flexion places more demand on the hip extensors (i.e., the gluteus maximus and hamstrings) and less demand on the knee extensors (i.e., the quadriceps). To maximally stimulate the desired muscle group, consistent technique is required.

A leg press is a viable alternative to develop these muscle groups while reducing the compressive and shearing forces on the lower back. A leg press machine provides greater control in all of the various planes of movement during the exercise. Although the leg press has the same number of joints involved in the movement as the squat, it has a lower potential of movement at the joints—otherwise known as degrees of freedom (Figure 18.3). Reducing the variability in a movement ensures that an exercise is placing a demand on the intended muscle (Hay et al. 1983). When a leg press is performed correctly, the machine provides stability to the athlete, thereby decreasing the strain on the lower back. The machine, however, should not be angled at the traditional forty-five degrees. Rather, the machine should apply several biomechanical

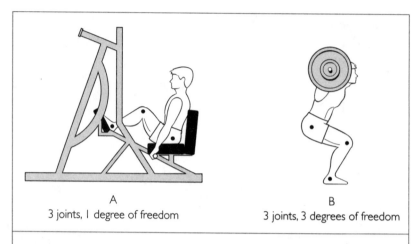

A	B
3 joints, 1 degree of freedom	3 joints, 3 degrees of freedom

FIGURE 18.3 **The Number of Joints at Which Motion Occurs and the Number of Degrees of Freedom (adapted from Hay et al. 1983). In "A," the axis of the leg press machine limits the degrees of freedom at the joint. The machine allows 1 degree of freedom at each hip (for flexion/extension). In "B," the squat allows 3 degrees of freedom at each hip (for flexion/extension, abduction/adduction and medial/lateral rotation) because the bar is free to move.**

principles. It should allow full hip extension; the foot plate should move in an arc; and the foot plate must be fixed perpendicular to the frontal plane of the hip during the arc of motion. A leg press machine following these principles comes close to replicating the squat (Palmitier et al. 1991).

4. *Use slow lifting speeds.* Only competitive weightlifters should perform the clean and jerk and snatch or their subdivision lifts. When lifting speed is increased there are correspondent increases in compressive and shear forces in the lumbar area. The increased forces may result in an injury to intervertebral discs, lumbar vertebrae, ligaments, and muscles. Slow technique training is preferable for conditioning programs. This requires at least a 2-second concentric (or raising) phase and a 4-second eccentric (or lowering) phase. This technique allows for maximum strength gains by incorporating the equally important concentric and eccentric loading phases of the muscle (Johnson et al. 1976).

The clean and snatch movements actually are a series of different exercises—namely the deadlift, shrug, and upright row—combined into one movement. (A leg press can be substituted for the deadlift.) Although the jerk is an explosive movement originating at the hips, a shoulder press exercise would stress the same upper-body muscles. Performance of these exercises separately in a slow manner using low force and moderate repetitions will improve the productivity of the exercises.

5. *Use proper lifting technique.* Variation in lifting technique may result in undue stress on the musculature and connective tissue, increasing the opportunity for injury. A lifter should avoid a forward lean and rounded-back position because these positions are potentially dangerous due to high compression and shear forces present in the lumbar spine. Proper technique includes lifting with the legs, squatting rather than stooping, and keeping the upper torso erect (Roozbazar 1974).

When performing pulling movements like the snatch and clean, the bar should follow the proper path. Once the bar leaves the floor, it has a significant effect on the lifter's center of gravity. Proper bar path helps the lifter maintain balance and enables the largest muscle groups to perform the action, thereby reducing the forces on the lower back. Proper lifting position includes a slight arch (lumbar curve) in the lower back with the shoulders back (shoulder blades pushed together) and the chest pushed forward (Baker). Maintaining this position minimizes the stress on the lumbar area. Incorrect technique may result in body parts absorbing unexpected forces.

REDUCE YOUR RISK!

Inadequate coaching, weight training at home without adult supervision, and the use of free weights without spotters are all factors that increase the risk of injury. Lack of experience also can play a significant role (Risser, Risser, and Preston 1990). By avoiding these risks as well as following the previously mentioned principles, potential injuries to the lower back will be dramatically reduced in the weight room.

REFERENCES

Alexander, M. J. L. 1985. Biomechanical aspects of lumbar spine injuries in athletes: A review. *Canadian Journal of Applied Sport Sciences* 10 (1): 1–20.

Baker, G. *The United States weightlifting federation coaching manual: Technique* 1: 13.

Bates, F. 1976. The editor's desk. *International Olympic Lifter* (1): 3.

Brady, T. A., B. R. Cahill, and L. M. Bodnar. 1982. Weight training-related injuries in the high school athlete. *American Journal of Sports Medicine* 10 (1): 1–5.

Brown, E. W., and A. Kaveh. 1985. Kinematics and kinetics of the deadlift in adolescent power lifters. *Medicine and Science in Sports and Exercise* 17 (5): 554–563.

Brown, E. W., and R. G. Kimball. 1983. Medical history associated with adolescent powerlifting. *Pediatrics* 72 (5): 636–644.

Buseck, M., O. D. Schipplein, G. B. J. Andersson, and T. P. Andriacchi. 1988. Influence of dynamic factors and external loads on the moment at the lumbar spine in lifting. *Spine* 13 (8): 918–921.

Dunn, B., T. Baechle, R. Elam, P. Etcheberry, R. Ball, B. Montgomery, and D. Semenick. 1983. Coaches' roundtable: Off-season strength & conditioning for basketball. *National Strength and Conditioning Association Journal* 5 (1): 19–29, 54–55.

Ebben, W., and D. Blackard. 1997. Survey: Strength and conditioning practices of National Football League (NFL) strength and conditioning coaches. Questionnaire sent to NFL strength and conditioning coaches. Marquette, MI: U.S. Olympic Education Center/Northern Michigan University.

Fleck, S. J., and W. J. Kraemer. 1987. *Designing resistance training programs.* Champaign, IL: Human Kinetics.

Fortin, J. 1996. Weight lifting. In *The spine in sports*, ed. R. Watkins, 484–498. St. Louis: Mosby-Year Publishing.

Gargan, M. F., and J. C. T. Fairbank. 1996. Anatomy of the spine. In *The spine in sports*, ed. R. Watkins, 2–12. St. Louis: Mosby-Year Publishing.

Garhammer, J. 1984. Weight lifting and training. In *Biomechanics of sport*, ed. C. L. Vaughn, 169–211. Boca Raton, FL: CRC Press.

Goss, K. 1998. Texas city stingarees: Hearts of champions. *Bigger Faster Stronger* 17 (2): 55–57.

Granhed, H., and B. Morelli. 1988. Low back pain among retired wrestlers and heavyweight lifters. *American Journal of Sports Medicine* 16 (5): 530–533.

Hall, S. 1985. Effect of attempted lifting speed on forces and torque exerted on the lumbar spine. *Medicine and Science in Sports and Exercise* 17 (4): 440–444.

Hay, J. G., J. G. Andrews, C. L. Vaughn, and K. Ueya. 1983. Load, speed, and equipment effects in strength training exercises. In *Biomechanics* VIII-B, eds. H. Matsui and K. Kobayashi, 939–950. Champaign, IL: Human Kinetics.

Jesse, J. P. 1977. Olympic lifting movements endanger adolescents. *Physician and Sportsmedicine* 72 (5): 61–67.

Johnson, B. L., J. W. Adamczyk, K. O. Tennoe, and S. B. Stromme. 1976. A comparison of concentric and eccentric muscle training. *Medicine and Science in Sports* 8 (1): 35–38.

Lamb, D. R. 1984. *Physiology of exercise: Responses and adaptations.* New York: Macmillan Publishing Company.

McLaughlin, T. M., C. J. Dillman, and T. J. Lardner. 1977. A kinematic model of performance in the parallel squat by champion powerlifters. *Medicine and Science in Sports* 9 (2): 128–133.

Palmitier, R. A., K. N. An, S. G. Scott, and Y. S. Chao. 1991. Kinetic chain exercise in knee rehabilitation. *Sports Medicine* 11 (6): 402–413.

Peterson, J. A. 1982. Strength training: Health insurance for the athlete. In *Strength training by the experts*, ed. D. Riley, 8–9. Champaign, IL: Leisure Press.

Pollock, M. L., S. H. Leggett, J. E. Graves, A. Jones, M. Fulton, and J. Cirulli. 1989. Effect of resistance training on lumbar extension strength. *American Journal of Sports Medicine* (17) 5: 624–629.

Quinney, H. A., D. E. R. Warburton, A. L. Webster, and M. J. Haykowsky. 1997. Pain and injuries associated with elite powerlifting: A Canadian perspective. *Canadian Journal of Applied Physiology* 22: 49P.

Riley, D. 1979. Power line. *Scholastic Coach* 49 (November): 10–16.

Risser, W. L., J. M. H. Risser, and D. Preston. 1990. Weight training injuries in adolescents. *American Journal of Diseases of Children* 144: 1015–1017.

Roozbazar, A. 1974. Biomechanics of lifting. In *Biomechanics* IV, eds. R. C. Nelson and
C. A. Morehouse, 37–43. Baltimore: University Park Press.

Stiggins, C. 1992. Testing and evaluation of athletes. In *Essential principles of strength training and conditioning*. Colorado Springs, CO: National Strength and Conditioning
Association, 74–83.

Twomey, L., J. R. Taylor, and C. Flynn. 1995. The lumbar region. In *Sports physiotherapy:
Applied science and practice*, ed. M. Zuluaga, 485–506. Melbourne: Churchill
Livingston.

Zatsiorsky, V. M. 1995. *Science and practice of strength training*. Champaign, IL: Human
Kinetics.

19

The Reality of the Power Clean

Jim Kielbaso, M.S., C.S.C.S.
Strength and Conditioning Coach
University of Detroit-Mercy
Detroit, Michigan

Of all the exercises available to develop muscular strength, size, and power, one of the most misunderstood and misused is the power clean. Along with the power clean, one could easily include the other Olympic-style lifts and their analogs, as these exercises are misused nearly as often. The majority of this discussion will focus on the power clean, but because of the similarities, other ballistic movements will also be included.

While the power clean has managed to mainstream itself into many strength and conditioning programs, its inclusion does not seem practical, well-investigated, or thoroughly analyzed. In fact, including the power clean in an athlete's preparation for competition may not only be a mistake, but it could be perceived as negligence on the part of the practitioner who suggests its use.

The purpose of this discussion is not to offend or discredit the intelligence or competency of anyone who uses the power clean; many well-respected and highly successful professionals advocate its use. Instead, the goal is to stimulate some critical thought on a subject that is not often thoroughly investigated. This is an attempt to get individuals to consider all of the information objectively and decide whether the benefits of the power clean truly outweigh the associated risks. The critical question in this discussion is whether or not it is really necessary to include the power clean in a strength and conditioning program.

Unlike some other sections of this book, this chapter does not present new ideas related to productive training. Rather, the focus is on why a certain movement should not be performed. Why is it important to discuss what *not* to do in training? What did power cleans do to deserve such cruel treatment? The reason this discussion is included is that there is so much misuse and misinformation about the power clean that it is necessary to address the issue. This is not an attack on the innocent power clean or any of its advocates but rather an impetus for thought and discussion related to the topic. The reality of the power clean should be analyzed for safe and productive training. If, after digesting the following information with an open mind, the decision is made to include power cleans in your program, at least you have made an informed decision and hopefully have a better understanding of the ramifications involved.

BACKGROUND OF THE POWER CLEAN

The first version of the power clean was probably performed hundreds of years ago when someone tried to figure out the easiest way to hoist an object to the shoulders for carrying. To its credit, a clean is a very easy way to lift an awkward object to the shoulder. In the late 1800s, physical conditioning increased in popularity, and men looked for new ways to display their masculinity. Again, a version of the power clean was used to hoist a barbell or heavy object to the shoulders and a jerk or push press-type movement was used to raise the object overhead; holding objects overhead was considered a true display of masculinity.

Of course, it was not long before simply displaying strength proved inadequate. People's competitive spirits took over and competitions were created to determine who could lift the most weight. The sport of weightlifting was born and finally found its way into the Olympic games in 1896. At first, the lifts were called one- and two-handed lifts but the modern form of weightlifting took shape in the 1928 Olympics with the press, snatch, and clean and jerk. The press was taken out after the 1972 games while the snatch and clean and jerk have remained since the beginning.

When strength training for athletes began to gain popularity in the 1960s and 1970s, many colleges and professional athletic teams hired former competitive Olympic weightlifters to train their athletes. Because the background of these individuals was primarily in Olympic-style weightlifting, they naturally began implementing training programs centered around these movements. The historical cycles of competitive athletics continued this practice for several years. This cycle shows that many athletes turn to coaching when their playing careers end. The cycle also reveals that many coaches develop programs based on the training they did when they competed. So, the fact that they were forced to perform the power clean when they competed was reason enough for many coaches to include the power clean in their later training regimes. Unfortunately, many of these coaches did not take the time to examine their own training philosophies and analyze why they were including competition-style movements in their programs. They perpetuated the use of power cleans in a way that can be compared to military or fraternity hazing; nobody is really sure of the purpose but because it's traditional it must be the right thing to do. This kind of thinking can lead to big problems.

There simply is not enough research available on the power clean to validate its extensive use in athletics today. While further research must be done, the following information suggests that the power clean is an unnecessary and potentially dangerous form of strength training.

WHAT'S THE BIG DEAL?

While many believe the power clean is a necessity in athletic preparation, there are plenty of reasons why it should not be a part of a strength and conditioning program. For simplicity, these factors have been organized into three categories. More detailed discussions of each heading can be found elsewhere in this book but the following will relate this information specifically to the power clean.

The three major areas of analysis in this discussion are strength gains, skill transfer, and safety.

Strength Gains

Gaining strength is the primary reason athletes engage in strength training, so it is vital that the program you adopt produces strength gains in the most efficient manner possible. Contrary to the beliefs of many individuals, performing power cleans is not a very efficient way to gain strength. It is well documented that high-resistance slow-velocity movements produce much greater strength gains than do high-velocity movements (Moffroid and Whipple 1970; Rosentswieg, Hinson, and Ridgway 1975; Poliquin 1990; Hedrick 1993; Brzycki 1995). In fact, hypertrophy and increases in contractile strength are directly related to the amount of tension developed within the muscle during training (Goldberg et al. 1975; Hedrick 1993). Because much more force and tension is generated during slower velocity contractions, it is obvious that a slow speed of movement is superior to fast speeds when the goal is to improve muscular strength. The force/velocity curve shows that force literally drops as the concentric speed of contraction increases (Figure 19.1). Interestingly, the greatest amount of force is created using very fast eccentric contractions. But is this either safe or practical? No. This would require very heavy weights to be thrown forcefully at the lifter while he or she attempted to decelerate them. Throwing and catching heavy weights is a dangerous practice; yet that is essentially what occurs during a power clean.

Many proponents of the power clean have voiced the opinion that to move your body explosively you have to move weights explosively. Some of these people also believe that moving heavy weights in a slow, controlled fashion will create slow athletes. Nothing could be further from the truth. These opinions have

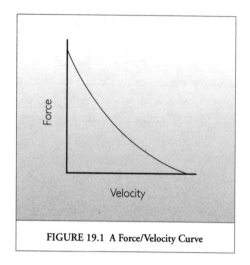

FIGURE 19.1 A Force/Velocity Curve

not been, and probably never will be, validated by legitimate scientific or empirical evidence. It is true that several studies have shown that high-velocity strength can be improved through high-speed training but other studies have disputed these findings, suggesting that there is no real difference in power development between training at high versus low speeds (Van Oteghen 1975; Kanehisa and Miyashita 1983; Garnica 1986; Palmieri 1987; Poliquin 1990; Wenzel and Perfetto 1992; Young and Bilby 1993). It has also been shown that any velocity-specific effects of training are based upon the *intended* movement speed rather than the *actual* speed of movement (Behm and Sale 1993). This means that you can gain the same velocity-specific effects by simply *attempting* to move heavy weights quickly. At the end of a slow and controlled set when you can barely move the weight, you can achieve results similar to fast movements simply by trying to lift the weight quickly. Fatigue will alter the neural firing patterns so that the weight will not actually be moving rapidly at this point but it does not appear to matter; it is the intent to move quickly that is of importance. So, you do not actually have to lift weights in a fast manner to gain the desirable effects.

Fiber Types

Related to the speed of movement is the issue of training fast-twitch (FT) Type IIb and slow-twitch (ST) Type I muscle fibers. To clarify, just because the name of Type IIb fibers has the word *fast* in it does not mean that these fibers are solely responsible for fast movements. Yes, there are some neuromuscular factors that allow FT fibers to contract more rapidly than ST fibers but the two fiber types are actually separated more by their oxidative and metabolic properties than by their neural innervation patterns.

Regardless of what they are called, the nervous system recruits muscle fibers in a very orderly fashion according to the force requirements of a movement rather than by the speed. The well-accepted Size Principle of Recruitment shows that motor neurons are recruited from smallest to largest, depending upon the need (Henneman 1957). This means that every movement starts with the smaller ST fibers and, depending upon the amount of force necessary, intermediate and larger FT fibers may be progressively recruited to perform the work. So as an exercise reaches maximal intensity, more and more fibers must contribute to generate the necessary tension. Thus, when the largest FT fibers are recruited, all fibers are being utilized.

This sequential recruitment pattern enables the body to utilize only the necessary number of muscle fibers to complete a movement, but the speed of movement is of absolutely no consequence to this process; the movement is dependent only on the intensity of the contraction. Furthermore, the suggestion that power cleans can selectively train only the FT fibers has been shown to be physiologically impossible (Palmieri 1983; Bell and Wenger 1992). Just because power cleans move a weight quickly does not mean that nervous-system mechanisms suddenly change to bypass the smaller motor units.

Fast-twitch fibers can be trained with slow movements as long as the force requirements are high enough. (photo by Matt Brzycki)

Keeping this recruitment pattern in mind, it is obvious that FT fibers can be trained with slow movements as long as the force requirements are high enough (MacDougall et al. 1980; Hedrick 1993; Stone 1993). In fact, assuming a maximal effort is given, it has been shown that FT fibers are utilized equally in slow and fast contractions (Desmedt and Godaux 1979; MacDougall et al. 1980; Sale and MacDougall 1981; Hedrick 1993). In other words, in an effort to train the larger FT muscle fibers, it is unnecessary to employ high-speed contractions such as seen in the power clean. The same results can be elicited through the use of controlled high-intensity muscular contractions.

Skill Transfer

Another reason many people advocate the use of power cleans involves the concept of specificity. Some people think that a clean looks like a football lineman performing a blocking motion, a swimmer's start, a basketball player rebounding, a volleyball player blocking, a sprinter coming out of the blocks, or nearly anything that happens in athletic competition. Is it possible for one movement to be specific to so many activities? Could performing the power clean possibly make you better at all of these sporting activities? No, absolutely not. In fact, there is no strength training exercise that will make you significantly better at any sport skill. The only skill that the power clean will make you better at is the skill of performing the clean and jerk in weightlifting competition. Attempting to improve athletic skills in the weight room is completely missing the point of strength training. Your primary goal should be to increase strength. Remember, it is not called *skill training*; it is called *strength training*.

As a result of increasing your strength through an organized strength and conditioning program, several benefits may be seen. First and foremost is the reduced risk of injury. Second, many individuals experience the psychological benefits of pushing themselves through the pain of hard work, thus giving them the comfort of knowing they can push their bodies through the rigors of competition. Third, body-composition changes can occur as a result of engaging in strength training. And, finally, increased levels of strength enable an athlete to perform any activity with a greater amount of force; many people refer to this as performance enhancement. Performance of many activities can be enhanced as total-body strength levels increase. Performance enhancement through strength training, however, is often misunderstood.

Many people attempt to replicate sport movements in the weight room thinking that this will help them perform more effectively in competition. What is misunderstood is the fact that while strengthening the musculature will indeed prove beneficial, the actual movements employed are relatively inconsequential to the sport performance. The sport skills should be practiced on the field. When the skills are mastered, increased levels of strength (gained through proper strength training) will allow those skills to be performed with greater force. Trying to isolate certain muscles and simulate sport movements in the weight room, however, is a waste of valuable time. Remember, the goal of strength training is to increase strength, and the goal of sport practice is to improve athletic skills and tactics. These are separate goals that should be addressed individually. Strength training produces *general* results; skill training produces *specific* results.

Although some professionals may disagree, this concept is well supported by the motor-learning literature (Adams 1987; Magill 1989). For a long time, people believed that performing certain movements in the weight room would improve specific skills. Research, however, shows that for skill transfer to take place from one movement to another, the movements must include four basic components (Freedman 1990):

1. muscle specificity—the same muscles used in the skill must be trained
2. movement specificity—the exact movement patterns on the field must be replicated by the exercise
3. speed specificity—the exact speed of movement used in competition must be employed by the exercise
4. resistance specificity—the exact resistance encountered in the sport skill must be identical to the resistance used in the exercise

For a power clean or any other movement to be specific to any sport skill, all four of these requirements must be met. Satisfying just one of them would be difficult enough, but there is absolutely no way a power clean can meet all four requirements. In fact, a study of lower-body movement during the snatch pull, which is nearly identical to the clean pull, showed that while it is similar in speed of movement, the motion of the pull is significantly different than the vertical jump (Canavan, Garret, and Armstrong 1996). This single study shows that the snatch is not specific to a vertical jump, and although it is speculation, there is an extremely good chance that the results would be the same if the clean pull were used. The vertical jump is one movement that many people think is specific to the Olympic lifts. If the snatch isn't specific to a vertical jump, it probably isn't specific to any other movement. It is not exactly like a football lineman blocking. It is not exactly like a sprinter's start. It is not exactly like any movement except the power clean itself. Actually, if you really look carefully, power cleans are not even close to any other movement. And the resistance involved in a power clean cannot be exactly like any athletic skill. After all, in what sport activity are you running around with a loaded barbell in your hands?

Another difference between the power clean and most sport skills is the fact that the clean is a closed skill; most athletic movements are open skills (Poulton 1957; Brzycki 1995). A closed skill is performed in a predictable environment where the athlete can begin the movement when he or she is ready. It is performed exactly the same way each time and environmental factors are negligible. Examples of closed skills are tossing the shot put, performing on the balance beam, and weightlifting (competitive or recreational). An open skill, on the other hand, is performed in a constantly changing environment where the athlete must react to outside stimuli. Even though open skills can be rehearsed, they may be slightly different each time. Basketball, football, soccer, wrestling, and baseball are examples of sports in which open skills are predominantly performed. With this in mind, why use a closed skill to prepare for a sport that primarily uses open skills?

Finally, if cleans truly enhance athletic skills, there would be a positive transfer of learning. This means that practicing one skill would improve performance on the other and vice versa. Many people have claimed that cleans help different sports skills, but have you ever heard anyone claim that practicing a sport skill would make you better at doing power cleans? No. Nobody would ever believe anything that ludicrous, let alone write about it. If the skill does not improve your power-clean performance then the power clean will not improve your sport skill. There is no significant skill transfer.

Safety

Up to this point I have shown that high-force, controlled-velocity movements are much more effective for gaining strength than high-velocity movements. I have also shown that power cleans do not directly improve sport skills. I have not, however, suggested that power cleans will produce no strength gains at all. Actually, if progressive overload is employed, just about any movement can strengthen the musculature. While it cannot be refuted that power cleans can improve strength, it should be obvious that there are more efficient ways of eliciting the same results.

But even if they did provide some terrific benefit that cannot be proven, a risk/benefit analysis would reveal that the potential for injury is too great to include the clean in most programs.

As stated before, one of the most important reasons for engaging in a strength and conditioning program is to reduce the risk of injury. This should be of paramount importance to you when designing any resistance-training program. Each exercise carries a certain amount of risk. You must weigh the risks associated with each exercise against its benefits to determine whether it should be included in the routine. This is where the power clean should be thoroughly analyzed.

It is well documented and generally accepted that compressive force, shear force, and torque drastically increase as the speed of movement increases (Andrews, Hay, and Vaughan 1983; Hall 1985; Hattin, Pierrynowski, and Ball 1989; Reid, Yeater, and Ullrich 1987; Behm 1991; Wenzel and Perfetto 1992; Behm and Sale 1993). These increased forces can cause muscular and connective tissue injuries such as strains, tears, tendinitis, and other chronic overuse injuries. So, as the speed of movement increases so does the risk of sustaining one or more of these injuries. This does not mean that we should all walk around extremely slowly and never train just to eliminate risk. Some speed is necessary, and the body is capable of withstanding certain forces. Unfortunately, we do not know exactly how much force each muscle can withstand, and we probably never will. The only way to ascertain exactly how much force our tissues can withstand is to apply force until they tear—but by that time it is obviously too late. And, because of individual differences this concept may never be completely understood. What we do know is that these forces will eventually damage a muscle or joint so it is in our best interest to avoid this dangerous threshold.

Because power cleans force the athlete to move the weight in a ballistic fashion, we know that greater forces are associated with this movement than with slower, more controlled movements. One study that specifically examined the clean and jerk reported dramatic increases in compressive force, shear force, and torque in the lumbar region as the speed of movement increased (Hall 1985). This does not necessarily mean that these forces were great enough to produce an injury. It can be deduced, however, that the power clean heightens the risk of injury by increasing the dangerous forces placed on the body. Although power cleans were not specifically cited, other studies have shown that lifting weights in an explosive fashion drastically increases the forces encountered by the body, thereby increasing the risk of injury (Kuland et al. 1978; Brady, Cahill, and Bodnar 1982; Andrews, Hay, and Vaughan 1983; Alexander 1985; Reid, Yeater, and Ullrich 1987; Hattin, Pierrynowski, and Ball 1989; Risser 1991; Wenzel and Perfetto 1992; Behm and Sale 1993; Mazur, Yetman, and Risser 1993).

While there is not a great deal of valid research available that specifically addresses the danger involved with the power clean, there is absolutely no evidence that suggests the power clean is as safe as a controlled movement. Further research must be done in this area, yet there must be some reason why both the American

Orthopaedic Society for Sports Medicine and the American Academy of Pediatrics (1983) contraindicate the use of Olympic weightlifting movements in exercise protocols. And why would so many professionals, including two former presidents of the American College of Sports Medicine and numerous college and professional strength coaches, suggest omitting ballistic weight training (including the power clean) from athletic preparation (Duda 1987; Mannie 1994; Brzycki 1995)?

There is, in fact, specific research that points out the stress placed on the low-back region as a result of repeated performance of the power clean and other Olympic lifts. The thought of placing additional stress on the already fragile lumbar spine should be enough to deter anyone from performing the power clean. The repetitive forced hyperextension of the lumbar spine can lead to several conditions such as lumbar sprain, strain, disc injury, and spondylolysis or *spondy* (Kotani et al. 1971; Duda 1987; Mannie 1994). Spondy is a fracture of the pars interarticularis of the vertebrae. You can think of this as a cracked vertebra. This condition can and will end an athlete's career. A worsening of the condition can lead to greater problems such as nervous-system damage. It should be noted that spondy only occurs in 6–7 percent of the general population. However, several researches have found a greatly increased incidence of the condition—up to 44 percent—in experienced Olympic weightlifters (Kotani et al. 1971; Alexander 1985; Duda 1987). One study even found that 24 of 26 experienced Olympic weightlifters suffered from recurrent episodes of low-back pain (Kotani et al. 1971). This does not mean that power cleans, or any other movements, were the sole cause of all of these back problems. But these studies do demonstrate the fact that there are many low-back problems associated with this kind of training.

Less examined than low-back pain, but equally problematic, are potential injuries to the wrists, elbows, shoulders, and knees. Again, the increased compressive and shear forces created by the power clean have the same potential to cause injury to these areas as they do to the lower back. While all of these injuries can occur while performing the clean, it is extremely important to note that long-term exposure to these damaging forces may weaken and degrade the joints and muscles. This degradation will predispose the body to injuries that may occur during other activities. So, even though all of the injuries may not occur while actually performing the movement, the clean could be the cause of many other injuries as a result of its degenerative effect on the body.

SUPERVISION AND INSTRUCTION

One issue related to the power clean that commonly results in injuries to athletes is the lack of quality instruction and supervision. While there are a great number of qualified instructors available, many athletes are still given incorrect information and are not properly supervised in the weight room. In addition, many weight rooms are simply not large enough or set up properly to allow athletes to perform power cleans safely. Insufficient space can lead to interference from other weight room users or a bar being dropped on someone during a failed lift. Rapidly moving Olympic barbells in a confined area can lead to problems when someone is not absolutely alert. If, after considering all of the information, you still decide to include power cleans in your program, it is absolutely imperative that supervision, instruction, and facility planning are given special attention.

FINAL THOUGHTS

Certainly, some intriguing questions have been raised regarding the efficacy of performing the power clean for athletic preparation. If you choose to perform power cleans, I hope this discussion prompts you to investigate your methods. Remember that controlled movements are the most effective way to produce strength gains. Consider the motor-learning literature that shows a lack of skill transfer from power cleans to other sport skills. Acknowledge the fact that there is absolutely no research or empirical evidence available that suggests a power clean will enhance a sport skill more than any other controlled strength training exercise. Finally, keep in mind that strength and conditioning is not just about preparing for the next competition. We need to consider the long-term ramifications and injury potential of everything we do in the weight room. Power cleans may produce results, but there are better methods available. Step up to the challenge of developing a program that not only produces results but is in the best interest of everyone involved.

REFERENCES

Adams, J. A. 1987. Historical review and appraisal of research on the learning retention and transfer of human motor skills. *Psychological Bulletin* 101: 41–74.

Alexander, M. J. L. 1985. Biomechanical aspects of lumbar spine injuries in athletes: A review. *Canadian Journal of Applied Sport Sciences* 10: 1–20.

American Academy of Pediatrics. 1983. Weight training and weight lifting: Information for the pediatrician. *Physician and Sportsmedicine* 11 (3): 157–161.

Andrews, J. G., J. G. Hay, and C. L. Vaughan. 1983. Knee shear forces during a squat exercise using a barbell and a weight machine. In *Biomechanics* VIII-B, ed. H. Matsui and K. Kobayashi, 923–927. Champaign, IL: Human Kinetics.

Behm, D. G. 1991. An analysis of intermediate speed of resistance exercises for velocity-specific strength gains. *Journal of Applied Sports Science Research* 5 (1): 1–5.

Behm, D. G., and D. G. Sale. 1993. Intended rather than actual movement velocity determines velocity-specific training response. *Journal of Applied Physiology* 74: 359–368.

Bell, G. J., and H. A. Wenger. 1992. Physiological adaptations to velocity-controlled resistance training. *Sports Medicine* 13 (4): 234–244.

Brady, T. A., B. R. Cahill, and L. M. Bodnar. 1982. Weight training–related injuries in the high school athlete. *American Journal of Sports Medicine* 10: 1–5.

Brzycki, M. 1995. *A practical approach to strength training.* 3rd ed. Indianapolis, IN: Masters Press.

Canavan, P. K., G. E. Garret, and L. E. Armstrong. 1996. Kinematic and kinetic relationships between an Olympic-style lift and the vertical jump. *Journal of Strength and Conditioning Research* 10 (2): 127–130.

Desmedt, J. E., and E. Godaux. 1979. Voluntary motor commands in human ballistic movements. *Annals of Neurology* 5: 415–421.

Duda, M. 1987. Elite lifters at risk of spondylolysis. *Physician and Sportsmedicine* 5 (9): 61–67.

Freedman, A. 1990. Specificity in exercise training. *Strength and Fitness Quarterly* 1 (3): 9.

Garnica, R. A. 1986. Muscular power in young women after slow and fast isokinetic training. *Journal of Orthopaedic and Sports Physical Therapy* 8: 1–9.

Goldberg, A. L., J. D. Etlinger, D. F. Goldspink, and C. Jablecki. 1975. Mechanisms of work induced hypertrophy of skeletal muscle. *Medicine and Science in Sports and Exercise* 7: 185–198.

Hall, S. 1985. Effects of attempted lifting speed on forces and torque exerted on the lumbar spine. *Medicine and Science in Sports and Exercise* 17: 440–444.

Hattin, H. C., M. R. Pierrynowski, and K. A. Ball. 1989. Effect of load, cadence, and fatigue on tibio-femoral joint force during a half squat. *Medicine and Science in Sports and Exercise* 21: 613–618.

Hedrick, A. 1993. Literature review: High speed resistance training. *National Strength and Conditioning Journal* 15 (6): 22–30.

Henneman, E. 1957. Relation between size of neurons and their susceptibility to discharge. *Science* 126: 1345–1347.

Kanehisa, H., and M. Miyashita. 1983. Specificity of velocity in strength training. *European Journal of Physiology* 52: 104–106.

Kotani, P. T., N. Ichikawa, W. Wakabayashi, T. Yoshii, and M. Koshimune. 1971. Studies of spondylolysis found among weightlifters. *British Journal of Sports Medicine* 6: 4–8.

Kuland, D. N., J. B. Dewey, L. E. Brubaker, and J. R. Roberts. 1978. Olympic weightlifting injuries. *Physician and Sports Medicine* 6 (11): 111–116, 119.

MacDougall, J. D., G. L. B. Elder, D. G. Sale, J. R. Moroz, and J. R. Sutton. 1980. Effects of strength training and immobilization on human muscle fibers. *European Journal of Applied Physiology* 43: 25–34.

Magill, R. A. 1989. *Motor learning: Concepts and applications.* 3rd ed. Dubuque, IA: W. C. Brown Publishing.

Mannie, K. 1994. Some thoughts on explosive weight training. *High Intensity Training Newsletter* 5 (1): 13–18.

Mazur, L. J., R. J. Yetman, and W. L. Risser. 1993. Weight training injuries: Common injuries and preventative measures. *Sports Medicine* 16: 57–63.

Moffroid, M. T., and R. H. Whipple. 1970. Specificity of speed of exercise. *Physical Therapy* 50: 1692–1699.

Palmieri, G. A. 1983. The principles of muscle fiber recruitment during ballistic movements. *National Strength and Conditioning Journal* 5 (5): 22–24, 63.

———. 1987. Weight training and repetition speed. *Journal of Applied Sport Science Research* 1 (2): 36–38.

Poliquin, C. 1990. Theory and methodology of strength training: At which speed should repetitions be performed? Part III. *Sports Coach* (April–June): 35–38.

Poulton, E. C. 1957. On prediction in skilled movements. *Psychological Bulletin* 54: 467–478.

Reid, C. M., R. A. Yeater, and I. H. Ullrich. 1987. Weight training and strength, cardiorespiratory functioning, and body composition in men. *British Journal of Sports Medicine* 21: 40–44.

Risser, W. L. 1991. Weight training injuries in children and adolescents. *American Family Physician* 44 (6): 2104-2110.

Rosentswieg, J., M. Hinson, and M. Ridgway. 1975. An electromyographic comparison of an isokinetic bench press performed at three speeds. *Research Quarterly* 46: 471–475.

Sale, D. G., and D. MacDougall. 1981. Specificity in strength training: A review for the coach and athlete. *Canadian Journal of Sport Sciences* 6: 87–92.

Stone, M. 1993. Literature review: Explosive exercise and training. *National Strength and Conditioning Journal* 15 (3): 6–19.

Van Oteghen, S. L. 1975. Two speeds of isokinetic exercise as related to the vertical jump performance in women. *Research Quarterly* 46: 78–84.

Wenzel, R. R., and E. M. Perfetto. 1992. The effect of speed versus non-speed training in power development. *Journal of Applied Sport Science Research* 6: 82–87.

Young, W. B., and G. E. Bilby. 1993. The effect of voluntary effort to influence speed of contraction on strength, muscular power, and hypertrophy development. *Journal of Strength and Conditioning Research* 7: 172–178.

This chapter is dedicated to three powerful and supportive leaders in my life: Dan, Donna, and Sheryl. Thank you.

20

Improving Speed, Power, and Explosiveness

Tim Wakeham, M.S., C.S.C.S.
Assistant Strength and Conditioning Coach
Michigan State University
East Lansing, Michigan

Which abilities do coaches and athletes want to improve more than any others? Virtually all individuals involved in sports would agree that the answer is speed and power, and with good reason. Speed and power are essential ingredients in numerous sports. The expression of sport-specific speed and force (widely referred to as explosiveness) strongly influences the rate of success in many of today's popular sports. In a sport like football, for example, the players who demonstrate the greatest amount of explosive power (all other variables being equal) should dominate their opponents. In track and field, the shot putter or hammer thrower who overcomes his or her implement's resistance with the greatest possible speed of movement should, in theory, produce the longest throw.

Hay and Reid (1988) define *speed* as "distance covered divided by the time taken to cover it." They propose focusing on the form, pattern, or sequencing of movements with respect to time when trying to enhance movement speed. In many competitive racing events, this recommendation means trying to improve an athlete's stride length and/or stride frequency. Hall (1991) supports these suggestions. She states that a major difference between highly skilled sprinters and ice skaters when compared to their novice counterparts is much higher stride frequencies seen in the elite group. She also notes that elite cross-country skiers are usually distinguishable from their slower (less-skilled) counterparts by longer-than-average stride lengths.

In scientific terms, power is expressed by this equation: power = force × distance/time (Bryant 1988). According to this description, training that involves all or various parts of the power equation can affect explosiveness in sports.

Power output can be enhanced in three general ways. The first method is to increase the force-producing capabilities of the muscles (i.e., keeping the distance moved and the time it took to move the distance constant). Since increases in explosiveness can be brought about by an increase in force, a hockey player who improves full-body strength (other power variables remaining constant) should be more explosive when skating up and down the ice.

The second way to enhance power is to decrease the time it takes to move across a given distance because of faster speed (i.e., keeping the force generated and the distance moved constant). Using the concept that improvements in power can be brought about through increased speed of movement, elite swimmers repetitively practice their stroke mechanics in an effort to improve skill coordination. Improved coordination of the muscles involved in a sport skill should increase overall speed and power output (other power variables remaining constant).

Increasing the distance that a force acts on a body or implement (i.e., keeping the force generated and the time elapsed constant) is another technique used to enhance explosive power. A volleyball player or track jumper who drops down into a deeper (optimum) crouched position than normal may exhibit an improvement in explosion provided that the force applied and the time it is applied remain constant (Myers and Munroe 1981).

Most sports require speed and power for success. There are many general areas that can be addressed to enhance the expression of explosiveness in sport. There are also specific strategies available to effect greater movement speed and power output. The question is "What areas and strategies should be emphasized to enhance the expression of speed, power, and explosiveness in sport?" The purpose of this chapter is to suggest probable physical and mental strategies to effect improvement in all three areas. Specifically, the objectives are (1) to identify methods that directly enhance movement speed and power output and (2) to review areas of motor learning and sport psychology that may positively affect the expression of speed and power.

WEIGHT TRAINING

Weight training, resulting in increased strength, is important for improving explosiveness. Whenever the force-producing capabilities of the muscles are increased, the potential to improve speed and power for skill execution is enhanced. Recent studies have shown that a progressive weight training program can increase sprint speed and throwing velocity (Napier 1991; Wooden et al. 1992). Some of this increase is due to greater amounts of muscle proteins (actin and myosin), which means an increase in the ability to generate force. Understanding and adhering to the following guidelines may help one to achieve speed and power enhancements through weight training.

1. *Train the entire body.* Current research suggests that strengthening opposing muscle groups (agonists and antagonists) enhances movement speed (Jaric et al. 1995). According to these data, strengthening a major muscle group such as the hamstrings may result in faster leg deceleration during high-speed activities such as sprinting. If the hamstrings need less time to decelerate the leg (while running), this leaves a longer period of time for the quadriceps to increase leg acceleration, resulting in faster lower-limb speeds.

Maximal strengthening of all the major muscle groups of the body may increase the time available for movement acceleration. The end result should be faster movement speeds and explosiveness in potentially all sport skills.

2. *Make the muscles work harder over time in a systematic manner.* To increase muscular strength, make the muscles work progressively harder. The four most common methods to make the muscles work harder are to increase the repetitions, increase sets, or increase load—or to systematically decrease the rest time between sets/exercises.

3. *Diminish momentum* (i.e., lift slowly). Momentum is always present when lifting weights. However, the less momentum allowed into the performance of each repetition, the more work the muscles have to perform; the more work the muscles have to perform, the greater the gains in force-generating capacity, speed, and explosiveness.

4. *Continue lifting to a point of demonstrated fatigue.* For years, coaches have asked, "Should we have our players lift to a point of all-out fatigue for maximum results?" Exercise scientists do not currently know what level of fatigue should be demonstrated before the termination of a set for optimal strength in each muscle and individual. However, training to a point where no complete concentric (positive portion of the repetition) contraction can be achieved ensures that athletes have surpassed their intensity threshold (amount of fatigue) for optimal results, whatever the level of intensity may be (Carpinelli 1997).

STRETCHING AND FLEXIBILITY

Flexibility has been defined as "the range of motion about a joint" (Fox, Bowers, and Foss 1993). Flexibility is important for improving speed and power because the greater the range of motion about a joint, the greater the distance available to apply force. When the distance to apply force is increased while force and time remain constant, explosiveness is improved. For instance, the quarterback possessing the greatest amount of shoulder-girdle flexibility should also have the greatest power output on each throw (all other variables being equal). Speed and power enhancements through flexibility training can be achieved by understanding and applying the guidelines that follow.

1. *Develop a program that is sport-specific.* Stretch all the major muscles involved in the performance of the sport. Pay careful attention to stretching opposing muscle groups and limbs to avoid imbalances in flexibility. There is some research suggesting a greater incidence of injury in populations with flexibility imbalances (Knapic et al. 1991).

2. *Stretch after a warm-up or after the training activity.* Beaulieu (1981) suggests that a warm-up period decreases a muscle's chance of injury when stretched because of greater extensibility. He also suggests increased gains in flexibility occur when stretching is performed after the muscle is warmed.

3. *Ease into each stretch (without bouncing) to a point where a slight tug is felt.* Easing slowly into each stretch brings about relaxation in the muscle, enabling further extensibility (Noakes and Granger 1990). Along with stretching slowly, it is important not to overstretch since this may lead to injury. Signs of going beyond a relative tolerance can include accelerated breathing and burning sensations in the targeted muscle.

4. *Hold each stretch for about 15–20 seconds.* One of the latest reviews on stretching reveals that there are no meaningful differences between holding a stretch 15 seconds, 45 seconds, or 2 minutes (Smith 1994).

5. *Stretch each muscle three to five times per session.* Current research suggests that this is the proper amount of stretching for maximal flexibility adaptations (Smith 1994).

TECHNIQUE

In sports, the nature of the activity and the equipment that is used usually control the distance over which force can be applied. By modifying performance technique, however, some athletes may be able to improve explosiveness by increasing the distance over which they apply force. For example, a shot putter who switches to a short-long technique where the glide across the ring is shorter and the length of the push (force application) is longer may see improved power, provided that all other variables (i.e., time and force) remain constant (Myers and Munroe 1981).

EQUIPMENT

More and more sport scientists are pursuing ways to alter sports equipment to increase the distance a competitor has to apply force. As with modifications to technique, an increase in the distance to apply force may result in greater power output.

One of the latest examples of this theory in action is the new skate blade used by some Olympic long-track speed skaters. The back portion of the blade is not completely attached to the heel. This skate modification increases the distance the skater applies force against the ice before the blade has to snap back up against the skate boot. In theory, this increased distance to apply force should result in more explosive skating strides (provided other power variables remain constant).

RATE OF FORCE DEVELOPMENT

Increasing the size of one's engine (muscles) should allow the mass of the body (during jumping or sprinting) or an external object (such as a competitor in football or wrestling) to be accelerated more explosively. To be optimally successful in many speed and power sports, it is also important to be able to develop (the engine's) force rapidly. Having a big engine but not being able to get it to top speed quickly is like driving a Cadillac in a quarter-mile race. All that power may still result in an unsuccessful performance in this particular race if the driver cannot get to maximum speed until the half-mile mark. For optimal sport success, speed-and-power athletes should have a large engine that reaches top speed quickly.

The rate of force development is the ability of the neuromuscular system to develop as much force as possible in a short period of time (Newton and Kraemer 1994). A rate of force development enhancement improves explosiveness by decreasing the time it takes to move over a given distance (provided other power variables are constant). Researchers suggest that the key stimulus for enhancing the rate of force development is maximum voluntary effort (i.e., the intent) to develop force as fast as possible, not the external speed of movement while training (Young and Bilby 1993).

Coaches and athletes have the option of trying to enhance the rate of force development in the weight room, the sport setting, or both. They also have the choice of training using high-speed or slow-speed movements with an intent to develop force quickly such as trying to accelerate a heavy weight explosively.

Recent research suggests that some options may be more practical than others. For example, there is evidence to suggest an increased probability of injury from the performance of some types of explosive weight training movements such as Olympic lifts, Leaper training, and exercises using chain-operated equipment (Brady, Cahill, and Bodnar 1982; Hall 1985; McCarroll, Miller, and Ritter 1986; Reid, Yeater, and Ullrich 1987). However, since most subjects in the reviewed studies were unsupervised, it is unknown whether it was the movements that caused the injuries or the improper execution of the movements. Regardless, explosive training in the weight room has a higher probability of causing

Explosive training in the weight room has a higher probability of causing musculotendinous injury, compared to slowly performed movements, since greater forces of momentum are generated at higher speeds. (photo by Kevin Fowler)

musculotendinous injury, compared to slowly performed movements, since greater forces of momentum are generated at higher speeds (Behm 1988). Furthermore, most weight-room injuries appear to occur from breaks in technique. Explosive lifts requiring large amounts of technique (e.g., the Olympic-style lifts) certainly add to the likelihood of improper execution and musculotendinous injury.

A more practical and perhaps optimal method to increase the rate of force development may be for coaches and athletes to implement explosive sport-specific drills. Currently, some motor-learning researchers suggest that because weight training movements are different from those executed on the field and court in dynamic situations, the explosive transfer may be less than optimal (Schmidt 1988). Furthermore, Sage (1984) proposes that training tasks (i.e., movements that are dependent upon practice and experience for their execution) must be virtually identical for meaningful transfer to performance to occur.

To improve the rate of force development in a sport setting, coaches should study game film and design explosive drills incorporating identical sport performance movement patterns. When implementing sport-specific power workouts, athletes should explode at the start and try to accelerate for the duration of each drill. For instance, to enhance sport-specific explosiveness, basketball players should perform jumps, defensive position lateral slides, and diagonal, forward, and backward sprints explosively. Execution of sport movements with maximum voluntary effort to develop force as fast as possible enhances an athlete's rate of force development in an exact (specific) manner. There may be no better form of movement-

and velocity-specific power training to ensure that explosive sport training carries over to explosive sport performance.

The necessity of preparing in the exact manner as one is expected to perform cannot be overstated. Students do not study algebra to take a geometry test even though those are similar subjects. Both subjects are under the umbrella of mathematics, and because of their similarities, studying one may positively affect test results in the other. But it should be obvious that the best results would come from preparing for an algebra test by studying algebra.

WARM-UP

McArdle, Katch, and Katch (1991) state that speed of contraction can be significantly increased by raising body temperature. A proper warm-up should include activities that incorporate the large muscle groups of the body in a rhythmic and repetitive manner. Warm-up activities should be specific to the training exercise(s) but performed with a lower level of effort for about 7–15 minutes.

DRAG

In many sports, movement speed and power may be improved by reducing drag. Drag can be described as *an external resistance that slows forward motion* (Lamb 1995). Examples of drag in sport include headwind on the forward speed of a track sprinter, water on the movement speed of a swimmer, and an offensive tackle on the pass rush of a defensive lineman in football.

Equipment

To reduce drag, sport scientists have developed various forms of aerodynamic and hydrodynamic sport apparatus. For example, newly designed rowing shells have reduced water drag while cycling helmets have reduced air drag, thus improving competitive velocities and performance power. Athletes who are involved in competitive sports that require movements against the resistance of air or water are advised to research sport-specific apparatus to find the most drag-reducing equipment available.

Body Composition

Modifications in body composition may also lead to the enhancement of movement speed and power through reductions in drag. In explosive jumping sports (e.g., high jumping, long jumping, and triple jumping), a loss in body mass results in a reduction in the drag of gravity (a limiting factor to success in jumping sports). If the lost body mass is muscle tissue, however, a decrease in the ability to produce force and explosiveness may also be expected. Strategies for body-composition alteration should be carefully considered before they are implemented so that power performances are enhanced rather than inhibited.

To improve explosiveness through enhanced body composition, athletes should (1) consult with a registered dietitian who can provide a body-composition analysis, evaluation of current diet, determination of optimal and realistic body-composition expectations, and diet-modification strategies; (2) perform a weight training program following the suggestions previously discussed; and (3) acknowledge and accept that there does not currently appear to be a safe and effective nutritional supplement that provides consistent body-composition improvements in athletes.

Biomechanical Factors

Also influencing drag and sport explosiveness are biomechanical factors. Changing body posture may decrease air drag in some racing sports. For example, elite cyclists and downhill skiers gain speed and power output by dropping into crouched postures, thereby diminishing the body surface area that is exposed to air resistance.

Track coaches and runners have made an art out of reducing drag through efficient biomechanical positions and postures. Although track experts utilize a variety of technique cues, their general recommendations remain the same: demonstrate straight-line movements and reduce vertical lift and time spent in the air.

Successfully performing the following cues may enhance movement efficiency, thereby reducing drag and improving explosiveness. Start by driving with both legs explosively in a straight-line direction. Gain as much ground as possible with the first step. Run with the head erect and still. Relax the jaw and face. Focus the eyes straight ahead. Keep the torso straight, trying not to turn or flex. Rotate the arms at the shoulder (with very little lift of the shoulders). Keep the arms tight to the torso. Do not allow the hands to cross the midline of the body. Consistently drive the front leg forcefully toward the ground. Point the toes and knees straight ahead and toward the target or finish line (Riley 1996).

Strategic Play

In many contact sports, strategic play and game planning are other methods that can be implemented to reduce external resistance to movement. For example, an opponent's resistance (body mass) can be overcome through practiced techniques under the instruction of intelligent coaches. A case in point: Wisely executed misdirection movements by a wrestler can deceive a countering opponent into resisting in the wrong direction. The reduction in external resistance by the opponent increases the countering movement velocity and the opportunity for successful power movements and performances.

Skill Execution

Drag and explosiveness can also be affected by skill execution. A good illustration of the impact of skill on power is the contrast in blitz performances of rookie and veteran defensive ends in football. The rookie may produce the same power output as the veteran but because the rookie is less skillful in the execution of each explosive movement, power output is misdirected. Because less wasted movement encounters less resistance, the veteran defensive end gains greater forward velocity and expresses more functional explosiveness.

To improve explosiveness through enhanced skill demonstrations, athletes need to learn efficient techniques from competent sport coaches and to study film of themselves executing the sport skills. Athletes should then practice the exact sport movement patterns demonstrating their most skillful technique. The specific goal of these procedures is to reduce drag resistance while demonstrating the movement pattern as a purposeful conditioned reflex rather than as a skill that must be thought about before execution.

ATTENTIONAL FOCUS AND REACTION TIME

The ability to focus one's attention, read situations, and react accordingly in explosive sports appears to be at least as important as movement time for successful power performances. Watching a football linebacker get flattened by the off-side guard on a misdirection play illustrates this point. In many cases, the linebacker gets crushed not because of lack of explosiveness but because he had an incorrect focus and/or did not demonstrate good reaction time. Athletes can have awesome explosive capabilities from the neck down but never get to use them effectively because of limiting factors from the neck up (i.e., mental focus problems and reaction time deficiencies); athletes may have a big, powerful gun (body) but if they cannot pull the trigger (read and react appropriately) under competitive conditions, the size of the gun and speed of the bullet (explosive movement speed) become irrelevant (Lambrinides 1998). Few, if any, other factors influence the expression of sport explosiveness more than attentional focus and reaction time.

Attentional Focus

Attentional focus has been described in the scientific literature as a process whereby athletes put a conscious effort into gathering appropriate information from a specific situation (Posner 1971). Nideffer (1976) says that attentional focus can be broad or narrow and internal or external. A broad-external focus is usually used to assess situations quickly. A quarterback in football should be able to keep this type of focus because relevant cues for success come from stimuli that are in the external environment (e.g., the defensive scheme, weather, and so on).

The broad-internal focus is customarily employed to analyze a game plan. A coach or athlete who is developing game strategies uses this type of attentional focus.

A narrow-external focus is practiced when minimal external cues must be focused on for success. A golfer focusing attention on the ball he or she is about to drive is using this type of concentration.

The last type of attention is the narrow-internal. This focus is used to systematically rehearse a performance or to control arousal. An example of narrow-internal focus is a gymnast who mentally rehearses an explosive vault or who is focused on his or her arousal level and is taking slow deep breaths to relax. This type of focus is also used in competitive weightlifting where the focus is on effort.

Each explosive sport and event requires distinct attentional demands at specific times for proper reads. For instance, as offensive linemen in football walk to the line of scrimmage they have a broad-external focus on the environment (i.e., the position of the defensive linemen, linebackers, and defensive backs). Once they have gathered this external information, their focus shifts to broad-internal as each member of the line plans his duty within their shared assignment. After the line calls are made, attention focuses to a narrow-internal as the linemen monitor their tension and make sure that they are calm yet optimally aroused and aggressive. During this focus, the linemen may also mentally rehearse the moves they plan to use against their individual opponents. Finally the linemen shift their attention to narrow-external as they focus on the quarterback's signals and their opponent.

By watching football linemen on film, we can see when they do not look explosive, miss their assignments, and mess up plays. What we cannot tell is why. Did a lineman miss picking up the blitzing defensive back because his movement speed was too slow? Possibly, but a lack of explosiveness could also be attributed to improper focus and a bad read. If, for example, linemen stay focused internally on their nervousness and do not switch over to the appropriate narrow-external focus (i.e., the quarterback's cadence and their opponent's position) at the right time, they can get off the line too late and miss their opponent.

Implementing the following recommendations may improve attentional focus, leading to an enhanced ability to read, react, and dominate explosive play: Operationally define the terms *focus* and *concentration* to ensure a common vernacular among coaches and athletes. Recognize which type(s) of attentional focus are appropriate during specific sport situations. Practice the proper focuses mentally while physically practicing the sport skills. The combination of both physical and mental training may help individuals learn to lock into a correct focus that allows faster and more accurate reads. Improvements in attentional focus may lead to faster, more accurate reaction times and successful performances in high-speed interactive sports.

Reaction Time

Reaction time refers to "the time it takes to initiate a motor response to a presented stimulus" (Grouios 1992). Reaction time can be improved by implementing the following suggestions: Instruct athletes through film study to identify a small number of relevant variables. The fewer situational and opponent cues they must read and react to, the shorter the response times (Nemish 1995). Watching a hockey goalie demonstrates this point. Most goalies have higher save success rates when they have to react to only one player on a breakaway as opposed to two or three.

Limit the number of possible responses an athlete has to consider before reacting. For example, a basketball player defending a three-on-one fast break who has been told to pressure the ball will read and respond faster than a player defending the break who has been told he or she has three defensive options to analyze before choosing a correct response.

Scouting brings knowledge of opponent tendencies that may allow athletes to invest in early reads and responses. For instance, in baseball a batter may know that the pitcher has a tendency to throw a fastball for his out pitch. Knowing this, the hitter primes his concentration and physical readiness for the fastball on a three-and-two count, thereby improving response time and the probability of hitting the fastball.

APPROPRIATE CONDITIONING

Most sports require competitors to express their explosive power and speed repeatedly to excel. A wide receiver who can run a 4.3-second 40-yard dash in the first quarter and a 5.5-second 40-yard dash in the fourth quarter is a potentially explosive athlete who is unable to produce at a critical time in the game. All athletes must be conditioned in a sport-specific manner to maximize their explosive endurance capacity.

There are two important methods to improve absolute speed and explosiveness through conditioning. First, systematically train the specific energy system used in the performance using identical sport movement patterns. This way, the athletes accomplish cardiovascular and muscular conditioning in the identical manner that they will be asked to perform. Second, practice repeated sport movements (e.g., starts, sprints, jumps) at maximal speed and effort with total recovery between work intervals. The reason for repeated practices in this manner is that during the conditioning process, a majority of athletes pace their effort to make it through the workout. To see optimal gains in explosiveness, athletes need to train in a nonfatigued state. This teaches the players to demonstrate consistent maximal efforts and coordinate their movements efficiently at high speeds.

CONCLUSION

Many sports require the expression of great speed and power for success. There are many areas and strategies currently available to improve sport explosiveness. At the present time, there does not appear to be one best method or recipe to improve speed and power for all athletes in all sport situations.

Each sport, position, and circumstance should be analyzed to decide how speed and power can be enhanced to maximize performance. Realistic training and performance goals should then be set based upon the greatest speed and power improvement possible. Coaches and athletes need to understand that motor abilities such as speed of limb movement, explosiveness, and flexibility are, to a large degree, genetically determined. For example, Wilmore (1982) suggests that sprint speed may only be enhanced about 10 percent through training. Olympic history supports this hypothesis. In 1900, Francis Jarvis from the United States set the men's Olympic 100-meter dash at 11.0 seconds; in 1980, Allan Wells from Great Britain set a new men's 100-meter dash mark of 10.25, an improvement of only 0.75 over an 80-year period (Komarek 1998). This tells us that speed and explosiveness can be improved but not to a large degree. It suggests to coaches that recruitment of gifted (explosive) athletes should be the first priority if speed and explosiveness are an important part of the game. More importantly, it tells competitors that the purchase of magical training recipes and equipment are ill-advised at best. Meaningful sport-specific speed and power improvements do not come from running along the yellow brick road with a parachute or by paying the wizard for magic pills, powders, and potions. The demonstration of sport-specific explosiveness comes from a combination of genetic traits, intelligent coaches who know how to communicate their training knowledge, and athletes who are motivated to use that knowledge.

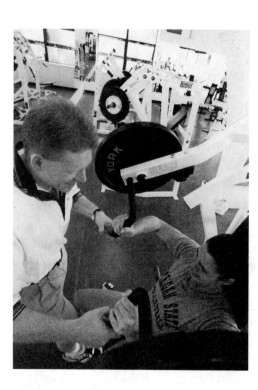

Coaches and athletes need to understand that motor abilities such as speed of limb movement, explosiveness, and flexibility are, to a large degree, genetically determined. (photo by Kevin Fowler)

REFERENCES

Beaulieu, J. E. 1981. Developing a stretching program. *Physician and Sportsmedicine* 9: 59–69.

Behm, D. G. 1988. Surgical tubing for sport and velocity specific training. *National Strength and Conditioning Journal* 10 (4): 66–70.

Brady, T. A., B. R. Cahill, and L. M. Bodnar. 1982. Weight training-related injuries in the high school athlete. *American Journal of Sports Medicine* 10 (1): 1–5.

Bryant, C. X. 1988. *How to develop muscular power.* Grand Rapids, MI: Masters Press.

Carpinelli, R. 1997. More on multiple sets and muscular fatigue. *Master Trainer* 7 (1): 15–17.

Ewing, M. 1998. Personal communication with the author (June 22).

Fox, E., R. W. Bowers, and M. L. Foss. 1993. *Physiological basis for exercise and sport.* 5th ed. Dubuque, IA: W. C. Brown Publishers.

Grouios, G. 1992. On the reduction of reaction time with mental practice. *Journal of Sport Behavior* 15: 141–157.

Hall, S. J. 1991. *Basic biomechanics.* St. Louis, MO: Mosby Year Book, Inc.

———. 1985. Effect of attempted lifting speed on forces and torque exerted on the lumbar spine. *Medicine and Science in Sport and Exercise* 17 (4): 440–444.

Haubenstricker, J. 1998. Personal communication with the author (June 15).

Hay, J. G., and J. G. Reid. 1988. *Anatomy, mechanics and human motion.* Englewood Cliffs, NJ: Simon & Schuster.

Jaric, S., R. Ropret, M. Kukolj, and D. Ilic. 1995. Role of agonist and antagonist muscle strength in performance of rapid movements. *European Journal of Applied Physiology* 71: 464–468.

Knapic, J. J., C. L. Bauman, B. H. Jones, J. M. Harris, and L. Vaughan. 1991. Preseason strength and flexibility imbalances associated with athletic injuries in female collegiate athletes. *American Journal of Sports Medicine* 19: 76–81.

Komarek, A. R. 1998. A history of speed. Unpublished essay. Tampa, FL: Tampa Bay Buccaneers.

Lamb, D. R. 1995. Basic principles for improving sport performance. *Gatorade Sports Science Exchange* 8 (2): 1–5.

Lambrinides, T. L. 1998. Personal communication with the author (April 3).

McArdle, W. D., F. I. Katch, and V. L. Katch. 1991. *Exercise physiology: Energy, nutrition, and human performance.* Malvern, PA: Lea & Febiger.

McCarroll, J. R., J. M. Miller, and M. A. Ritter. 1986. Lumbar spondyloysis and spondylolisthesis in college football players. *American Journal of Sports Medicine* 14 (5): 404–406.

Myers, B., and R. Munroe. 1981. Theory of training for explosive power. *Modern Athlete and Coach* 19 (4): 3–6.

Napier, M. E. 1991. Effects of two different weight training regimens on twenty meter sprinting speed. Unpublished master's thesis. Starkville, MS: Mississippi State University.

Nemish, M. 1995. Reaction time: Implications for its reduction in an effort to enhance sport performance. Unpublished essay. Grand Forks, ND: University of North Dakota.

Newton, R. U., and W. J. Kraemer. 1994. Developing explosive power: Implications for a mixed methods training strategy. *National Strength and Conditioning Association Journal* 11: 20–31.

Nideffer, R. M. 1976. *The inner athlete: Mind plus muscle for winning.* New York: Crowell.

Noakes, T. D., and S. Granger. 1990. *Running injuries.* Cape Town, South Africa: Oxford University Press.

Pivarnik, J. 1998. Personal communication with the author (June 22).

Posner, M. I. 1971. Components of attention. *Psychological Review* 78: 391–408.

Reid, C. M., R. A. Yeater, and I. H. Ullrich. 1987. Weight training and strength, cardiovascular functioning and body composition of men. *British Journal of Sports Medicine* 21 (1): 40–44.

Riley, D. 1996. *Washington Redskins strength and conditioning manual.* Ashburn, VA: Washington Redskins.

Sage, G. H. 1984. *Motor learning and control: A neuropsychological approach.* Dubuque, IA: W. C. Brown Publishers.

Sale, D., and D. MacDougall. 1981. Specificity in strength training: A review for the coach and athlete. *Canadian Journal of Applied Sport Sciences* 6: 87–92.

Schmidt, R. A. 1988. *Motor control and learning: A behavioral emphasis.* 2nd ed. Champaign, IL: Human Kinetics.

Smith, C. A. 1994. The warm-up procedure: To stretch or not to stretch—a brief review. *Journal of Orthopedic Sports Physical Therapy* 19 (1): 12–17.

Ulibarri, D. 1998. Personal communication with the author (June 25).

Wilmore, J. H. 1982. *Training for sport and activity: The physiological basis of the conditioning process.* 2nd ed. Boston: Allyn and Bacon, Inc.

Wooden, M. J., B. Greenfield, M. Johanson, L. Litzelman, M. Mundrane, and R. A. Donatelli. 1992. Effects of strength training on throwing velocity and shoulder muscle performance in teenage baseball players. *Journal of Orthopedic Sports Physical Therapy* 15 (5): 223–228.

Young, W. B., and G. E. Bilby. 1993. The effect of voluntary effort to influence speed of contraction on strength, muscular power, and hypertrophy development. *Journal of Strength and Conditioning Research* 7 (3): 172–178.

This chapter is dedicated to my lovely and patient wife, Alicia, and our wonderful and impatient son, Ryan.

21

Metabolic Conditioning

Matt Brzycki, B.S.
Coordinator of Health Fitness, Strength and Conditioning
Princeton University
Princeton, New Jersey

Most people perform their strength training separate from their aerobic conditioning. Yet, many individuals—especially athletes—are required to integrate their muscular strength with their aerobic conditioning.

Metabolic conditioning is essentially a combination of intense strength training (or other anaerobic efforts) and aerobic conditioning. It involves three major biological systems: the musculoskeletal, respiratory, and circulatory systems. To improve your metabolic fitness, these three systems must share the physiological demands.

Unfortunately, conditioning of the metabolic system is rarely emphasized or even addressed. However, a thorough understanding of metabolic conditioning and an application of specific training techniques can enhance your functional fitness.

PROJECT TOTAL CONDITIONING

In the early 1970s, research designated as Project Total Conditioning was conducted at the United States Military Academy in New York. The research used members of several athletic teams at the academy as test subjects. Project Total Conditioning actually consisted of a number of different studies. For example, one study examined the effects of a strength training program on the neck size and strength of rugby players. Another study investigated the effects of two different training protocols on the vertical-jump ability of volleyball players.

However, the main portion of Project Total Conditioning was a six-week study that examined metabolic conditioning. An experimental group consisted of 18 varsity football players from the academy (a nineteenth subject was injured during spring football practice). This group performed a strength training workout three times per week on alternate days with two days of rest after the third workout of the week. Each workout consisted of 10 exercises and took an average of about 30 minutes to complete. (The subjects also performed six neck exercises twice per week.) Each subject was required to perform as many repetitions as possible using proper technique in every exercise of every workout. One set of each exercise was done to the point of muscular fatigue (or failure) within 5–12 repetitions. The group took a minimal amount of recovery time between exercises.

In order to minimize the influence of the learning effect, the experimental group followed the training protocol for two weeks prior to the study. (The "learning effect" refers to the often dramatic increases initially attained by individuals, which are attributable to improvement in their neurological functioning, not muscular strength.) Prior to the six-week study, the subjects were pretested in several areas—including body composition, strength, cardiovascular fitness, the 40-yard dash, the vertical jump, and flexibility. They were retested following the study.

The study produced very compelling results. After six weeks of training, the subjects increased the resistance they used between their first and seventeenth workouts by an average of 58.54 percent. The minimum improvement in strength was 45.61 percent while the maximum increase in strength was 69.70 percent. (Incidentally, the average increase in the resistance that was used between the second and sixteenth workouts was 43.06 percent.) The subjects also increased the number of repetitions they performed between their first and seventeenth workouts by an average of 6.59 percent.

Interestingly, the time that the subjects needed to complete their workouts decreased substantially. Comparing the first workout to the seventeenth, the experimental group reduced the average duration of their workouts by 24.09 percent—from an average of 37.73 minutes to an average of 28.64 minutes. Two individuals literally cut their workout times almost in half—one from 49 to 25 minutes and the other from 43 to 22 minutes—yet increased their strength levels by 68.32 percent and 65.59 percent, respectively. A third individual reduced his workout time from 42 to 27 minutes and increased his strength level by 66.32 percent.

Besides the tremendous improvements in muscular strength, the subjects also reduced their average time in the two-mile run by 88 seconds—from an average of 13:18 to an average of 11:50. This represented an average improvement of 11 percent—without having performed any running except during the course of spring football practice (which occurred during the first four weeks of training). The subjects also had lower resting heart rates following the six weeks of training. In addition, the experimental group had lower exercising heart rates at various workloads on a stationary cycle, and they were able to perform more work before reaching heart rates of 170 beats per minute.

At the end of the six-week study, members of the experimental group had reduced their average time in the 40-yard dash from 5.1467 seconds to 5.0933 seconds—a 1.04 percent improvement. Their vertical jump had increased from an average of 22.6 inches to an average of 24.067 inches—an average improvement of 6.49 percent. Finally, their average improvement in three flexibility measures was 10.92 percent.

These striking results are even more impressive when you consider that they were accomplished in such a time-efficient manner. In fact, the total amount of actual training time performed by each individual during the six-week program averaged less than 8.5 hours—which is less than 30 minutes per workout. It should be noted that the test subjects were highly conditioned football players who were already quite strong and fit at the start of the program. Nevertheless, the study demonstrated the favorable effects of short-duration, high-intensity strength training on metabolic conditioning.

TYPES OF METABOLIC WORKOUTS

Your metabolic fitness may be improved by simply performing your strength training with a high level of intensity while taking very little rest between your exercises. Performed in this fashion, the shared demands placed on your major biological systems creates a metabolic conditioning effect that cannot be approached by traditional methods of training. The two most popular types of metabolic workouts are high intensity training (HIT) and circuit training.

High Intensity Training

One form of metabolic conditioning that has recently seen a renewed interest is high intensity training or, simply, HIT. In the early 1970s, Nautilus® inventor Arthur Jones popularized the brief, intense strength training workouts that would later become known as HIT in the mid-1980s. In recent years, HIT has become increasingly popular among highly competitive male and female athletes in a variety of sports and activities. HIT is currently used by professional athletes in the National Basketball Association (NBA), the National Hockey League (NHL), and Major League Baseball (MLB), as well as nearly a dozen teams in the National Football League (NFL). In addition, HIT is utilized by literally thousands of collegiate athletes who participate in virtually every sport imaginable—and the numbers are growing. The United States Women's Basketball Team also used HIT on their way to the 1996 Olympic gold medal.

There are many interpretations and variations of HIT. However, most versions have several common denominators. As the name implies, HIT is characterized by

Your metabolic fit-
ness may be
improved by simply
performing your
strength training
with a high level of
intensity while tak-
ing very little rest
between your
exercises. (photo by
Kevin Fowler)

intense, aggressive effort—each exercise is typically performed to the point of muscular fatigue (or failure). A minimal number of sets is usually performed—often only one set of each exercise but sometimes as many as three sets. Another characteristic of HIT is the emphasis on progressive overload—whenever possible, an attempt is made to increase either the repetitions performed or the resistance used from one workout to the next. With safety a major concern, HIT doesn't include explosive movements or momentum—all repetitions are done with a controlled speed of movement. Additionally, HIT is comprehensive—training all of the major muscle groups is a priority.

In general, HIT also involves very brief workouts with a minimum amount of recovery taken between exercises. The short recovery interval between exercises enables a person to maintain a fairly high heart rate for the duration of the workout. Like other forms of metabolic conditioning, the length of the recovery interval taken between exercises depends upon your present level of metabolic fitness. The recovery period isn't structured, timed, or predetermined. Initially, however, a recovery time of perhaps three minutes may be necessary between efforts; with improved fitness, your pace should increase to the point where you are moving as rapidly as possible between exercises.

In short, HIT places an incredible workload upon every major muscle in your body and, at the same time, stresses your circulatory and respiratory pathways. Furthermore, this type of workout can be used to improve your metabolic fitness in a safe and time-efficient manner.

The 3 × 3 Workout

One of the most strenuous of all HIT workouts is sometimes referred to as a 3 × 3 (i.e., three by three) and, for this reason, deserves special note. A 3 × 3 workout simply means that you do three exercises that are repeated three times. For example, the most popular and demanding version of a 3 × 3 workout looks like this: leg press, dip, chin-up; leg press, dip, chin-up; leg press, dip, and chin-up. However, this routine is just one of many possible versions of a 3 × 3 workout. This form of metabolic conditioning can actually be modified in countless ways. (Detailed information on specific exercises mentioned throughout this chapter can be found in my book *A Practical Approach to Strength Training*, published by Masters Press.)

Essentially, a 3 × 3 workout consists of a multi-joint hip movement, followed by a multi-joint chest movement, followed by a multi-joint upper-back movement, and repeated two more times with as little rest as possible between exercises. These three types of movements address every major muscle in your body including your hips/gluteals, quadriceps, hamstrings, chest, upper back, shoulders, biceps, triceps, and forearms.

The most demanding multi-joint exercises for your hips/gluteals (along with your quadriceps and hamstrings) are some type of leg press, squat, or deadlift (with an Olympic bar, a trap bar, or dumbbells). Dips and chin-ups certainly represent the most challenging options for your chest and upper back, respectively. Those who cannot perform dips and/or chin-ups with their body weight can do alternative multi-joint movements that exercise the same muscles. Any kind of multi-joint movement that involves a pushing motion—such as the bench press, incline press, or push-ups—can be used to influence your chest musculature (as well as your shoulders and triceps). Any type of multi-joint movement that involves a pulling motion—such as a lat pulldown or seated row—is suitable for targeting the muscles of your upper back (along with your biceps and forearms).

The first time through the three movements, you should reach muscle fatigue at about 20 repetitions for the hip/gluteal exercise, 12 for the chest exercise, and 12 for the upper-back exercise. When the sequence is repeated the second time, the repetition goals would be 15 for the hip/gluteal exercise, 10 for the chest exercise, and 10 for the upper-back exercise. The third time through the movements should have goals of 12 for the hip/gluteal exercise, 8 for the chest exercise, and 8 for the upper-back exercise. In summary, the repetition goals for these movements should be 20, 15, and 12 for the hip/gluteal exercise and 12, 10, and 8 for the chest and upper-back exercises.

A 3 × 3 workout is extremely time-efficient—most variations can be performed in about 20 minutes or less. The simplicity of this specific type of HIT workout can be deceptive. Though it may not appear demanding, a 3 × 3 workout—if done as outlined above—can place a Herculean workload upon your physiological systems, which translates into tremendous metabolic stress.

Circuit Training

One of the oldest and most popular forms of metabolic conditioning has been dubbed *circuit training*. The birth of circuit training can be traced back to

England in the 1950s. The idea is to perform a series of exercises (or activities) in a sequence (or circuit) with a very brief recovery period between each station. In a sense, therefore, circuit training is a form of interval training.

Circuit Weight Training

The merger of circuit training with weight training is known as *circuit weight training* or, simply, CWT. Usually, CWT is performed on a multi-station apparatus—such as a Universal® Multi-Gym. There are several advantages in using multi-station equipment for CWT. First of all, the exercises of multi-station equipment are in close proximity to each other, which allows you to move quickly around the circuit. Second, the selectorized weight stacks of multi-station equipment enable you to make faster and easier adjustments in resistance. Nevertheless, CWT can also be performed with single-station pieces and/or free weights, provided that the distance between the equipment isn't too great.

CWT is very versatile—you can manipulate the number of exercises/stations, the number of repetitions performed, and the amount of recovery taken between movements. The number of exercises you do in the circuit and the amount of recovery taken between the exercises is a function of your level of fitness. However, a comprehensive session of CWT involves a series of about 12–14 exercises or stations that target each of your major muscle groups. A total-body circuit on a Universal® Multi-Gym might be as follows: leg press, leg curl, leg extension, bench press, dip, pull-up, lat pulldown, seated press, shoulder shrug, bicep curl, tricep extension, wrist flexion, and sit-up. (Several other productive exercises can be done on most multi-station equipment including the upright row, knee-up, and side bend.)

At each station, you can either perform a given number of repetitions or do as many repetitions as possible during a specified time frame (with a controlled speed of movement). At a pace of 60 seconds per exercise with 30 seconds of recovery between stations (including the set-up for the next exercise), a circuit of 12–14 stations can be completed in as little as 18–21 minutes. It should be noted that the resistance you use at each station should permit you to reach muscle fatigue by the end of the allotted exercise time.

To ensure that you obtain continued metabolic improvements from CWT, you can progressively overload your metabolic system in the following ways.

1. Increase the resistance you use at a given station.
2. Increase the length of the work interval (thereby doing more repetitions).
3. Decrease the length of the recovery interval taken between stations.
4. Use any combination of the three previous options.

To summarize CWT: You begin at a particular station and complete one set of an exercise. After this, you move to the next station in the circuit where you set up for your next exercise and rest for the remainder of your recovery period. This cycle is repeated over and over again until the entire circuit is complete.

Circuit Aerobic Training

In the last few years, there's been a growing interest in circuit aerobic training (CAT), which involves a series of aerobic cross-training activities or stations. The circuit can be designed a number of different ways; you can vary the number of cross-training activities, the duration and intensity of each activity, and the amount of recovery taken between stations. Most of these variables are dependent upon your fitness level. Your goal, however, is to perform the equivalent of about 20–60 minutes of aerobic activity with an appropriate level of effort. Keep in mind that 30 minutes of exercise can be done as one 30-minute session, two 15-minute sessions, three 10-minute sessions, or even six 5-minute sessions. So, you might exercise for 10 minutes on a stationary cycle, 10 minutes on a rower, and 10 minutes on a stair-climbing machine for a total of 30 minutes of cross-training activity. Or, you might perform each of those same three activities for 5 minutes but repeat the circuit twice for a total of 30 minutes. Regardless, your level of intensity should be as high as possible during your efforts. (It probably wouldn't be practical—or permissible—for you to monopolize a group of activities for intervals of less than five minutes per station in a commercial facility.)

Other Variations

Yet another version of circuit training is to integrate weight training exercises with one or more aerobic activities. For instance, you might do a strength training exercise, pedal a stationary cycle for 1–3 minutes, do another strength training exercise, pedal a stationary cycle for another 1–3 minutes and so on. Along these lines, a simple but brutal form of metabolic conditioning can be done by alternating dips and chin-ups with running. In other words, you might do a set of dips, run a short distance, do a set of chin-ups, run a short distance, and repeat this circuit several times. (If you work out indoors, you can run on a motorized treadmill.)

The Fitness Trail is a form of circuit training that was originated in several of the Scandinavian countries. This method of circuit training is performed outdoors in a natural environment such as a park. A typical Fitness Trail consists of numerous stations that are positioned several hundred yards apart and arranged along a circuitous route. You would walk, jog, or run to a station; stop and perform some type of agility movement (e.g., hurdles, log walks, and vaults), calisthenic activity (e.g., push-ups, sit-ups, chin-ups, and dips), or flexibility exercise; and then proceed to the next station.

METABOLIC DYNAMICS

At rest, your body doesn't consume much oxygen and your energy needs are easily satisfied by your aerobic system. As your metabolic demands increase during exercise, you require more energy immediately. Your aerobic system cannot transport and deliver oxygen fast enough to address this physiological urgency. Therefore, you must rely upon your anaerobic systems to provide energy until your aerobic system is able to meet your needs.

For the most part, metabolic conditioning involves all-out efforts that last about 60–90 seconds (though the time of activity can approach 120 seconds when performing strength training exercises for your hips/gluteals). In the early stages of intense exercise, a limited amount of energy can be supplied rapidly by your two anaerobic sources: the ATP-PC system and anaerobic glycolysis. During intense efforts, your ATP-PC system exhausts your phosphagen stores in a matter of seconds; as a result of anaerobic glycolysis, the glycogen content of your working muscles drops progressively. As additional oxygen becomes available, your aerobic system is used to a greater degree. After a few minutes, your aerobic system is able to furnish all the energy needed for mild exercise.

Metabolic conditioning presents an enormous physiological challenge to your musculoskeletal, respiratory, and circulatory systems. In response to this metabolic stress, your systems make a number of sudden temporary adjustments that return to resting levels once you complete your effort. The degree of your metabolic response increases in direct proportion to your intensity and the duration of the activity and is also related to other factors such as your body size, gender, and level of fitness. Therefore, detailing your precise biological reaction to general metabolic conditioning is impossible. However, your metabolic adjustments can be estimated with a reasonable degree of accuracy. When going from a resting state to an exercising state, you will experience musculoskeletal, respiratory, circulatory, and general responses.

Musculoskeletal Responses

When performing a strength training exercise, your intensity is lowest during the first repetition. At this point, only a small percentage of your available muscle fibers is recruited (or innervated) by your nervous system—just enough to move the weight. When the muscular intensity is low, your metabolic needs are met by your slow-twitch fiber population. As you do each repetition, your intensity increases progressively and deeper inroads are made into your muscles. Some of your muscle fibers fatigue and are no longer able to keep up with the increasing metabolic demands. Fresh fibers are simultaneously called upon to assist the fatigued fibers in generating ample force. Your fast-twitch fibers are recruited by your nervous system only when your fatigue-resistant slow-twitch fibers have depleted their energy stores and cannot meet the force requirements. This process continues until the last repetition when you reach concentric muscular fatigue and your intensity is at its highest. Now, the collective efforts of your remaining fibers cannot produce enough force to raise the weight. During this final repetition, the cumulative effect of each preceding repetition has fatigued your muscles, thereby providing a sufficient—and efficient—stimulus for muscular growth. It should be noted that your first few repetitions are the least productive because your intensity is low. On the other hand, your very last repetition is the most productive because your intensity is very high.

Your very last repetition is the most productive because your intensity is very high. (photo courtesy of Richard Winett)

Respiratory Responses

The most obvious respiratory response to intense metabolic activity is an increase in the frequency and depth of your breathing. Indeed, rapid and deep breathing is an unmistakable indicator of intense activity. Your labored breathing leads to a heightened sense of respiratory distress, general discomfort, and widespread fatigue. Specifically, your number of breaths per minute (breaths/min) may increase from a resting rate of about 10–12 breaths/min to about 40–50 breaths/min.

Tidal volume refers to the amount of air entering or leaving your lungs during a single breath and is measured in liters per breath (L/breath). During intense activity, your tidal volume may rise to more than six times its resting level—from about 0.5 L/breath to about 3.0 L/breath or more.

The amount of air you inhale or exhale each minute is known as your pulmonary ventilation. It is measured in liters per minute (L/min) and is calculated by multiplying the frequency of your breathing (breaths/min) by your tidal volume (L/breath). Because of the combined increases in your rate and depth of breathing, your pulmonary ventilation may increase from 5 L/min (10 breaths/min × 0.5 L/breath) to more than 150 L/min (50 breaths/min × 3.0 L/breath). To aid in forced expiration during intense efforts, there is also a greater involvement of your respiratory muscles—that is, your abdominal and internal intercostal muscles (which lie between your ribs). In fact, your respiratory muscles may demand 8–10 percent of your oxygen consumption during intense exercise.

Circulatory Responses

When you exercise, your heart beats faster to meet the demands of your muscles for more blood and oxygen. Specifically, your heart rate may climb from a resting level of about 60–70 beats per minute (bpm) to as much as 80–90 percent of your age-predicted maximum or more for brief periods. (Your heart rate actually increases above resting levels prior to your efforts due to the so-called anticipatory response.) The more intense the exercise or activity, the faster your heart beats. The increase in your heart rate is greatest when you perform exercises involving your larger muscle groups—particularly your hips and legs. Monitoring your heart rate during exercise provides a very accurate reflection of the metabolic intensity of the exercise.

Stroke volume refers to the volume of blood pumped by your heart and is measured in liters per beat (L/beat). During intense efforts, your stroke volume may rise from about 0.08 L/beat to perhaps 0.2 L/beat or more. As a result of the combined increases in your stroke volume and heart rate, your cardiac output may increase from about 5 L/min (e.g., 0.08 L/beat × 60 bpm) to more than 30 L/min (e.g., 0.2 L/beat × 150 bpm). Once your stroke volume reaches your physiological limit, further increases in your cardiac output are only possible through increases in your heart rate.

Your cardiac output is distributed to your organs and tissues according to their functions and needs at any given moment. During intense activity, your blood flow is redistributed from areas where it isn't very critical to areas where it is absolutely essential. Specifically, there is a diminished blood flow to your inactive muscles and less active tissues such as your liver, kidneys, and digestive organs (i.e., your stomach and intestines). At rest, 15–20 percent of your systemic blood flow is to your muscles—the majority of the blood goes to your digestive organs and brain. During intense exercise, your blood flow is redirected to your working muscles. In fact, your exercising muscles may receive 85–90 percent of the total blood flow. This means that for a cardiac output of 30 L/min, more than 25 liters of blood can be delivered to your active muscles every minute. Your heart also receives an increased supply of blood during intense efforts—from a resting level of about 0.25 L/min to about 0.75 L/min. (The blood flow to your brain is unchanged.)

Your blood pressure is measured in millimeters of mercury (mm Hg). Your systolic blood pressure increases in proportion to your exercise intensity and can rise from a resting level of about 120 mm Hg to more than 200 mm Hg. During intense activity, the diastolic blood pressure of healthy individuals remains at about 70 mm Hg or drops slightly. Maximum blood pressure usually occurs at maximum heart rate.

Your body temperature rises during intense exercise—especially in hot, humid conditions. Your body has a temperature-regulatory mechanism and, like a thermostat, tries to maintain its temperature at a relatively constant value of roughly 98.6°F (or about 37°C). During vigorous activity, your body temperature may exceed 102°F (or about 39°C). As your body temperature rises, there is an increased blood flow from your warmer core to the surface of your skin. This process facilitates heat dissipation and allows heat loss. Unfortunately, this also reduces the amount of blood available to supply your working muscles with oxygen.

Your expenditure of calories per minute is also elevated during intense activity.

(photo by Matt Brzycki)

General Responses

Short-term high-intensity activity increases the production of carbon dioxide and lactic acid. This, in turn, lowers your pH. Your muscle pH may briefly decrease from a resting value of about 7.0 to as low as 6.4. The lactate spreads from your muscles into the surrounding tissues and eventually spills into your blood. This causes your blood pH to temporarily drop from a resting value of perhaps 7.4 to as low as 6.8. As the lactic acid begins to accumulate, it irritates your nerve endings and causes feelings of muscular pain, discomfort, distress, and fatigue. As lactic acid accumulates, it also causes your breathing to become labored.

Your oxygen consumption can be measured in either milliliters per kilogram per minute (ml/kg/min) or liters per minute (L/min). During intense metabolic conditioning, your oxygen consumption may increase from about 3.5 ml/kg/min at rest to about 26.0 ml/kg/min or more. For a 165-pound person, this equates to an increase from a resting level of roughly 0.25 L/min to about 2.0 L/min or more. Compared to pure aerobic training, these oxygen-consumption values are somewhat low. Such low values are primarily due to the intermittent nature of metabolic conditioning. At any given heart rate, the metabolic demands—in terms of oxygen consumption—are lower for strength training compared to aerobic training. Research has shown that the oxygen consumption during strength training averages 68 percent of that seen during aerobic training at the same exercising heart rate. To express this idea in different terms, at a given level of oxygen consumption, heart rates are higher during strength training compared to aerobic training. For instance, an oxygen consumption of 25 ml/kg/min elicits a heart rate of about 180 bpm during strength training compared to a heart rate of about 155 bpm for aerobic training. During strength training, the heart rate is disproportionately elevated relative to oxygen consumption.

Your expenditure of calories per minute (cal/min) is also elevated during intense activity. Like most of your other metabolic responses, the rate of your caloric expenditure largely depends upon your intensity and your body weight. The rate of caloric expenditure for a 165-pound individual may increase from about 1.3 cal/min to perhaps 10.0 cal/min or more. Finally, it should be noted that your oxygen consumption and caloric expenditure are greatest when training the larger muscles in the body such as your hips and legs.

REFERENCES

Asimov, I. 1992. *The human body: Its structure and operation.* Revised ed. New York: Mentor.

Bryant, C. X. 1995. Understanding crossaerobic training. In *The StairMaster fitness handbook,* 2nd ed., ed. J. A. Peterson and C. X. Bryant, 81–105. St. Louis: Wellness Bookshelf.

Brzycki, M. 1997. *Cross training for fitness.* Indianapolis, IN: Masters Press.

Fox, E. L. 1984. Physiology of exercise and physical fitness. In *Sports medicine,* ed. R. H. Strauss, 381–456. Philadelphia: W. B. Saunders Company.

Fox, E. L., and D. K. Mathews. 1981. *The physiological basis of physical education and athletics.* 3rd ed. Philadelphia: Saunders College Publishing.

Gettman, L. R., P. Ward, and R. D. Hagman. 1982. A comparison of combined running and weight training with circuit weight training. *Medicine and Science in Sports and Exercise* 14: 229–234.

Hempel, L. S., and C. L. Wells. 1985. Cardiorespiratory cost of the Nautilus express circuit. *Physician and Sportsmedicine* 13 (4): 82–86, 91–97.

Howley, E. T., and B. D. Franks. 1992. *Health fitness instructor's handbook.* 2nd ed. Champaign, IL: Human Kinetics.

Hurley, B. F., D. R. Seals, A. A. Ehsani, L. J. Cartier, G. P. Dalsky, J. M. Hagberg, and J. O. Holloszy. 1984. Effects of high-intensity strength training on cardiovascular function. *Medicine and Science in Sports and Exercise* 16: 483–488.

Messier, S. P., and M. Dill. 1985. Alterations in strength and maximal oxygen uptake consequent to Nautilus circuit weight training. *Research Quarterly for Exercise and Sport* 56: 345–351.

Peterson, J. A. 1975. Total conditioning: A case study. *Athletic Journal* 56 (September): 40–55.

Porcari, J., and J. Curtis. 1996. Can you work strength and aerobics at the same time? *Fitness Management* 12 (June): 26–29.

Wilmore, J. H. 1982. *Training for sport and activity: The physiological basis of the conditioning process.* 2nd ed. Boston: Allyn and Bacon, Inc.

We dedicate this chapter to our wives—Susan and Ginger—who continually provide us with immeasurable strength and support.

22

Strength Training and Women: Dispelling the Myths

James A. Peterson, Ph.D., FACSM
Sports Medicine Specialist
Monterey, California

Cedric X. Bryant, Ph.D., FACSM
Vice President of Product Management and Sports Medicine
StairMaster® Sports/Medical Products, Inc.
Kirkland, Washington

If you ask a group of individuals about their opinions concerning strength training, in all likelihood the responses you receive will vary widely. Some will like the activity a lot while others will view the prospect of "pumping iron" as totally foreign to their sense of reality. Unlike the other components of physical fitness, muscular fitness is often clouded by a cloak of mysticism, baffling practices, and unfathomable explanations. In numerous instances, the foundation for this aura of misunderstanding has been the seemingly endless array of myths and misconceptions concerning strength training that has proliferated over the years.

These baseless elements have at least one attribute in common: They misrepresent the truth. Their continued existence is due to many factors, not the least of which is a general lack of effort in the popular literature to refute them. In reality, many of the more popular muscle magazines and strength development texts marketed for public consumption often seem to reinforce them with an unfortunate lack of propriety. Among the most common misguided viewpoints attendant to strength training are the 13 myths we'll describe in this chapter.

MYTH 1: WOMEN CAN'T GET STRONG

Not true. Women can (and should) develop muscular fitness. For example, since the first admission of women to the United States Military Academy (USMA) at West Point, this national institution has had several women graduates who could perform more than 100 straight-back push-ups (the so-called male push-ups) in two minutes or less. A number of USMA women graduates were able to perform at least 10 properly executed pull-ups. In addition, the average female West Point cadet has been able to do more sit-ups in a set period of time than her male counterpart. The point to be drawn from these statistics is not that average women can or should do as well as the women at West Point but rather that women have a potential for muscular fitness—particularly upper-body muscular fitness—that is virtually untapped. In reality, the average woman tends to gain strength at a slightly faster rate than the average man. This apparent gender-based difference is thought to be due to the fact that most women initially have low levels of muscular strength.

MYTH 2: STRENGTH TRAINING DEFEMINIZES WOMEN

Not true. What right does anyone have to suggest to a woman that her body is less important to her than a man's is to him? On what rational basis could anyone possibly confine the potential health, functional, mental, and cosmetic benefits of strength training to members of the male sex? The short answer? No one could or should.

Proper strength training—by helping a woman increase her physical working capacity, improve her body composition, and lower her risk of injury—will make her look and feel better about herself. Tight, firm muscles have nothing whatsoever to do with the objectionable (and patronizing) term "defeminizing."

MYTH 3: LIFTING WEIGHTS CAUSES BULKY MUSCLES

Not true. The overwhelming majority of women simply don't have the genetic potential to develop large muscles. Most don't have sufficient amounts of testosterone—the hormone largely responsible for the development of muscle bulk. At the onset of puberty, the endocrine systems of young women begin to secrete estrogen, which is often referred to as the *female hormone*. Estrogen helps to initiate the process of menstruation and the development of specific female traits. At the same time, however, young men begin to produce testosterone (the *male hormone*), which helps partially explain why many young men, from that point in their lives, are able to outperform their female counterparts on strength-related tasks. Understanding how hormonal factors can affect the process of muscular growth also helps to explain how most of the women with an extraordinarily high level of muscular development who frequently adorn the covers of the so-called muscle magazines or appear on national television got that ultra-buffed look. They didn't do it the old-fashioned way . . . they didn't earn it naturally. Many apparently had chemical assistance—usually either steroids or synthetic derivatives of growth hormones.

MYTH 4: STRENGTH TRAINING MAKES WOMEN MUSCLE-BOUND

Not true. "Muscle-bound" is a term that connotes a lack of flexibility. Contrary to popular belief, to be muscle-bound has little to do with either the size of your muscles or proper strength training. Proper strength training won't make a woman less flexible; in fact, it could make her more flexible. Each of the dozens of skeletal joints in the body is surrounded by muscle. If skeletal muscles are kept loose and supple by regularly requiring them to go through a full range of motion (ROM), joint flexibility is maintained or improved.

The overwhelming majority of women simply don't have the genetic potential to develop large muscles.

(photo courtesy of StairMaster® Sports/ Medical Products, Inc.)

In other words, the elongated muscles will permit the skeletal joints to move through a normal ROM. If, however, strength training exercises are not performed through a full ROM (a practice that is contrary to proper strength training techniques), the muscles will tighten and shorten, resulting in a loss of flexibility (i.e., the development of muscle-boundness). If this happens, joints will no longer be able to move through a full ROM (i.e., they have become muscle-bound). Proper strength training can prevent that.

MYTH 5: MORE IS BETTER

Not true. More might be better in some things—such as loyal friends, good music, leisure time, and so on—but not with regard to any form of exercise, including strength training. Sooner or later, a point of either diminishing or no returns will be reached. Eventually, individuals who subscribe to the more-is-better philosophy encounter the negative effects associated with overuse or over-training. Too much of a good thing is seldom beneficial for the human body. Individuals take a very real chance of injuring themselves if they don't approach their training with common sense. Exercise scientists, for example, have shown that an individual who runs seven days a week is not significantly more aerobically

If a muscle is not actively used, it will literally waste away (i.e., atrophy). (photo courtesy of StairMaster® Sports/ Medical Products, Inc.)

fit than an individual who properly trains three to four times a week. In other words, it is the quality of strength training exercise performed that is important, not the quantity of time spent. At West Point, for instance, several studies found that challenging strength training workouts that are brief and infrequent could be used to develop muscular fitness effectively and safely.

MYTH 6: NO PAIN, NO GAIN

Not true. A sensible strength training program should not be painful—challenging and uncomfortable perhaps, but not painful. A sound resistance-training regimen should place a reasonable demand on the muscular system without subjecting the entire musculoskeletal system to an unreasonable risk of injury. Knowing when to say when is one of the keys to engaging in resistance exercise in a sensible manner. The old adage "no pain, no gain" is incomplete. What the person who coined this phrase was really trying to say was "no pain equals no gain equals no sense."

MYTH 7: MUSCLES CAN TURN TO FAT

Not true. Muscles cannot turn into fat. They simply do not have the physiological capability of changing from one type of tissue to another. In an attempt to justify their apprehensions about strength training, many people advance the argument that, in the long run, strength training is bad for a person because when individuals stop strength training their muscles turn into fat. In reality, muscles have to use it or lose it. If a muscle is not actively used, it will literally waste away (i.e., atrophy). The process is perhaps best illustrated when someone has to wear a cast on a broken leg. When the cast is eventually removed, the unused leg muscles are considerably smaller than they were prior to the injury. If muscle can turn to fat, a "fat ball" should be seen when the cast is removed, not a highly atrophied set of leg muscles.

MYTH 8: PROTEIN SUPPLEMENTS ARE ESSENTIAL FOR DEVELOPING A MUSCULAR PHYSIQUE

Not true. The argument that the development of a muscular physique is somehow enhanced through the ingestion of protein supplements has no scientific basis. The human body is simply unable to store extra protein. Protein consumed in excess of the body's needs—which the average American adult easily gets by eating a normal, balanced diet—is not used to build muscle tissue. Instead, it is used for nonprotein bodily functions. If protein is consumed in excess of caloric and protein needs, the extra protein will not be stored as protein but converted to and stored as fat. As a result, if a woman consumes large amounts of extra protein in addition to her regular diet, any weight gain will very likely be in the form of fat. In addition, excess protein can lead to dehydration because protein metabolism (breakdown) requires extra water for utilization and excretion. Excess protein consumption can also lead to an increased loss of urinary calcium. Chronic calcium loss—which can result from excess protein intake—is of particular concern because it increases the risk of osteoporosis, especially in women. If a woman wants to be muscularly fit, her best option is to engage in a sound strength training program, not search for a quick-fix solution in a "promise-them-the-impossible-as-long-as-they-pay-for-it" product.

MYTH 9: PROPER STRENGTH TRAINING MUST BE COMPLEX

Not true. In reality, it's just the opposite. To a point, the more basic and straightforward the strength training program, the more likely it is to be successful. Part of the complexity that some individuals incorporate into the strength training arena is a by-product of a conscious—or subconscious—effort to make the process appear to be more technical and scientific, which people misinterpret as being authoritative. Unfortunately, such an approach frequently leads to confusion—confusion that can result either in a woman's strength training efforts being compromised or in increasing the possibility that she won't stick with her training program. Neither alternative is desirable. At West Point, the women cadets train using an extremely basic muscular development program—one that emphasizes effectiveness, efficiency, and safety over complexity—and produces extraordinary results.

MYTH 10: STRENGTH TRAINING IS A CONTEST

Not true. Strength training is not a contest—against yourself or anyone else. Individuals who focus on the competitive aspects of this particular form of exercise tend to either injure themselves or get more easily discouraged with the results of their efforts and drop out of their programs. In general they try to do too much too soon. They compare their training numbers—particularly the amount lifted during a specific exercise—with those of other participants. What do such numbers really mean other than offering a simplistic means of keeping score? How much a woman lifts on a given day is a by-product of several factors, over most of which she has no control—including the length of her arms or legs, her muscle-fiber composition, the insertion points of her muscles, and so on. As trite as it may sound, the old adage "do your best and leave the rest" should govern a woman's efforts to develop muscular fitness. A woman's goal with regard to strength development should be to reach her unique potential. An Ancient Greek word, *arete*, best represents this philosophy. Literally translated, it means "be the best you can be."

MYTH 11: STRENGTH TRAINING IS FOR YOUNG PEOPLE

Not true. In reality, your biological clock is not a factor. It's never too late to experience an improved quality of life. It's never too late to enjoy the benefits of a higher level of muscular fitness. It's never too late to extend an individual's functional life span, perhaps making the difference between a person's living at home independently or becoming institutionalized. The literature is replete with instances of women of all ages reaching a decision to initiate a strength training program at a particular point in their lives and benefiting from that decision. Recent research conducted at Tufts University in Boston showed that older women experienced significant health improvements following participation in a strength training program. By adhering to a strength training regimen, the postmenopausal women in the study realized substantial increases in bone density and muscle mass. These positive physiological changes resulted in their becoming stronger, more active, and less susceptible to osteoporotic bone fractures. After one full year, their bodies were physiologically more youthful—almost 20 years younger. As with any form of exercise, older participants should check with their physicians before initiating a strength training program.

MYTH 12: STRENGTH TRAINING CAN RID THE BODY OF FAT

Not true. Research consistently shows that strength training can firm and tone muscles and, therefore, help to preserve or increase resting metabolic rate. However, it does not totally eliminate fat. Keep in mind that some fat is needed for normal bodily functions and that a woman shouldn't want to eliminate all body fat even if she could. The total amount of fat in the body consists of two types: essential fat and storage fat. Essential fat is necessary in specific body structures such as the brain, nerve tissue, heart, bone marrow, and cell membranes. Adult women have approximately 12 percent of their body weight in essential fat.

Exercise adherence is always higher (all other factors considered) in those individuals who enjoy what they're doing. (photo courtesy of StairMaster® Sports/ Medical Products, Inc.)

Storage fat represents the excess energy that has been stockpiled as fat. The total amount of storage fat in an individual varies considerably from person to person. For health reasons, the minimum optimal level of total body fat should range from 13 to 18 percent for women.

MYTH 13: STRENGTH TRAINING CAN'T BE FUN

Not true. Strength training can and should be an enjoyable endeavor. If a woman does not find strength training to be particularly enjoyable, it is very likely that she will give it up for greener pastures. Fortunately, almost anyone can design an enjoyable strength training program that meets her individual needs. Not surprisingly, exercise adherence is always higher (all other factors considered) in those individuals who enjoy what they're doing.

REFERENCES

American College of Sports Medicine (ACSM). 1998. *ACSM's resource manual for guidelines for exercise testing and prescription.* 3rd ed. Philadelphia, PA: Williams & Wilkins.

Colletti, L. A., J. Edwards, L. Gordon, J. Shary, and N. H. Ball. 1989. The effects of muscle-building exercise on bone mineral density of the radius, spine, and hip in young men. *Calcified Tissue International* 45 (1): 12–14.

Ebben, W. P., and R. L. Jensen. 1998. Strength training for women: Debunking myths that block opportunity. *Physician and Sportsmedicine* 26 (5): 86–97.

Fiore, C. E., E. Cottini, C. Fargetta, D. S. Giuseppe, R. Foti, and M. Raspagliesi. 1991. The effects of muscle-building exercise on forearm bone mineral content and osteoblast activity in drug-free and anabolic steroids self-administering young men. *Bone and Mineral* 13 (1): 77–83.

Fleck, S. J., and W. J. Kraemer. 1997. *Designing resistance training programs.* 2nd ed. Champaign, IL: Human Kinetics.

Gleeson, P. B., E. J. Protas, A. D. LeBlanc, V. S. Schneider, and H. J. Evans. 1990. Effects of weight lifting on bone mineral density in premenopausal women. *Journal of Bone and Mineral Research* 5 (2): 153–158.

Holloway, J. B. 1994. Individual differences and their implications for resistance training. In *Essentials of strength training and conditioning*, ed. T. R. Baechle, 151–162. Champaign, IL: Human Kinetics.

Kraemer, W. J., and S. J. Fleck. 1993. *Resistance training for young athletes.* Champaign, IL: Human Kinetics.

National Strength and Conditioning Association (NSCA). 1989. Strength training for female athletes: A position paper: Part I. *National Strength and Conditioning Association Journal* 11 (4):43–55.

———. 1989. Strength training for female athletes: A position paper: Part II. *National Strength and Conditioning Association Journal* 11 (5): 29–36.

Nieman, D. C. 1990. *Fitness and sports medicine: An introduction.* 2nd ed. Palo Alto, CA: Bull Publishing Company.

Peterson, J. A., and C. X. Bryant, eds. 1995. *The StairMaster fitness handbook.* 2nd ed. Champaign, IL: Sagamore Publishing.

Peterson, J. A., C. X. Bryant, and S. L. Peterson. 1995. *Strength training for women.* Champaign, IL: Human Kinetics.

Petranick, K., and K. Berg. 1997. The effects of weight training on bone density of premenopausal, postmenopausal and elderly women: A review. *Journal of Strength and Conditioning Research* 11 (3): 200–208.

This chapter is dedicated to my father, Warren Westcott, for his superb example of senior fitness through sensible strength training and for his even greater model as a man of God.

23

Strength Training for Older Adults

Wayne L. Westcott, Ph.D., C.S.C.S.
Fitness Research Director
South Shore YMCA
Quincy, Massachusetts

During the past few years there has been considerable interest in the aging process, and several studies have examined strategies for delaying various degenerative responses (Frontera et al. 1988; Fiatarone et al. 1990; Koffler et al. 1992; Menkes et al. 1993; Risch et al. 1993; Campbell et al. 1994; Nelson et al. 1994; Tufts University Diet and Nutrition Letter 1994; Westcott and Guy 1996).

Perhaps the most obvious and misunderstood aspect of the aging process is the undesirable change in body composition and physical appearance. It is estimated that approximately 80 percent of Americans are sedentary (Anderson et al. 1997) and that 75 percent of adults are overweight (Scripps 1996), and there would appear to be a strong association between doing too little exercise and having too much body weight.

Generally, men and women add about 10 pounds of body weight every decade during their midlife years. The typical response is dieting and, according to a Tufts University study (1994), about 40 percent of American adults are presently following restricted-calorie diets. Unfortunately, dieting without exercise does not have a very strong record of success. First, only 50 percent of those who begin dieting complete the program (McClernan 1992). Second, of those individuals who do lose weight, more than 90 percent regain it within one year (Brehm and Keller 1990). Third, about 25 percent of the weight lost during low-calorie diets is actually muscle tissue, which is already in short supply among most older adults (Ballor and Poehlman 1994).

Research shows that adult men and women lose more than five pounds of lean body mass (mostly muscle) every decade of life due to disuse (Forbes 1976; Evans and Rosenberg 1992). So the 10-pounds-per-decade increase in body weight actually represents a 20-pound problem with respect to body composition. That is, on a decade-by-decade basis, the aging adult has about 5 pounds less muscle and about 15 pounds more fat for a 20-pound change in physical appearance. This process is illustrated in Table 23.1.

Because our muscles are the engines of our bodies, muscle loss has a profound impact on our physical ability and functional capacity. Losing muscle is similar to going from an eight-cylinder engine to a four-cylinder engine. As engine size is closely associated with fuel utilization, it is not hard to understand why less muscle leads to a lower metabolic rate. In fact, the progressive reduction in muscle tissue is largely responsible for a 2–5 percent decrease per decade in our resting metabolism (Keyes, Taylor, and Grande 1973; Evans and Rosenberg 1992).

When our resting metabolic rate slows down, calories that were previously used by muscle tissue are routed into fat storage. In other words, the progressive weight gain known as *creeping obesity* is typically due to fewer calories being expended rather than more calories being consumed. That is why dieting does not solve the problem. In fact, dieting exacerbates the problem by further reducing muscle tissue and metabolic rate.

While adults should perform regular endurance exercise to enhance their cardiovascular function (such as walking and cycling), aerobic activities do little to prevent the gradual deterioration of the musculoskeletal system. In a study of elite middle-aged runners, the subjects lost about five pounds of muscle over a 10-year period in spite of extensive aerobic training (Pollock et al. 1987).

If losing muscle is the basic problem, then adding muscle should be the logical solution. But is it possible for older adults to replace the muscle they have already forfeited? Absolutely. In fact, several studies have shown that both strength and muscle mass can be increased at essentially any age through systematic strength training (Frontera et al. 1988; Fiatarone et al. 1990; Campbell et al. 1994; Westcott and Guy 1996).

With respect to reversing body-composition problems, strength exercise is effective for adding muscle, losing fat, raising resting metabolic rate, and increas-

Table 23.1 Average American Woman's Changes in Body Composition During Midlife Years

Age	20	30	40	50
Body Weight (lbs.)	126	136	146	156
Muscle Weight (lbs.)	45	40	35	30
Fat Weight (lbs.)	29	44	59	74
Percent Fat (%)	23	32	40	47

ing daily energy expenditure. Consider the results of a Tufts University study conducted by Campbell and his colleagues (1994). After 12 weeks of strength training (about 30 minutes per session, three days per week), 12 senior men and women added about three pounds of lean (muscle) weight, lost about four pounds of fat weight, raised their resting metabolism by almost 7 percent and increased their daily energy expenditure by 15 percent. That is, three months of relatively brief strength training sessions enabled these older adults to replace muscle, reduce fat, and eat about 350 more calories per day in the process.

In a similar study conducted at the South Shore YMCA (Westcott 1995), 85 senior men and women performed about 30 minutes of strength exercise and 20 minutes of endurance exercise two days per week for a period of eight weeks. On average, the exercisers added two pounds of lean (muscle) weight, lost four pounds of fat weight, and increased their overall muscle strength by about 50 percent.

In addition to replacing muscle tissue, research reveals that men and women of all ages can increase their bone mineral density through regular strength training. Studies with senior men (Menkes et al. 1993) and senior women (Nelson et al. 1994) have shown significant gains in bone mineral density, indicating that strength exercise may reduce the risk of osteoporosis.

Another benefit of strength training is an enhanced glucose metabolism that may reduce the risk of adult onset diabetes. Research at the University of Maryland (Hurley 1994) showed a 23 percent improvement in glucose metabolism after four months of strength exercise.

Another study at the University of Maryland (Koffler et al. 1992) demonstrated a 56 percent increase in gastrointestinal transit speed following three months of strength exercise. Because faster gastrointestinal transit speed may reduce the risk of colon cancer, this finding has important implications for older adults.

Researchers at the University of Florida (Risch et al. 1993) have demonstrated that properly performed strength training can significantly reduce low-back pain, and researchers at Tufts University (Tufts University Diet and Nutrition Letter 1994) have determined that strength exercise can alleviate arthritic discomfort.

Contrary to popular opinion, regular strength training results in lower resting blood pressure in seniors (Westcott, Dolan, and Cavicchi 1996), as well as in mildly hypertensive individuals (Harris and Holly 1987). Strength exercise has also been shown to improve blood cholesterol profiles (Hurley et al. 1988).

In addition to the physiological benefits associated with strength training, a recent Harvard University study (Singh, Clements, and Fiatarone 1997) showed significant psychological improvements as well. After 12 weeks of strength exercise, 14 of 16 depressed senior subjects no longer met the criteria for clinical depression.

Of course, for most men and women the major outcomes of strength training are simply looking better, feeling better, and functioning better on a day-to-day basis. Fortunately, seniors respond just as well to strength exercise as younger adults.

SENIOR STUDY RESULTS

A large-scale study conducted at the South Shore YMCA (Westcott and Guy 1996) compared the results of young, middle-aged, and older adults following an eight-week training program. The program consisted of two to three workouts per week. Each workout involved about 30 minutes of strength exercise and 20 minutes of endurance exercise.

The 1,132 participants in this study included 238 young adults (21–40 years), 553 middle-aged adults (41–60 years), and 341 older adults (61–80 years). As shown in Table 23.2, all three age groups began the program with similar body weights (172.7–179.9 pounds) and similar percent-fat readings (25.6–27.2 percent). After eight weeks of exercise, the body weight and body-composition changes were comparable for the three age groups. The 21-to-40-year-olds lowered their body weight by 2.6 pounds and their percent fat by 2.3 percent. The 41-to-60-year-olds decreased their body weight by 2 pounds and their percent fat by 2.1 percent. The 61-to-80-year-olds reduced their body weight by 1.7 pounds and their percent fat by 2 percent.

Changes in fat weight and lean (muscle) weight were similar for the three age groups. The young adults lost 4.9 pounds of fat weight and added 2.3 pounds of lean weight. The middle-aged adults lost 4.4 pounds of fat weight and added 2.3 pounds of lean weight. The older adults lost 4.1 pounds of fat weight and added 2.4 pounds of lean weight.

These findings indicate that senior men and women experience similar body-composition improvements to those of young and middle-aged adults in response

Table 23.2 Changes in Body Weight and Body Composition for Young, Middle-Aged, and Older Program Participants (N = 1,132)

Age	Body Weight Pre (lb.)	Body Weight Post (lb.)	Body Weight Change (lb.)	Body Fat Pre (%)	Body Weight Post (%)	Body Weight Change (%)	Fat Weight Pre (lb.)	Fat Weight Post (lb.)	Fat Weight Change (lb.)	Lean Weight Pre (lb.)	Lean Weight Post (lb.)	Lean Weight Change (lb.)
21–40 years (N=238)	176.5	173.9	-2.6*	27.2	24.9	-2.3*	49.1	44.2	-4.9*	127.4	129.7	+2.3*
41–60 years (N=553)	179.9	177.9	-2.0*	27.0	24.9	-2.1*	48.9	44.5	-4.4*	130.8	133.1	+2.3*
61–80 years (N=341)	172.7	171.0	-1.7*	25.6	23.6	-2.0*	44.7	40.6	-4.1*	128.0	130.4	+2.4*

*Statistically significant change (p<.01).

to a basic program of strength and endurance exercise. It is interesting to note that the older exercisers replaced muscle at the same rate as the younger program participants.

In addition to body-composition assessments, 785 of the study subjects had resting blood pressure readings taken before and after the eight-week exercise program. As presented in Table 23.3, all three age groups began with similar diastolic blood pressure readings (76.1–80.1 mm Hg). However, the systolic blood pressure readings were considerably higher for the 61-to-80-year-olds (143.1 mm Hg) than for the 41-to-60-year-olds (127.9 mm Hg) and 21-to-40-year-olds (121.2 mm Hg).

Although all three age groups recorded significant reductions in resting blood pressure, the senior participants experienced the greatest improvement. Their diastolic blood pressure decreased 3.7 mm Hg, and their systolic blood pressure decreased 6.2 mm Hg. Perhaps most important, the older adult group began the exercise program with a systolic blood pressure above the hypertensive level (143.1 mm Hg), but ended within the normal systolic range (136.9 mm Hg).

The results of this large-scale research study should be encouraging news for senior men and women. Consider the following key findings for the 341 older adults who completed the two-month strength training program:

1. Seniors can safely participate in well-designed and carefully supervised programs of strength exercise, contingent upon a physician's approval.
2. Seniors can reduce their body weight and improve their body composition. The participants in this exercise program decreased their body weight by 1.7 pounds and improved their body composition by 2 percent.

Table 23.3 Changes in Resting Blood Pressure for the Young, Middle-Aged, and Older Program Participants (N = 785)

Age	Systolic BP Pre (mm Hg)	Systolic BP Post (mm Hg)	Systolic BP Change (mm Hg)	Diastolic BP Pre (mm Hg)	Diastolic BP Post (mm Hg)	Diastolic BP Change (mm Hg)
21–40 years (N=144)	121.2	116.7	-4.5*	76.1	72.9	-3.2*
41–60 years (N=375)	127.9	125.4	-2.5*	79.0	76.6	-2.4*
61–80 years (N=266)	143.1	136.9	-6.2*	80.1	76.4	-3.7*

*Statistically significant change (p<.01).

3. Seniors can decrease their fat weight and increase their lean (muscle) weight. The subjects in this study lost 4.1 pounds of fat and added 2.4 pounds of muscle.

4. Seniors can reduce their resting blood pressure. The participants in this exercise program experienced a 3.7 mm Hg decrease in their diastolic blood pressure and a 6.2 mm Hg decrease in their systolic blood pressure.

5. Seniors can develop physically active lifestyles, even after decades of sedentary behavior. More than 90 percent of the study subjects continued to strength train after completing the exercise program.

It would appear that older adults have much to gain from strength exercise, including increased physical capacity, enhanced personal appearance, improved athletic performance, and reduced injury risk. However, many have limited time and energy to participate in a traditional strength training program. Fortunately, properly performed strength exercise requires a relatively small time commitment. For example, the significant improvements in body composition and muscle strength experienced by 1,132 subjects in the Westcott and Guy (1996) study resulted from just two or three brief training sessions per week.

It would appear that older adults have much to gain from strength exercise, including increased physical activity, enhanced personal appearance, improved athletic performance, and reduced injury risk.

(photo by Matt Brzycki)

RECOMMENDATIONS FOR SENSIBLE SENIOR STRENGTH TRAINING

Several national organizations have developed guidelines for safe and effective strength training, including the YMCA of the USA (1987), the American College of Sports Medicine (1990) and the American Council on Exercise (1996). In general, all of these organizations promote the following program recommendations for adult strength exercise.

Training Exercises

The training guidelines call for one exercise for each of the major muscle groups. Table 23.4

Table 23.4 Standard Machine and Free-Weight Exercises for the Major Muscles of the Body

Major Muscle Group	Machine Exercise	Free-Weight Exercise
Quadriceps	Leg Extension	Dumbbell Squat
Hamstrings	Leg Curl	Dumbbell Squat
Pectoralis Major	Arm Cross	Dumbbell Bench Press
Latissimus Dorsi	Pullover	Dumbbell Bent-Over Row
Deltoids	Lateral Raise	Dumbbell Lateral Raise
Biceps	Bicep Curl	Dumbbell Bicep Curl
Triceps	Tricep Extension	Dumbbell Tricep Extension
Erector Spinae	Low Back Extension	Body Weight Back Extension
Rectus Abdominis	Abdominal Curl	Body Weight Trunk Curl
Neck Flexors/Extensors	Four-Way Neck	

presents standard machine and free-weight exercises for the major muscles of the body.

If training time is really limited, one study (Westcott 1990) reported excellent results from just three multiple-muscle exercises. These were the leg press (gluteals, quadriceps, and hamstrings), bench press (pectoralis major, deltoids, and triceps), and compound row (latissimus dorsi and biceps).

Training Frequency

Strength exercise may be productively performed two or three days per week. In terms of strength development, a recent study by DeMichele and coworkers (1997) found two and three training sessions per week to be equally effective. With respect to body-composition changes, subjects in the Westcott and Guy (1996) study who trained twice a week attained almost 90 percent as much improvement as subjects who trained three times a week (see Figure 23.1).

Because two and three training sessions per week appear to produce similar muscular benefits, the exercise frequency factor may be a matter of personal preference and scheduling ability.

Training Sets

Single- and multiple-set training protocols have proven effective for increasing muscle strength and mass in senior men and women (Frontera et al. 1988; Campbell et al. 1994; Fiatarone et al. 1994; Nelson et al. 1994; Westcott and Guy 1996; Westcott, Dolan, and Cavicchi 1996). However, studies comparing one and three sets of exercise have found no significant developmental differences during the first few months of training (Starkey et al. 1996; Westcott and Baechle 1998). It is

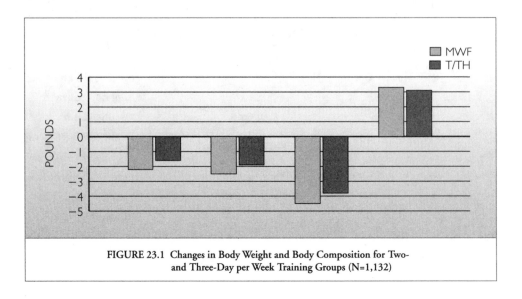

FIGURE 23.1 Changes in Body Weight and Body Composition for Two-
and Three-Day per Week Training Groups (N=1,132)

therefore suggested that seniors begin strength training with one properly performed set of each exercise. This time-efficient approach to strength exercise is
safe, effective, and well-received by seniors.

For example, in the Westcott and Guy (1996) study, the 341 older adults added
2.4 pounds of muscle and lost 4.1 pounds of fat after two months of single-set
strength training. Perhaps more important, 90 percent of the participants continued to strength train after completion of the exercise program. Of course, as the
senior exercisers become better conditioned, they may perform additional training sets if they so desire.

Training Resistance

There is a range of training weight loads, generally between 60 and 90 percent of
maximum resistance, that is productive for developing muscle size and strength.
Weight loads below 60 percent of maximum are relatively light and provide less
muscle-building stimulus. Conversely, weight loads above 90 percent of maximum are relatively heavy and may present more injury risk.

For most practical purposes, training with 70–80 percent of maximum resistance represents a safe and effective weight load range. In fact, many of the
studies with senior subjects have successfully used 70–80 percent of maximum
resistance in their training programs (Frontera et al. 1988; Fiatarone et al. 1994;
Nelson et al. 1994; Westcott and Guy 1996). As these studies have reported no
training-related injuries and high rates of muscle development, exercise weight
loads between 70 and 80 percent of maximum resistance are recommended for
senior strength training programs.

Training Repetitions

Research (Westcott 1995) indicates that most people can perform about 8 repetitions with 80 percent of their maximum resistance and about 12 repetitions with 70 percent of their maximum resistance. This represents a moderate number of repetitions per set and requires about 50–70 seconds of continuous training effort when performed at a moderate speed. The recommended number of training repetitions for senior exercisers is therefore between 8 and 12 repetitions per set.

Training Progression

Although it is not problematic to train with more than 12 repetitions, the key to muscle development is progressive increases in the exercise resistance. Therefore, it is advisable to add a little weight whenever 12 repetitions can be completed in proper form. The recommended training approach is to work with a given resistance until 12 repetitions are performed, then to raise the weight load by about 5 percent or less. For most senior exercisers, this corresponds to about 2.5–5 pounds more weight, which in turn reduces the number of repetitions that can be completed. This double-progressive training system gradually increases the exercise demands and reduces the risk of doing too much too soon.

Training Speed

There is general consensus that older adults should use controlled movement speeds when performing strength exercise. One study (Westcott 1994) showed significant and similar strength gains for subjects training with 4-second, 6-second, 8-second, and 14-second repetitions, indicating that there is a wide range of effective training speeds. Because 6-second repetitions have a long and successful history, this repetition speed is recommended for senior exercisers. The preferred cadence is 2 seconds for the more demanding lifting phase (concentric muscle action) and 4 seconds for the less demanding lowering phase (eccentric muscle action). However, the slow 14-second training speed may be even more productive for those who prefer to exercise in this manner.

Training Range

Due to age-related decreases in muscle function and joint flexibility, it is important for seniors to develop strength throughout their full range of joint movement. Research has shown that full-range exercise movements are necessary for building full-range muscle strength (Jones et al. 1988). That is, strength gains appear to be limited to the movement range that is trained. For best results, seniors should perform each strength exercise through the complete range of joint movement, working the muscles from their fully stretched position to their fully contracted position. However, if any part of the exercise action causes discomfort, the movement range should be abbreviated accordingly.

Training Technique

In addition to controlled movement speed and full movement range, exercise technique is a critical training factor for older adults. Seniors should always practice proper posture when performing strength exercises, with particular emphasis on position stability and back support. To avoid unnecessary blood pressure elevation, older adults should breathe continuously throughout every repetition. The preferred breathing pattern is to exhale during the more demanding lifting movement (concentric muscle action) and to inhale during the less demanding lowering movement (eccentric muscle action). Most importantly, senior strength trainers should never hold their breath (valsalva effect) or hold the resistance in a static position (isometric effect).

SUMMARY

There are many reasons why men and women over 50 years of age should perform regular strength training. The physiological benefits encompass the muscular, skeletal, cardiovascular, and digestive systems.

However, the major advantage of strength exercise is to replace the muscle tissue that is lost at the rate of about one pound per year in older adults. Regular strength training has been shown to increase muscle mass by more than one pound per month and to increase resting metabolism by more than 2 percent per month, thereby reversing some of the degenerative processes associated with aging.

Senior exercisers should follow general guidelines for safe, sensible, effective, and efficient strength training programs. The basic recommendations for successful strength training experiences are as follows:

1. Include exercises for all of the major muscle groups.
2. Train two or three nonconsecutive days per week.
3. Perform one set of each exercise.
4. Use between 70 and 80 percent of maximum resistance.
5. Perform between 8 and 12 repetitions per set.
6. Add about 5 percent more resistance (or less) whenever 12 repetitions are completed.
7. Use moderate movement speeds, such as 6 seconds per repetition.
8. Exercise through the full range of joint movement.
9. Practice proper posture.
10. Breathe continuously throughout every exercise repetition.

Research indicates that 90 percent of previously sedentary seniors who complete a well-designed short-term strength training program continue to do strength exercise.

REFERENCES

Andersen, R., S. Blair, L. Cheskin, et al. 1997. Encouraging patients to become more physically active: The physician's role. *Annals of Internal Medicine* 127: 395–400.

Ballor, D. L., and E. T. Poehlman. 1994. Exercise training enhances fat-free mass preservation during diet-induced weight loss: a meta analytic finding. *International Journal of Obesity* 18: 35–40.

Brehm, B., and B. Keller. 1990. Diet and exercise factors that influence weight and fat loss. *IDEA Today* 8: 33-46.

Campbell, W., M. Crim, V. Young, and W. Evans. 1994. Increased energy requirements and changes in body composition with resistance training in older adults. *American Journal of Clinical Nutrition* 60: 167–175.

DeMichele, P., M. Pollock, J. Graves, et al. 1997. Isometric torso rotation strength: Effect of training frequency on its development. *Archives of Physical Medicine and Rehabilitation* 78: 64–69.

Evans, W., and I. Rosenberg. 1992. *Biomarkers.* New York: Simon & Schuster.

Fiatarone, M., E. Marks, N. Ryan, et al. 1990. High-intensity strength training in nonagenarians. *Journal of the American Medical Association* 263 (22): 3029–3034.

Fiatarone, M., E. O'Neil, N. Ryan, et al. 1994. Exercise training and nutritional supplementation for physical frailty in very elderly people. *New England Journal of Medicine* 330 (25): 1769–1775.

Forbes, G. 1976. The adult decline in lean body mass. *Human Biology* 48: 161–173.

Frontera, W., C. Meredith, K. O'Reilly, et al. 1988. Strength conditioning in older men: Skeletal muscle hypertrophy and improved function. *Journal of Applied Physiology* 64 (3): 1038–1044.

Harris, K., and R. Holly. 1987. Physiological response to circuit weight training in borderline hypertensive subjects. *Medicine and Science in Sports and Exercise* 19: 246–252.

Hurley, B. 1994. Does strength training improve health status? *Strength and Conditioning* 16: 7–13.

Hurley, B., J. Hagberg, A. Goldberg, et al. 1988. Resistance training can reduce coronary risk factors without altering VO_2 max or percent body fat. *Medicine and Science in Sports and Exercise* 20: 150–154.

Jones, A., M. Pollock, J. Graves, et al. 1988. *Safe, specific testing and rehabilitative exercise for muscles of the lumbar spine.* Santa Barbara, CA: Sequoia Communications.

Keyes, A., H. L. Taylor, and F. Grande. 1973. Basal metabolism and age of adult man. *Metabolism* 22: 579–587.

Koffler, K., A. Menkes, W. Redmond, et al. 1992. Strength training accelerates gastrointestinal transit in middle-aged and older men. *Medicine and Science in Sports and Exercise* 24: 415–419.

McClernan, J. 1992. The great American fat rip-offs. *IDEA Today* 10: 48–49.

Menkes, A., S. Mazel, R. Redmond, et al. 1993. Strength training increases regional bone mineral density and bone remodeling in middle-aged and older men. *Journal of Applied Physiology* 74: 2478–2484.

Nelson, M., M. Fiatarone, C. Morganti, et al. 1994. Effects of high-intensity strength training on multiple risk factors for osteoporotic fractures. *Journal of the American Medical Association* 272 (24): 1909–1914.

Pollock, M., C. Foster, D. Knapp, et al. 1987. Effect of age and training on aerobic capacity and body composition of master athletes. *Journal of Applied Physiology* 62 (2): 725–731.

Risch, S., N. Nowell, M. Pollock, et al. 1993. Lumbar strengthening in chronic low-back pain patients. *Spine* 18: 232–238.

Scripps Howard News Service. 1996. Study: Nearly 75 percent in U.S. are overweight. *Quincy Patriot Ledger Newspaper*, November 26.

Singh, N., K. Clements, and M. Fiatarone. 1997. A randomized controlled trial of progressive resistance training in depressed elders. *Journal of Gerontology* 52A (1): M27–M35.

Starkey, D., M. Pollock, Y. Ishida, et al. 1996. Effect of resistance training volume on strength and muscle thickness. *Medicine and Science in Sports and Exercise* 28 (10): 1311–1320.

Tufts University Diet and Nutrition Letter. 1994. Never too late to build up your muscle. 12 (September): 6–7.

Westcott, W. 1990. How much exercise is necessary? *American Fitness Quarterly* 9 (2): 38–47.

———. 1994. Exercise speed and strength development. *American Fitness Quarterly* 3 (3): 20–21.

———. 1995. *Strength fitness.* 4th ed. Dubuque, IA: W. C. Brown Publishers.

Westcott, W., and J. Guy. 1996. A physical evolution: Sedentary adults see marked improvements in as little as two days a week. *IDEA Today* 14 (9): 58–65.

Westcott, W., F. Dolan, and T. Cavicchi. 1996. Golf and strength training are compatible activities. *Strength and Conditioning* 18 (4): 54–56.

Westcott, W., and T. Baechle. 1998. *Strength training past 50.* Champaign, IL: Human Kinetics.

24

Strength Training for Prepubescents

Frank Furgiuele, B.A., B.Ed., NCCP—Level III
Head of Physical Education and Athletic Director
Iona Catholic Secondary School
Mississauga, Ontario, Canada

The term *prepubescent* is used to designate boys aged 13–14 and girls aged 11–12. The lifestyles of these youngsters are heavily influenced by parents, teachers, and coaches, as well as by their peers. For strength training to become a meaningful and regular part of their lifestyle, prepubescent boys and girls must be educated about the effects and benefits of proper strength training and learn the differences between weightlifting and strength training. Once prepubescents understand and appreciate the value of strength training, they need to be taught the basic fundamentals of that activity. Thereafter, they can initiate a safe and productive program.

THE IMPORTANCE OF EDUCATION

The effects and benefits of regular exercise have been well documented. While many people believe in the importance of physical activity, we continue to allow our children to learn about the subject by chance. Many years ago, the topic of sex education was kept out of the classroom. Children were forced to learn about the topic by watching movies and television shows, listening to older siblings, reading magazines, and hearing glorified stories told by friends. Not surprisingly, this approach led to a wide variety of myths and misconceptions. The move to provide formal education about this particular subject earlier in life has led to healthier attitudes and a better understanding of the topic.

For strength training to become a meaningful part of their lifestyle, pre-pubescent boys and girls need to be educated about the effects and benefits of proper strength training and learn the differences between weightlifting and strength training.

(photo by Mike Lynch)

For information and attitudes about strength training, we allow our youths to learn by listening to gym jockeys and bodybuilders, reading muscle mags, and hearing anecdotes told by friends. In many cases, these sources have had no formal schooling in the area of proper strength training. Many of the training programs that have been glamorized and implemented are essentially copies or variations of weightlifting, not strength training. Fortunately, strength training is now a valued part of many high school curriculums and, as a result, has generated significant improvements in the level of accurate knowledge and understanding.

Weightlifting Versus Strength Training

An important consideration is how the terms *weightlifting* and *strength training* are actually defined. Weightlifting is based upon numerous principles that date back many years. These principles include the notions of explosive lifting, specificity, periodization, and one-repetition maximum (1-RM) attempts.

The perception of explosive lifting is advertised every four years when the Olympics are televised. Viewers watch the Olympic-style weightlifters perform the snatch and the clean and jerk in a rapid, explosive manner and assume that if it works for the lifters then it will work for everyone else. So people have adopted these particular movements—or mutations of them such as the power clean—and performed their repetitions explosively in the weight room. Fortunately, we have finally realized that these movements and others done explosively are not very efficient and are in fact potentially dangerous.

Because of the influence of the competitive weightlifters, many coaches believed that explosive lifting would improve explosiveness in a wide variety of sports. As such, many athletes began to lift weights with high speeds of movement in the sincere hope that this would directly improve their performance. Recent discoveries have proven that there is no carryover or transfer of explosiveness from the weight room to the athletic forum. This is best explained by the

Principle of Specificity, which states that to produce optimal transfer, an activity must be specific to an intended skill. *Specific* means "exact," not "similar." No skill done in the weight room is ever repeated elsewhere in the exact way—except perhaps in a weightlifting meet.

Periodization is another concept that has been popularized by weightlifters. This theoretical approach involves cycles of training that eventually lead to peak strength—in this case measured by a 1-RM—during a later phase or stage. Periodized training allows for maximal strength performance during a very limited period of time. How is this practical or useful for athletes who need to peak on a weekly or even a daily basis? Periodization is also flawed because of the inflexible nature of computer-generated, preplanned workouts. There is no room in this system for the inevitability of illness, injury, and individual rates of progression.

Finally, success in the sport of weightlifting is measured by the amount of weight that is lifted in a 1-RM attempt. Remember, this practice only measures the ability to demonstrate strength with a limited number of muscles. It does not give an indication of the functional strength of the overall body nor does it illustrate how well athletes will perform competitively in their sport. The use of low-repetition movements can also lead to several serious problems, such as an unhealthy rise in blood pressure as well as an unreasonable—and unnecessary—amount of orthopedic stress. Simply stated, if you are not a competitive weightlifter you should not be training like one.

How then is the term *strength training* defined? Like weightlifting, strength training involves the use of progressive resistance methods that increase a person's ability to exert or resist a force. However, strength training typically includes a wide range of modalities and equipment, whereas weightlifting usually expresses a distinct favoritism toward the use of free weights (i.e., barbells and dumbbells) and certain core movements. Strength training can be done using equipment that is traditional—such as free weights and machines—as well as nontraditional. For example, a person's own weight could be used to improve strength by implementing body-weight exercises—such as push-ups, sit-ups, and chin-ups—with or without assistance/resistance from a partner. These exercises do not require special equipment or skill and they can be performed virtually anywhere at any time. Additionally, resistance can be supplied by a partner as a lifter endeavors through a series of manual-resistance exercises. A number of innovative strength and conditioning coaches who are progressive thinkers also implement other forms of nontraditional equipment, using chains, sandbags, and tires as the resistance. These options allow for a wide range of choices without the need for expensive or specialized equipment.

From an athletic perspective, the primary purposes of strength training should be to protect the athletes from injury and enhance their performance potential. Proper resistance training keeps the athlete in peak strength throughout the year—not just during a small portion of it. Unlike periodization, this type of training also allows for program adjustments necessitated by injury, illness, and individual timetables relating to progression. Finally, strength training does not prepare individuals to become better weightlifters.

Strength Training Benefits

In 1985, a group of physicians, physiologists, and other sports-medical professionals conducted a conference called "Strength Training and the Prepubescent," which was sponsored by the American Orthopaedic Society for Sports Medicine. The consensus was that "strength training, with proper program design, instruction, and supervision is a safe activity for prepubescent boys and girls."

In a study conducted at McMaster University (in Ontario, Canada) by Ramsay and coworkers (1990), 13 prepubescent boys (aged 9–11) performed weight training three days per week for 20 weeks. They increased their voluntary strength significantly—more than 30 percent in some exercises (Figure 24.1).

Besides improving strength, prepubescents can obtain a number of other benefits from strength training. These benefits include:

1. enhancing performance potential in sports and recreation activities
2. improving motor strength
3. protecting against injury
4. increasing muscle endurance
5. encouraging positive psychological qualities
6. providing a forum for introduction of proper training techniques

During discussions with parents, I have often asked the question "Why do you think that it will be a bad idea for your child to begin strength training?"

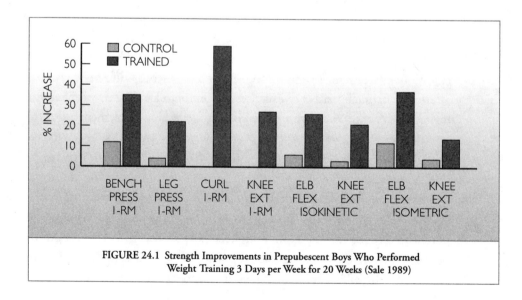

FIGURE 24.1 Strength Improvements in Prepubescent Boys Who Performed Weight Training 3 Days per Week for 20 Weeks (Sale 1989)

Their responses usually ranged from "Well, it will prevent them from growing tall [i.e., stunt their growth]" to "They are too young to work out because they will get hurt."

As a follow-up question to the parents I ask, "What is the source of your information?" Their replies include "I just read it somewhere," "My neighbor told me and he has been a weightlifter for years," "My daughter's summer coach told me," and so on.

Consider the fact that prepubescent children are getting involved with sports and recreational activities at increasingly

Technique is what makes the exercise effective and, as always, safety should be emphasized. (photo by Mike Lynch)

younger ages. By the age of 11 or 12, many boys already suffer from shoulder and elbow injuries due to the wear and tear of pitching/throwing. This is because baseball coaches are specializing young athletes as pitchers, which has led to overuse injuries. Over the long term, this overuse can lead to acute/chronic injuries that will affect performance. Question: What can be done to prevent or lessen the severity of injuries? Answer: Improve strength in the muscles that are primarily used. This is a simple concept but one that many coaches and parents fail to understand.

FUNDAMENTALS OF STRENGTH TRAINING

In T-ball, young children are taught fundamentals such as throwing, catching, and hitting a ball off a tee. Once this foundation has been laid, the players are taught more complex skills such as hitting a pitched ball. In youth football, children are taught fundamentals such as blocking, tackling, running, throwing, catching, kicking, and assuming a stance. After the young athletes have learned these basic skills, they progress to more advanced skills such as running after and tackling an opponent and catching the football on the run.

So, why is it that children are not taught the fundamentals of strength training in the beginning? If children learn the basics from an experienced strength coach it will lay a foundation that can be built upon for years to come.

The fundamentals are clearly the heart and soul of a strength training program. When starting a program, children should be taught the following fundamentals of strength training.

Fundamental 1: Provide Overload

One of the most important foundational concepts in strength training is the Overload Principle (Hellebrandt and Houtz 1956). The term *overload* refers to an exercise task that requires considerable voluntary effort to complete. Regardless of the strength training program utilized, the muscles must be overloaded to increase strength—that is, greater demands must be experienced than in the previous workout. This can be accomplished by doing more repetitions than the last time, increasing the weight used, taking less rest between sets of exercises, increasing the intensity, or performing more sets than in the previous workout (although the latter possibility isn't necessarily recommended). Doing any of these options in a systematic manner will improve muscular strength (Shibinski 1996).

Dr. Digby Sale of McMaster University states clearly that minimum overload requires maximum voluntary effort (Sale 1989). Two goals in strength training are (1) to fully activate the prime movers and (2) to induce hypertrophy in all of the muscle fibers that are able to contribute force in the intended direction of movement. As such, maximal effort can be achieved by doing brief maximal contractions or submaximal contractions-to-fatigue—that is, until no further repetitions can be done with a given load or until a given force of contraction cannot be maintained any longer.

In the second way, full activation of motor units does not occur at the beginning of an exercise; rather, activation increases as fatigue develops and may be complete at the point of fatigue (Sale 1989).

When applying the Overload Principle to prepubescent training, a variety of methods should be used such as calisthenics, free weights, machines, body-weight exercises, and manual resistance. Nonconventional equipment can also be utilized as the resistance (for example, water-filled jugs and small sandbags). This will provide a greater amount of variety for the children and prevent boredom that can be associated with doing the same exercise over and over again for lengthy periods of time.

Fundamental 2: Use Appropriate Intensity

According to many authorities, intensity of effort is the most important controllable factor in determining the degree of response from strength training. Prepubescents must be taught and experience the different levels of intensity—the key word here being *experience*. Ideally, children should begin with a resistance or load in which muscle fatigue is reached within a prescribed number of repetitions.

To get prepubescent children to achieve the goal of muscle fatigue, the primary emphasis should first be given to learning and mastering the new motor skills. Initially, the exercises can be practiced with minimal resistance such as an empty bar without weights. Once correct exercise technique has been learned, the resistance can be increased. Technique is what makes the exercise effective and, as always, safety should be emphasized. Remember, momentum makes the exercise very unsafe and can lead to an injury. Once children are taught the proper technique with low resistance, it then becomes an easier challenge for them to train safely and effectively.

The natural progression from low resistance and high repetitions to higher resistance and fewer repetitions is the ultimate goal for the youth. As coaches, we must remember that preadolescents may not be comfortable training to the point of muscular fatigue. It is then up to us to make the necessary adaptations in the strength training program to achieve this goal. In this case, have the youth terminate the exercise a few repetitions short of muscular fatigue. As they develop physically and mentally (in terms of maturity), their intensity can be gradually increased. Remember this point: A submaximal effort will yield submaximal results.

Fundamental 3: Incorporate Double Progression

Double progression is a systematic method of overloading the muscles. Earlier, it was noted that for muscle growth to occur, the muscle must be overloaded—that is, it must be worked progressively harder than during a previous workout. The easiest way to do this is to have the youth simply add weight once a specified number of repetitions is reached. The increase in resistance should be kept to about 5 percent or less.

When using the method of double progression, a range of repetitions is used for an exercise. An example would be 10–15 repetitions in which an application in the weight room would be as follows: Initially, the youth should use a weight with which 10 perfect repetitions can be done and no more. The youth should use this weight each workout until he or she can achieve 15 repetitions. When this is accomplished, increase the weight by about 5 percent or less. Progressions are made by first increasing the number of repetitions and then by increasing the weight used; hence the term *double progression* (Shibinski 1996). The following is an illustration using a repetition range of 10–15:

Workout	Weight/Repetitions
1	100/10
2	100/11
3	100/12
4	100/13
5	100/14
6	100/15
7	105/10
8	105/11

Prepubescents should perform about 20–25 repetitions for their hips, 15–20 repetitions for their legs, and 10–15 repetitions for their upper torso. As they mature physically and emotionally, the repetition range can be lowered to a level usually recommended for older individuals.

Fundamental 4: Perform Full Range of Motion

When youths are exercising, it is critical that they do quality repetitions. This can be accomplished by having them exercise throughout a full range of motion (ROM). Exercising the muscle through a full ROM will maintain (or increase) their flexibility. A joint that has increased its flexibility will generally have a lower potential for injury.

To perform quality repetitions, a basic guideline is to raise the weight to the midrange position in about a 2-second count, pause briefly, and then lower the weight to the starting/stretched position in about a 4-second count. This means that each repetition will take approximately 4–6 seconds to complete.

In strength training, momentum is undesirable. The use of momentum to lift a weight is unavoidable. Otherwise, the weight would never move. But it is the degree to which momentum is involved that makes it undesirable. Lifting weights with sudden jerking movements that are ballistic or explosive makes the exercise less productive and less efficient. By minimizing momentum, the muscles are forced to work harder throughout their entire ROM. Momentum also subjects the muscles, joints, and connective tissue to potentially dangerous forces that increase the possibility of injury. Therefore, the weight should be lifted in a controlled manner so that momentum does not play a significant role in the safety or effectiveness of the exercise.

Olympic weightlifting movements can only be done in an explosive manner. The American Academy of Pediatrics (1983) has recommended against the use of the Olympic-style lifts for young individuals. When defining strength training, the proceedings of the aforementioned conference on strength training and the prepubescent noted that "competitive or Olympic weightlifting is not included in this definition, since they are considered sport rather than training modalities and are activities that the prepubescent should not be involved in." Note that this group of exercise specialists used the term *sport* rather than *training modality* to characterize the Olympic lifts. Yet, some individuals continue to incorporate these risky exercises in their strength training programs. If these movements are so questionable in terms of safety and require such a large amount of time to learn correct technique, why are they endorsed by coaches and prescribed to athletes? Don't forget, we are training young individuals, not competitive weightlifters for the next Olympic Games.

Fundamental 5: Train 2–3 Times per Week on Nonconsecutive Days

In the beginning, youths should train two days per week. If they trained on a Monday, for example, they would then train again on Wednesday or Thursday.

When lifting weights, muscles get stressed and fatigued. The recovery of the muscles is just as important as the workout itself. Remember, muscles grow when you are recovering, not when you are exercising. When they first begin weight training, many eager youths think that more is better. They increase the frequency of their workouts from two days to three days to four days and sometimes six days with one day of recovery per week. These youths often reason that if they are seeing results by working out just two or three days each week then their results will be magnified if they lift six days each week.

Failing to allow for adequate recovery contributes to overtraining and can eventually lead to serious overuse injuries. Since between 48 and 72 hours is usually needed for the body to recover from an intense workout, a youth will settle on a lifting schedule of either Monday-Wednesday-Friday or Tuesday-Thursday-Saturday with recovery occurring on the nonlifting days.

Alternating body parts on different days—known as a *split routine*—is not recommended for several reasons. First, the body needs a minimum of 48 hours to fully recover its energy stores—namely carbohydrates—that were exhausted during intense activity. Split routines are also inefficient in terms of time and in today's busy society, there is less and less time available to do various activity programs. Further, a strength training program should not be the focal point of a youth's entire week since he or she will most likely be involved in other sports. Finally, split routines will likely lead to overtraining and—due to the increased volume and inadequate recovery—produce more wear and tear on the body.

Fundamental 6: Exercise the Muscles from Largest to Smallest

When designing a strength training program, youths should always begin their workout with the exercises that influence their largest muscles and finish with those that involve their smallest muscles. The following order is recommended:

1. hips
2. upper legs (hamstrings and quadriceps)
3. lower legs (calves or dorsi flexors)
4. upper torso (chest, upper back, and shoulders)
5. upper arms (biceps and triceps)
6. lower arms (forearms)
7. abdominals
8. lower back

Here's why the sequence of exercises is important: When performing multijoint movements, the smaller muscles are used to assist in the exercise. Since they are smaller, they are the weak link in the movement. If these smaller muscles are fatigued first, then the weak link will be weakened even further. This means that the workload that is placed upon the larger muscles will be limited, which will, in turn, make the exercise more difficult to complete and restrict the development of the larger muscles. As a rule of thumb, the arms are the weak link when performing multi-joint movements for the upper body and the legs are the weak link when performing multi-joint movements for the hips.

A few words about training the neck muscles: Neck exercises are important for prepubescents but must be closely supervised by an experienced adult. Many coaches and parents fail to understand the importance of training the neck. A number of strength training programs omit neck movements from their menu of exercises. This is quite puzzling since the neck muscles are used in many sports. In some combative sports—such as wrestling and football (where youths can begin participating as young as nine years old)—a strong neck is an obvious necessity. Strengthening the neck is important in other sports as well. In hockey, for instance, many injuries occur when players are body checked or cross checked by a stick, which can result in a whiplash. Soccer players use their neck muscles to head the ball. A strong neck is even important in some nonathletic situations. When automobile accidents occur, one of the most common injuries suffered by the driver and passengers is whiplash. The bottom line is that the neck muscles have a major role in the total development of the body. If neck exercises are prescribed, they should be placed at the beginning of a workout. By the end of a workout, youths will be fatigued both physically and mentally, which will lead to very little enthusiasm and poor technique.

Fundamental 7: Perform About 9–14 Exercises Each Workout

A prepubescent should start with no more than about nine exercises. Once the youth has performed the exercises safely and correctly, he or she can progress to about 14 exercises. A lower volume of exercises decreases the potential for overuse injury.

Younger and physically immature individuals should choose one exercise to target each of the following nine muscle groups: the hips, hamstrings, quadriceps, calves (or dorsi flexors), chest, upper back (the lats), shoulders, abdominals, and lower back. Older and more physically mature individuals should select one exercise to address the following eight muscle groups: the hips, hamstrings, quadriceps, calves (or dorsi flexors), biceps, triceps, abdominals, and lower back. They should also include two exercises for each of the following three muscle groups: the chest, upper back, and shoulders.

Fundamental 8: Maintain Accountability—Record All Workouts

When prepubescents begin strength training, it is of vital importance that they understand the need to maintain accurate records of their performance. Why? Their record keeping will provide them with immediate feedback concerning the sequence of their routine as well as their improvements in resistance and repetitions. When prepubescents use workout cards as a motivational tool, they can see progression in their weights and repetitions.

Remember, youths should not be solely focused on or completely obsessed with simply gaining muscular size. Rather, they should concentrate on feeling good about themselves and successfully achieving and maintaining an active lifestyle using productive strength training activities.

Prepubescents are motivated by achievement, which means their success will be dictated by the extent to which they will continue the activity. Recording data on their workout cards can provide the needed stimulus.

REVIEW OF PREPUBESCENT FUNDAMENTALS

The following is a detailed summary of the fundamentals that have been discussed in this chapter, along with several other considerations for prepubescents who want to start strength training:

- Undergo a physical and a medical check-up before beginning.
- Receive constant and experienced adult supervision.
- Include a warm-up before training and flexibility exercises after training.
- Use calisthenics initially to improve muscular endurance and strength.
- Utilize strength training as one of a variety of sport and fitness activities.
- Incorporate a number of different training modalities, such as calisthenics, free weights, machines, body-weight exercises, and manual resistance.
- Develop proper technique first with low resistance.
- Progress from low resistance and high repetitions to higher resistance and fewer repetitions as they advance physically and mentally.
- Increase the resistance by about 5 percent or less once the maximum number of prescribed repetitions is performed in good form.
- Exercise muscles throughout a full ROM.
- Perform one set of each exercise with an age-appropriate level of intensity.
- Do about 20–25 repetitions for the hips, 15–20 repetitions for the legs, and 10–15 repetitions for the upper torso.
- Take a minimal amount of time between sets to stimulate metabolic conditioning.
- Begin with about 9 exercises and progress to a maximum of about 14 exercises.
- Train all the major muscle groups.
- Provide equal emphasis for antagonistic muscles.
- Exercise for approximately 20–40 minutes per session.
- Restrict strength training to no more than three times per week.

- Use a workout card to record performance information.
- Refrain from doing 1-RMs, Olympic-style movements, or explosive repetitions.
- Avoid using negative-only exercise (i.e., lowering very heavy weights).
- Recognize joint pain as a warning signal and seek medical advice (Blimkie 1989).
- Incorporate achievement goals to encourage progress.
- Receive motivational feedback on a regular basis.
- Remember that strength training is only one aspect of a total fitness program.
- Practice sports skills regularly and never replace skill training with strength training.

SAMPLE ROUTINES

The following sample routines are based upon beginner, intermediate, and advanced levels. As a 10-minute warm-up, a youth can (1) ride a stationary bicycle; (2) run on a motorized treadmill; or (3) run laps around the gymnasium or track. After the warm-up, the youth should stretch all the muscle groups.

Keep in mind that the exercises in a routine will depend upon the equipment available. One set of each exercise should be done 2–3 times per week using the suggested repetition ranges.

Sample Routine: Beginner

Leg press: 20–25
Leg curl: 15–20
Leg extension: 15–20
Calf raise: 15–20
Dip: 10–15
Chin-up: 10–15
Upright row: 10–15
Sit-up: 10–15
Back extension: 15–20

Total workout time: about 30 minutes (including warm-up)

Sample Routine: Intermediate

Leg press: 20–25
Leg curl: 15–20
Leg extension: 15–20
Dorsi flexion: 15–20
Bench press: 10–15
Bent-arm fly: 10–15
Seated row: 10–15

Shoulder shrug: 10–15

Shoulder press: 10–15

Lateral raise: 10–15

Bicep curl: 10–15

Tricep extension: 10–15

Knee-up: 10–15

Back extension: 15–20

Total workout time: about 45 minutes (including warm-up)

Sample Routine: Advanced

Neck flexion: 8–12

Neck extension: 8–12

Leg press: 15–20

Leg curl: 10–15

Strength training—and other healthy activities—should be accepted by prepubescents in such a way that it leads to a continuation as adolescents and adults. (photo by Mike Lynch)

Calf raise: 10–15

Incline bench press: 8–12

Bent-arm fly: 8–12

Bent-over row: 8–12

Pullover: 8–12

Shoulder press: 8–12

Front raise: 8–12

Bicep curl: 8–12

Tricep extension: 8–12

Curl-up: 8–12

Back extension: 10–15

Total workout time: about 55 minutes (including warm-up)

TOWARD AN ACTIVE LIFESTYLE

In conclusion, strength training—and other healthy activities—should be practiced by prepubescents in such a way that it leads to a continuation as adolescents and adults. In the distant future, the effectiveness of this will be revealed as part of our history and culture by anthropologists. These days anthropologists who study mummies can tell a laborer from a noble by the density and quality of the bone that became thickened far more than someone of leisure. People who have regularly followed a strength training program that is physically challenging will enjoy the benefits of a healthy life—benefits that may be noted by future civilizations.

REFERENCES

American Academy of Pediatrics. 1983. Weight training and weight lifting: Information for the pediatrician. *Physician and Sportsmedicine* 11 (3): 157–161.

Blimkie, C. 1989. Strength training for young athletes. *Scholastic Coach* 59 (3): 9.

Blimkie, C., and D. Sale. 1998. Strength development and trainability during childhood. In *Pediatric anaerobic performance, part III: Anaerobic trainability and training*, ed. E. Van Praagh, 193–224. Champaign, IL: Human Kinetics.

Brady, T. A., B. R. Cahill, and L. M. Bodnar. 1982. Weight training-related injuries in the high school athlete. *American Journal of Sports Medicine* 10 (1): 1–5.

Brier, B. 1998. *The murder of Tutankhamen: A true story*. New York, NY: G. P. Putnam's Sons.

Brown, E. W., and R. G. Kimball. 1983. Medical history associated with adolescent powerlifting. *Pediatrics* 72 (5): 635–644.

Brzycki, M. 1996. *Youth strength and conditioning*. Indianapolis, IN: Masters Press.

Cahill, B. R., ed. and mod. 1985. Proceedings of the conference on strength training and the prepubescent. *American Orthopaedic Society for Sports Medicine.* Indianapolis, IN.

Charters, P. 1990. Strength training considerations for the child and adolescent. *Fitness for All Seasons Review* 1 (1): 1–4.

Hellebrandt, F. A., and S. J. Houtz. 1956. Mechanisms of muscle training in man: Experimental demonstration of the overload principle. *Physical Therapy Review* 36: 371–383.

Jacobson, B. H., and F. A. Kulling. 1989. Effect of resistive weight training in prepubescents. *Journal of Orthopaedic and Sports Physical Therapy* 11 (3): 96–99.

Leistner, K. 1998. Training the adolescent athlete. *Hard Training Newsletter* 4: 1–4.

Mannie, K. 1998. The spartan strength program. Presented at the Hammer Strength and Conditioning Seminar. Cincinnati, OH.

Mentzer, M. 1998. Personal communication with author (April 25).

Nelson, M., B. Goldberg, S. Harris, G. Landry, and W. L. Risser. 1990. Strength training, weight and power lifting, and body building by children and adolescents. *Pediatrics* 86 (5): 801–803.

Ramsay, J. A., C. J. Blimkie, K. Smith, S. Garner, J. D. MacDougall, and D. G. Sale. 1990. Strength training effects in prepubescent boys. *Medicine and Science in Sports and Exercise* 22 (5): 605–614.

Rians, C. B., A. Weltman, B. R. Cahill, C. A. Janney, S. R. Tippett, and F. I. Katch. 1987. Strength training for prepubescent males: Is it safe? *American Journal of Sports Medicine* 15 (5): 483–489.

Riley, D. 1982. *Maximum muscular fitness: How to develop strength without equipment.* West Point, NY: Leisure Press.

———. 1982. *Strength training by the experts.* 2nd ed. West Point, NY: Leisure Press.

Risser, W. L., J. M. Risser, and D. Preston. 1990. Weight training injuries in adolescents. *American Journal of Diseases of Children* 144 (9): 1015–1017.

Sale, D. 1989. Youth, exercise, and sport. In *Perspectives in exercise science and sports medicine,* volume 2, ed. C. V. Gisolfi and D. R. Lamb, 165–222. Indianapolis, IN: Benchmark Press.

———. 1998. Personal communication with author (June 15).

Sewall, L., and L. Micheli. 1986. Strength training for children. *Journal of Pediatric Orthopedics* 6 (2): 143–146.

Shibinski, M. 1996. *Viking strength training manual.* Cincinnati, OH: Princeton High School.

Webb, D. R. 1990. Strength training in children and adolescents. *Pediatric Clinics of North America* 37 (5): 1187–1210.

Weltman, A., C. A. Janney, C. B. Rians, K. Strand, B. Berg, S. Tippett, J. Wise, B. R. Cahill, and F. I. Katch. 1986. The effects of hydraulic resistance strength training in pre-pubertal males. *Medicine and Science in Sports and Exercise* 8 (6): 629–638.

This chapter is dedicated to my wife, Joni, who tempers my frequent flights of fancy with a foot grounded in reality; to my sons, Evan and Nathan, who remind me daily of the only true essentials in life; and my parents, Harvey and Fran, who blessed me with a body to build and a mind to expand.

25

Bodybuilding HIT

Steve Weingarten, B.A.
NPC Bodybuilding Champion/Personal Trainer
Louisville, Kentucky

High intensity training (HIT) for bodybuilding involves the application of maximum effort to build maximum muscle in minimum time. HIT bodybuilders don't waste energy trying out the latest super routines in the muscle magazines. They don't train "instinctively." They generally don't squander training time with light pumping exercises. They don't adopt the attitude that performing a few extra sets will make up for earlier sets that were poorly executed.

Instead, successful HIT bodybuilders focus mostly on compound exercises such as the deadlift, squat, bent-over row, chin-up, and heavy pressing movements. These bodybuilders endeavor to gradually build their poundages—by adding a repetition or so each workout or two and/or increasing the weight by small increments as often as possible—because they know that getting stronger on the big movements is the best way to stimulate real gains in size. They know exactly what exercises and weights they're going to use when they arrive at the gym. They strive to get the most out of every repetition and every set.

"HIT bodybuilding doesn't work," claim the naysayers. "It's useful only as a short-term change from typical bodybuilding workouts," say others. Nonsense. HIT bodybuilding comprises the soundest application of the principles of exercise physiology. It's a methodical, disciplined, uncomplicated approach to physique development. If you're a drug-free trainee interested in maximizing your natural bodybuilding potential, HIT is the fastest route to your destination.

HIT BODYBUILDING GUIDELINES

The following guidelines can be used to realize your bodybuilding potential:

Keep Volume Low and Intensity High

Some claim that you must do a certain number of sets per body part to induce muscular hypertrophy. While it's true that the volume of work performed is a consideration, if volume were the primary stimulus for growth then marathon runners would have massively muscled legs. Instead, a casual observation of distance runners almost always reveals thin legs that appear nearly devoid of appreciable muscle.

Intensity—that is, the amount of effort applied to each set—supersedes volume when it comes to producing results. Coupled with a gradual progression in poundage, intensity is the key to growth. In fact, one set performed at 100 percent intensity is far more productive than 10 sets performed at 75 percent intensity.

Understand that HIT bodybuilding presumes a definition of intensity different from that of periodization. Periodizers define intensity as *a percentage of their one-repetition maximum* (1-RM); according to this definition, if you're capable of a 200-pound bench press then 100 percent intensity would be a set of one repetition with 200 pounds. Bodybuilders who follow this philosophy are frequently advised to exercise at 75–80 percent intensity for 6–8 repetitions. Part of the problem with this advice is that people are endowed with different muscle fiber-type distributions. Some individuals have inherited a higher percentage of fast-twitch (strength) fibers while others have more slow-twitch (endurance) fibers. In addition, fiber-type distribution differs from muscle to muscle within the same person. All of this means that poundages based upon 80 percent of a 1-RM provide varying levels of difficulty from person to person and from body part to body part within the same person.

As defined by HIT, 100 percent intensity means performing a set until you are unable—despite your most aggressive effort—to squeeze out one more repetition in good form. This is also known as training to muscle fatigue (or failure). It's simple in concept but difficult in execution. Most trainees who think that they are training to fatigue actually terminate their sets well before reaching true fatigue—particularly when it comes to heavy leg exercises. The mind gives out well before the body.

HIT bodybuilding is based upon the notion that muscular hypertrophy is the result of the body's effort to protect itself from the stress of heavy training. The more intense the stress, the greater the body's protective response. This is why the highest possible intensity—taking each work set to the point of muscular fatigue—is required for the fastest progress.

Pushing each set to muscular fatigue is the most efficient way to train because it ensures that the greatest number of muscle fibers are stimulated within the shortest amount of time and with the lowest possible volume of work. The All-

or-None Principle of muscle-fiber recruitment states that a muscle uses only the minimum number of fibers necessary to complete a given task and that those fibers contract with maximal force. As you proceed through a set, the muscle fibers that initially lifted the weight become fatigued, forcing fresh fibers to assist in continuing the set. By the time you reach muscular fatigue, most or all of the target muscle's fibers have been exhausted. Training to fatigue also ensures that you use the heaviest possible weight for a given number of repetitions. Both of these scenarios set the stage for the fastest possible growth.

Intensity—that is, the amount of effort applied to each set—supersedes volume when it comes to producing results. (photo by Matt Brzycki)

This begs the question: If one set to fatigue is good, aren't two sets better and three sets better still? No. Performing an excessive number of sets of a given exercise does not increase intensity, it increases volume. It's essential to understand that the body possesses a limited ability to cope with the demands of any stressor, including exercise. The right amount of HIT leads to results; too much HIT leads to overtraining. Needless to say, muscular hypertrophy will not occur in an overtrained body.

Train Briefly and Infrequently

Once you understand that training as hard as possible ensures maximum growth stimulation, the next point to grasp is that training as briefly as possible ensures the body the resources it needs to provide growth. Bear in mind that the body's first priority after a workout is to recover the energy it expended during that workout. Only after the body returns to its preworkout state will it then begin the process of supercompensation (growth). It stands to reason that a trainee should perform the minimum amount of work required to stimulate growth to preserve enough energy to foster the growth process.

There exists no ideal workout length or set count. These parameters vary among trainees, depending upon individual genetic makeup, training history, and lifestyle. But it's safe to say that if you're training in proper HIT style, one or two sets of any exercise is plenty, with six sets being the maximum one should perform for any single body part. Less is probably better for most people.

In general, two workouts per week or a workout once every 3–4 days is sufficient for most to make progress. This applies to advanced trainees as well as beginners. In fact, advanced trainees may need to work out even less often than beginners because their increased strength and ability to generate more effort places their bodies under greater stress. Whatever frequency you initially choose, you should add more rest days between your workouts if you find that you're still tired and sore by the time of your next workout or if you fail to increase poundages/repetitions regularly.

Train for Strength

Imagine that you currently bench press a maximum of 150 × 8—that is, 150 pounds for 8 repetitions. You spend the next 12 months performing supersets, drop sets, continuous tension, muscle confusion, and other alleged muscle-building techniques. At the end of the 12-month period, you can still bench press a maximum of 150 × 8. How much muscle do you think you'll have gained? The answer is none. Yes, none, even after a year's worth of effort.

That's because a relationship exists between a muscle's strength and its size. Sadly, many trainees never comprehend this reality. Instead of making a conscious effort to increase their poundages regularly, they fall into the trap of trying every new technique glorified in the bodybuilding magazines. But because they don't get stronger, they don't get bigger.

Don't be swayed by the throng of so-called bodybuilders who perform set after set of an exercise with the goal of achieving a maximum pump. A pump has nothing to do with true growth; it is merely a temporary state in which the muscle is engorged with blood.

If you want to build real, lasting muscle tissue, you must make the muscle stronger. This means training for strength. When you're able to do a target number of repetitions with a given weight, it's time to increase that weight. This increase should be small—about 5 pounds on leg exercises and 2½ pounds on upper-body exercises is usually plenty. Keep in mind that you'll need 1¼-pound plates for a 2½-pound increase on barbell exercises. Most gyms don't have 1¼ pounders but you can purchase your own pair and keep them in your gym bag. With machines, it's simple to increase the resistance incrementally by pinning a 2½- or 5-pound plate to the weight stack. Making small jumps in weight with dumbbells requires a bit of creativity since they typically come in 5-pound increments—which is equivalent to a 10-pound increase with a barbell. One simple solution is to tie 1¼-pound and 2½-pound plates to the dumbbells with shoelaces; another way to make slight increases in resistance when using dumbbells is to use 1¼- or 2½-pound ankle weights on your wrists.

Most people—when they even bother to increase their weights—make the mistake of increasing them too much. This leads to a rapid deterioration of form. Don't be impatient; over time, small increases add up to a large increase.

Use an Appropriate Repetition Range

Many authorities believe that hypertrophy can be maximized by a repetition range of about 8–12. This is a useful principle to follow but, in truth, there can be a significant difference in productive repetition ranges among individuals and among body parts within the same individual.

In general, sets of about five repetitions or less should be avoided by bodybuilders because such low repetitions *demonstrate* strength rather than *build* it. In addition, sets of about five repetitions or less at a typical cadence heavily stress the joints and connective tissue without keeping the muscle fibers loaded long enough to provoke hypertrophy. Sets of about 15 repetitions or more promote greater metabolic and muscular endurance adaptations rather than strength/hypertrophy. This leaves a usable repetition range for bodybuilding purposes of about 6–15.

A compelling amount of anecdotal evidence suggests that the lower body responds better than the upper body to higher repetition ranges. As such, it may be best to use about 10–15 repetitions for lower-body work and about 6–10 repetitions for upper-body work. Experiment with both the upper and lower end of these repetition ranges to discover what works best for you.

Focus on the Major Muscle Groups

If you want to get big, you're going to have to pay the price in the form of agonizing effort on exercises that allow you to use relatively heavy weights. The focus should be on compound (or multi-joint) movements that work several muscle groups at the same time, such as the squat, deadlift, chin-up, bent-over row, and bench press. In fact, a very productive routine that stimulates serious growth from head to toe could be built around just these five exercises.

That's not to say that calf raises, arm exercises, and abdominal work should be avoided. They can be part of your program—especially once you're an advanced trainee. Just understand that you'll stimulate more biceps growth by doing heavy chin-ups and rows than you will by doing set after set of concentration curls.

The majority of the muscle mass in your body is found in your hips, legs, back, and chest. The only way to gain the pounds of muscular body weight that will accentuate your appearance is by increasing the size of these muscles. Train the large muscle groups heavy and hard and the smaller groups will gain as well. Think about it: If you increase your maximum bench press from 150×8 to 250×8, you'll possess not only vastly larger pecs and delts but bigger triceps, too—without doing a single set of specific triceps work.

Compose the heart of your routine from the following compound movements:

Hips/legs: squat (barbell or machine), front squat, leg press

Upper/lower back: deadlift (barbell), bent-over row (barbell or dumbbell), chin-up, pull-up, pulldown

Chest: bench press (barbell, dumbbells, or machine), incline press (barbell, dumbbells, or machine), dip

Shoulders: overhead press (barbell, dumbbells, or machine)

Triceps (if needed): close-grip bench press, dip

Biceps (if needed): bicep curl (barbell, dumbbells, or machine)

Use Proper Training Style

For best results, it's not enough to lift heavy weights—you must lift them properly. Heaving, thrusting, jerking, and bouncing should be avoided at all costs. As a bodybuilder, your mission in the gym is to exhaust your muscles so that they are forced to rebuild larger and stronger. Weights and machines are the tools you use for that purpose. While you want to lift as much weight as possible for a given number of repetitions, you want to do so within the context of proper form.

Jerky, bouncing motions may allow you to lift more weight than you otherwise might be able to handle but such motions minimize the load on the muscle(s) you're trying to work. Such motions also multiply the stress on your joints and connective tissue, setting you up for injury.

Some training authorities suggest following a 2/4 protocol in which the positive (lifting) motion takes 2 seconds and the negative (lowering) motion takes 4 seconds. This is fine general advice but what's important to remember is that you want to keep the muscle loaded throughout the entire repetition. Lift a weight with power, precision, and focus; pause for a second in the fully contracted position; then lower the weight reasonably slowly while feeling the muscle resist the weight all the way down. (An explanation of the proper performance for specific exercises is well beyond the scope of this chapter. Such information can be found in detail in *The Insider's Tell-All Handbook on Weight Training Technique* by Stuart McRobert. For ordering information, contact cs Publishing, Ltd., P.O. Box 390, CY-2151 Nicosia, Cyprus.)

Go Beyond Positive Fatigue Infrequently

It is generally sufficient to take each set to the point of positive muscular fatigue, where you are unable to raise the weight with good form. Occasionally—how often is an individual matter determined by one's recovery ability—it can be beneficial to take a set beyond positive fatigue. This is known as extending the intensity.

Common intensity-extending techniques include:

Forced repetitions—in which a partner helps you barely complete one or two extra repetitions

Negative repetitions—in which a partner lifts the weight and you resist the negative (downward) motion. These should be continued only until you cannot control the descent of the weight.

Rest pause—where after reaching positive fatigue, you rest for about 15–30 seconds and then attempt to squeeze out 1–3 extra repetitions

Drop set—where after reaching positive fatigue, the weight is immediately reduced by about 20–25 percent and you perform as many repetitions as possible

Unfortunately, too many trainees abuse intensity-extending techniques by doing too many too often. It is a mistake to use intensity-extenders for every set of every workout as the body cannot accommodate such extreme stress. Such a well-meaning but foolish practice can quickly lead to overtraining, a possible loss in size and strength, and injury. Use intensity-extending methods judiciously— perhaps only once a week and for only one body part in a given workout.

Emphasize Recovery

Training provides the stimulus for growth but the growth process does not take place while you train. It takes place later when you rest and especially when you sleep.

Taking an adequate number of days off between workouts is only part of the recovery equation. You must also ensure that your rest days are true rest days. If your goal is to add substantial muscle to your frame, minimize your activity level outside the gym. Playing full-court basketball may be fun but doing so regularly will deplete energy that would otherwise be directed toward recovery and super-compensation. Determine your priorities and act accordingly.

Nor can you afford to frolic until the wee hours of the morning if your dream is to get big. Sleep is critical to the growth process and must not be overlooked. Six hours a night is the minimum you should sleep and seven or eight hours is preferable. Understand that even the most painstakingly devised and religiously followed training program will yield little or no gains if you're sleep deprived.

Eat Well and Often

If training serves as the catalyst for growth and sleep provides the opportunity for growth, then food provides the raw materials required for growth.

The ideal eating plan to get big is based around lean protein sources (e.g., lean beef, chicken breast, turkey breast, fish, egg whites, and low-fat dairy products), complex carbohydrates (e.g., oatmeal, brown rice, yams, and potatoes), fibrous carbohydrates (e.g., vegetables and whole fruits), and a small-to-moderate amount of healthy fats (e.g., egg yolks, vegetable oils, nuts, and nut butters). The occasional inclusion—perhaps several times weekly—of sweets and fast foods is fine, but keep in mind that a steady intake of sugar-and-fat-laden foods can lead to a rapid accumulation of body fat.

Structure your eating plan to include five or six moderate-size meals each day. Smaller, more frequent feedings provide your muscles with a constant supply of the nutrients they need for growth without promoting excessive fat storage. Such an eating plan will keep your energy level stable and minimize cravings.

For those who wish to gain fat-free mass, a general rule of thumb is to eat between 15 and 20 calories per pound of body weight each day. Bodybuilders with fast metabolisms may need to consume more than 25 calories per pound of body weight to gain weight while those with sluggish metabolisms may find it best to eat a bit less than the preceding recommendations.

Supplements such as protein powders and meal replacements should be viewed as conveniences rather than necessities. Natural food should form the cornerstone of your nutrition program, but when time is short a meal replacement or protein drink is preferable to fast food or no food.

Of the hundreds of supplements that have been touted as performance enhancers, only one has proven itself both in the laboratory and in the gym: creatine monohydrate. This supplement reportedly increases a muscle's ability to contract under heavy loads, enabling users to lift more weight or obtain more repetitions. Individual response to creatine varies. Some trainees report dramatic gains in strength; some note minor improvements; others gain nothing at all. Beginners should not concern themselves with creatine but those who have been training for a while may want to experiment with this compound. Creatine users typically begin with a loading dose of 5 grams taken four to five times daily for five days, followed by a maintenance dose of 5 grams a day. Some research indicates that creatine works better if it is taken with a simple carbohydrate such as fruit juice. Please note, however, that unpublished anecdotal evidence has linked creatine use to muscle strains or pulls, muscle cramps, and renal failure. The long-term effects of creatine use are currently unknown.

Combine Machines and Free Weights

The arguments in support of both free weights and machines are loud and long. Free-weight supporters claim that the balance required to lift free weights provides a stronger growth stimulus to the muscles while machine aficionados point out that machine users can work their muscles harder precisely because they don't have to balance the weight. Free weights are said to be a more natural form of resistance while machines, say others, are designed to make up for the inherent shortcomings of barbells and dumbbells.

Each side has valid arguments, so why not get the benefits of both by combining free weights and machines in your program? A very productive routine can be designed around barbells, dumbbells, and whatever machines you have access to. Hammer Strength®, Nautilus®, and Med-X® machines are particularly suited for the needs of the serious bodybuilder, but these are by no means the only worthwhile machines on the market.

Suppose that you work your entire body in a single workout. Here's what such a routine might look like incorporating free weights and machines (sets × repetition range):

Deadlift (barbell): 2 × 8–10

Leg press (machine): 2 × 8–10

Chin-up (body weight): 2 × 8–10

Bench press (machine): 2 × 6–8

Overhead press (dumbbells): 2 × 6–8

Bicep curl (machine): 2 × 8–10

Let's say that you use a split routine and perform more than one exercise per body part. Here's how a chest/back workout might appear:

Incline press (dumbbells): 2 × 6–8

Iso-lateral chest press (machine): 1 × 6–8

Dip (body weight): 1 × 8–10

Deadlift (barbell): 2 × 6–8

Iso-lateral pulldown (machine): 1 × 8–10

Row (dumbbell): 1 × 8–10

The point is, it's silly and counterproductive to label yourself a *free-weight fiend* or *machine maven*. Both modalities can help you reach your goals, so mix 'em and match 'em for best results.

Use Split Routines with Care

You can make fine progress by training the entire body in one workout repeated 2–3 times weekly or once every 3–4 days. But as you become more advanced and able to handle both greater poundages and a somewhat larger workload, lack of energy near the end of a workout can prevent the necessary effort on the final exercises.

Many trainees try to solve this problem by exercising the whole body over two or three different workouts. The proper application of a split routine can provide a workable solution, but too often a split routine actually compounds a bodybuilder's problem. That's because a split routine often prompts one to add sets and exercises in excess of what is required for optimal results.

Let's say that this is your routine (for two sets each):

Deadlift

Squat

Bench press

Chin-up

Bicep curl

Let's further assume that you've made good progress from this routine twice weekly but the weights you're lifting have increased so much that you're completely exhausted by the time you get to chin-ups and cannot produce a desirable level of effort. In this case, it might make sense to try a split as follows (again for two sets each):

Workout A
Squat
Bench press

Workout B
Deadlift
Chin-up
Bicep curl

You might perform Workout A on Monday, Workout B on Wednesday, and Workout A on Friday, then return the next Monday with Workout B. Or you might want to rest two days between each workout—the ideal protocol depends upon your particular recovery ability.

What you would not want to do is add more sets and repetitions to the above workouts, as this would defeat your purpose for doing a split in the first place. You'd end up even more tired and overtrained and with no progress to show for your doubled efforts.

Beginners shouldn't even consider a split routine. Most newcomers will make terrific progress performing one or two sets of 3–6 compound exercises once every 3–4 days.

Keep Detailed Records

Most trainees have no idea where they're going or how to reach their destination because they don't keep track of where they've been. That is, they don't keep a training diary.

To make the most of HIT bodybuilding, you're going to have to keep meticulous records. Don't trust your memory—put your performances on paper. For every work set completed, you should write down the weights used and repetitions obtained. Refer to your workout diary during your next training session and try as hard as possible to better your previous performance.

This implies, of course, that the only frequent changes in your routine should be in repetitions and poundages, not exercises. While some variety is reasonable, continually changing exercises doesn't give you the benefit of establishing linear progression from workout to workout, which is the basis for long-term improvement. This does not mean you should use the same exercises for years on end. It only means that you should stick with a given exercise until it ceases to work for you. Leave the so-called Instinctive Training Principle—which states that one should "confuse" the muscles by constantly changing exercises from workout to workout—for those who are more interested in being avant-garde than in making progress.

Specialize Wisely

As a bodybuilder's physique becomes more advanced, he or she may find one or more body parts lagging behind the rest. Since the most eye-pleasing physique showcases harmonious, symmetrical development, a lagging body part can be a source of frustration to the dedicated bodybuilder. The solution could be a thoughtfully designed body-part specialization routine.

A body-part specialization routine is not a license to overtrain a muscle by bombing it with a multitude of sets. Rather, it is a short-term (6–8 week) program of slightly increased focus, volume, and intensity for one muscle, accompanied by a maintenance routine for the remainder of the body. For most trainees, attempting to specialize on a body part while training the whole body for growth results only in overtraining.

Most trainees are best served by training twice weekly or once every 3–4 days. The same protocol should be applied to specialization. Use one workout to perform one (or at the most, two) sets for each major muscle group. These sets should be taken to the point of positive muscle fatigue or even one or two repetitions shy of fatigue; your goal is to maintain your strength in these exercises.

Structure your second workout around your target body part. Select two, three, or at the most, four exercises and perform one or two sets each, adding intensity-extending techniques to half of these sets. Perform some of your sets using a 6–8 repetition range and some using a 10–12 or 12–15 range. As always, keep meticulous records and endeavor to increase poundages as often as possible while adhering to proper form.

Let's say that you've been using the following routine twice weekly (for two sets each):

Squat

Deadlift

Bench press

Chin-up

Dumbbell press

Barbell curl

Let's further say that this routine is stimulating growth in every body part except your arms. You can set up a 6–8 week arm-specialization program like this (for one set per exercise using the repetition ranges noted):

Workout 1
Squat: 12–15
Deadlift: 10–12
Bench press: 6–8
Chin-up: 8–10
Overhead press: 6–8

You would delete barbell curls in Workout 1 since the biceps receive substantial work during chin-ups. In addition, the biceps are stressed heavily in the second workout (for two sets per exercise using the repetition ranges noted):

Workout 2
Close-grip bench press: 6–8
Tricep pushdown: 10–12
Bicep curl: 6–8
Incline bicep curl: 10–12

Specialization workouts for other body parts might consist of the following (sets × repetition range):

Chest
Bench press: 2 × 6–8
Incline press: 2 × 8–10
Dip: 1 × 10–12

Back
Deadlift: 2 × 6–8
Reverse-grip pulldowns: 2 × 8–10
Bent-over row: 1 × 10–12

Shoulders
Military press: 2 × 6–8
Alternate press: 2 × 8–10
Bent-over lateral raise: 2 × 10–12

Hips/Legs
Squat: 2 × 8–10

Leg press: 2 × 12–15
Leg curl: 2 × 8–10

Diet to Obtain Muscular Definition

While getting bigger is the primary goal of the typical trainee, most serious body-builders eventually develop the urge to improve their muscular definition. After all, the source of the unique appearance of bodybuilders—the thing that distinguishes them from just another big person who pumps iron—is crisp, sharply delineated musculature.

In truth, training for definition is a fallacy. Definition is not a quality that can be trained into a muscle; it is nothing more than the absence of fat over a well-developed muscle. The peaks, valleys, separations, and veins that characterize a defined physique exist in anyone who has developed a respectable degree of muscle mass. If these muscular details cannot be seen, it's because they're obscured by body fat.

The best way to train for definition, then, is to adopt a sensible fat-loss plan. Put simply, you'll have to eat less. But you want to eat only a little less—starvation diets burn more muscle than fat. A slight reduction (of perhaps 300–400 calories daily) should be sufficient to set the fat-loss machinery in motion. Aim for a loss of just one pound weekly; more rapid weight loss will quickly eat into your hard-won muscle mass.

The peaks, valleys, separations, and veins that characterize a defined physique exist in everyone who has developed a respectable degree of muscle mass.

(photo by Matt Brzycki)

The best fat-loss diets are based around frequent feedings. Eat five or six small meals a day consisting of lean protein, a moderate amount of carbohydrates, and a small amount of fat. While mainstream nutritionists typically promote high-carbohydrate eating plans, many competitive bodybuilders find that they get their best fat-loss results by consuming a moderate amount of carbohydrates—perhaps 40 percent or less of their calories—with 30–40 percent of their calories coming from protein and fats supplying the remaining 20–30 percent of calories. These bodybuilders also find it better to taper their carbohydrates as the day goes on by eating starchy carbohydrates (e.g., oatmeal, yams, and brown rice) for breakfast and maybe lunch and fibrous carbohydrates such as broccoli—a staple source of fibrous carbohydrates for bodybuilders—during the late afternoon and the evening.

A moderate amount of cardiovascular activity can assist in fat loss. Whether you choose to run or walk at a fast pace outdoors or indoors on a treadmill, ride a bike indoors or outdoors, or use one of the numerous cardio machines available at commercial gyms, start out by performing the activity two or three times weekly for 20 minutes at a moderate intensity. Gradually increase the duration and number of cardio sessions. Since excessive cardiovascular work can cut into muscle size, perform the minimum amount of cardio activity required to keep fat loss occurring until you reach your goal. Try not to exceed five 45-minute cardio sessions weekly.

While trying to get lean, your approach to weight training should be the same as when you're striving to add mass: Train intensely, briefly, and infrequently. At this point, increasing your volume is an even bigger mistake than it is when you're training for size, as a decreased caloric intake and the inclusion of cardio work renders you more susceptible to overtraining.

Although it's not likely that you'll gain appreciable strength during this leaning-out process, you must strive to at least maintain your poundages. The weights that built your muscles to their current size will maintain that size as you shed the fat. Lifting lighter weights will only lead to a reduction in muscle size. Likewise, so-called shaping movements—such as the concentration curl, leg extension, tricep kickback, pec dec fly, and the like—are a waste of time for shaping. Muscle shape is a genetically determined variable that is realized by increasing the size of the muscle. You can't shape a muscle through specific exercises as if you were molding a lump of clay. Stick to the heavy, basic, compound movements even when you're focusing on muscular definition.

What about developing an impressive "six-pack" abdominal region? This again is a matter of eliminating excess body fat through diet and cardio. Performing countless crunches, sit-ups, and leg raises in hopes of bringing out the abs is a waste of time and effort. As your percentage of body fat lowers, your abs will become more prominent. To display a truly impressive rock-hard midsection, you'll need to lower your percentage of body fat to well under 10 percent—an undertaking that requires discipline and diligence. (Women would need to drop their percentage of body fat to the low teens.)

SAMPLE HIT BODYBUILDING TRAINING SCHEDULES

The following training schedules show how HIT workouts can be devised for trainees at different levels of experience. These are sample routines only, not proclamations set in stone. Bear in mind that the beginner routine could be perfectly appropriate for an advanced trainee whose limited recovery ability permits progress with only a minimal number of sets. When in doubt, always perform fewer sets rather than more sets.

Sample Routine: Beginner

Perform the following exercises for one or two sets each twice weekly or once every 3–4 days using the repetition ranges noted:

>   Barbell squat or leg press: 10–12
>
>   Bench press: 8–10
>
>   Reverse-grip pulldown or chin-up: 8–10
>
>   Military press (optional): 8–10

Sample Routine: Intermediate

Perform two sets of the following exercises twice weekly or once every 4–5 days using the repetition ranges noted:

>   Squat: 8–10
>
>   Deadlift: 8–10
>
>   Incline press: 6–8
>
>   Chin-up: 8–10
>
>   Seated press: 6–8
>
>   Bicep curl: 6–8
>
>   Incline sit-up: 12–15

Sample Routine: Advanced

Alternate the following workouts, performing one workout every 4–5 days (sets × repetition range):

>   **Workout A**
>   Squat: 2 × 8–10
>   Leg press: 1 × 12–15

Dip: 2 × 6–8
Incline press: 2 × 8–10
Overhead press: 2 × 6–8
Calf raise (sitting): 2 × 12–15

Workout B
Deadlift: 2 × 8–10
Leg curl: 2 × 8–10
Reverse-grip pulldown: 2 × 8–10
Bent-over row: 2 × 10–12
Incline bicep curl: 2 × 6–8
Abdominal crunch machine: 2 × 12–15

Here's a triple-split program that is appropriate only for a very advanced trainee with above-average recuperative ability. Alternate these three workouts, taking 2–3 complete days off between sessions.

Workout A: Chest/Back
Bench press: 2 × 6–8
Incline press: 2 × 8–10
Dip: 1 × 10–12
Deadlift: 2 × 8–10
Reverse-grip chin-up 2 × 6–8
Bent-over row: 2 × 8–10

Workout B: Shoulders/Arms
Military press: 2 × 6–8
Alternate press: 2 × 8–10
Bicep curl: 2 × 6–8
Preacher curl: 1 × 8–10
Reverse curl: 1–2 × 8–10
Close-grip bench press: 2 × 6–8
French press: 2 × 10–12

Workout C: Legs/Abs
Leg press: 2 × 8–10
Front squat: 2 × 10–12
Seated leg curl: 2 × 8–10
Stiff-leg deadlift: 1 × 10–12
Calf raise (standing): 2 × 12–15
Abdominal crunch machine or incline sit-up: 2 × 12–15

This chapter is dedicated to my wife, Kim, and our children, Ryan and Amanda.

26

Powerlifting HIT

Bill Piche, M.S.
Marion, Iowa

The sport of powerlifting is simple: The person who lifts the most combined poundage in the squat, bench press, and deadlift wins the contest. For this reason, the squat, bench press, and deadlift should be the core of a powerlifter's training routine. High intensity training (HIT) for powerlifters consists of hard, brief, and infrequent workouts using these three exercises as the focal point of a training routine. Since HIT is so versatile, powerlifters can use this type of training regardless of whether they are preparing for a contest (pre-contest) or trying to increase overall muscle strength and endurance (off-contest).

OFF-CONTEST: THE BASICS

Off-contest training should focus on increasing muscle strength and endurance by performing relatively high repetitions (8–20). A powerlifter's off-contest strength training does not need to differ from that of other athletes. Athletes in all sports can use the squat, bench press, and deadlift for strength training; but for a powerlifter, these are the specific skills of the sport that need to be mastered. Therefore, powerlifters should not exclude these exercises from their off-contest training. The off-contest strength training program should be comprehensive; it should include areas of development often neglected by a powerlifter, such as grip training and abdominal work.

Sets

Unfortunately, the norm for powerlifting training has not been HIT. Instead, the norm has been to perform multiple low-repetition sets with long rest intervals between sets. It's no surprise that by the end of a powerlifting contest, many competitors often miss their deadlifts due to poor conditioning.

Many powerlifters don't believe that one or two work sets of squats, bench presses, or deadlifts are all that is needed to get stronger. The quality of a set is more important than the quantity of sets. If your intensity is high, you don't need to do more than one or two sets per exercise. In fact, if your intensity is truly high, you literally will not be able to do more than one or two sets. You can work out hard, but not long and hard. Hard and long are mutually exclusive in strength training. They are mutually exclusive in powerlifting as well.

In addition to the competitive lifts, many powerlifters make the mistake of performing too many additional exercises and, therefore, too many additional sets. This practice often results in overtraining. The additional exercises are commonly referred to as *assistance exercises*. An assistance exercise is one that targets a particular muscle or group of muscles that are used to perform one of the powerlifts. An example of an assistance exercise for the bench press would be the tricep extension because the triceps are used when performing a bench press. The term *assistance* is actually a misnomer because the purpose of the exercises is to build overall body strength, not assist the performance of the powerlifts. An erroneous belief among many powerlifters is that assistance exercises build specific strength that will carry over to an increase in the powerlifts. The true purpose of assistance exercises is to build overall strength.

Repetitions

How many repetitions should be performed? A powerlifter does not need to use repetition ranges that are any different from athletes in any other sport. Based upon a 6-second repetition, for example, a general guideline would be to perform 10–20 repetitions for lower-body exercises and 8–15 repetitions for upper-body exercises. Powerlifters should experiment within these guidelines for continued progression. Remember, too, that the repetitions should be performed in a smooth and deliberate manner.

Before a contest, powerlifters must practice the squat, bench press, and deadlift in the same manner as these lifts will be performed in the contest. This means that the number of repetitions must be decreased and the amount of weight must be increased. However, there is no reason to reduce the number of repetitions during off-contest training. Lifting heavy weights for low repetitions takes a toll on the body that should be avoided during off-contest training. As the number of repetitions decreases, the margin for error in technique decreases and the potential for injury increases. This is contrary to the purpose of off-contest training.

Many powerlifters frequently use low repetition ranges—even during their off-contest training—and this often results in injury, overtraining, and lack of progression.

With respect to progression, many powerlifters increase their poundage too much between workouts. Smaller, almost imperceptible weight increases over a six-month period will add up to far more progress than will larger increases in a month's time that can lead to stagnation and possible injury. These small poundage increases can be accomplished by the use of small plates. Unfortunately, incorporating small plates (e.g., one-pound plates) is virtually unseen in powerlifting circles. Systematic and sensible progression is often sacrificed because of ego.

Frequency

The sport of powerlifting is lifting weights. Unlike basketball players who may practice sport-specific skills every day to improve their performance, powerlifters should not train or practice for their sport with such frequency. Strength training, and HIT in particular, is very stressful to the body. The body must be given an adequate amount of time to recover and to adapt to the stress and hence get stronger.

Many powerlifters use split routines where each of the competitive lifts are trained twice in the same week. This amount of training is unnecessary and is counterproductive to long-term progression in the powerlifts. The powerlifts should not be trained more than once per week. For the advanced lifter, it may even be more conducive to recovery to train the deadlift once every other week.

A powerlifter should perform at least two of the three competitive lifts during a workout. This will help to maximize recovery between workouts. An effective minor split would be to perform the squat and deadlift in one training session and the bench press in another. This would maximize the recovery of the hips, legs, and lower back, which are the prime movers in both movements. A full-body workout can also be performed once a week to maximize recovery between workouts.

The ability to recover from a workout varies according to many factors including age, genetics, and training experience as well as other factors not often mentioned such as family and job responsibilities. For most, two workouts per week are more than adequate. Contrary to popular belief, your muscles will not lose size and strength if more than 48 hours or even 96 hours elapses between workouts. The roadblock for the use of such infrequent workouts is not physical but psychological. The psychological barrier for reducing the frequency of workouts can be overcome once lifters start to see favorable results in their training.

Duration

A typical powerlifting contest has the competitors sitting around and waiting for their attempts on the platform. Ten- to twenty-minute time periods between attempts are quite common. During pre-contest training, some simulation of this environment is necessary. When the contest is atypical and there are few competitors, lifters may find themselves on the platform with little rest between attempts. Powerlifters who use lengthy, split, multi-set routines rarely succeed at these contests—a direct result of their lack of conditioning.

There is no reason for prolonged recovery intervals between exercises. Powerlifters should only rest long enough so they are able to proceed to the next exercise. How long should a workout be? Long enough to get the job done. With a minor split based on the powerlifts and two weekly workouts, the total weekly workout time need not exceed 90 minutes.

PRE-CONTEST: THE BASICS

When it comes to contest day, one must perform a one-repetition maximum (1-RM). Training for a contest does not have to be complicated nor does it need to change significantly from off-contest training. Off-contest training should have focused on increasing overall body strength and muscle endurance by emphasizing higher repetitions (8–20). The pre-contest training should consist of the same core off-contest strength training with the addition of specific skill practice for the powerlifts. If supportive equipment (e.g., a tight lifting suit) will be used for the contest, this equipment must be worn when performing the skill set. (A skill set is a set performed specifically to master the exact technique of the squat, bench press, and deadlift that will be used in the contest.) If possible, the contest environment should be simulated as well.

Sets

The number of sets performed in pre-contest workouts increases but only by one set per powerlift. The skill sets should be performed first in the workout. The purpose of the skill set is not to build strength but to hone technique and get the body used to a heavy weight when performing a 1-RM. In addition, the skill set should be terminated one or two repetitions short of muscular fatigue. The set should be performed in a manner that simulates the contest environment. Why? It's the same reason why a basketball player does not practice free throws from three feet beyond the free throw line: To maximize performance, a skill must be practiced exactly as it will be used in competition. The warm-ups for the skill set should be duplicated as they will be performed in the contest. There is no need to perform many warm-up sets before the skill set. The purpose of the warm-up sets is simply to warm up.

The second set should be performed in the same manner as during off-contest training. No supportive equipment should be used for this set. The supportive equipment does not make the lifter stronger. Rather, the supportive equipment robs the muscles of the adaptive stress that is required for increasing strength. Lifters who use equipment for all of their sets before a contest will likely lose strength. Strength can be increased during pre-contest training.

Repetitions

Lower repetitions should only be done as part of pre-contest training. Performing lower repetitions means doing 5-repetition sets and finally 3-repetition sets before the contest. A powerlifter should prepare for a contest by decreasing repetitions over the course of a 6–12 week period. A powerlifter should never perform a 1-RM before a contest. Lower repetitions should only be used for the skill set.

Decreasing the repetitions for the skill set should be done gradually. Many lifters make the mistake of decreasing repetitions and increasing weight too quickly. This leads to degradation in the skill set. The number of repetitions in the skill set is decreased and the lifter ends up performing 1-RMs in the gym. Some lifters erroneously plan for singles in training. Their poundage expectations that are based on these singles are seldom fulfilled in the contest.

Frequency

The frequency of pre-contest training does not need to differ from off-contest training. The use of supportive equipment may make it necessary for a minor split based upon the powerlifts because the equipment takes time to put on and take off. A full-body workout where all three skill sets are performed in the same workout may not be practical due to time considerations.

Duration

A pre-contest workout will take longer because of the performance of skill sets and the simulation of contest conditions. As noted previously, there are often long periods of time between attempts in a powerlifting contest. To an HIT powerlifter, this can seem like an eternity. The skill sets should be preceded by a time period comparable to contest conditions. The amount of time between attempts can vary significantly. Most often it is between 10 and 20 minutes. After the skill sets are performed, the rest of the workout can be performed in the same manner as off-contest training.

SAMPLE TRAINING ROUTINES

There are no magic routines. Any routine, no matter how good, will fail if the lifter does not provide the effort to succeed. The routines that follow are suggested based on the material provided in this chapter.

Exercises

It is beyond the scope of this chapter to describe how to perform the powerlifts and other common exercises. Detailed exercise descriptions can be found in many books such as *A Practical Approach to Strength Training* by Matt Brzycki (Indianapolis, IN: Masters Press). However, some of the exercises that will be listed in this chapter are not usually described in other books. Therefore, the following exercises are illustrated and detailed in this chapter: ball squat, trap bar deadlift, and pinch grip.

Ball Squat

Muscles used: hips, quadriceps, hamstrings

Suggested repetitions: 10–20

Starting position: A smooth, unobstructed wall is needed to perform ball squats. Stand up straight and put a medium-size pliable ball behind your lower back against the wall.

Description: Position your feet so that when leaning against the ball on the wall, your upper and lower legs form a 90° angle in the parallel squat position. A stance in which the feet are slightly wider will work well for most lifters. Slowly lower your hips until the tops of your thighs are in line with where your hip joint bends. Pause briefly in the bottom position and return slowly to the starting position. Most of your body weight should be centered on your heels.

The ball squat is a productive exercise that strengthens the hips, quadriceps, and hamstrings. (photo by Kim Piche)

Performance points:
- Don't lean too hard against the ball.
- Don't bounce in the bottom position.
- Don't lock or "snap" your knees when returning to the starting position.
- This movement can be performed with added resistance by holding dumbbells or using a hip belt.

Trap Bar Deadlift

Muscles used: hips, quadriceps, hamstrings, erector spinae

Suggested repetitions: 10–20

Starting position: While standing inside the diamond-shaped trap bar, position your feet slightly wider than shoulder-width apart. The middle of your feet should be approximately in line with the center of the bar. Reach down and grab the parallel handles. Your hips should be low enough so your back is flat (i.e., not rounded). Look straight ahead.

The trap bar deadlift is a movement that utilizes the buttocks, quadriceps, hamstrings, and erector spinae. (photo by Kim Piche)

Description: Stand upright by straightening your legs and upper torso. Pause briefly in the standing position and return slowly to the starting position.

Performance points:

- If the trap bar tips, move your hands on the handles to prevent further imbalance.
- Try to push your feet "through the floor" at the beginning of each repetition.
- Keep your arms straight and don't jerk the weight.
- Keep your back flat.
- For those with low-back pain, this exercise is a good alternative to the regular deadlift performed with a barbell.

Pinch Grip

Muscles used: finger flexors, forearms

Suggested repetitions: 8–12

Starting position: Place two weight plates together in a vertical position on a bench with the smooth sides facing outward. Grasp the plates with one hand so that your thumb is on one side and the rest of your fingers are on the other side. Grip the plates with the full length of your fingers and thumb.

Description: Pinch and lift the plates off of the bench until your hand is waist high. Slowly return the plates to the bench. Keep the same grip on the plates.

The pinch grip is an excellent exercise for strengthening the finger flexors and forearms. (photo by Kim Piche)

Performance Points:
- Keep the plates from resting up against the side of your body.
- Timed holds can also be performed.

Sample Off-Contest Routine

A routine for off-contest training can have infinite variations within the context of being brief, intense, and infrequent. It is important to vary the strength training routine for continued progression. One simple variation is to change the exercises performed. Another would be changing the number of repetitions.

Two sample workouts are presented in Figure 26.1. In these examples, only barbells and dumbbells are used and one set is performed for each exercise. Machines can also be used if available. The repetition guidelines given previously apply.

Sample Pre-Contest Routine

A pre-contest routine should include an extra skill set for the powerlifts that should be performed in a manner as close as possible to contest conditions. The amount of weight for the skill set should be increased and the number of repetitions decreased as the contest approaches. The other exercises in the routine should be performed in the same manner as during off-contest training.

A sample pre-contest routine is presented in Figure 26.2. The number of repetitions for the skill sets is specified for a 12-week period prior to the contest. If used, supportive equipment should be introduced gradually.

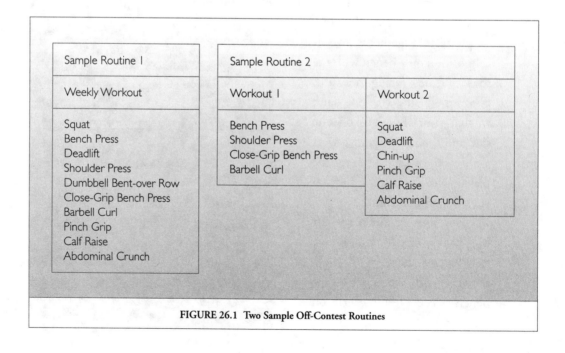

Sample Routine 1	Sample Routine 2	
Weekly Workout	Workout 1	Workout 2
Squat	Bench Press	Squat
Bench Press	Shoulder Press	Deadlift
Deadlift	Close-Grip Bench Press	Chin-up
Shoulder Press	Barbell Curl	Pinch Grip
Dumbbell Bent-over Row		Calf Raise
Close-Grip Bench Press		Abdominal Crunch
Barbell Curl		
Pinch Grip		
Calf Raise		
Abdominal Crunch		

FIGURE 26.1 Two Sample Off-Contest Routines

Sample Routine	Week											
Workout 1	1	2	3	4	5	6	7	8	9	10	11	12
Bench Press Shoulder Press Close-Grip Bench Press Barbell Curl	12	10	10	10	8	8	8	5	5	5	3	3
Workout 2	1	2	3	4	5	6	7	8	9	10	11	12
Squat Deadlift Chin-up Pinch Grip Calf Raise Abdominal Crunch	20 15	15 12	15 12	12 10	10 8	8 8	8 8	5 5	5 5	5 5	3 3	3 3

NOTES
1. The numbers under each week are the suggested repetitions to be performed.
2. In Week #8, introduce the equipment to be used in the contest and then use for the remaining weeks.

FIGURE 26.2 Sample Pre-Contest Routine

The routine specified in Figure 26.2 is just an example. Some experimentation is necessary and recommended.

THE FINAL ATTEMPT

To excel in any sport, the specific skills of the sport must be practiced to perfection. In powerlifting, this means practicing the lifting of heavy weights for low repetitions in the squat, bench press, and deadlift. Skill practice should not be confused with what is necessary to build muscle: hard, brief, and infrequent training. HIT provides the means to build the muscle and it's muscle that moves the weight on the powerlifting platform.

27

Athletic Skill Development: An Open and Closed Case

Ken Mannie, M.S., C.S.C.S.
Strength and Conditioning Coach
Michigan State University
East Lansing, Michigan

Skill development remains the most critical element in athletic performance. A strong, well-conditioned, genetically endowed athlete with a poor skill level is akin to a high-performance race car with flat tires.

No one can disagree with that. The problem lies in determining the best way to achieve an optimum skill level. And that has to begin with a clear understanding of the neuromuscular and cognitive processes involved in the teaching and learning progression.

Coaches and athletes alike thrive on searching for new-and-improved methods for enhancing athletic skills. Everyone wants to discover an innovative teaching technique or try the latest gimmick on the market that purports to be skill specific. There are certainly many helpful teaching aids and highly efficient modalities for training purposes. However, we should never lose sight of the basic principles of athletic skill development.

ABILITIES VERSUS SKILLS

Oftentimes—and wrongly so—the words *ability* and *skill* are used interchangeably. An ability can be defined as "a general trait or capacity of an individual that is related to the performance of a variety of motor skills" (Magill 1993).

Motor abilities—such as static and dynamic balance, reaction time, response time, speed of limb movement, eye–hand/foot coordination, visual acuity, and so on—can be viewed as the foundational components of motor-skill development and performance. While abilities enhance (or limit) an individual's performance level in various athletic skills, they are not considered skills per se.

Most motor-learning researchers maintain that motor abilities are determined more by genetics than by experience. Simply put, the ultimate ability level of an individual is controlled primarily by inherited constituents. However, research also indicates that people can often compensate for a lack of certain specific abilities with experience, training, and quality practice in an activity.

These processes, which develop the actual science and application of coaching, are often conducted with confusion and/or misinterpretations of the scientific literature.

THE THREE STAGES OF LEARNING

Skills are learned over time in three specific stages (Schmidt 1991): (1) the cognitive stage; (2) the associative stage; and (3) the autonomous stage.

The Cognitive Stage

This is the beginning stage of learning, one in which the learner has many unanswered questions: What stance should I use? What type of grip should I use on this bat, racket, golf club, football, or baseball? What are my steps on a lead, trap, or pass block?

Obviously, numerous errors, variability in performance, and needed quality repetition mark the cognitive stage. The learner requires specific information to help in making the correct decisions and adjustments.

You will know that athletes are still in this stage when there is an awareness of "doing something wrong," but the corrective measures are a mystery.

The Associative Stage

As athletes enter this stage, they know many of the basic mechanics of the skill. They make fewer, less serious mistakes, and, more importantly, they are capable of recognizing many of their errors and are aware of the proper steps to correct them. The goal now is to refine the skill.

It is vital for the coach to continue to provide the athletes with useful specific information and constructive feedback throughout this stage.

The Autonomous Stage

This final stage of learning is realized only after much practice, quality repetition, and experience with the specific task. The skill has now become habitual or automatic. Obviously, this stage is not achieved overnight; depending on the complexity of the skill, it may take years.

The athletes are now able to recognize their errors and are cognizant of the process needed to correct them. Optimal performance is impossible until the athletes are operating in the autonomous mode.

Even when this level of learning has been achieved, mistakes will still be made. However, the athletes will be able to tell their coach what they did wrong, why they did it, what should have been done, and the proper techniques for doing it. As a coach,

The final stage of learning is realized only after much practice, quality repetition, and experience with the specific task.
(photo by Kevin Fowler)

the only way to discern whether the athletes have achieved this higher level of learning is by quizzing them rather than lecturing them.

Questions like "What should have been done in that situation?" or "What did you see?" and "Why did you make that decision?" will give the coach a better handle on where the players are in the learning progression. It will also motivate the athletes to learn by challenging their recall capabilities.

THE NERVOUS SYSTEM AND MOVEMENT CONTROL

Movement control involves a highly complex system for central and peripheral nervous system structures. The central nervous system (CNS) is the command center for human movement; primarily the cerebral cortex, basal ganglia, cerebellum, and the brain stem. The functions of these structures are as follows.

Cerebral cortex. This structure is responsible for receiving and interpreting sensory signals and sending these signals to the appropriate effectors via the correct neural pathways to store and organize information.

Basal ganglia. These are three large nuclei that play an important role in controlling coordinated movement. They plan rapid complex responses to stimuli. Research is showing that the basal ganglia may be even more critical for movement control than was once thought.

Cerebellum. Though traditionally thought to relate primarily to balance, postural adjustments, locomotion, and reflex activity, there is current speculation that the cerebellum is also a vital center of control for pro-grammed movements. Some refer to it as the seat of motor learning.

Brain stem. The brain stem has four main areas: thalamus, pons, medulla, and reticular formation. They are responsible for transmitting sensory information, regulating vital internal processes, and integrating sensory and motor impulses.

OPEN-LOOP AND CLOSED-LOOP SYSTEMS

The spinal cord interacts with a variety of systems related to the transmission of both sensory and motor information. Afferent feedback (i.e., sending information to the CNS) is sent via the proprioceptors (muscle spindles and joint receptors).

All coordinated movements are controlled by the open-loop or closed-loop systems. Both systems contain control centers that issue movement commands to the effectors (the muscles and joints involved in producing the desired move-ment). They also involve a feedback pathway that travels from the effectors to the CNS. However, the two systems do have very distinct, inherent differences. First, the closed-loop system relies on feedback from the movement effectors to the movement control center (thus closing the loop). This is the same afferent infor-mation sent by the proprioceptors as well as the feedback sent by the auditory and visual systems. This feedback updates the control center about the correctness of the movement while it is in progress.

The other important difference between the open-loop and closed-loop systems is yielded by the nature of the commands emitted from the control center. The open-loop system directives contain all of the information needed for the effectors to execute the planned movement. Although feedback is both produced and avail-able, it is not used to control the ongoing movement. However, this feedback can help plan a future response, especially if there was an error in the first one.

The movement commands differ in the closed-loop system because there is an initial command to the effectors that is only sufficient to initiate the movement. After initiation, feedback information is required for the execution and comple-tion of the task. Control of the ongoing movement and help in planning the next movement is dependent upon this feedback.

Most types of movement have a predominant system, but complex voluntary movement typically exhibits characteristics of both open-loop and closed-loop systems.

CLOSED SKILLS AND OPEN SKILLS

Athletic skills can be placed on a continuum of closed and open categories.

When doing open skills, decisions and adjustments must be made while the performer is on the run. (photo by Kevin Fowler)

Closed skills are at the low end of the continuum and take place under fixed, unchanging environmental conditions. They are predictable and have clearly defined beginning and ending points. Once the skill is initiated, feedback plays a minor role. In addition, the skills are usually self-paced in the sense that the performer begins movement when ready. Bowling, golf, archery, and competitive weightlifting are consummate closed-skill sports.

Open skills, which are at the high end of the continuum, usually take place under the conditions of a temporarily or spatially changing environment. Decisions and adjustments must be made while the performer is on the run.

A major distinction of open skills is the reliance on feedback in the decision-making process. It may be a visual cue (e.g., a tennis player reacting to an opponent's serve), an auditory cue (e.g., an offensive lineman's reaction to the snap count), a pressure cue (e.g., a defensive lineman's reaction to the type and/or angle of the block he is facing), or some other external stimulus or sensory indicator.

A player's ability to respond quickly, properly, and precisely to the information being sent is of utmost importance in determining success in that particular sport.

(photo by Kevin Fowler)

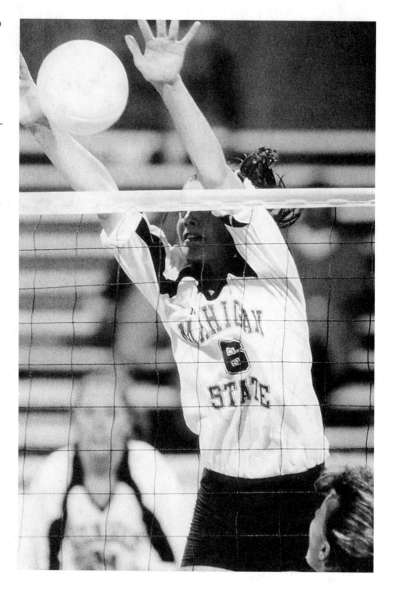

These are known as *forced-pace skills* and they are extremely complex due to the fact that athletes must make quick decisions and get their bodies to react with precision in a very short period of time.

Due to the variability, dependence on feedback, and the mental pressure to make instant judgments under duress, it is evident that open skills require a higher level of learning than closed skills. It is vital that coaches understand the distinction between these two categories of skills when designing training programs.

SPECIFICITY REVISITED

Without question, the most misused term in much of the current training literature is *specificity*. We are led to believe by various individuals and organizations that any number of strength training movements are specific—in either a neuro-muscular or skill sense—to sport-specific or position-specific movements.

Two tasks may appear at first glance to have many general underlying features in common, but they most likely use completely unique neuromuscular pathways. The fact that individuals are skilled (or unskilled) in one activity does not indicate their skill level in a different activity. To be specific—at least in the case of a motor/athletic skill—requires that an athlete use exactness (not similarity) in all of the involved variables (i.e., limb positioning, equipment, audio and visual cues, environmental conditions, ever-changing feedback, and so on) so that the practice situation mirrors that of the actual competition.

Specificity can be put into proper perspective when it is understood that the more complex the skill, the greater the importance of exactness when practicing it. This precept is known in the motor-learning literature as the Encoding Principle of Specificity and it is the cornerstone in the teaching progression of any skill. The Encoding Principle of Specificity states that "the closer the influence of practice on the test context characteristics (i.e., the competition situation), the better the practiced movements will be recalled during the test. Simply put, practice sessions should be designed to replicate the game conditions—especially when preparing for the schemes of a specific opponent—as often as possible.

PRACTICE: WHOLE OR PART?

A common problem among coaches is whether to teach a skill as a whole (and allow the athlete to get a better feel for the flow and timing of all of the elements involved) or to have the athlete practice the skill in parts (to emphasize each important detail).

Before making this decision, the coach must analyze both the complexity and organizational requirements of the skill. Complexity refers to how many parts or components are involved in the skill along with the information-processing demands it carries. The organizational requirements refer to how the components of a skill are interrelated. If the parts of the skill are rather independent, it would be considered low in organization.

Researchers tell us that if a skill is low in complexity and high in organization, practice as a whole is a better choice. In other words, a simple skill with highly related component parts can be most efficiently learned through the whole-practice approach.

If the skill is high in complexity and low in organization, the part method would be the better choice. This would involve a skill that has many components, but these components are independent.

What if the skill ranks high in both complexity and organization? A progressive-part method would be a wise choice in this case: organizing all of the parts in the order in which they occur in performing the skill, then progressively linking these parts one by one. In other words, after part one is learned, part two is practiced independently. Then parts one and two are practiced together. Part three is then practiced independently before being combined with parts one and two.

IMPROVING RESPONSE TIME

Response time is an often overlooked and usually underestimated element in the preparation process of athletes. What we refer to as explosiveness is often actually great response time.

Think about it: In just about all sports you will find a constant series of reactions to auditory and visual cues. A player's ability to respond quickly, properly, and precisely to the information being sent is of utmost importance in determining success in that particular sport. Decreasing response time to various stimuli is just as vital in overall development as the strength and conditioning protocols you implement.

Before we outline a game plan for getting this done, however, it is necessary to clarify some vital points. The term *reaction time* is often incorrectly substituted for *response time.* Reaction time (RT) is defined in the motor-learning literature as "the interval of time between the onset of a signal (i.e., a stimulus) and the initiation of a response." It is important to note that reaction time does not include the movement itself but only the time prior to the beginning of the movement.

Movement time (MT) is the term used to define the interval between the initiation and completion of the movement. Response time defines the total time interval involving both RT and MT (i.e., RT + MT).

As you can see, improvement in response time is predicated on improving RT, MT, or both. The following four points will assist you in developing a strategy for helping athletes improve their response times to the various cues they receive.

1. *Reduce the number of stimulus-response choices.* There are numerous ways to accomplish a task, but some are better than others. You would be well advised to teach your athletes the best responses to various stimuli. The average individual has a limited ability to acquire, store, and use meaningful information when it comes to learning and repeating specific tasks. In simple terms, teach them to do a few things very well as opposed to doing a lot of things poorly or below average.

2. *Search for predictors.* How often have you heard an athlete make the comment, "I knew what was coming because they telegraphed their intentions"? What is actually happening in this situation is that the athletes have more time to prepare a response because they have anticipated the stimulus eventually sent by their opponents. The more predictable the stimulus, the quicker and more accurately a person can respond.

For a task utilizing large muscle actions and requiring high levels of force and speed, the performer should generate a maximum arousal level. (photo by Kevin Fowler)

This element is closely related to reducing the number of stimulus-response choices, as the process of elimination will usually kick in before a response is required. In other words, the main cue (i.e., visual, auditory, or other sensory indicator) will often narrow the possible options to one or two good ones. The main reason why coaches study opponents so closely and intensely through videotape, scouting, and so on is to identify these predictors and utilize them in the preparation scheme.

3. *Ensure an optimal arousal level.* Get fired up! How often is that said before or during an athletic contest? Of course, we are speaking primarily of an emotional mind-set—an intangible, intrinsic component that is usually a product of motivation. There are those who maintain that as arousal increases, performance increases proportionately.

You must be careful, however, to influence arousal so as not to negatively affect performance. If the task involves complicated decision making or fine movement control, the performer's arousal level should be adjusted to a relatively low level. Conversely, for a task utilizing large muscle actions and requiring high levels of force and speed, the performer should generate a maximum arousal level.

Experienced coaches know that emotion will carry an athlete or team only so far in a contest. Basically, emotion without proper preparation and confidence in one's abilities usually results in bitter disappointment. Proper preparation breeds confidence, which usually results in successful performance (with, as they say, all else being equal).

The key here is to build confidence and security with a concurrent reduction in anxiety. This can be accomplished by properly preparing the mind as well as the spirit.

4. *Design quality, task-specific practices.* Once the best responses have been defined for all of the possible situations to be faced in competition, the players should be drilled with both the correct cues (keys) and appropriate reactions. Repetition of the proper responses in game situations is the best way to develop the motor memory so that the correct information can be recalled when needed.

Proper practice—i.e., practice that is very specific by design— reduces uncertainty in situations where much preparation is needed to translate unfamiliar stimuli or new stimulus–response relationships. This is especially true of tasks that are extremely complex and require a great deal of organization in the acquisition process.

THE BOTTOM LINE

The teaching and learning of athletic skills doesn't happen by chance, nor is it just a matter of improving physical components. The outstanding strength and fitness professionals who have addressed the various elements of conditioning throughout this book have given you scientifically sound, safe, and practical information in those areas. By combining this information with the motor-learning principles discussed in this chapter, you can make inroads with regard to the perceptual, sensory, and movement aspects of performance enhancement.

REFERENCES

Magill, R. 1993. *Motor learning: Concepts and applications.* 4th ed. Madison, WI: W. C. Brown Publishers.

Rosenbaum, D. 1991. *Human motor control.* San Diego, CA: Academic Press, Inc.

Schmidt, R. 1991. *Motor learning and performance.* Champaign, IL: Human Kinetics.

Dedicated in loving memory to Sophie E. Snyder (1906–1964), Hazel Hill (1906–1989), Richard G. Snyder (1901–1990), William S. Picone (1908–1991), and Anthony Pazienza (1938–1995).

28

Improving Functional Flexibility

Rachael E. Picone, B.S.
Graduate Student
University of Massachusetts-Amherst
Amherst, Massachusetts

Flexibility can be defined as the *range of motion (ROM) available at a specific joint or group of joints.* When applied to the physical attributes of a person, flexibility describes the capability to bend or flex freely through a normal and full ROM without injury. Each movable joint in the body has an ROM that can be measured, evaluated, and improved until an optimal range is met.

In a sports program, flexibility is one of many interrelated components of conditioning that plays a crucial role in the functioning of an athlete. Flexibility complements cardiovascular endurance and muscular strength. Without it, total fitness cannot be achieved. Unfortunately, flexibility is often misunderstood and neglected by coaches and athletes alike. Both tend to undervalue the true potential of an effective stretching program and often lack patience to view it as anything more than a time-consuming nuisance. This may be due in part to the fact that stretching is a low-intensity activity and its results are not noticeable by way of appearance.

Athletes and coaches must understand, however, that maintaining a flexible body is important as it has the potential to maximize performance while minimizing injury. On a professional or amateur level, goals of optimal performance can be attained through a balanced, synchronized, commonsense approach to fitness. Athletes will function at their personal best only when flexibility training becomes a serious part of their conditioning program.

Athletes and coaches must understand that maintaining a flexible body is important as it has the potential to maximize performance while minimizing injury. (photo courtesy of Rutgers University Sports Media Relations and Information)

MOVEMENT MECHANOLOGY

Basic knowledge of the musculoskeletal organization is essential to fully explore, understand, and appreciate the movement and stretching mechanics of the human body. Like individual musicians playing together to create a harmonious symphony, our complex system of bones, muscles, connective tissue, and joints perform as a unit. While the various parts involved in the process of movement are often weighed one by one, keep in mind that the body never acts in isolation; its parts function together as a whole.

Skeletal Muscle

Skeletal muscle, also referred to as *voluntary* or *striated muscle*, attaches to the bony framework of the body and has four fundamental properties. First, muscles are excitable and are able to receive and react to stimuli. Second, they are unique in their ability to contract by shortening and thickening. Third, they are extensible and have the ability to be stretched. And fourth, like a rubber band, muscles are elastic and can return to resting length after being stretched. Extensibility and elasticity are important considerations in a flexibility program; when proper techniques are applied, muscles can be safely stretched.

Connective Tissue

A vast network of elastic fascia (pronounced *fay-shuh*), from the fine sheath around each individual muscle fiber to the covering around the entire muscle, connects and supports the muscle fibers. This connective-tissue webbing extends and tapers, merging imperceptibly at the ends of muscles to form strong, inelastic, collagenous, cord-like tendons. Tendons cross over a joint and act as the most important stabilizing factor for most articulations. They attach the muscle to the outermost covering of the bone and are kept taut by constant low-level muscle tone.

In muscle contraction, a nerve stimulates the muscle cells to contract. The force originates in the muscle, pulling the connective tissue toward it, which in turn tugs on the tendon. Tendons pull on the bone where they attach, transmitting the force, and this is what ultimately moves the skeleton. Conversely, when the muscle lengthens, its intertwining connective tissue stretches along with it.

Movable Joints

Articulations or joints are connections between bones. Depending upon the structure and function of the joint, they permit a large ROM or virtually no movement at all. The majority of the body's joints, called *freely movable* or *synovial joints*, are designed for a variety of movements in multiple directions. Joints enable us to execute various physical activities, from returning a tennis serve to passing a volleyball.

Synovial joints—such as the shoulder and knee—have several distinguishing features including articular cartilage, a joint cavity, a synovial membrane, and synovial fluid. Hyaline cartilage, which lacks nerves or blood supply, covers the end surfaces of connecting bones in movable joints. Physical contact occurs between the bones and the hyaline cartilage and provides a smooth, porous cushioning

Joints enable us to execute various physical activities— from returning a tennis serve to passing a volleyball. (photo by J. Anthony Roberts)

which acts to reduce friction and absorb shock. A joint cavity or capsule is formed and protected by dense, fibrous bands of connective tissue known as *ligaments*. Ligaments are responsible for connecting bone to bone. They provide stability to the joint by imposing limits on the ROM. Unlike muscles, ligaments are primarily inextensible and can become injured when taxed beyond their limits. The synovial membrane, which lines the joint capsule, secretes thick, transparent fluid to bathe, nourish, and lubricate the inner capsule and moving joint.

Coordinated Motion

Although bones and joints provide the body with structure, a simultaneous pair of contracting and relaxing muscles permits ROM. Muscles—such as the biceps and triceps in the upper arm—are conveniently arranged in opposing pairs; their particular ROM is known as *flexion* and *extension*. The agonist or prime mover is the muscle that generates a contraction and causes movement to occur. For example, the biceps is the agonist when you flex your arm. Its opposite or antagonist is the triceps.

Muscles can only pull like a rope, they can not push. When a muscle contracts and pulls in one direction, its opposing muscle cooperates by relaxing. In this example, the triceps is inhibited from contracting and must relax. To reverse direction and extend the arm, the antagonist often becomes agonist and contracts. This seesaw relationship between opposing muscles around a joint is known as *reciprocal inhibition*. Reciprocated motion is complementary and interchangeable. Muscles constantly alternate from contracting to relaxing—that is, from acting as agonist to antagonist—but the end result is steady, smooth motion.

Smooth motion is viable only if the agonist–antagonist relationship is balanced. Flexible muscles that can easily lengthen support the contraction of the prime mover. The balance between strength and flexibility of opposing muscle groups clearly becomes a significant training factor in athletics.

The contract–relax working relationship is the foundation of athletic movements such as running where the quadriceps and hamstrings work in constant opposition to each other. (photo courtesy of the University of Massachusetts Media Relations)

The contract-relax working relationship is the foundation of athletic movements such as running where the quadriceps and hamstrings work in constant opposition to each other. All physical activities involve muscle contractions; stretching restores their length. Restoring suppleness gives us the capacity to adjust to a wide range of physical demands. Being flexible prepares us for action, maintains the health of soft tissues, and speeds recovery.

WHAT DETERMINES RANGE OF MOTION?

Restriction of movement is controlled by multiple internal and external factors including genetics, physiologic changes, specific diseases, and lifestyle habits. While there is not much to be done about traits for which we are predisposed, some factors we can control. As a coach or athlete, you need to be aware that these should be considered of primary importance and focus. The following breakdown of factors and their influence on optimal flexibility will help you understand how you can develop the most effective program.

Activity Level

Activity—by far the most influential controllable factor of flexibility—has the capability of restoring, improving, and maintaining a healthy ROM. Conversely, inactivity promotes a loss of flexibility, increasing the chances of injury. Regular moderate-level activity along with stretching promotes greater flexibility. The frequency, intensity, duration, and technique of stretching will determine its effectiveness.

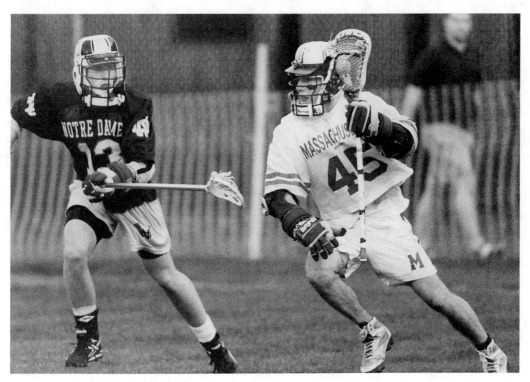

Activity—by far the most influential controllable factor of flexibility—has the capability of restoring, improving, and maintaining a healthy range of motion. (photo courtesy of C. W. Pack Sports)

Age

The relationship between children, adolescents, and flexibility remains unclear. Research data are often difficult to interpret and compare due to factors such as a lack of testing-method standardization; large variations in populations studies; the joint-specificity differences; and ranges of physiologic growth. Although it appears that children are quite flexible, research generally demonstrates that only very young children benefit from high levels of flexibility. During the school years, flexibility decreases until puberty, possibly as a result of bone growth which causes tightness around joints. This childhood period of rapid growth and lowered flexibility potentially increases the young athlete's susceptibility to injuries due to overextension of muscles and joints. Flexibility levels have been shown to increase throughout adolescence, level off at physical maturity, and finally decrease in adulthood. It has been proposed that when body tissue such as ligaments reaches maturity in late adolescence, a plateau of flexibility is reached.

By comparison, older adults see a decline in flexibility and have a tendency to become stiff and tight. As part of the normal aging process, unwelcome changes occur. The musculoskeletal system grows weaker, discs in the spine begin to deteriorate, hormone levels decrease, and connective tissue loses its elasticity. The unfortunate end result is joint stiffness and pain along with a decline in mobility and stability. This decline plays a major role in all aspects of an individual's life. Loss of flexibility contributes to disease and an increased vulnerability to injury. Quality of life may deteriorate as leisure activities and simple day-to-day chores become increasingly difficult. Research confirms that exercise can slow or reverse the loss of flexibility associated with aging. Although it is never too late in life to begin a flexibility training program, the best time to educate our athletes about the many benefits of stretching is unquestionably while they are young.

Anatomy

Since joints are regularly pulled, they must be stabilized so that they do not stretch beyond their optimal range and dislocate. Therefore, natural characteristics of joints, ligaments, tendons, muscles, and bones restrict ROM. The specific type and shape of the joint structure determines the extent of movement it allows. Ball-and-socket joints—such as those in the hips and shoulders—offer extensive circumduction motion as compared with the knee, which is designed to permit only angular hinge-like movement. The shape and positioning of bones also determines joint motion. It is not possible, for example, to turn your ankle completely and lay the side of your foot on the ground because bone impinges on bone and motion is stopped. Size, position, and elasticity of ligaments, muscles, tendons, and skin also play a role in determining flexibility. The number of stabilizing ligaments will affect joint movement to a large degree; more ligaments equal a stronger joint. When other stabilizing factors are inadequate, however, undue tension develops within the ligaments and they fail. Ligaments can only stretch about 6 percent beyond normal length before they snap.

Body Composition

Excess body fat imposes restriction of motion simply by interfering with the ability of the body to move and stretch in certain positions. Excess abdominal fat, for instance, has been shown to interfere with the Sit-and-Reach Test. Naturally, a reduction of body fat will usually lead to improvements in flexibility.

Body Temperature

Elevating the temperature of deep muscle tissue increases fiber elasticity, helping muscles become more pliable and supple. As muscles and connective tissue are more easily lengthened, ROM improves. Increasing blood flow and warming a joint through dynamic movements—such as walking or cycling—improves flexibility and, therefore, positively affects athletic performance. Stretching cold muscles is not only ineffective but may also present the risk of injury.

Disease

Joint disease commonly affects ROM due to the pain, stiffness, and inflammation that it causes. Arthritis, as an example, reduces ROM in several ways. In rheumatoid arthritis, the joint becomes severely inflamed causing pain and stiffness. Osteoarthritis is characterized by degeneration of the joint; the protective cartilage between the two connecting bones begins to wear away, leaving the bone ends exposed and unprotected, resulting in painful distortion of joints. Other conditions that may affect ROM include neurological disease or injury, orthopedic spinal conditions, bone cancer, osteomalacia, and chronic fatigue syndrome.

Gender

Females generally seem to have greater flexibility than males, attributed in part to anatomical differences in joint structure. For instance, the female pelvis exhibits many differences—such as broader hips and a shallower pelvic cavity—that lead to greater pelvic ROM. It has also been speculated that the cyclical effects of women's hormones contribute to increased joint laxity. During pregnancy, hormones soften connective tissues mainly to accommodate the enlarging uterus as the baby grows—though all joints throughout the body are affected.

Injury

Injuries to muscle, connective tissues, and bone can limit movement depending upon their severity. Symptoms of pain and swelling are often restricting factors in limiting ROM. Acute ligament sprains and muscle/tendon strains occur when the tissue is simply overstretched, usually by either a sudden twisting motion or a direct blow. In chronic and repetitive-motion injuries—such as bursitis and tendinitis—the pain leads to disuse. Inactivity further impairs ROM by shortening connective tissues and opposing the healing of inelastic scar tissue. An athlete may experience complete loss of function with more severe injuries such as bone fractures, tendon ruptures, ligament tears, and dislocations. Flexibility levels and functional movement will vary over the course of rehabilitation.

Hypermobility

Being hypermobile or overflexible refers to those who are more flexible than normal. The term *double-jointed* is also commonly used, though these people do not have any extra anatomical joints as the name might suggest. Because the joint ligaments and capsule have greater laxity, the joints can move much farther than normal. Hypermobility may be seen in all of the joints throughout the body or at specific joints—most commonly the wrist, fingers, thumb, and toes. It may also be present in the hinge joints of the knees and elbows where both are able to extend past the average 180 degrees of motion. The degree of joint laxity may be affected by a combination of factors including muscle tone and muscle-fiber length, connective tissues, temperature, hormones, training, gender, and genetics.

Hypermobility may not necessarily impose a problem or disadvantage. Maintaining joint stability through strength training is critical, though, especially with increasing age, since excessive flexibility in joints may potentially increase the risk of injury. Hypermobility might even benefit certain athletes. For example, an ice hockey goalie may have an easier time getting down into position on the ice to make a save.

Flexibility Evaluation

Flexibility is only one component of a physical fitness screening. Other tests include cardiovascular endurance, muscular strength, muscular endurance, and body composition. Although these tests are independent of each other, their combined results reflect the current physical condition of a participant and the risk of disease. Flexibility is not in itself a sign of fitness. It is very possible for a person to be healthy but not flexible and vice versa.

Flexibility assessment is performed for a number of reasons. Most people have a good idea of whether or not they are flexible without any scientific testing. However, formal testing is needed to evaluate injuries and rehabilitation progress, to diagnose strengths and weaknesses, and to prescribe exercise or sports drills. Once flexibility is assessed and baseline information is recorded, reasonable and attainable fitness goals can be set. Periodically monitoring progress can be helpful in two ways. First, it helps determine if goals are being met through the initially designed program and what modifications, if any, need to be made. Second, seeing measured progress—or lack of it—motivates athletes.

There is no general test to measure overall flexibility because flexibility is specific to each joint being tested. Consider again all of the determining factors that affect flexibility and it becomes easy to see why each joint—as well as each individual—has such a distinct ROM. Indeed, some athletes have great shoulder flexibility but lack hamstring flexibility. It is quite common to have bilateral differences in flexibility—that is, one side of your body is more flexible than the

Hypermobility might benefit certain athletes such as an ice hockey goalie who may have an easier time getting down into position on the ice to make a save.
(photo courtesy of the University of Massachusetts Media Relations)

other. Many athletes demonstrate increased flexibility in relation to their specific athletic movements or unique positions. A baseball pitcher, for example, may have increased ROM in the dominant shoulder. Flexibility also changes depending upon the direction the joint is moving and the speed of movement.

Although it is difficult to assess general flexibility, you can measure specific movements either directly or indirectly and repeat the tests to at least monitor progress. Direct measurements are commonly obtained with a goniometer (pronounced *go-nee-AH-me-ter*) or, in some cases, a flexometer. A goniometer is used to measure the actual degrees of ROM available in various joints. Similar to a protractor, a goniometer has a circular dial labeled with degrees (from 0 to 180 in each direction) and two protruding arms—one stationary and one fully movable—that are used to measure the static (nonmoving) angle of a joint. This versatile measuring device can be used for most movable joints in the body by positioning the center of the goniometer over the axis of rotation at a joint such as at the hip. The arms are aligned with the long axis of the bones of the two adjoining body segments—in this case, the femur and spine. The joint angle, read in degrees, can tell us if the athlete's flexibility level is below average, average, or above average. A flexometer is another direct measuring device that is attached to the limb. Changes in angles are noted from one position to another.

Direct angular testing can be time-consuming and expensive and usually requires an experienced evaluator. More practical tests that are indirect and linear have been developed—such as shoulder elevation, trunk flexion and extension, and hip flexion—many of which can easily be performed in a gym or even at home. Stationary positions are assumed and maintained and the maximal ROM is measured. Devices used for an indirect measurement of flexibility include a ruler, sliding caliper, or pass/fail test. Similar to goniometry measurement results, indirect tests are rated on a scale of poor, good, or excellent.

Choosing which test to administer depends upon the equipment available, the evaluator's experience, and the intended use of the results. Many indirect flexibility tests have several limitations and have been criticized for their validity. Trunk flexion—commonly referred to as the Sit-and-Reach Test (i.e., a sitting toe touch)—may return low scores in the overweight population due to excessive, ROM-limiting body-fat stores in the abdomen rather than low flexibility. Those with variations in leg, trunk, and arm length may score higher based on their limb-length advantage rather than their flexibility level. Finally, assessing low-back flexibility in this way involves more than one muscle; results involve not only the flexibility of the lower back but, more correctly, the tightness of the hamstrings. However, lack of flexibility in the hamstrings may increase the risk of back injuries. Although the Sit-and-Reach Test has its limitations, it is quick, affordable and simple enough for mass testing; it is, therefore, commonly accepted and administered as part of a typical fitness screening. More research is needed to determine the best way to evaluate the lower back and the exact correlation between hamstring and low-back flexibility and pain.

THE VALUE OF STRETCHING

The benefits of having a normal or high degree of ROM are numerous and diverse. Most athletes are aware that they should be stretching, but many fail to do so—or fail to do so properly. Perhaps the best way to convince athletes to spend quality time stretching is to explain and continually emphasize how flexibility directly relates to their athletic performance and personal health. Understanding all of the benefits derived from developing and maintaining optimal flexibility will allow you to educate your athletes and, in turn, help them stay motivated to continue with a program of regular stretching. The benefits include:

I. *Improvement in skills, muscular efficiency, and sports performance.* An athlete depends upon a large degree of functional flexibility for successful sports participation. Stretching promotes a greater ROM, which makes executing skills easier and improves the quality of movement. Due to less resistance in the joint, motions require less energy and are simply more efficient. Flexibility training can also increase neuromuscular coordination and fine-tune the agonist–antagonist relationship. An increase in flexibility has the potential to directly enhance and refine technique, which will invariably lead to improved performance. With more flexibility, runners can increase their stride lengths, golfers can generate more power in their swings, and divers can enhance their grace.

2. *Prevention, decreased severity, and treatment of injury/disease.* Injury prevention is one of the main reasons that stretching becomes so vitally important for those participating in sports. Stretching—which increases and maintains ROM—protects against injuries that may result from the physical demands imposed by athletics. Tight muscles are weak; they offer no joint protection and may contribute to cramping. If one area of the body is tight and inefficient, other

With more flexibil-
ity, runners can
increase their
stride lengths,
golfers can gener-
ate more power in
their swings, and
divers can enhance
their grace. (photo
courtesy of Ben
Barnhart Photo Services)

parts of the body will attempt to compensate, and the risk of injury increases. When an athlete jumps over a hurdle, for example, the explosive movement demands a great degree of skill and flexibility. It is easy to see how an athlete might be prone to injury without adequate—or even exceptional—flexibility.

In addition to decreasing the initial risk for injury, the severity of a sustained injury will—in all likelihood—be less if the individual has been conditioned with an effective flexibility program. This translates into less pain and less recovery time for the athlete. Rehabilitation from an injury always involves stretching. Even with gentle ROM exercises, early mobilization (i.e., moving the tissue) increases circulation to the joint, may decrease pain, and greatly aids in recovery. For the athlete to return to participation, a full ROM is essential and must be regained through rehabilitation. Other painful conditions—such as temporomandibular disorder (TMD) or arthritis—can also be treated through a program of regular stretching.

3. *Improvement in posture and muscle symmetry.* Posture affects energy level, appearance, efficiency, and freedom of movement as well as sports performance. Sitting and standing habits, occupational tasks, and bone density directly influence posture. Poor posture leaves you vulnerable to problems including back, neck, and shoulder pain, all of which affect daily activities. Proper alignment of the body minimizes stress to the spine and such problems.

Tight muscles caused by exercise, aging, or stress can also affect posture by creating muscular imbalances. An imbalance occurs when muscles on one side of a joint become far weaker or less flexible than muscles on the opposing side of the joint. Maintaining a balance between the strength and flexibility of each muscle group is the key to improving posture and achieving muscular symmetry. Stretching emphasizes proper body alignment and awareness of correct posture. Restoring muscles to their optimum length and balancing opposing muscle groups strengthens the working condition and efficiency of the human body.

4. *Prevention and alleviation of delayed-onset muscle soreness.* Vigorous physical activity often causes delayed-onset muscle soreness, commonly referred to as *DOMS.* Symptoms—inevitable to some degree with strenuous athletics—usually appear when athletes have been overworked or overstressed to a point that they have not yet adapted. Typical symptoms of DOMS include stiffness, weakness, loss of ROM, and tenderness of the muscle. Pain develops 6–12 hours after exercise, peaking at 24–48 hours.

There are several current theories regarding the cause of delayed soreness. The symptoms may be caused by residual waste products that have accumulated within the muscle or from the pooling of blood, which leads to pain. Damage to the muscle from microtears and localized spasm of individual muscle motor units may contribute to muscle soreness as well. Perhaps a more supported theory is the connective-tissue theory based upon the observation that muscle soreness is common after unaccustomed eccentric muscle contractions (or negative exercise). Microtears in the connective tissue may occur due to the strain of the eccentric contraction (lengthening) rather than the stress (i.e., the force applied). This damage is accompanied by edema, which results in swelling and stiffness with maximal damage at 48 hours.

Adequate warm-up and stretching have been shown to prevent and reduce the pain associated with DOMS. Stretching may prevent adhesions from occurring in the muscle, thereby speeding recovery. Though there may not be any long-term benefit or effect on total recovery time, gentle ROM exercises and stretching can help reduce the severity of DOMS.

5. *Preventing loss of ROM associated with aging.* As joints are exercised through their full ROM, tissue temperature increases and blood supply—which is rich in nutrients—is circulated to the joint structure. Within the joint capsule itself, the synovial fluid decreases in thickness and increases in quantity, fully lubricating the joint and allowing a greater ROM. More nutrients can then be transported to the articular cartilage as both the joint circulation and the quality of the synovial fluid improves. This combined effect opposes the loss of elasticity and joint deceleration often seen with aging. Strengthening and stretching muscles through their full ROM also prevents adaptive shortening of deeper muscle layers commonly seen in adults.

6. *Reduction in low-back pain and injury.* Painful and debilitating low-back problems—experienced by a staggering 60–80 percent of the entire population—are most often seen in the 25- to 60-year-old sedentary population. Most back problems develop gradually from multiple causes including low levels of muscular strength and flexibility, muscular imbalances, poor posture, overweight or pregnancy, repetitious work, and psychological stress. When the muscles and ligaments in the spine become stressed and mechanical imbalances occur, the soft tissues that support the lower back become vulnerable to sprains and strains. Movement and stretching nourish the spine and keep it healthy, which prevents back discomfort and injuries. Developing a healthy body and maintaining the natural curves of the spine allows greater freedom and efficiency of movement in all directions, improvement in posture, and a marked decrease in muscular tension. A balanced, consistent stretching program that focuses on the muscles of the hamstrings and lower back is recommended to prevent and reduce low-back pain.

7. *Reduced muscular tension and stress.* Everyday physical and emotional stress in our lives damages many systems in our bodies. In response to stress, we tense our muscles. Unconscious habits of contracting muscles can cause chronic discomfort including back, shoulder, jaw, and neck pain along with headaches, fatigue, and vulnerability to injury and illness. Stretching to relieve tension and stiffness is a natural desire. We stretch when we have been in one position too long or whenever we merely feel the need to relax our muscles or our minds.

Stretching and relaxation go hand in hand. Awareness of varying levels of tension—the first step toward relaxation—is better understood through stretching. As we hold a stretch and direct our attention to the way our bodies feel, muscle tension is gradually released. Stretching for relaxation—rather than as an attempt to increase flexibility—is commonly recommended. For example, stretching can benefit an athlete who may be experiencing pregame anxiety. Returning the body to its natural, relaxed, balanced state helps normalize physical, mental, and emotional processes.

8. *Women's health benefits.* Stretching often relieves muscle cramps, backache, and general fatigue associated with the female menstrual cycle and stages of pregnancy. Exercises should focus on proper posture to minimize stress on the spine. Slow stretching and proper breathing will further promote relaxation. Gentle stretching is encouraged throughout the day as often as needed. Fitness instructors working with pregnant clients should be well trained and familiar with pregnancy-related flexibility changes, low-back pain, exercise modifications, contraindications, and precautions.

FLEXIBILITY TODAY

For centuries, stretching has formed an integral and rudimentary part of physical training and sports. Although stretching is not a new idea, the popularity of fitness and wellness has brought both new and ancient forms of flexibility training to our attention today. Several styles of movement training, movement therapy, or mind-body programs are now practiced in the rehabilitation, dance, athletic, and fitness arenas. Taking each joint through its full ROM is part of the overall concept of many of these techniques. Even though these approaches vary widely, many are performed for the same reason—simply to enhance flexibility as well as overall well-being.

These disciplines—now mainstreamed into our lives—aim to awaken and unite our physical, mental, and spiritual selves. Engaging the mind to focus on body sensations heightens body awareness, giving the athlete a better understanding and sense of movement. By developing this subtle but precise awareness of body alignment, muscular tension, balance, breathing, and posture, movements become more efficient and fluid. The emphasis on body positioning—which corrects posture and balances each body part—can only help athletes learn to use their bodies to perform at their utmost potential. Methods of movement training often include a relaxation component—such as meditation or progressive relaxation—accentuating the mind-body conjunction and easing emotional stress. This gentler type of workout is frequently a welcome addition or alternative approach to typical forms of exercise—such as weight training and aerobics—and is highly recommended for most athletes. Examples of movement training exercise include yoga, tai chi, Chi Gung, Feldenkrais, Pilates, and the Alexander technique.

CLASSIFYING RANGE OF MOVEMENT

Deciphering the nomenclature of various flexibility types and stretching techniques can be puzzling. There is no common standardization in terminology usage among subdisciplines and experts within the exercise science field. The professional scientific community finds it helpful to classify exercises for the purpose of explanation. Remember, strength and fitness professionals may prefer to use the correct terminology but it is far more important for an individual to understand the principles behind the stretching technique rather than the type or name of stretch being performed.

Active, Passive, and Dynamic Flexibility

The ROM in a joint will vary depending upon the specific type of movement being performed. The three types of ROM—referred to as *active*, *passive*, and *dynamic* flexibility—all play a part in athletic conditioning and performance. Although each sport has its own flexibility requirements, it is important to include a combination of all three methods to achieve true functional flexibility.

Active flexibility represents the ROM that we are capable of achieving by consciously contracting our muscles around a joint. The term *active* refers to the active force the athlete supplies for the stretch and is not intended to mean that dynamic movement is occurring. Extending and holding your leg to the side without any assistance is an example of active flexibility. During an active stretch, the contraction of the agonists helps relax the muscles being stretched (the antagonists) by reciprocal inhibition; in this case, the adductors are stretched by contracting the opposing muscles—namely the abductors. The person attains this position by performing an unassisted voluntary movement that requires both strength and flexibility. Since active flexibility is usually thought of and measured in stationary—or static—positions, it has also been labeled *static-active flexibility*.

Extending and holding your leg to the side without any assistance is an example of active flexibility. (photo courtesy of the University of Massachusetts Media Relations)

In contrast, passive flexibility involves the use of a partner or therapist, support of your limbs, or apparatus such as a towel, ballet barre, or chair. The force for this type of flexibility and the ability to hold the stretch does not come solely from the muscles but rather from an outside force. A passive ROM is an additional amount of movement beyond our active range. Each movable joint has a small amount of available motion that is not under voluntary control. The extra ROM aids in protection by allowing the joint to absorb extrinsic force. Holding an extended leg by grasping your foot with your hands demonstrates passive flexibility; it is much easier to attain a greater ROM with assistance from external support. Extra caution should be used, however, to avoid overstretching. Passive stretches are normally performed as static, hence the term static-passive flexibility.

Dynamic flexibility occurs when movement is applied through a complete ROM. Dynamic motions are usually circular or back and forth, representing the body's range of flexion/extension, abduction/adduction, and

Holding an extended leg by grasping your foot with your hands demonstrates passive flexibility. (photo courtesy of Rutgers University Sports Media Relations and Information)

In demonstrating dynamic flexibility, movements can be general (such as performing an arm circle) or sport specific (such as executing a swimming stroke). (photo courtesy of the University of Massachusetts Media Relations)

rotation. Movements can be general (such as performing an arm circle) or sport specific (such as executing a swimming stroke). Dynamic flexibility refers to the amount of resistance in a joint (e.g., the shoulder) during movement. Dynamic flexibility—which obviously has the highest correlation to sports performance—is developed by a combination of methods. An increase in passive ROM enhances active ROM—which in turn potentially develops a greater dynamic ROM.

Specific exercises intended to improve dynamic flexibility utilize a slightly different approach than stretching methods. Mobility or ROM exercises incorporate active movements, whereas a stretch involves assuming and holding a position to elongate the muscle. The difference lies in the emphasis placed on the joints rather than in the muscles. General mobility exercises—such as knee lifts and arm circles—improve joint circulation and synovial fluid lubrication and aid an athlete during warm-up, conditioning, and cool-down periods.

THE STRETCH ITSELF

Although limiting factors do exist, improvements in flexibility result when ROM is progressively overloaded by elongating the tissue beyond its resting length. When you stretch a muscle, it resists with a lengthening tension. Once the muscle fibers have been stretched to their full length, the surrounding fascia—which supplies the most resistance to the stretch—takes up the remaining slack and becomes

Although limiting factors do exist, improvements in flexibility result when range of motion is progressively overloaded by elongating the muscle tissue beyond its resting length. (photo courtesy of the American Tae Kwon Do Academy)

taut. One of the fundamental properties of skeletal muscle is elasticity; when it is stretched, the increase in length is only temporary and the tissue recovers to its original resting length. The connective tissue harness, however, functions with both elastic and plastic stretching properties. In a plastic stretch, tissue deformation still remains even after the force for the stretch is removed. Therefore, stretches should be directed at the muscle's fascia since it has the most elastic tissue and will gain plastic or more permanent deformation thus achieving improvement in the resting length of a muscle. Increasing connective-tissue length and attaining plastic deformation is dependent upon the amount of force and the duration of the stretch.

Despite the fact that ligaments are pliable enough to allow freedom of movement in the joint, they can only stretch so far before their tough fibers become taut. In addition, tendons should not be stretched at all. Attempting to stretch further than a muscle's natural limit places too much stretch on ligaments and tendons. Once stretched, these soft tissues remain stretched and have too much slack. Overstretching beyond anatomical limits may lead to permanent structural damage and loss of stability in the joint, especially in weight-bearing joints such as the hip, knee, and ankle. The need for a well-balanced strength and flexibility program is recommended to keep muscles and joints strong as well as supple.

NATURAL DEFENSE

The body has built-in protective mechanisms related to stretching that prevent too much stretch and too much tension from occurring within the muscles. Proprioceptors—known as *sensory receptors*—monitor changes in movement,

If the stretch within the muscle is too extreme or occurs too fast, the spinal cord sends a reflex message back to the muscle causing it to contract, which helps prevent over-stretching and injury. (photo courtesy of the University of Massachusetts Media Relations)

position, or tension within the body. This natural line of defense—which relies on sensory receptors and their ability to convey information to the spinal cord—guards us against injury.

Neural receptors—called *muscle spindles*—lie parallel to the muscle fibers and are sensitive to change and the rate of change in muscle length. As a muscle is stretched, the muscle spindle is stimulated along with it and sends a signal to the spinal cord. If the stretch within the muscle is too extreme or occurs too fast, the spinal cord sends a reflex message back to the muscle causing it to contract. This involuntary contraction—known as the *stretch reflex* or *myotatic reflex*—helps protect against overstretching and injury.

Just as the muscle spindle serves as protection against too much stretch, another sensory receptor—the golgi tendon organ (GTO)—protects against generating too much contractile force. When too much tension develops—either from excessive stretch or muscle contraction—the GTO (which is located in the musculotendon junction) activates the inverse stretch reflex or inverse myotatic reflex. This causes the contraction to stop and immediately relaxes the entire muscle, preventing injury in the muscle and its connective tissues.

TECHNIQUES TO IMPROVE FLEXIBILITY

Improving flexibility can be accomplished by several distinct—but somewhat controversial—methods. Although variations and combinations exist, the three basic types of stretches to increase flexibility include ballistic, static, and proprioceptive neuromuscular facilitation (PNF). Stretches aimed at improving the available ROM are designed to reduce the internal resistance of the muscles and connective tissues. Decreasing the resistance of muscles is accomplished by either increasing connective tissue length or attaining a greater degree of relaxation within the muscle. Careful application of a relaxed, low-force, prolonged stretch utilizes both of these principles. The best method may depend upon your physical condition and whether or not you wish to increase or maintain your ROM.

Ballistic Stretching

Ballistic stretching is a high-force, short-duration stretch that utilizes repetitive bouncing movements to create a stretch. For example, the athlete assumes a seated straddle-stretch position and then bounces toward the floor to stretch the hamstrings. Though well-intentioned, ballistic stretching presents the risk for serious injury. The movements are uncontrolled and rapid, having the potential to overstretch soft tissues beyond their normal limits and cause damage to the muscle. The excessive momentum and extreme stretch of a ballistic motion may cause the body to react with the stretch reflex by contracting (or shortening) the target muscle. Because attempting to stretch a muscle that is contracted is dangerous and contradictory to the goal of increasing flexibility, ballistic stretching is not advisable.

Ballistic stretching remains controversial because some advanced athletes practice rapid stretches for their sport. These dynamic movements should not be confused with ballistic stretching, however. The movements are controlled and do not have the same bouncing, jerky motions as ballistic stretches. A football punter, for example, may be seen on the field performing high kicks in preparation for a punt. These kicks mimic the actual motion required in the sport and are more closely related to dynamic flexibility and mobility exercises than to ballistic stretching.

Static Stretching

Static stretching—the most common flexibility training technique—is simple, convenient, safe, and effective. It is the best method for beginners, general fitness programs, and flexibility maintenance. Slow, deliberate movements teach awareness of body position and posture as well as muscle tension and relaxation. Learning to recognize limits of flexibility—an important factor in avoiding injury—is another value of static flexibility training.

To benefit from static stretching, a muscle is pulled slightly beyond its resting length and held at a point of slight tension; force is then slowly applied to produce further stretching. Passive assistance is usually necessary since active stretching does not always produce enough force to increase muscle length. For example, a person assumes a quadricep stretch to the point of light tension. Additional torque is passively applied by gently pulling the foot toward the hips. The position is held and the body relaxes to stretch even further. The movement is never pulled to the point of pain but is mild and executed gradually, carefully, and under complete control.

Static stretching is of such low force that the muscles and connective tissue require a greater time to elongate. Although it requires a longer time than a high-force ballistic stretch, the proportion of lengthening that remains is greater. Slow, sustained, static stretching also diminishes the stretch reflex. The muscle spindle adapts to the lengthened position, lessens the reflex signaling and allows the muscle to relax and stretch further. Through proper and regular stretching, the stretch reflex adapts and resets to a higher level so that your muscle will relax further into the stretch. Static stretching is the preferred type of stretching because it imposes less risk of overstretching the tissues and may result in less muscle soreness when compared to other methods.

Proprioceptive Neuromuscular Facilitation

As its name implies, proprioceptive neuromuscular facilitation (PNF) is slightly more complex than static stretching and can intimidate a person unfamiliar with the term or its theories. It was originally designed in the 1950s to rehabilitate paralysis patients and is successfully used today by many top athletes. PNF goes one step beyond static stretching by incorporating an isometric contraction of either the muscle being stretched or its opposite. Various forms of PNF stretching are used depending upon the condition of the person and the situation. Two common techniques are contract-relax (CR) and contract-relax-agonist-contract (CRAC).

In a CR sequence—also known as hold-relax (HR)—the tight muscle group is first gently stretched; this is followed by an isometric contraction of the same muscle group against the resistance of your own hands or a partner's for approximately 6–15 seconds. The muscle is then relaxed and immediately taken into a greater ROM. The reasoning behind the CR technique is rooted in the inverse stretch reflex; the contraction is thought to produce a relaxation phase in the same muscle. Based upon concepts of reciprocal inhibition, the CRAC technique follows the same sequence as CR with one additional phase. A contraction of the agonist—or the muscle opposite the one you wish to stretch—follows the relaxation phase; the athlete actively moves the limb into a new ROM and then proceeds with a contraction to elicit reciprocal inhibition of the target muscle, allowing a deeper stretch. Isometric contractions should not be explosive but should gradually build to a less-than-maximal contraction. PNF sequences are usually repeated several times.

PNF stretches are at least as effective—if not superior—to other techniques in developing flexibility. This may be the preferred method when trying to improve flexibility, especially in extremely tight muscles. Although PNF may be modified for individual use, a partner usually assists with the contraction and final stretch phases. Coaches, athletic trainers, and training partners have successfully applied PNF techniques, but to prevent injury it is imperative that assistants are adequately instructed in the technique. Subjects need to give verbal feedback to the assistant, and in turn assistants must use caution in the amount of force that they provide.

WARMING UP

The terms *warm-up* and *stretching* have mistakenly been used interchangeably since each can be performed prior to activity. Stretching is not inclusively considered a warm-up; it is, however, part of the entire warm-up process which usually includes one to three distinct phases. Increasing blood flow to muscles and elevating core body temperature by about 1–3 degrees is the goal of phase one. Steady-state, full-body, aerobic exercise best accomplishes this general warm-up. Low to moderate intensity activity—such as walking, cycling, or jumping rope—should be done for approximately five minutes or until you break a light sweat. The activity should gradually increase in intensity and sufficiently warm up the body without creating fatigue. A general warm-up is recommended for both fitness enthusiasts and serious athletes.

In phase two, general dynamic exercises are performed. This will continue to prepare the body's synovial joints for more vigorous activity. Following the general warm-up, general mobility exercises can include the following: shoulder, hip, ankle and wrist rotations, shoulder rolls, knee lifts, trunk flexion/extension, and partial squats. These dynamic movements should be slow and controlled through a complete and natural ROM, gradually increasing in speed and intensity with the purpose of loosening up muscles and joints. You should perform sets of 3–6 repetitions for general fitness workouts and 8–12 repetitions for more strenuous sports conditioning.

Preactivity stretching—also included in phase two—is only intended to prepare the body for activity and should not be viewed as a means of increasing flex-

Stretching is suggested before numerous sports including baseball, volleyball, racket sports, golf, and downhill skiing. (photo courtesy of the University of Massachusetts Media Relations)

ibility. Stretching prior to a conditioning session is imperative for sports that call for immediate and extreme physical demands that an athlete must be prepared to meet. Stretching is suggested before numerous sports including baseball, volleyball, racket sports, golf and downhill skiing. Pre-competition stretching is also a good idea, since the length of a stride or stroke can be crucial to performance. Stretching prior to weight-bearing activity should focus on the lower back, hamstrings, calves, chronically tight muscles, and areas most susceptible to injury. If you are exercising purely for fitness benefits and your workout includes low to moderate intensity activities—such as walking, cycling, or jogging—prestretching is not always necessary.

Sport-specific movements and stretches—depending upon the type and level of activity to be done—comprise the third phase of a total warm-up. For example, gymnasts would practice handstands and pike jumps along with performing different positions such as splits. The sport-specific phase of a warm-up gives the athlete time to rehearse both physically and mentally.

The best time to improve long-term flexibility is at the end of a workout when muscles are tight from being contracted and are still warm and pliable. An effective post-activity stretching program also harmonizes mind and body, creating a calming mood and positive shift of focus to conclude a workout.

DESIGNING A FLEXIBILITY PROGRAM

Individual safety is undoubtedly the primary consideration in designing a flexibility training program. Secondly, take into account the following: personal goals, maturity level, experience, and physical condition. Training can be personalized to meet different needs, though programs should be designed with the same overall goal: to keep muscles and connective tissue supple, healthy, and functional while maintaining the strength and integrity of the joint. Since there are different approaches to increasing flexibility, it is important to find a method with which you are comfortable and successful; keep in mind that personal preference and rates of progress will vary from person to person.

Stretching as a team can promote camaraderie while giving the athletes a chance to perform stretches with a partner, if necessary. It is strongly suggested that coaches view stretching as a part of practice and allow athletes ample time for flexibility training. Coaches and instructors should be sure that athletes actually take the necessary time to stretch and provide supervision so that exercises are performed safely and correctly.

Frequency, Intensity, and Duration

Although the debate concerning stretching frequency, intensity, and duration still continues, athletes are encouraged to follow general guidelines. Mobility and flexibility training should be included at least three days per week, preferably on a daily basis. Spontaneous stretching throughout the day is not enough to improve flexibility; a consistent stretching program can mean the difference between making progress and not. Athletes need to stretch before and after activity and may benefit from additional stretching on their own time.

Stretching intensity may greatly depend upon whether or not the athlete is attempting to rehabilitate, increase, or maintain ROM. During stretching, intensity—which is subjective—involves two factors: body position and the force or torque applied. Stretching positions can be modified for beginner, intermediate, and advanced levels thus varying intensity. Stretches should be gradual and gentle and only to the point of mild discomfort. Athletes should progress into a greater ROM by applying slightly more force.

It is generally recommended for healthy individuals to hold each stretch for about 15–60 seconds. The use of a clock or stopwatch is suggested initially to help athletes learn an appropriate amount of time to spend in a stretch. Athletes should stay in the stretched position as long as it feels comfortable, taking extra time whenever needed. Focusing on feeling the muscle release and relax is recommended to make the stretch more effective. For maximum results, stretches can be repeated up to four times with an increase in repetitions as training progresses.

Keys to Proper Stretching

1. Evaluate flexibility and monitor progress. Attempt to maintain or improve upon the previous workout.

2. Wear comfortable clothing that does not restrict movement. Removing footwear may be helpful to stretch the lower body (quadriceps, hamstrings, calves, shins, and feet).

3. Work at your own pace. Begin slowly and listen to your body. Since flexibility will vary greatly from person to person, stretching should never be competitive and should always be practiced within one's own individual limits. Overstretching beyond your body's natural limits will only weaken joints, making you more susceptible to injury.

4. Perform the movements through a comfortable, pain-free ROM.

5. Always include a general warm-up before preactivity stretching. Perform flexibility exercises at the end of a workout when body temperature is elevated and tissues are warm and pliable.

6. Perform a balanced routine that includes at least one stretch for each muscle group. Because flexibility is specific to each joint, it cannot be easily improved or maintained with one or two quick stretches. Stretch opposing muscles and emphasize chronically tight areas such as the lower back and hamstrings.

7. Incorporate sport-specific stretches that will be used during physical activity or sport participation such as shoulder stretches for volleyball and neck stretches for wrestling.

8. Concentrate on technique by focusing on proper body alignment and isolating the target muscles involved in the stretch.

9. Become aware of your breathing rhythm. Inhale and exhale properly by taking deep, slow breaths that originate from the abdomen not the chest. Do not hold your breath.

10. Relax before and during the stretch. A relaxed muscle will move through a greater ROM.

A WORD ABOUT STRENGTH TRAINING

Flexibility training and strength training clearly complement each other. One should not be sacrificed for the other. There does not need to be a trade-off between strength and flexibility and both should be included as part of a total conditioning program. A common fallacy about the relationship between strength training and flexibility is that strength training will decrease your ROM. Strength training does not limit flexibility and may maintain or actually improve it if athletes regard the following guidelines:

1. Strengthen and stretch opposing muscle groups (agonist/antagonist) in a balanced fashion.
2. Perform each repetition through a complete ROM.
3. Emphasize the negative (or lowering) phase of each repetition.
4. Include regular mobility and stretching exercises in your training program.

Stretching prior to a strength training session is not always essential presuming a relatively high number of repetitions are performed and the weight is lifted in a controlled manner. Athletes may consider the added benefit of gentle stretching during a workout, immediately after each set or exercise.

CONTRAINDICATED EXERCISES

If safety precautions are not followed, advanced flexibility training presents the potential for injury to vulnerable areas such as the neck, spine, lower back, and knees. Although some sports require advanced stretches for skill development and performance, certain exercises may be dangerous for the general population. Children, the elderly, deconditioned participants, or those with musculoskeletal conditions and other health concerns have a higher possibility of injury with such contraindicated movements. Since the risks far outweigh any benefit that might be gained, these populations should explore safer alternatives. If these stretches are incorporated into a training program, extreme caution should be used to reduce the risk of injury. Learning the exercise in sequential stages as well as having a knowledgeable instructor can also minimize the risk of injury.

- Full circular neck rotations are dangerous to the cervical spine because they compress the cervical discs and impinge on nerve structures. A safer option is to perform isolated static stretches for the neck.
- The plough—or reverse trunk flexion—also places excessive stress on the cervical spine. The subject lies down and sweeps the legs up and over the torso, trying to touch the knees to the ears. This position places stress on

the lower back as well and compresses internal organs, possibly making it difficult to breathe.

- The banana (or rocker) involves lying in the prone position; the subject reaches back and grasps the ankles while lifting the head and upper body. This stretch places unnecessary pressure on the lower back, hips, and knees.
- In the traditional hurdler's stretch, the subject places one leg outstretched and the other bent at the knee and turned backward. This stretch has the potential to damage the inner structures of the bent knee such as the medial ligaments and places undue stress on the lower back. The kneecap can also be injured from being twisted and compressed. Lying backward in this position forces the lower back to hyperextend and stresses the hip and anterior lower leg. An alternate hamstring stretch that is safer is the modified hurdler's stretch where the knee is turned outward and the foot rests on the inside of the outstretched leg.
- In the straight-leg standing toe touch (straddle or nonstraddle), pressure is placed on the lower back, hip, knees, and lower legs. This position overloads the discs in the lower lumbar region and may cause the knees to hyperextend. Touching your toes with locked knees and legs crossed is just as dangerous and places strain on the hamstrings, gluteals, calves, and lower back.
- The traditional backbend known as a bridge compresses the discs in the spine and impinges on nerve structures in the lower back. The neck bridge also places considerable stress on the cervical spine.
- The cobra—or extreme hyperextension of the lower back—places unnecessary pressure on the lower back and hips. The subject is prone and raises the torso up on the hands, placing the lower back and neck in hyperextension. Raising the legs and arms at the same time also places unnecessary stress on the lower back.

CORE STRETCHES

The following routine of core stretches is appropriate for the healthy adult. It is a balanced program covering all of the major muscle groups and should take approximately 10–15 minutes to complete. The exercise order is purposely designed for convenience; there should be a comfortable and smooth transition between exercises as well as a natural progression from lying to sitting to standing positions (or vice versa). The level of difficulty should be adapted to meet individual needs. Start flat on your back with a full-body stretch. Take a deep breath and a few moments to relax before beginning:

1. *Spinal rotation and chest stretch combo.* Lie flat on your back and bring your right knee to your chest. Gently turn onto your left side, placing your right knee and ankle on the floor. Lower both of your shoulders to

Spinal Rotation and Chest Stretch Combo (photo by Rachael E. Picone)

Gluteals (photo by Rachael E. Picone)

Inner Thigh (photo by Rachael E. Picone)

Single Lying Hamstring (photo by Rachael E. Picone)

the floor. Interlace your fingers and place your hands behind your head. Look toward the ceiling and slowly stretch your elbows to the floor. Return to the starting position and repeat with your left leg.

2. *Gluteals.* Lie flat on your back with your arms at your sides and your knees bent. Cross your left ankle over your right knee, turned out from your hip. Reach forward and wrap both of your hands under and around your right hamstring. Pull your right leg toward your chest keeping your head, back, and shoulders on the floor and relaxed. Return to the starting position and repeat with your right ankle over your left knee.

3. *Inner thigh.* Lie flat on your back with your knees bent. Bring your knees toward your chest and place the soles of your feet together, turned out from your hip. Grasp the tops of your feet and pull toward your chest while keeping your knees turned out, your heels close to your groin, and your feet together.

4. *Single lying hamstring.* Lie on your back with your knees bent and your heels close to your buttocks. Extend your right leg upward from your hip, keeping your lower back on the floor. Place both of your hands behind your calf and slowly pull the raised leg toward your chest. The extended leg can vary from straight to slightly flexed. Return to the starting position and repeat with your left leg.

Side Lying Quad (photo by Rachael E. Picone)

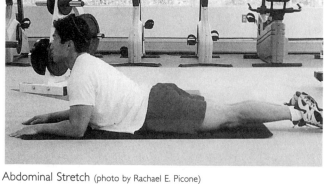

Abdominal Stretch (photo by Rachael E. Picone)

Stacked Hamstring and Calf (photo by Rachael E. Picone)

Side Bend (photo by Rachael E. Picone)

5. *Side lying quad.* Lie on your left side supported on your left forearm while pulling in your abdominal muscles. Bend your right leg, keeping your knee parallel to the floor. Grasp your right foot with your right hand and gently pull your heel toward your hips. Don't arch your back or twist your pelvis. Repeat on your right side with your left leg.

6. *Abdominal stretch.* Roll into a relaxed prone position. Support your body by resting on your forearms and pull upward from your abdomen and chest. Keep your hips on floor and look forward.

7. *Stacked hamstring and calf.* Extend your legs forward with your feet together, assuming a sitting pike position. Place your right heel on top of your left foot. Place your hands below your knee and gently pull your chest toward the floor. Slide your arms toward your ankle and lower your head to your knee to deepen the stretch. Return to the starting position and repeat with your left heel on top of your right foot.

8. *Side bend.* Remain seated with your back straight and your legs crossed. Place your right palm on the floor for support. Lift your left arm straight above your head, pull up through your abdomen and slowly lean to the right. Keep your chest, head, and torso facing forward without twisting your upper body.

9. *Back release and hip stretch.* Sit with your back straight and place your hands on the floor in front of you with your palms down. Lean forward very gently, flexing your spine and relaxing your neck. Move your torso and your hands slightly

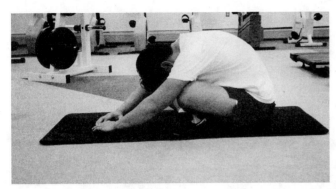

Back Release and Hip Stretch (photo by Rachael E. Picone)

Standing Calf and Posterior Shoulder Combo (photo by Rachael E. Picone)

to the left and hold the stretch. Repeat to the right and hold the stretch. Return to the starting position and repeat with your legs crossed the opposite way.

10. *Standing calf and posterior shoulder combo.* Step forward with your right foot. Bend your right knee and keep your left leg straight. Lean forward, keeping your hands on your thigh to support your upper body. Keep both of your feet facing forward (parallel), your heels flat on the floor and your knees over your toes. Grasp the back of your left upper arm and gently pull it horizontally across your body. Repeat with your right calf and right shoulder.

11. *Single triceps.* Stand straight with your feet about shoulder-width apart. Keep your toes pointed forward and your knees slightly flexed. Lift your right arm above your head and bend your elbow, releasing your arm toward your back. Grasp the outside of your right arm with your left hand and pull toward the left. Keep your body facing forward and avoid twisting at the waist. Repeat with your left arm.

Single Triceps (photo by Rachael E. Picone)

12. *Single biceps.* While standing, place your left arm behind you with your elbow bent. Grasp onto a piece of exercise equipment or a door frame.

Single Biceps (photo by Rachael E. Picone)

Wrist Flexors (photo by Rachael E. Picone)

Wrist Extensors (photo by Rachael E. Picone)

Slowly step forward and bring your upper body to a front-facing position until your elbow is straight. Keep your feet shoulder-width apart and your knees bent. Repeat with your right arm.

13. *Wrist flexors.* Place your hands palms down on a bench. Keeping your elbows straight, turn your fingers toward your body and gently lean backward. Keep your wrists on the bench. This stretch can also be performed kneeling on the floor.

14. *Wrist extensors.* Place the tops of your hands against a bench with your fingers pointing toward you. Keeping your elbows straight, gently lean backward. Keep your wrists on the bench. This stretch can also be performed kneeling on the floor.

15. *Lateral neck.* Stand with your arms at your sides. Place your right hand on the left side of your head and slowly pull your head to your right shoulder. Slowly straighten and repeat to your left side.

16. *Neck rotation.* Stand with your feet shoulder-width apart and your knees bent. Keeping your shoulders relaxed, slowly look over your right shoulder. Keep your back straight and your shoulders down. Slowly look to the center and repeat to your left side.

17. *Neck flexion.* Stand with your feet shoulder-width apart and your knees bent. Slowly bend your head forward, bringing your chin to your chest.

Lateral Neck (photo by Rachael E. Picone)

Neck Rotation (photo by Rachael E. Picone)

Neck Flexion (photo by Rachael E. Picone)

Interlock your fingers behind your head. Gently pull your head forward and down toward your chest. Tilt your head slightly to the right and then to the left to vary the position of the stretch.

18. *Neck extension.* Stand with your feet shoulder-width apart and your knees bent. Gently move your head backward and look to the ceiling. Keep your shoulders relaxed and do not arch your back. Use optional assistance by placing your hands under the outer borders of your jaw or on your forehead.

Neck Extension (photo by Rachael E. Picone)

REFERENCES

Allen, O. E., and editors of Time-Life Books. 1981. *Building sound bones and muscles.* Alexandria, VA: Time-Life Books.

Alter, M. J. 1996. *Science of flexibility.* 2nd ed. Champaign, IL: Human Kinetics.

———. 1998. *Sport stretch.* 2nd ed. Champaign, IL: Human Kinetics.

American College of Sports Medicine (ACSM). 1988. *Resource manual for guidelines for exercise testing and prescription.* Philadelphia: Lea & Febiger.

———. 1995. *ACSM's guidelines for exercise testing and prescription.* 5th ed. Philadelphia: Williams & Wilkins.

American Council on Exercise (ACE). 1991. *Personal trainer manual: The resource for fitness instructors.* San Diego: ACE.

American Medical Association (AMA). 1992. Bones, muscles, and joints. Newark, NJ: *Reader's Digest.*

Anderson, B. 1980. *Stretching.* Bolinas, CA: Shelter Publications, Inc.

Appleton, B. Stretching and flexibility: Everything you never wanted to know. Available at: http://www.enteract.com/~bradapp/docs/rec/stretching/stretching_toc.html

Arendt, E. A. 1996. Common musculoskeletal injuries in women. *Physician and Sportsmedicine* 24 (7): 39.

Arnheim, D. D. 1985. *Modern principles of athletic training.* 6th ed. St. Louis: Times Mirror/Mosby College Publishing.

Baechle, T. R., ed. 1994. *Essentials of strength and conditioning.* Champaign, IL: Human Kinetics.

Brzycki, M. 1997. *Cross training for fitness.* Indianapolis, IN: Masters Press.

———. 1995. *A practical approach to strength training.* 3rd ed. Indianapolis, IN: Masters Press.

Buckwalter, J. A. 1997. Decreased mobility in the elderly: The exercise antidote. *Physician and Sportsmedicine* 25 (9): 126.

Colliton, J. 1996. Back pain and pregnancy: Active management strategies. *Physician and Sportsmedicine* 24 (7): 89.

Cooper, R. K. 1989. *Health & fitness excellence.* Boston: Houghton Mifflin Company.

Crisp, T. 1998. Delayed onset muscle sorenes. FitPro (April/May). Available at: http://www.fitpro.com/News/0298/doms.html

Golding, L. A., C. F. Myers, and W. E. Sinning. 1982. *The Y's way to physical fitness.* Revised ed. Champaign, IL: Human Kinetics.

Gray, H. 1974. *Gray's anatomy.* Philadelphia: Running Press.

Howley, E. T., and B. D. Franks. 1986. *Health/fitness instructor's handbook.* Champaign, IL: Human Kinetics.

Jerome, J. 1987. *Staying supple.* New York: Bantam Books.

Knudson, D. 1998. Stretching: From Science to Practice. *Journal of Physical Education, Recreation and Dance* 69 (3), 38–42.

Kravitz, L., and V. H. Heyward. 1995. Flexibility training. *Fitness Management* 11 (February): 32–38.

Marieb, E. N., and J. Mallatt. 1996. *Human anatomy.* 2nd ed. Menlo Park, CA: Benjamin/Cummings.

Martins, P. 1997. *New York City Ballet workout.* New York: William Morrow and Company, Inc.

Mattes, A. L. 1990. *Flexibility: Active and assisted stretching.* Sarasota, FL: Aaron L. Mattes.

McArdle, W. D., F. I. Katch, and V. L. Katch. 1986. *Exercise physiology: Energy, nutrition, and human performance.* 2nd ed. Philadelphia: Lea & Febiger.

McAtee, R. E. 1993. *Facilitated stretching.* Champaign, IL: Human Kinetics.

Moloney, K., and the staff of Canyon Ranch. 1989. *The Canyon Ranch health and fitness program.* New York: Simon & Schuster.

Norkin, C. C., and D. J. White. 1985. *Measurement of joint motion: A guide to goniometry.* Philadelphia: F. A. Davis Company.

Plowman, S. A. 1992. Physical activity, physical fitness, and low back pain. In *ACSM exercise and sport sciences reviews* 20, 221-242. Philadelphia: Williams & Wilkins.

Roos, R. 1996. On the mend. Healthtrack. A supplement to the *Physician and Sportsmedicine* for the waiting room. July. Available at: http://www.physsportsmed.com/issues/jul_96/mend.htm

Solomon, E. P., and P. W. Davis. 1978. *Understanding human anatomy and physiology.* New York: McGraw-Hill Book Company.

St. George, F. 1997. *Stretching for flexibility and health.* Freedom, CA: The Crossing Press, Inc.

Tobias, M., and M. Stewart. 1985. *Stretch & relax.* Tucson: The Body Press.

Tufts University Health & Nutrition Letter: December 1997. To stretch or not to stretch?

United States Olympic Committee Online. Sports Medicine. Flexibility. Available at: http://www.olympic-usa.org/inside/in_1_3_5_7.html#TOC

Voight, K. 1996. *Precision training for body & mind.* New York: Hyperion.

Wharton, J., and P. Wharton. 1996. *The Whartons' stretch book.* New York: Times Books.

White, T. P., and editors of the University of California at Berkeley Wellness Letter. 1993. *The wellness guide to lifelong fitness.* New York: Rebus.

Wood, R. Rob Wood's Home of Fitness Testing. Flexibility Tests. Available at: http://www.general.uwa.edu.au/u/rjwood/flex.htm

Zemach-Bersin, D., K. Zemach-Bersin, and M. Reese. 1990. *Relaxercise.* San Francisco: Harper & Row Publishers.

This chapter is dedicated to my mom, Evelyn Schmidt. Her optimism, sense of commitment, and unwavering faith during times of adversity will forever be an inspiration to me.

29

Fueling the Active Lifestyle

W. Daniel Schmidt, Ph.D.
Assistant Professor
Department of Physical Education and Health Promotion
University of Wisconsin-Oshkosh
Oshkosh, Wisconsin

The perfectly balanced diet for an active lifestyle. One would be hard pressed to find an area of scientific research that has proven more elusive or created more controversy. For years, consumers have been constantly bombarded with the latest findings that "seem to suggest" this or "may indicate" that. As professionals working to bring out the best in the athletes we train, the process of separating nutritional fact from fiction becomes even more challenging. Generally speaking, athletes have an acute understanding of the role that sound nutrition plays with regard to conditioning for peak performance. Inches and/or seconds often mean the difference between success and failure, so athletes realize how crucial it is to provide their bodies with the optimal raw materials (nutrients) to fuel their activity. Unfortunately, athletes are also prone to try anything to gain an edge over an opponent, a fact that makes them extremely vulnerable to fad diets and nutritional gimmicks. To quote Chip Harrison, head strength and conditioning coach at Penn State University, "If an athlete said that eating rhinoceros hair helped to make him stronger, many athletes would start including rhinoceros hair as part of their daily diet!"

A common approach used by the manufacturers of nutritional supplements is the time-honored tradition of soliciting testimonials from world-class athletes. The individual looking for any slight advantage will reason, "If that supplement worked for them, maybe it can work for me." This is where the strength training and conditioning professional must be willing to serve as a resource and differentiate scientific evidence from anecdotes and hearsay about nutritional strategies.

This is no simple task. Findings from highly respected and reputable research groups often contradict previous results found in other studies, leaving the practitioner wondering what to believe and, more importantly, what to prescribe to their athletes. In the purist sense, nutritional research must be viewed as a large picture; a continuously evolving process. It is very unusual for one study to answer all questions and/or end all controversy about a nutritional topic. On the contrary, most research studies address one or possibly two issues while generating even more questions. For this reason, the scientific process can be painstakingly slow. Still it remains the single best method we have for learning the truth. To the disappointment of some of you reading this, there is no top-secret diet that will benefit every individual or every athlete. This chapter is not about presenting a new dietary twist that will make a good athlete into a world-class athlete. However, individuals who do not follow a balanced and well-planned dietary program may be selling themselves short as far as their optimal performance is concerned. The main objective of this chapter will be to help you sort through what is known and what is not known based upon the best available research regarding optimal nutrition for fueling the active lifestyle.

THE SIX BASIC NUTRIENTS

Which nutrient is the most important? This is like asking a parent to tell you which of their children they love the most. If asked, most parents would likely tell you that they love all of their children the same and that each child has his or her own unique characteristics and personality which makes him or her a special part of the family as a whole. When describing a healthy diet, the same principles apply. Like members of a family or an athletic team, each nutrient plays a specific role or roles with regard to proper bodily function; we simply require these nutrients in different amounts. When describing the nutrients and the amounts necessary for a balanced diet, reference will be made to a recommended dietary allowance (RDA). The RDAs were developed by the National Academy of Sciences and represent the daily suggested intake of nutrients for normal, healthy people.

Carbohydrates

The main function of carbohydrates is to supply us with energy, and without question, on a percentage basis, they represent the single most highly utilized energy source during exercise. Carbohydrates come in different forms. Simple carbohydrates, commonly referred to as simple sugars, are classified as monosaccharides (glucose, fructose, or galactose) or disaccharides (sucrose, lactose, or maltose), which are simply two monosaccharides connected together. Fruit juices, soft drinks, and candy are usually high in simple sugars as well as calories. Complex carbohydrates (or starches) are three or more glucose molecules combined and represent the storage form of carbohydrates in the body known as glycogen. Pasta, rice, potatoes, and whole grains are excellent sources of complex carbohydrates. The current RDA for Americans is to consume 55–60 percent of your total daily caloric intake in the form of carbohydrates with 10 percent or less of these coming from simple sugars. Plainly speaking, complex carbohydrates give you more bang for your buck. They have a greater nutrient value in that they contain more essential nutrients per calorie than simple carbohydrates. Dietary fiber is a nondigestible form of carbohydrate often lacking in the typical American diet. Fiber can be either water soluble (such as pectin which is found in apples and pears) or water insoluble (as in cellulose).

Because fiber is not digested, it plays an important role in the process of decreasing food transit time through the gastrointestinal tract. Whole grains, fruits, and vegetables are good fiber sources. It is recommended that we consume 20–35 grams of fiber per day.

Has the high-carbohydrate diet been overrated?

Obviously, a diet that relied exclusively on carbohydrates would not be healthy for anyone including the heavy-duty endurance athlete (e.g., a marathoner or triathlete) who has perhaps the greatest carbohydrate need. On the other hand, there have been reports of some athletes taking the high-carbohydrate notion too far by substituting carbohydrates for other important nutrients—most notably protein (Walsh 1996). However, do not be misled. Athletes—as well as everyday fitness enthusiasts—must have a readily available supply of blood glucose along with adequate levels of muscle glycogen to perform effectively. Carbohydrates are the

The main function of carbohydrates is to supply us with energy. Without question, on a percentage basis, they represent the single most highly utilized energy source during exercise.
(photo by Matt Brzycki)

primary source of adenosine triphosphate (ATP) production during high-intensity exercise and must also be available if we are to effectively utilize fat as an energy source. Physically active individuals who train heavily on consecutive days should consume anywhere from 60–70 percent of their total calories as carbohydrates (ADA and CDA 1993).

Should I carbo-load prior to my event?

The concept of carbo-loading has been popular among athletes, especially distance runners, for several years. Traditionally, this process has involved consuming a low-carbohydrate diet in the week leading up to a competition while simultaneously training intensely with the intention of depleting muscle glycogen stores. Two to three days before the competition the athlete reverses the trend, performing only very light workouts while consuming high-carbohydrate foods such as rice, pasta, and cereal. Due to the previous depletion of glycogen earlier in the week, the body will tend to overcompensate when fed carbohydrates and retain more glycogen than would be stored under normal circumstances, thus becoming glycogen loaded.

This approach has been proven effective for high-intensity exercise lasting beyond 60–80 minutes and is still practiced by many athletes. With more glycogen available, the athlete is better able to delay early fatigue during exercise. There may be some drawbacks to this practice, however, at least for some people. If individuals deprive themselves of carbohydrates one week prior to competition, their training will likely be compromised. An equally effective adaptation to the traditional carbo-loading technique may be to simply consume a high-carbohydrate diet on a consistent basis without throwing in a new twist the week of a competition. The week before a competition is not a good time to experiment with a diet that differs from what you have been following as part of your regular training routine. Imagine preparing for a race for several months and then, the week before the race, dramatically changing your eating patterns, which are an essential part of your training routine. Fuel the workouts that are preparing you for the competition.

What about this thing called the *glycemic index*?

The glycemic index is the magnitude of the increase in blood glucose that follows ingestion of a food. In response to increased levels of blood glucose, the pancreas secretes insulin, which is responsible for glucose uptake by the cells as well as glycogen synthesis. There is some evidence to indicate that ingestion of food with a high glycemic index (e.g., such as cereal or a baked potato) 30–60 minutes prior to exercise may cause a greater-than-normal decrease in blood glucose when exercise commences as a result of an increased secretion of insulin (Walberg-Rankin 1997). Therefore, it may be more effective to consume foods with a lower glycemic index—such as spaghetti or fruit yogurt—prior to exercise. It must be emphasized, however, that the relationship between glycemic index and performance is still unknown.

I've heard that high-carbohydrate diets make you fat. Is this true?

Unfortunately, the media has helped to perpetuate this myth. A few years ago, an article was published in the *New York Times* stating that pasta makes people fat. The article was based upon the premise that approximately 25 percent of all Americans cannot effectively utilize the glucose in carbohydrates and consequently store this glucose as fat (a term known as insulin resistance). It was speculated that fat storage and subsequent weight gain occur more readily. Obviously, eating excess amounts of any food can cause weight gain; high-carbohydrate foods are no exception to this. If you consume more calories than you expend, you will most likely gain weight. However, to single out pasta as having a direct cause-and-effect relationship with obesity is, at best, faulty reporting. Quite often, diets that restrict carbohydrate intake result in weight loss. This is not due to some magic formula in your body; if you decrease caloric intake, as you would on most low-carbohydrate diets, you will probably lose weight. Is the weight loss permanent? Hardly. This is a difficult diet to sustain yourself on especially if you are a regular exerciser or an athlete and your muscles demand a ready supply of carbohydrate to perform effectively. There is little scientific evidence to suggest that eating a low-carbohydrate diet will be beneficial with regard to long-term weight loss.

Fats/Lipids

Fats (also known as lipids) are a highly concentrated energy source that contribute more significantly as exercise becomes more aerobic in nature. More than 95 percent of the fat we consume and store in our bodies is in the form of triglycerides. A triglyceride is made up of three fatty acids attached to a glycerol molecule (also called the backbone), thus the name triglyceride. Fatty acids are composed of carbon chains with hydrogen atoms attached to the carbons. If the carbons are carrying the maximum number of hydrogen atoms, the chain is called a saturated fatty acid. If, due to a chemical reaction, two carbons located side by side each lose a hydrogen, a double bond forms between the two carbons and the fatty acid is now classified as a monounsaturated fatty acid. When two or more double bonds form in the chain of carbons, it is known as a polyunsaturated fatty acid. Perhaps the easiest way to distinguish between fats is to remember that saturated fats, which are derived primarily from animal sources, are solid at room temperature while unsaturated fats are liquid at room temperature. Americans should consume 30 percent or less of their total daily calories in the form of fat with 10 percent or less of their total calories from saturated fat (ADA and CDA 1993).

I'm an active person; do I really need to worry about excess fat intake?

There is no question that athletes and active people can take in more calories than sedentary individuals. If you exercise, you have a greater caloric need. The problem with consuming a high-fat diet with ice cream, cookies, and pastries is the caloric density of such foods. By consuming foods that are high in complex carbohydrates—such as whole grains, fruits, and vegetables—you get more readily available energy with fewer empty calories (i.e., those that have a low quantity of other nutrients). There is also a strong correlation between a diet high in saturated fat and heart disease. Some forms of cancer may be associated with this as well.

Should I cut fat out of my diet altogether?

Ask any college student what nutrient causes them the most concern and they will probably tell you fats. The American culture has an obsession with thinness. Realistically, the only way one could accomplish a no-fat diet would be to stop eating completely; not a very realistic approach for sustaining life, much less fueling an active lifestyle!

Without question, your body needs fat for a variety of important functions including hormone synthesis, vitamin absorption, and proper immune function. Obesity is a major health problem in the United States, but athletes sometimes go a bit overboard with low-fat regimens. Consuming fatty foods from time to time will not ruin a person for life. As mentioned earlier dietary fat should make up 30 percent or less of a person's daily caloric intake.

Proteins

Proteins are similar to fats and carbohydrates in that they are a potential fuel source, especially when the body is low on glucose. However, unlike fats and carbohydrates, only proteins contain nitrogen and can be used as building material for body tissues. When nitrogen is combined with carbon, hydrogen, and oxygen, amino acids are formed that can be further combined to form proteins. There are nine amino acids that cannot be produced in the body and therefore must be consumed in the diet. These are called essential amino acids. The other 11 amino acids can be manufactured in the body and are called nonessential amino acids (see Figure 29.1). A complete protein contains all nine essential amino acids while an incomplete protein is deficient in one or more of them. It is recommended that we consume 10–15 percent of our total daily calories in the form of protein or approximately 0.8 grams per kilogram of body weight (ADA and CDA 1993).

Does an athlete have an increased need for protein?

As with carbohydrates, it seems that athletes may have protein requirements that exceed the RDA. Increases in training volume and/or intensity have been shown to cause a negative nitrogen balance (Lemon 1987)—that is, a lack of protein for

Table 29.1 The Essential and Nonessential Amino Acids

Essential Amino Acids	Nonessential Amino Acids
Histidine	Alanine
Isoleucine	Arginine
Leucine	Asparagine
Lysine	Aspartic Acid
Methionine	Cysteine
Phenylalanine	Glutamic Acid
Threonine	Glutamine
Tryptophan	Glycine
Valine	Proline
	Serine
	Tyrosine

anabolic purposes—in both endurance- and strength-trained athletes. It has therefore been suggested that during times of heavy training, athletes should consume 12–15 percent of their caloric intake in the form of proteins, assuming that caloric intake has increased with the concurrent increased energy requirement. If for some reason caloric intake decreases during heavy training, then the percentage of protein should be slightly more than 15 percent (Stone 1994).

Will protein or amino acid supplements help me gain size and strength?

Despite an increased protein requirement during heavy training, there is little evidence to suggest that supplementation (i.e., consumption above and beyond even the athlete's increased requirement) will improve physical performance beyond

Despite an increased protein requirement during heavy training, there is little evidence to suggest that supplementation will improve physical performance beyond what would be attained with a balanced diet.

(photo by Kevin Fowler)

Table 29.2 Essential Vitamins: Their Primary Functions and Main Sources

Fat-Soluble

Vitamins	Primary Functions	Main Sources
Vitamin A	Important for vision as well as maintenance of skin and mucous membranes	Carrots, sweet potatoes, green leafy vegetables, cheese, margarine, butter
Vitamin D	Enhances calcium absorption to promote bone growth and teeth formation	Dairy products, margarine, sunlight
Vitamin E	Protects cell membranes and polyunsaturated fats	Green leafy vegetables, whole grains, vegetable oil
Vitamin K	Blood clotting	Eggs, green leafy vegetables, pork, beef, liver

Water-Soluble

Vitamins	Primary Functions	Main Sources
Thiamine (Vitamin B_1)	Aids energy production as a coenzyme; central nervous system function	Lean meat, ham, whole grains, legumes
Riboflavin (Vitamin B_2)	Aids energy production as a coenzyme	Dairy products, green leafy vegetables
Niacin	Aids energy production as a coenzyme; blocks release of free fatty acids	Lean meat, fish, poultry, whole grains
Vitamin B_6	Coenzyme for protein metabolism; helps form red blood cells	Green leafy vegetables, fish, poultry, whole grains
Vitamin B_{12}	Coenzyme for DNA and red blood cell synthesis	Exclusive to animal foods
Folic Acid	Coenzyme for DNA and red blood cell synthesis	Green leafy vegetables, legumes, whole wheat
Biotin	Coenzyme for metabolism of carbohydrates, fats, and proteins	Milk, whole grains, green vegetables
Pantothenic Acid	Assists with the metabolism of carbohydrates, fats, and proteins	Whole grains, lean meats, green vegetables
Vitamin C	Forms collagen; maintains bones and teeth	Citrus fruits, broccoli, green leafy vegetables

what would be attained with a balanced diet. Unfortunately, many athletes translate "increased protein requirement" to mean protein and amino acid pills and powders, which are often quite expensive. These supplements may be convenient for the busy student-athlete and are certainly lower in fat than certain meats that are often consumed as protein sources. However, these supplements should never be viewed as a substitute for a well-balanced diet.

Vitamins and Minerals

Vitamins are organic compounds that are required for several important bodily functions including growth and metabolism. A vitamin can be fat soluble (vitamins A, D, E, and K) or water soluble (vitamin C and the B-complex vitamins). Contrary to popular belief, the typical American diet supplies an individual with adequate amounts of vitamins, as only small quantities are necessary (see Figure 29.2).

Unlike vitamins, minerals are inorganic elements that exist in topsoil, rivers, and streams. Minerals can be found in all human cells and are especially prevalent in bones and teeth. They regulate the speed of specific reactions throughout the body and help to maintain both the water and acid-base balance. The minerals that have gained the most research attention in recent years are calcium (the body's most abundant mineral), iron, and sodium (see Figure 29.3).

What are antioxidants and how do they relate to exercise?

Antioxidants have become a hot topic in recent years as evidence has surfaced that this group of vitamins (i.e., beta carotene and vitamins C and E) may help prevent

Table 29.3 Selected Minerals: Their Primary Functions and Main Sources

Major Minerals	Primary Functions	Main Sources
Calcium	Bone and teeth formation; muscle contraction; blood clotting; nerve transmission	Dairy products, beans, dark-green vegetables
Phosphorus	Bone and teeth formation; acid-base balance; energy transfer	Meats, poultry, dairy products, whole grains
Magnesium	Bone growth; muscle contraction; protein synthesis	Whole grains, seafood, green leafy vegetables
Trace Minerals	**Primary Functions**	**Main Sources**
Iron	Formation of hemoglobin; enzyme function	Meat, fish, poultry, whole grains, green leafy vegetables
Chromium	Metabolizes glucose	Meats, whole grains, liver, beans
Selenium	Works with vitamin E	Meats, fish, whole grains

cardiovascular disease and cancer. It is believed that antioxidants may shield our cells by neutralizing oxygen-free radicals, which are formed in the body and are also found in pollutants and cigarette smoke. Despite the many benefits, high-intensity and/or long-duration exercise have also been shown to increase the number of free radicals in the bloodstream and cause damage to polyunsaturated fatty acids in membrane structures—a process known as *lipid peroxidation*. It is further established that some types of exercise result in muscle damage. Some researchers have suggested that trained individuals may have an increased antioxidant requirement. However, it is still unknown whether antioxidant supplements can prevent lipid peroxidation or muscle damage.

Will vitamin and/or mineral supplements improve physical performance?

A diet that is deficient in any nutrient will result in a less-than-optimal physical working capacity. However, there is no evidence that vitamin and/or mineral supplements above and beyond the RDA will provide any performance benefit whatsoever. With that statement, it is important to emphasize that many people—including athletes—do not follow a well-rounded diet plan. This can often lead to problems that manifest as a decline in athletic performance. Simply stated, if an athlete (or anyone, for that matter) is well nourished, there is no need for vitamin and mineral supplements. In fact, certain vitamin and mineral megadoses may actually be toxic if consumed for an extended period of time as the body slows down absorption to prevent an accumulation of these substances.

Water

Water, an inorganic and noncaloric nutrient, is made up of two hydrogen atoms bound to one oxygen atom. Our body mass is approximately 60–70 percent water. Nearly two-thirds of this water is stored as intracellular water, and one-third is stored as extracellular water. Water is the nutrient required in the greatest quantity by the body and is involved in nearly every bodily process, including digestion, absorption, circulation, and transportation. A minimum of 8–10 glasses of water per day should be consumed. Athletes or fitness enthusiasts should consume even more.

Which is better for me: water or a sports drink?

Sports drinks have become big business in the past decade; there are many different products on the market. The question is whether or not these drinks are effective with regard to physical performance. There is no debate that dehydration will not only cause a decline in performance but may pose a serious health risk as well. Athletes and weekend warriors alike must make a conscious effort to maintain a well-hydrated state by drinking plenty of fluids before, during, and after activity. If the event involves prolonged exercise with heavy sweat loss—such as an ultramarathon or triathalon—a glucose-polymer solution (i.e., a sports drink) would be a better choice than water because of the glucose and electrolytes (i.e., sodium, chloride, and potassium) such products can replace. However, if the event lasts less than 60 minutes, hydration is the major concern and can best be dealt with by consuming plenty of water. Some individuals prefer the taste of sports drinks over water; if it results in the person taking in more fluids, the sports drink may be a better choice.

CURRENT ISSUES IN SPORTS NUTRITION

There are several additional subjects that are important in fueling an active lifestyle.

The Precompetition Meal

The meal you consume prior to a competition or a workout has less influence on performance than the food patterns you have established as part of your overall training regimen. However, there are some precompetition strategies that can work to your advantage. First, it may be a good idea to experiment during your training to find out which foods your body seems to digest more efficiently. Meals that are high in complex carbohydrates and low in protein and fat will benefit glycogen storage and, just as important, be agreeable to most people from a digestive standpoint. The timing of this meal can range between three and five hours prior to competing yet this remains very much an individual matter. Precompetition nerves are a factor in determining both the composition and timing of this meal as digestive time can be delayed with stress and anxiety. Some athletes choose to consume carbohydrate drinks as their pre-event meal and this does provide the benefit of a reduced gastrointestinal workload.

Is there any benefit to ingesting carbohydrates during exercise?

For intense exercise lasting longer than one hour, it appears that carbohydrate ingestion may help the athlete maintain blood glucose levels and thereby prolong a high rate of energy production. A solution containing no more than 8 percent carbohydrate has been shown to have little detrimental effect on gastric emptying and would therefore be absorbed into the bloodstream at about the same rate as plain water. If the duration of the activity is less than one hour, there does not appear to be any performance benefit from carbohydrate ingestion.

What about the post-competition meal?

It has been estimated that at least 20 hours are required to restore muscle glycogen levels following exhaustive exercise (Coyle 1988), with the first two hours post-exercise being the most crucial for glycogen reloading (Ivy et al. 1988).

Simple carbohydrates ingested within the first six hours following exercise may actually enhance muscle glycogen resynthesis more readily than complex carbohydrates (Kiens et al. 1990).

Safe Weight-Loss Methods for Athletes

Rapid weight loss is a common practice among athletes involved in sports with weight classifications (e.g., wrestlers, boxers, and jockeys) or where aesthetics are important to success (e.g., figure skaters, divers, and gymnasts). Unfortunately, the techniques employed by these athletes to achieve weight loss are often severe and detrimental not only to performance but, more importantly, to the overall health of the athlete. The best approach to weight loss is for the athlete to begin before the competitive season gets underway. Ideally, this process would start with a body-composition assessment followed by a meeting with a nutritionist or registered dietitian to determine the best competition weight for the individual. Realistically, the athlete should lose no more than about 1–2 pounds per week and it has been further suggested that body fat should not drop below 5–7 percent in males and 14 percent in females (Walberg-Rankin 1998). Athletes who are obsessed with "making weight" on a weekly basis during the competitive season are less likely to concentrate their efforts on the real keys to success, training and skill development. Finally, athletes need to experiment a bit during the off-season to determine a weight where they feel the strongest and most competitive. This can apply to any athlete in any sport.

Is it possible to gain weight naturally?

In many sports, extra weight in the form of muscle mass can be an asset. Unfortunately, many individuals who attempt to bulk up do so using high-fat, high-sugar foods that provide very little benefit in the way of muscle building. Those interested in gaining weight must discipline themselves to eat at least three meals per day with portions that are larger than normal. Snacking can be beneficial if good foods are eaten such as bagels, yogurt, muffins, and healthful sandwiches. Juices and milk are the weight gainer's friends. Finally and most importantly, muscle-building exercises are essential to gaining muscle mass (Clark 1991). Unless you are an endurance athlete, all those excess calories you consume will likely stay with you as stored fat.

It is important to understand the role that genetics plays with regard to weight gain. Be realistic in your attempt and realize that your mother and/or father may have already had the final say on your weight-gain program!

What is the female athletic triad?

With excessive training and a growing emphasis on thinness, certain female athletes can develop eating disorders. They may start restricting their food intake as well as binging and purging—all in an attempt to lose weight. This will often lead to extensive bone loss (osteoporosis) and amenorrhea. Disordered eating, osteoporosis, and amenorrhea have been termed the *female athlete triad*. Women who compete in sports like gymnastics, cross-country running, and figure skating—where low weight is emphasized—appear to be the most at risk for developing eating disorders. The female athlete must be educated on proper caloric intake and nutrient consumption with dietary supplements a possibility during periods of heavy training. If a coach or trainer suspects that an athlete is suffering from an eating disorder, a registered dietitian or psychologist must be consulted.

EATING TO WIN

There is no magic bullet when it comes to eating right. An athlete or fitness enthusiast is likely to have an increased caloric need based upon a greater energy expenditure, but the nutritional recommendations are not that different from what would be recommended for a sedentary individual. However, the athlete who eats well will generally train well and the athlete who trains well will usually perform well.

REFERENCES

American Dietetic Association (ADA) and Canadian Dietetic Association (CDA). 1993. Position of the American Dietetic Association and the Canadian Dietetic Association. Nutrition for physical fitness and athletic performance for adults. *Journal of the American Dietetic Association* 93: 691–696.

Clark, N. 1991. How to gain weight healthfully. *Physician and Sportsmedicine* 19 (9): 53–54.

Coyle, E. F. 1988. Carbohydrates and athletic performance. *Sports Science Exchange* 1 (7).

Ivy, J. L., A. L. Katz, C. L. Cutler, W. M. Sherman, and E. F. Coyle. 1988. Muscle glycogen synthesis after exercise: Effect of time on carbohydrate ingestion. *Journal of Applied Physiology* 64: 1480–1485.

Kiens, B., A. B. Raben, A. K. Valeus, and E. A. Richter. 1990. Benefit of dietary simple carbohydrates on the early postexercise muscle glycogen repletion in male athletes. *Medicine and Science in Sports and Exercise* 22 (S): S88.

Lemon, P. W. R. 1987. Protein and exercise: Update 1987. *Medicine and Science in Sports and Exercise* 19 (S): S179–190.

Stone, M. H. 1994. Nutritional factors in performance and health. In *Essentials of strength training and conditioning*, ed. T. R. Baechle. Champaign, IL: Human Kinetics.

Walberg-Rankin, J. 1997. Glycemic index and exercise metabolism. *Sports Science Exchange* 10 (1).

———. 1998. Methods and strategies for weight loss in athletes. *Sports Science Exchange*, Roundtable 9 (1).

Walsh, J. 1996. Fuel for the flame. *Women's Sports and Fitness* (July/August).

OTHER SOURCES

Applegate, E. 1991. Nutritional considerations for ultraendurance performance. *International Journal of Sports Nutrition* 1: 118–126.

Baechle, T. R., ed. 1994. *Essentials of strength and conditioning.* Champaign, IL: Human Kinetics.

Butterfield, G. 1991. Fat as a fuel for exercise. In *Sports nutrition for the 90's*, ed. J. Berning and S. Steen. Gaithersburg, MD: Aspen Publishers.

Clark, N. 1991. Fueling up with carbs: How much is enough? *Physician and Sportsmedicine* 19: 68–69.

———. 1993. Athletes with amenorrhea: Nutrition to the rescue. *Physician and Sportsmedicine* 21: 45–48.

Clarkson, P. 1991. Minerals: Exercise performance and supplementation in athletes. *Journal of Sport Science* 9: 91–115.

Costill, D. 1990. Gastric emptying of fluids during exercise. In *Perspectives in exercise science and sports medicine: Fluid homeostasis during exercise*, ed. C. Gisolfi and D. R. Lamb. Indianapolis, IN: Benchmark.

Coyle, E. F. 1991. Timing and method of increased carbohydrate intake to cope with heavy training, competition, and recovery. *Journal of Sport Science* 9: 29–52.

———. 1992. Carbohydrate supplementation during exercise. *Journal of Nutrition* 122: 788–795.

DuPuy, N. A., and V. L. Mermel. 1995. *Focus on nutrition.* St. Louis: Mosby.

Grandjean, A. 1993. What are the protein requirements of athletes? *Food and Nutrition News* 65: 11.

Hoeger, W. W. K., and S. A. Hoeger. 1997. *Principles and labs for fitness and wellness.* 4th ed. Englewood, CO: Morton Publishing Company.

Howley, E. T., and B. D. Franks. 1997. *Health fitness instructor's handbook.* 3rd ed. Champaign, IL: Human Kinetics.

Kromhout, D. 1992. Dietary fats: Long term implications for health. *Nutrition Reviews* 50: 49–53.

Lemon, P. 1991. Effect of exercise on protein requirements. *Journal of Sport Science* 9: 53–70.

———. 1991. Protein and amino acid needs of the strength athlete. *International Journal of Sports Nutrition* 1: 127–145.

Nelson, D. 1997. *Perspectives: Nutrition.* Boulder, CO: Coursewise Publishing.

Noakes, T. 1993. Fluid replacement during exercise. In *Exercise and sports sciences reviews* 21, ed. J. Holloszy, 297–330. Baltimore, MD: Williams and Wilkins.

Sherman, W. 1991. Carbohydrate meals before and after exercise. In *Perspectives in exercise science and sports medicine: Ergogenics—the enhancement of sports performance*, ed. D. R. Lamb and M. H. Williams. Indianapolis, IN: Benchmark.

Williams, M. H. 1995. *Nutrition for fitness and sport.* 4th ed. Dubuque, IA: Brown and Benchmark.

This chapter is dedicated to my wife, Meg, and my sister-in-law, Kathy Bickhart, without whom this writing would not be possible.

30

The Straight Dope on Steroids

Kevin C. Tolbert, B.S.
Strength and Conditioning Coach (Basketball)
The University of Miami
Coral Gables, Florida

Athletes are continually looking for ways to improve their performance and thus improve their chances of being successful during a game or competition. This well-meaning quest to gain the competitive edge may lead to a dangerous win-at-all-costs attitude. In some cases, there can be a blatant disregard for the serious consequences of certain actions. Unfortunately, the temptation to achieve the ultimate level of success leads many athletes to use some type of performance-enhancing drug.

One class of drugs that has been used to improve athletic performance since at least the 1950s is steroids. Today, their use is widespread among both power and endurance athletes. Further, steroid use is prevalent among high school, college, and professional athletes—men as well as women. The ability to increase muscle mass and strength—along with significant improvement in recovery time—help to account for the popularity of these drugs.

WHAT ARE THEY?

Steroids are synthetic derivatives of the powerful male sex hormone testosterone. In males, this hormone is produced in the testes and is regulated by the pituitary gland in the brain. In females, it is primarily produced by the adrenal gland. From a scientific standpoint, steroids are referred to as anabolic-androgenic. The anabolic, or tissue-building, effects of testosterone include an increase in muscle mass and protein synthesis while its androgenic or masculinizing effects include a deepening of the voice, an increase in body and facial hair, and an altered libido.

Individuals—including nonathletes—take anabolic steroids for a number of reasons, such as the ability to increase strength, increase lean body mass, and improve physical appearance. Anabolic steroids can be taken orally or by intermuscular injection. They are usually used in cycles of 6 to 12 weeks and are frequently stacked, meaning that more than one type of steroid (or other drug) is used simultaneously.

POTENTIAL SIDE EFFECTS

Although steroid users—and potential users—envision only the positive effects from the use of the drug, there are a host of well-documented negative effects associated with steroid usage. The long-term effects of steroid use are uncertain. However, they pose serious threats to several organs and systems of the body, thereby presenting dangers to overall health. The potential for side effects is based upon the type and amount of steroid being used as well as individual tolerances. Nevertheless, the side effects from the use of steroids occur quite frequently and are heavily documented in the medical literature. The use of steroids has the potential for adverse consequences to the liver (peliosis hepatis, liver tumors, liver cancer, impaired excretory function, jaundice, and liver dysfunction); the kidneys (kidney dysfunction, kidney stones, and Wilm's tumor); and the cardiovascular system (hypertension and elevated cholesterol).

Steroid use also gives rise to a wide range of miscellaneous side effects. Adolescents who use steroids may experience stunted growth—which is irreversible. Steroid users also have a predisposition to connective-tissue abnormalities which can lead to tendon and ligament injuries. If steroids are injected into the body, the user risks blood poisoning and the spread of communicable diseases—including AIDS—from contaminated needles as well as neural dysfunction as a result of improperly placed needles. Additionally, there is a risk of sudden death accompanying an injection due to anaphylactic shock. Steroids can increase the production of oil by the sebaceous glands of the skin and cause acne to develop anywhere on the body—most commonly on the upper back. A number of other possible side effects are commonly noted in the literature including fluid retention, unprovoked nosebleeds, arthritis, peptic ulcers, and alopecia (hair loss). Finally, steroid use often leads to the use of other drugs—sometimes in an attempt to control the unwanted side effects. For example, amphetamines are taken to combat depression and diuretics are used to avoid fluid retention and to lower the blood pressure.

Many major psychological side effects have been linked to the use of steroids such as auditory hallucinations, delusions, extreme mood swings, sleep distur-

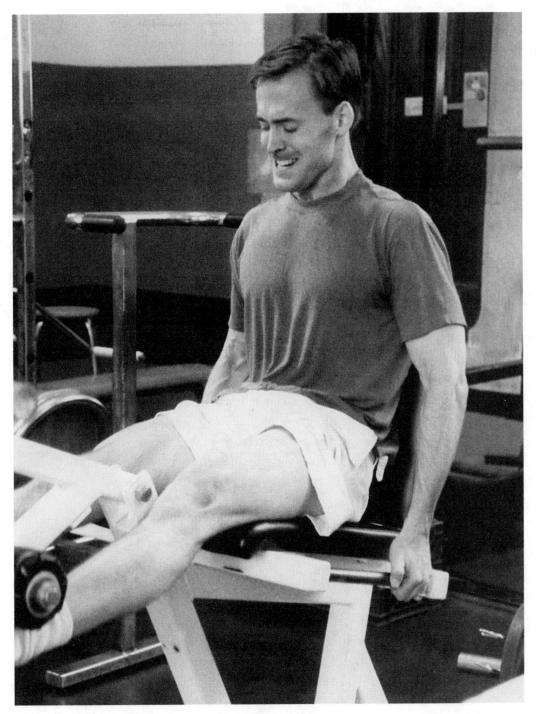

The ultimate goal of getting bigger, faster, and stronger can be achieved the old-fashioned way: through hard work, dedication, a strong will, and the desire to be the best. (photo by Matt Brzycki)

bances, euphoria, paranoia, irritability, anxiety, and an increased or a decreased libido. Steroid users may also experience psychological dependency, which can lead to depression-related withdrawal when steroid use is discontinued. However, the most frequently documented psychological side effect is probably an increased level of unpredictable hostility and aggression which is commonly referred to as *'roid rage.*

The use of steroids has a profound impact on the male reproductive system. In males, the main function of testosterone is to promote secondary sexual characteristics, increase muscle mass, and initiate and maintain sperm production. The body is designed to maintain its own hormonal balance. When external testosterone is introduced into the body, however, that balance is disturbed. The body perceives that there is too much testosterone being produced and responds by decreasing its own natural production of the hormone. This decrease in testosterone production can lead to assorted biological and physiological problems including a reduced sperm count, testicular atrophy, functional impotency, a high-pitched voice, prostate enlargement, sterility, and gynecomastia (the appearance of enlarged, female-like breasts on the male physique). In extreme cases, the body completely ceases production of its natural testosterone—which can cause a temporary or permanent demasculinization effect.

Women who take steroids are subject to gender-specific side effects as well. When a woman takes anabolic steroids, she is essentially a female turning male. Females may experience irreversible physical changes including an enlargement of the clitoris, a decreased breast size, a deepening of the voice and hirsutism (increased facial and body hair). Menstrual irregularities—such as diminution or cessation—have also been reported. In addition, women who use steroids increase their risk of bearing children with birth defects. When taken by pregnant females, steroids can cause masculinization of the fetus. The degree of masculinization is related to the amount of anabolic steroid being taken and the age of the fetus during the steroid usage. Other potential side effects include an increased risk of breast cancer and uterine atrophy.

LEGAL ISSUES

There are several legal repercussions associated with steroid use. Steroids and related compounds are controlled by the Food and Drug Administration (FDA). In fact, their use is restricted in the same manner as some narcotics, depressants, and stimulants. Currently, transportation or distribution of these agents is punishable by fines of up to $500,000 and/or a prison sentence of up to 15 years. It is important to note that steroids are banned by the National Collegiate Athletic Association, the United States Olympic Committee, and the International Olympic Committee.

THE STEROID ALTERNATIVE

In this society, there is an ever-increasing pressure to be a winner. Indeed, there is little glory in losing. It is this pressure among athletes to push their bodies to the limit and to outperform their opponents that may lead to the use of steroids.

The desire to be the biggest, fastest, or strongest is one of the things that differentiates a good athlete from a great one. However, this ultimate goal can be achieved without the use of steroids. It can be achieved the old-fashioned way: through hard work, dedication, a strong will, and the desire to be the best.

REFERENCES

Corrigan, B. 1996. Anabolic steroids and the mind. *Medical Journal of Australia* 165 (4): 222–226.

Deusterr, P. A., ed. 1997. The Navy SEAL fitness guide. *Department of Military and Emergency Medicine*: 221–233.

Pope, H. G., and D. L. Katz. 1994. Psychiatric and medical effects of anabolic-androgenic steroid use. *Archives of General Psychiatry* 51: 375–382.

Rogol, A. D., and C. E. Yesalis. 1992. Anabolic-androgenic steroids and athletes: What are the issues? *Journal of Clinical Endocrinology and Metabolism* 74: 465–469.

Su, T. P., M. Pagliaro, P. J. Schmidt, D. Pickar, O. Wolkowitz, and D. R. Rubinow. 1993. Neuropsychiatric effects of anabolic steroids in male normal volunteers. *Journal of the American Medical Association* 269: 2760–2764.

This chapter is dedicated to all of the athletes who took the time to participate in the ATLAS program.

31

Steroid Education: The ATLAS Program

Chris Green, M.Ed.
Eugene, Oregon

ATLAS stands for Athletes Training and Learning to Avoid Steroids. It was the first research study sponsored by the National Institutes of Health that attempted to prevent anabolic steroid use by high school football players. The ATLAS program began in the spring of 1994 with one high school participating in the pilot study. The results of this pilot program have subsequently been published (Goldberg et al. 1996a). In the fall of 1994, the ATLAS program was expanded to include 31 high schools in the Portland, Oregon, and Vancouver, Washington, areas. Of the 31 high schools chosen in the fall of 1994, 15 high schools were selected to receive the ATLAS educational intervention program. The other 16 high schools served as the control group to determine if the ATLAS program was successful in preventing anabolic steroid use among high school football players. The ATLAS program was slated for implementation at the same high schools for four consecutive years. Along with the first-year pilot program results, the results of the first full-year intervention of ATLAS have also been published (Goldberg et al. 1996b).

This chapter charts the evolution of the ATLAS program over a four-year span and highlights some parts of the program that can be used to build a successful steroid-prevention program. Hopefully this information will assist students, coaches, administrators, and research scientists who want to implement such programs at their schools. Beyond steroid prevention, however, there are lessons to be learned about how to implement any type of educational or drug-prevention program at the high school level. The main reason for this success level is that the ATLAS staff used a team-based learning and intervention approach in the ATLAS curriculum, which was found to be very powerful in delivering messages to high school students.

This chapter's intention is not to claim that there is only one way to develop, organize, and implement a drug-prevention program. In the words of Bruce Lee, "Remember, too, that I seek neither your approval nor to influence you towards my way of thinking. I will be more than satisfied if, as a result of this article, you begin to investigate everything for yourself and cease to uncritically accept prescribed formulas that dictate 'this is this' and 'that is that'" (Lee 1971). We must continually search for more effective ways to reach our goals, and we must be willing to apply our experiences and knowledge in an ever-changing, dynamic environment.

THE FIRST PILOT PROGRAM

In the spring of 1994, a high school in Portland, Oregon, was chosen to complete the first ATLAS pilot program. The essence of the ATLAS program rests with peers teaching peers. What this means is that athletes from the school's football team were chosen by the coaching staff to help teach part of the ATLAS program. These individuals were referred to as squad leaders or peer leaders. In the first pilot program, the entire ATLAS curriculum consisted of eight classroom sessions and eight weight training sessions.

The classroom sessions covered three main areas: nutrition, weight training, and drug education. Each classroom session was designed to be approximately one hour long and to be led by the school's football coach.

The weight training sessions were led by the research staff and took place in the weight room of the high school. The sessions were designed to be done in three stages. The first weight training stage consisted of a basic orientation for the athletes and took place during the first three sessions of the weight training curriculum. The second stage of weight training refined the knowledge received in the first stage and was covered in the next three sessions of the curriculum. The third phase of weight training emphasized and expanded upon the need for a proper warm-up, stretching, and cool-down when participating in any type of aerobic or anaerobic activity. It also emphasized the need to train using some type of speed and agility exercises in combination with weights. This stage was discussed and practiced in the last two curriculum sessions.

This weight training program was designed for the needs of the athletes at the specific pilot school, taking into account their present skill level and any other safety considerations related to the school. The goals of the weight training program included building confidence among the athletes in their ability to perform the exercises, enhancing their skill level, improving their knowledge about how to use weight training to reach their athletic goals, and increasing their safety in the weight room.

Reinforcing classroom material in the weight room was a valuable tool because it allowed the athletes to link the classroom sessions with the weight room activities. (photo by Mike Lynch)

Prior to the start of the pilot program, the squad leaders were trained in a one-day seminar at Oregon Health Sciences University (OHSU). It was important for them to become familiar with the classroom curriculum and practice the pieces of the program that they would be teaching. Once they were trained and the pilot program began at their school, we wanted to get feedback from the squad leaders as to the effectiveness of the activities. To get direct and timely feedback, the research staff met with the squad leaders at the school immediately after each weekly classroom session. The squad leaders discussed with the research staff which activities worked well in the classroom session and which activities did not.

A more detailed analysis of the pilot program can be found elsewhere (Goldberg et al. 1996a).

Summary of the First Pilot Program

Because the program took place during the football season, there were actually too many sessions. A pre-intervention questionnaire and a post-intervention questionnaire had to be collected as well as physical measurements such as vertical jump, submaximal bench press, height, weight, and skinfold measurements. As a result, the research staff decided to condense the entire program to seven classroom sessions and seven weight-room sessions. Modifications were also made to the classroom curriculum based on suggestions from the squad leaders during the feedback sessions.

The football coach was totally supportive of the ATLAS program, which enabled the staff to work very smoothly with the athletes in the weight room. The coach taught weight training at the school, so we had convenient access to every football player during the regularly scheduled physical education (PE) classes.

TRAINING THE COACHES FOR THE FULL-SCALE IMPLEMENTATION OF ATLAS

Between the first pilot program and the first large implementation program, a coach from each high school needed to become familiar with the overall ATLAS curriculum. The ATLAS staff scheduled a meeting with all of the coaches at OHSU. During a one-day training program, the coaches familiarized themselves with all aspects of the ATLAS program that they would teach to their athletes. A curriculum specialist facilitated this process. The ATLAS staff also brought in two weight training consultants to speak to the coaches about the weight training portion of the curriculum.

Before the full-scale implementation of the ATLAS program started, an effort was made to involve companies who would make donations to the program. The ATLAS staff used these contributions as incentives for the athletes to complete all of the required parts of the program. Some of these contributions actually became part of the ATLAS curriculum.

FIRST-YEAR IMPLEMENTATION

The ATLAS program was implemented for the varsity football teams at 15 different high schools. By then the ATLAS staff had six full-time trainers who were tasked with coordinating events at the schools. Each of the ATLAS trainers had previous athletic experience and was well qualified to teach weight training at the high school level. The coaches taught the classroom sessions, and the ATLAS trainers taught the weight-room sessions. The elements of the program were the same at each school, but the ways in which the program was actually implemented were different at each school. For example, some weight training sessions were done with the entire football team as a group at one specific time and other sessions were done as part of the normal PE classes held throughout the entire schoolday. In this latter situation, the entire team would not be together during the weight training sessions.

SUMMARY OF FIRST-YEAR IMPLEMENTATION

The ATLAS staff found that the weight training program—with specific exercises and repetitions—was too rigid to be adopted by the different schools. All of the coaches had their own weight training approach, and every time an athlete had to choose between the ATLAS program or the coach's program, the coach's program was always chosen. This may have been due, in part, to the fact that the athletes had more desire to impress the football coach than the ATLAS trainer but that is a subjective observation. It may also have been due to the fact that the athletes were more familiar with the previously instituted weight training program. Because the ATLAS program was new to the athletes, it may have been more difficult to follow. Also, when the weight training sessions were part of the PE classes, the athletes' grades were determined by their ability to do what the teacher required in the PE class. In some instances, the football coach was the PE teacher; therefore, the athletes had to perform certain requirements for the class—and for a grade—and could not give their full attention to the ATLAS trainer. It was also difficult for the ATLAS trainer to work with the ATLAS football players in the normal PE class with a large group of other students lifting weights at the same time (although this had been the situation at the initial pilot school). In these instances, it was difficult for the athletes to pay attention to the ATLAS instructors. In some cases, the environment was also very noisy, which made the situation even more distracting.

The ATLAS staff found that the coaches' teaching methods varied greatly in the classroom sessions. Some of the coaches prepared better than others. No standardization existed among the coaches' delivery of the curriculum. Also, some of the coaches found it too difficult to do the program during the football season. (The reason the football season was chosen was because the team met on a regular basis in a group setting.) From these findings, the following changes were made to the ATLAS program after the first year.

1. The weight training program was changed from a specific, predetermined routine to a more general, principle-based program.
2. The ATLAS program had to be standardized and the delivery of the program by the coaches had to be more consistent. The ATLAS trainers would be tasked with teaching the classroom curriculum along with teaching the weight training curriculum.
3. Feedback from the coaches indicated that the ATLAS program was difficult for them to implement during the season along with all of the other football responsibilities. Considerations were made to do the ATLAS program in the summer when the teams were doing their two-a-day football practices.

Off-Season Training for Coaches and Athletes

The ATLAS staff tried to maintain contact with the athletes and their coaches during the off-season with regard to the weight training portion of the program. The ATLAS staff was made available to the coaches for assistance with their off-season conditioning program. Overall, this wasn't accomplished. It was very difficult to get the football players together as a group after the end of the season. In the summer, there was less accountability on the part of the players. Therefore, the ATLAS staff was unable to assist in the team's off-season conditioning program.

SECOND-YEAR PILOT PROGRAM

In the second-year pilot program, the seven-session classroom curriculum was not repiloted. That seven-session program was now slated to become the curriculum for incoming freshmen. During this pilot, a four-session booster program was tested for the returning varsity players who had already completed the initial seven-session program. This booster program was designed to reinforce the material that the athletes had learned the previous year. During this pilot, the ATLAS staff also tested a three-session weight-room program. Earlier, it was found that it was too difficult to complete seven sessions with the athletes during the football season. The first two sessions of this new three-session weight-room program would consist of a demonstration of certain weight training exercises by the ATLAS trainers. Once the demonstrations were complete, the athletes would then have several minutes to actually perform the movements during these sessions under the supervision of the ATLAS trainers. The purpose was to give each athlete an opportunity to build weight training skills by getting a few minutes of one-on-one attention. The first two sessions had four different exercises to be demonstrated and used four different ATLAS trainers at four different stations. The athletes spent a few minutes at each station and then rotated to the next exercise. At each station, the ATLAS trainer was also tasked with reinforcing one principle from the ATLAS classroom curriculum. For example, the trainer might remind the athletes to make healthy choices if they ate at a fast-food restaurant. This created a link between what the athletes were doing in the weight room with what they were doing in the classroom. The adolescent athletes enjoyed being in the weight room but did not always enjoy the classroom. The ATLAS staff tried to reinforce the fact that if they did not follow the principles being taught in the classroom, then they would not make the best gains they could in the weight room. The third and final weight training session was a basic warm-up, stretch, and cool-down along with several minutes of fundamental agility drills. In each of the sessions, the goal was to make it short and simple enough so that every athlete could complete the required movements.

One change that was made in the classroom curriculum—which was tested during this second pilot—was the actual packaging of the ATLAS classroom curriculum material. The first year we used papers that were stapled together or just one-page handouts. It was difficult for the athletes to find the proper activity quickly. We tried to make a single activity guide with all of the information that was needed in one place for the athletes to use.

All of these elements seemed to work well and were integrated into the program for the second year of implementation. We now had a four-session booster program for the returning players, a seven-session freshman program for the new players, and the same three-session weight training program for both new players and returning players.

Second-Year Implementation

Using information learned from the first-year implementation, the ATLAS staff decided to give the football coach an opportunity to start the ATLAS program during the summer two-a-day practices. Most of the coaches chose this option for the simple reason that they would have most of the program accomplished before the season started and consequently they would have fewer distractions during the season. The freshman session was not able to be done during the summer because the coaches did not have access to those athletes until the beginning of the school year. Therefore, the freshman program began at the start of school in the fall. The weight training sessions were implemented using the three-session program.

Summary of the Second-Year Implementation

After the second year of implementation, the ATLAS staff found that the four-session booster program worked fine for the returning athletes. However, a problem area was the athletes who had not done the initial seven-session ATLAS program and who were not freshmen. These athletes may have transferred from another school or may have chosen not to participate in the ATLAS program the previous year. Since these athletes were not freshmen, they did not want to participate in the freshman program, so the decision was made to allow them to do the four-session ATLAS booster training with the rest of their teammates.

The ATLAS staff also realized that the seven-session freshman program was too long for their season due to the amount of information that had to be collected. This would equal at least 10 weeks; some freshman football seasons did not even last that long. After the second year, therefore, the freshman program was shortened to five classroom sessions. One other note: Certain sections of the material in the classroom curriculum that the ATLAS trainers had to read to the class were too long. These detracted from the interaction of the athletes and began to seem like traditional lectures instead of fun activities. The sections were shortened and modified so that most of the reading could be done by the ATLAS squad leaders instead of the ATLAS trainer.

Other observations were as follows.

1. The three-session weight training program worked well and was kept without making any changes.
2. Reinforcing classroom material in the weight room was a valuable tool because it allowed the athletes to link the classroom sessions with the weight-room activities.

Off-Season Training for Coaches

Following the second-year implementation, the ATLAS staff attempted to continue the off-season educational program for the football coaches. The staff set up a free two-day seminar for coaches that was specifically geared toward football conditioning. Many of the drills that were demonstrated were used by collegiate football players and at summer camps for high school football players. The coaches who attended the seminar really enjoyed interacting with each other and appreciated the new information.

THIRD-YEAR PILOT PROGRAM

The ATLAS staff decided not to pilot any new programs prior to the third year of implementation.

Third-Year Implementation

For the third year of implementation, the ATLAS staff had developed and started using a single activity guide for the classroom sessions. This was a major improvement because all of the information that the athlete needed to use was in one place. To put this activity guide together, the ATLAS staff solicited help from graphic designers and layout specialists in the local area who were not part of the initial research staff. These professionals helped immensely in making the curriculum look attractive for our audience. In this case, we found out that the packaging outside is sometimes just as important as the message inside.

Another big change for the third year was the use of female ATLAS trainers. Until this time, the ATLAS staff had always used male trainers in the classroom and the weight room. The staff also decided to hire more part-time trainers instead of using fewer full-time trainers. Regardless of gender, the only thing that made a difference for the athletes was the ability of the trainer—male or female—to teach and hold their attention.

The other parts of the curriculum worked well during this third year. The staff used the shortened five-session freshman curriculum, the four-session booster program, and the three-session weight training program for both the freshmen and the varsity players. One drawback of using the same booster program for the returning varsity players was that they had already done the activities, which made it difficult for them to understand why they were doing those same activities again.

Off-Season Training for Coaches

Nothing was planned for the coaches' off-season educational program.

Fourth-Year Pilot

The ATLAS staff decided not to pilot any new programs prior to the fourth year of implementation.

Fourth-Year Implementation

During the fourth year, the freshman program was implemented with no changes. However, some changes were made to the booster program. The booster sessions included similar information about nutrition, drug education, and weight training, but the specific activities were changed to hold the athletes' attention. The weight training portion of the curriculum remained unchanged.

SPECIFIC ELEMENTS OF THE ATLAS PROGRAM

Now that the history and chronological development of the four-year ATLAS intervention program has been detailed, several specific elements of the program should be mentioned.

Curriculum Material

The ATLAS staff eventually used two specific guides in the curriculum. These were given to every athlete involved in the program. One was a food guide that contained various nutritional information for the adolescent athlete. The other was a weight training guide that contained general information about the ATLAS weight training curriculum along with pictures of the correct way to perform different exercises. These two pocket-size books were designed as reference material for the athlete. The ATLAS program also had a family food guide that was distributed to the parents. The information presented there was similar to that in the student food guide but with added recipes for healthy preparation of food. These family food guides were larger than the student food guide. One other piece of the curriculum that grew out of these guides was wallet-sized sports menu cards that had information about fast food. These cards were provided to the athletes as a way for them to make healthy fast-food choices. The sports menu cards also included some basic nutritional information taught in the classroom curriculum such as the daily caloric and protein needs of an athlete. The cards seemed to work well among the players. They were excited about looking through the cards in the curriculum sessions and some actually asked for another card to replace a lost one—a good indication that the information was being utilized.

Incentives for Participation

Unfortunately, the incentives used by the ATLAS staff turned out to be a double-edged sword. Initially, each participating school was provided with $3,000 for the purchase of new weight-room equipment. This was done as an incentive for the high schools to participate in the program and to make their weight rooms more appealing to the athletes. The ATLAS staff felt that it would be better for the athletes to lift weights in their high schools under the supervision of their coaches rather than at the local gyms where steroids could be readily available.

The first year, the ATLAS staff ordered all of the weight-room equipment that each school wanted with their incentive money. An unusual problem occurred when a vendor suddenly went out of business right after making the deliveries. Fortunately, the high school received the equipment (although it no longer came with a warranty).

The ordering process was difficult for the ATLAS staff because some schools wanted specific equipment from vendors of their choice. In subsequent years, this problem was alleviated by giving the incentive money directly to the high school. The ordering and delivery of equipment were then the responsibility of the school and the coach. This was a much better situation for all parties involved. In the final two years of the study, the ATLAS staff sent a $500 check to the high school in the beginning of the season and another $500 check after the school had completed all of the scheduled ATLAS events. This was to ensure that the school completed every element of the ATLAS program.

The incentives for the students to participate in the curriculum and complete the questionnaires included such items as ATLAS T-shirts and water bottles. A local vendor also donated meals to the ATLAS program for the athletes. The ATLAS staff helped to design these meals so that they were appropriate for an active lifestyle. The staff wanted to show the athletes that they could make good choices for meals at fast-food restaurants. In summary, the athletes really enjoyed all of the incentives that they received for participation.

The High School Football Coaching Staff

The ATLAS staff found the football coach to be a very important linking agent in the success of a school-based program involving football players. The coaches need to be on board and fully supportive of any type of program for their teams. Ideally, the coach should have a thorough understanding of every element in the intervention program beforehand and be present for each of the curriculum sessions. However, this may not always be possible. Having the coach present with the athletes during the intervention program shows that the program is worthwhile and also helps with classroom discipline.

For future interventions, it is best to involve the coach in as many aspects of the program as possible. From the perspective of the research staff, the coach needs to be a satisfied customer but also has to understand that in research programs scientific protocol must be followed. The ATLAS staff found that it was best to keep the lines of communication open and continually inform the coaches of changes as they occurred. One way the ATLAS staff communicated to the coaches was through an ATLAS newsletter. The newsletter was given to the coaches and the students as a way of continuing communication throughout the school year. It is also important for the coaches and the research staff to be respectful of each other's time. Good communication and commitment to the elements of the intervention program are excellent ways to facilitate this mutual respect.

ATLAS Student Squad Leaders

The strength of the ATLAS program lies in its ability to involve the athletes, allow them to take an active role in learning the information, and pass that information on to their peers. The squad leaders were involved in all aspects of the classroom curriculum. To build upon this success and to make the program more effective and interactive, the squad leaders could also be involved with teaching the weight training curriculum. They would have to receive basic weight training instruction in the same manner that they received the basic classroom instruction for the classroom curriculum.

Squad leaders can create a positive environment for good nutritional and weight training practices among the team. They should be utilized as much as possible. The team members need to see examples of their peers following sound practices that lead to athletic success. Having someone from the outside coming in to tell them what to do and then leaving does not have the same impact. The ATLAS trainers only have access to the athletes for a few hours each fall; the athletes on the team see each other and their coach for several hours each day. Because of this, there is a greater opportunity for the coach and peers to influence team members to modify certain behaviors. This is how squad leaders—when involved in all aspects of the program—can enhance the overall success of the intervention.

As already mentioned, another strength of the ATLAS program was the high degree of interactivity among the students and research staff as well as among the students themselves. When a lecture-only approach is relied upon as the teaching method, it often detracts from the interaction. Just passing on information is a poor substitute for creating a desire in someone to investigate their own patterns and habits. Interaction among the students helps to build a team environment where the athletes can reinforce positive habits and behaviors.

After the intervention is completed and the staff and the coaches are gone, the athletes will probably interact in their groups on their own time. During this interaction, they are going to strongly influence each other while developing and reinforcing group norms. One objective of the classroom and weight-room curriculum is to give the students an interesting subject to discuss along with some tools on how to discuss it, mainly by encouraging them to use their own reasoning and investigative powers. It is important that they are not told how to think but rather to just think and share their thoughts with their peer group. This is one of the reasons that the ATLAS program uses a balanced approach to the risks of using anabolic steroids. The ATLAS staff has found that scare tactics do not necessarily work. Therefore, any drug intervention has to give the athletes the information to enable them to make their own choices.

Characteristics of the Squad Leader

A suggestion that may work better is to use older squad leaders with younger athletes. The ATLAS staff tried this informally when there was a shortage of certain squad leaders. However, this approach was never officially tested. This would send a powerful message to the younger athletes that the program is important and if they follow it they can become bigger, stronger, and healthier players. The squad leaders' attitudes and behavior are very important to the success of the program. If the squad leaders think that the program is a waste of time, then that negative attitude will be passed along to the team; if the squad leaders think that it is fun and worthwhile, then that positive attitude will be passed on. When selecting squad leaders, there is a tendency to pick the best athletes. Sometimes, however, the best athletes are not the best individuals to lead the classroom activities. Along with the best athletes, squad leaders should be selected who can speak in front of a group and who can lead classroom discussions.

FINAL OBSERVATIONS

To attempt a program of this magnitude in the high school setting is very difficult for both the research staff and the high school staff—including the administrators, coaches, and players. Many lessons can be learned along the way. Hopefully, the story of the development and implementation of the ATLAS program has shed some insight into what elements need to be present for a successful high school drug-prevention program.

The ATLAS program was successful in changing attitudes and increasing knowledge related to the use of anabolic-androgenic steroids. Some of the effective outcomes from the program are increased knowledge about the side effects of steroid use; increased knowledge regarding the number of individuals actually using anabolic-androgenic steroids; decreased intent to use anabolic-androgenic steroids*; and increased drug-refusal skills.

Another successful aspect of the program was the peer-teaching method that allowed the athletes to see the team and their peers as more reliable sources of information. Using this knowledge, the athletes were able to debunk numerous myths related to nutrition and weight training.

The program involved many different individuals who are influential in the life of an athlete at school and at home including school administrators, coaches, teachers, peers, and parents. In so doing, it is hoped that a positive environment can be created that offers the athletes access to knowledgeable people who are supportive of a drug-free lifestyle and, in turn, offers the athletes the best chance for success in their future.

REFERENCES

Goldberg, L., D. L. Elliot, G. N. Clarke, D. P. MacKinnon, L. Zoref, E. Moe, C. Green, and S. Wolf. 1996a. The Adolescents Training and Learning to Avoid Steroids (ATLAS) Prevention Program. *Archives of Pediatric Adolescent Medicine* 150 (July): 713–721.

Goldberg, L., D. L. Elliot, G. N. Clarke, D. P. MacKinnon, L. Zoref, E. Moe, C. Green, S. Wolf, E. Greffrath, D. J. Miller, and A. Lapin. 1996b. Effects of a multidimensional anabolic steroid prevention intervention: The Adolescents Training and Learning to Avoid Steroids (ATLAS) Program. *Journal of the American Medical Association* 276 (November 20): 1555–1562.

Lee, B. 1971. Liberate yourself from classical karate. *Black Belt Magazine* (September).

---

* The number of actual steroid users surveyed by the ATLAS program was very low. It was, therefore, difficult to show a significant decrease in the actual use of steroids between the control group and the experimental group.

Resource Section

Books

Brzycki, M. *A Practical Approach to Strength Training.*

——. *Cross Training for Fitness.*

——. *Youth Strength and Conditioning.*

Brzycki, M., and S. Brown. *Conditioning for Basketball.*

Johnston, B. *Strength Training: Objective Principles of an Exact Discipline.*

Kenney, W. L., R. H. Humphrey, C. X. Bryant, and D. A. Mahler. *ACSM's Guidelines for Exercise Testing and Prescription.* 5th ed.

McRobert, S. *Brawn: Bodybuilding for the Drug-Free and Genetically Typical.*

——. *Beyond Brawn: The Insider's Encyclopedia on How to Build Muscle & Might.*

Peterson, J. A., and C. X. Bryant. *The StairMaster® Fitness Handbook: A User's Guide to Exercise Testing and Prescription.* 2nd ed.

Peterson, J. A., C. X. Bryant, and S. L. Peterson. *Strength Training for Women.*

Westcott, W. L. *Be Strong: Strength Training for Muscular Fitness for Men and Women.*

——. *Building Strength and Stamina: New Nautilus Training for Total Fitness.*

——. *Strength Fitness: Physiological Principles and Training Techniques.*

Westcott, W. L., and T. R. Baechle. *Strength Training Past 50.*

Correspondence Courses

Desert Southwest Fitness
602 East Roger Road
Tucson, Arizona 85705
(800) 873-6759 (phone)
(520) 292-0066 (fax)
dswf@msn.com (e-mail)

Gyms/Fitness Centers

The Club at Woodbridge
585 Main Street
Woodbridge, New Jersey 07095
(732) 634-5000 (phone)

Gibson's Gym
75A East Washington Avenue
Washington, New Jersey 07822
(908) 689-9733 (phone)

Iron Island Gym
3465 Lawson Boulevard
Oceanside, New York 11572
(516) 594-9014 (phone)
(516) 594-9426 (fax)

National Fitness Institute and
 Exercise Center
15201 Shady Grove Road
Rockville, Maryland 20850
(301) 258-2687 (phone)

The Quality Repetition
1029 Broadway
Islip, New York 11751
(516) 737-8382 (phone)

Rocco's Complete Fitness Systems
519 Main Street
Covington, Kentucky 41011
(606) 581-3134 (phone)
rocco@hitfitness.com (e-mail)

South Shore YMCA
79 Coddington Street
Quincy, Massachusetts 02169
(617) 479-8500 (phone)

Ultimate Exercise, Inc. (a licensed
 SuperSlow® facility)
108 East North 1st Street
Seneca, South Carolina 29678
(864) 886-0200 (phone)

Whelan Strength Training
 "Building Physically Superior
 Athletes"
800 7th Street NW
Suite #1
Washington, D.C. 20001
(202) 638-1708 (phone)
bobwhelan@naturalstrength.com

Internet

American College of Sports Medicine
http://www.acsm.org/

Castellano, Rocco
http://hitfitness.com/newsite/index.html

Coaching Science Abstracts
http://www-rohan.sdsu.edu/dept/
 coachsci/index.htm

Cyberpump! The Home for HIT
 on the Web
http://www.cyberpump.com/

Desert Southwest Fitness
http://www.dswfitness.com/

Fitness Management magazine
http://www.fitnessworld.com/

Fitt Quarterly (formerly the Fitt
 Health Journal)
http://www.fittjournal.com/

Gatorade® Sports Science Institute
http://www.gssiweb.com/

Hammer Strength®
http://hammerstrength.com/
 hammerstrength.html/

International Association of
 Resistance Trainers
http://www.i-a-r-t.com/

Iron Island Gym
http://hometown.aol.com/IIGKPL/
 iron.html/

Master Trainer
http://ageless-athletes.com/

Medicine & Science in Sports
 & Exercise®
http://www.wwilkins.com/MSSE/

MedX® Corporation
http://www.medxonline.com/

The Physician and Sportsmedicine
http://www.physsportsmed.com/

StairMaster® Sports/Medical Products,
 Incorporated
http://stairmaster.net/

Whelan, Bob
http://www.naturalstrength.com/

York® Barbell Company, Inc.
http://www.yorkbarbell.com/toc.html

Organizations

American College of Sports Medicine
P. O. Box 1440
Indianapolis, Indiana 46206-1440
(317) 637-9200 (phone)
(317) 634-7817 (fax)

International Association of Resistance
    Trainers (Canada)
2545 Trout Lake Road
P.O. Box 24016
North Bay, Ontario P1B 9S1
Canada
(705) 476-6058 or toll free
    (877) 817-IART (phone)
logic@i-a-r-t.com (e-mail)

International Association of Resistance
    Trainers (United States)
P. O. Box 2219
Venice, California 90294
(310) 827-7661 or (phone)
(310) 574-0079 (fax)
mikementzer@worldnet.att.net (e-mail)

Periodicals

Fitt Quarterly (formerly the *Fitt Health
    Journal*)
2545 Trout Lake Road
P.O. Box 24016
North Bay, Ontario P1B 9S1
Canada
(705) 497-0814 or toll free
    (877) 817-IART (phone)
editor@fittjournal.com(e-mail)

Hard Training
P. O. Box 19446
Cincinnati, Ohio 45219
(513) 221-2600 (phone)
(513) 221-8084 (fax)

Exercise Protocol (Canada)
2545 Trout Lake Road
P.O. Box 24016
North Bay, Ontario P1B 9S1
Canada
(705) 476-6058 or toll free
    (877) 817-IART (phone)
editor@fittjournal.com (e-mail)

Exercise Protocol (United States)
P. O. Box 2219
Venice, California 90294
(310) 827-7661 (phone)
(310) 574-0079 (fax)
mikementzer@worldnet.att.net (e-mail)

Master Trainer
c/o Ageless Athletes
Suite 221
Memorial Building
610 North Main Street
Blacksburg, Virginia 24060-3349
(540) 951-3237 (phone)
ageless.athletes@pcr-inc.com (e-mail)

Personal Training by E-Mail

rocco@hitfitness.com (Rocco
    Castellano)
editor@fittjournal.com (Brian Johnston)
flexwriter@aol.com (Steve Weingarten)
ageless.athletes@pcr-inc.com (Richard
    Winett)

Personal Training by Phone

(606) 581-3134 (Rocco Castellano)
(705) 497-0814 (Brian Johnston)
(864) 886-0200 (M. Doug McGuff)
(540) 951-3237 (Richard Winett)

About the Authors

Tony Alexander, C.M.E.S., is the WorkSTEPS® coordinator for physical therapy sports rehab at The Club at Woodbridge in Woodbridge, New Jersey. In his current position he oversees an employment-testing program known as WorkSTEPS®, which matches a worker to a specific job based upon the results of situation-specific physical tests. His many responsibilities include marketing, administration, and coordination of this up-and-coming innovative enterprise. Mr. Alexander is also a popular personal trainer and has been a guest speaker at many local and regional strength and fitness seminars. Born in Princeton, New Jersey, he served in the United States Navy from 1983 to 1987. From 1992 to 1996, Mr. Alexander taught a variety of strength training classes at Princeton University. He has also served as a volunteer strength coach assistant for the Philadelphia Eagles. Mr. Alexander is accredited as a certified medical exercise specialist by the American Association of Fitness Professions. His hobbies include reading, gourmet cooking, strength training, playing softball and flag football, and tae kwon do (he recently completed the requirements for his purple belt). Mr. Alexander and his beautiful wife, Kirsten, reside in Plainsboro, New Jersey.

Michael Bradley, M.A., is the assistant strength and conditioning coach at Stanford University in Palo Alto, California. Coach Bradley has also served in similar capacities at the University of Miami (1995–1998), the United States Military Academy (1994-95), the University of South Carolina (1993–1994), and Southern Methodist University (1991–1993). He earned his bachelor of science degree in chemistry from San Diego State University (1989) and his master of arts degree in the same discipline from the University of California, Santa Barbara (1990).

Shaun Brown, M.S., is the strength and conditioning coach of the Boston Celtics. Previously, he served as the strength and conditioning coach at the

University of Kentucky (1992–1997) and Providence College (1988–1992). His coaching resume also includes stints at the University of Virginia, Ohio State, and Rutgers University. Coach Brown received his bachelor of science degree in physical education from Canisius College (NY) and his master of science degree in exercise physiology from Ohio State. He has written numerous articles on strength and fitness and coauthored the book *Conditioning for Basketball* with Matt Brzycki. He and his wife, Tracey, live in Massachusetts.

Cedric X. Bryant, Ph.D., FACSM, is the vice president of product management and sports medicine at StairMaster® Sports/Medical Products, Inc., in Kirkland, Washington. Before joining StairMaster® in 1992, Dr. Bryant was on the exercise science faculty at Arizona State University. Prior to that, he was an assistant strength and conditioning coach at Penn State where he helped design and implement strength and conditioning programs for the women's basketball, volleyball, gymnastics, track and field, softball, tennis, and swimming teams. In the late 1980s, Dr. Bryant served as the coordinator of strength development for the corps of cadets at the United States Military Academy at West Point. A fellow of American College of Sports Medicine (ACSM) and coeditor of *The ACSM Guidelines for Exercise Testing and Prescription* (5th edition), Dr. Bryant is a regular contributor to *Fitness*

Management and *Muscular Development* magazines. Currently, he lives in Redmond, Washington, with his wife, Ginger, and their four sons. In his spare time, Dr. Bryant enjoys reading, playing racket sports, and coaching youth teams.

Ralph N. Carpinelli, Ed.D., is an adjunct professor in the Department of Health, Physical Education and Human Performance Science at Adelphi University in Garden City, New York. A retired New York police officer, Dr. Carpinelli earned his master's degree in exercise physiology from Adelphi University and a second master's and a doctorate degree in applied physiology from Columbia University. He teaches a course at Adelphi University pertaining to the neuromuscular aspects of strength training.

Rocco Castellano, B.S., C.P.F.T., is the owner of Rocco's Complete Fitness Systems in Covington, Kentucky. He has been involved in fitness for more than 20 years, having owned and managed two health clubs even before earning his bachelor's degree in exercise science from Montclair State University (NJ). A former New York City Golden Gloves Champion, he is also accredited as a certified personal fitness trainer by the National Academy of Sports Medicine. Mr. Castellano has written more than 60 articles on fitness, published two newsletters, and been the host of a weekly radio show dedicated to fitness issues and trends ("Fitness Talk with Rocco"). His expertise and accomplishments have led him to be the subject of numerous newspaper and magazine articles across the country. Over the years, Mr. Castellano has received numerous awards for developing outstanding, new exercise programs for both children and adults. His innovative HIT (High Intensity Training) Fitness System® features manual resistance movements along with the use of simple, nontraditional equipment such as towels, broomsticks, and even buckets. As a personal fitness trainer, Mr. Castellano has worked with professional sports personalities, media celebrities, supermodels, and scores of everyday people looking to improve the quality of their lives. He believes that education is the key to motivation. Mr. Castellano's goal is to teach his clients about the process of exercise so that they have the knowledge to effectively incorporate it into their daily routine and can continue working out on their own.

Jan Dellinger, A.A., is employed by York® Barbell Company, Inc., in York, Pennsylvania. More than two decades of employment there has given him a front-row seat at the window to the world of strength training. In his capacities as the associate editor of *Strength & Health* and *Muscular Development* magazines (then editor of the latter publication) and, subsequently, a commercial/institutional sales representative, this lifelong aficionado of progressive resistance exercise was afforded the unique opportunity to enjoy ongoing contact with strength athletes and coaches as well as respected physical educators and researchers from a wide spectrum of backgrounds. These valued associations allowed Mr. Dellinger to gain familiarity with a broad gamut of trends, techniques, perspectives, and influences that impact on the fascinating topic of muscular contraction and its relationship to human physicality. Moreover, insights gleaned from these extraordinary sources have allowed him to author well-received articles for numerous publications including *Hard Training, Hardgainer,* and *Varsity* magazine. Being associated with an exercise equipment company whose pioneering presence did much to shape the modern-day strength/fitness industry also went a long way toward an awareness of and appreciation for the historical dimension of the Iron Game. He and his wife, Joan, reside in Red Lion, Pennsylvania, with their poodle, Moose.

Jeff Friday, M.S., is the strength and conditioning coach of the Baltimore Ravens in Maryland. Previously, he served as the assistant strength and conditioning coach of the Minnesota Vikings in Eden Prairie, Minnesota. Coach Friday came to the Vikings after spending almost four years as the assistant strength and conditioning coach at Northwestern University in Evanston, Illinois. Previously, he served two years as the assistant strength and conditioning coach at Illinois State University while pursuing his master's degree in exercise science. Coach Friday was the Redbirds' interim strength and conditioning coach for a two-month stint in January and February of 1991. A native of Milwaukee, he earned his bachelor's degree in physical education from the University of Wisconsin at Milwaukee. Coach Friday was certified by the National Strength and Conditioning Association in February 1992 and by the United States Weightlifting Federation in July 1989. He and wife, Jennifer, live in Minneapolis.

 **Frank Furgiuele,** B.A., B.Ed., NCCP—level III, is the head of Physical Education and athletic director at Iona Catholic Secondary School in Mississauga, Ontario, Canada. Born and raised in Toronto, he graduated from York Memorial Collegiate Institute in 1978. Coach Furgiuele earned his bachelor of arts degree in physical education and geography (1982) from Wilfrid Laurier University in Waterloo where he played three seasons for the Golden Hawks varsity football team. He also received the award for Outstanding Contributions to Athletics in 1981 and the Unsung Hero award in 1982. Coach Furgiuele earned his bachelor of education from the University of Toronto in 1983. He began teaching within the Dufferin Peel District Catholic School Board in 1984, starting at the elementary level (1984–1988) and later moving to the secondary level at Father Michael Goetz Secondary School (1988–1992). Coach Furgiuele has been at Iona Catholic Secondary School since 1992. His numerous responsibilities include serving as the head football coach, participating on the subject council, and acting as the chairperson for the Physical and Health Education subject council (1992–1998). He introduced a Strength Training Theory and Application course to the school board in 1990 and it is now being offered at almost all of the 18 secondary schools. Coach Furgiuele served as a consultant to the high schools throughout Ontario as the course was being initiated. He teaches the course during the school year, has hosted and coordinated many coaching clinics, and began a highly successful strength and conditioning summer camp for students and community members aged 12–65. Coach Furgiuele has trained numerous professional and collegiate athletes in a wide variety of sports including hockey, basketball, and baseball. He resides in Mississauga with his wife, Patricia, and three daughters, Erica, Jenna, and Frances.

 **Daniel I. Galper,** M.S., is a doctoral student in clinical health psychology at Virginia Tech in Blacksburg, Virginia. He is currently completing his predoctoral residency in the Department of Psychiatric Medicine at the University of Virginia. Mr. Galper has published and presented at international conferences in the areas of physical activity promotion, anabolic steroid use, and clinical hypnosis. His present interests center on the use of mind–body tech-

niques in pain management and cancer treatment. He and his wife, Sharon Kearns, are both avid weightlifters and certified personal trainers.

Sam Gannelli is the strength and conditioning coordinator of the San Diego Padres Baseball Club in San Diego, California. Coach Gannelli graduated from the United States Military Academy in 1993, where he was a four-year member of the football team. After graduation, he served in the United States Army as a field artillery officer. He was a graduate assistant in strength and conditioning at the United States Military Academy in 1993 and Michigan State University in 1995. From 1995 to 1996, he was the head strength and conditioning coach at the University at Buffalo (NY). Coach Gannelli currently lives in San Diego.

Kristi D. Graves, M.A., is a doctoral student in clinical health psychology at Virginia Tech in Blacksburg, Virginia. She graduated Summa Cum Laude with Distinction in psychology from James Madison University and earned her master's degree in health psychology from Appalachian State University. Ms. Graves was active in gymnastics for 14 years and continues to value health and fitness. She served as a health educator at James Madison University and coordinated a Wellness Peer Education program at Appalachian

State University. Ms. Graves hopes to encourage all fitness enthusiasts to appreciate the importance of the mind's interaction with the body in the pursuit of a healthy self.

Chris Green, M.Ed., graduated in 1987 from Penn State, where he was also a competitive decathlete on the track and field team. After graduation, he served a four-year enlistment in the United States Marine Corps as a commissioned officer. As a marine, Mr. Green competed on the World Cup bobsled team for four seasons, qualifying for two Olympic Trials and two World Championships. After earning his master's degree in health education from the University of Texas in 1993, Mr. Green served as a senior research assistant at Oregon Health Sciences University in Portland, Oregon. He is currently working toward an MBA from Portland State University.

Chip Harrison, M.S., is the head strength and conditioning coach at Penn State in University Park, Pennsylvania. He earned his bachelor of science in physical education (exercise science) and his master of science in physical education (exercise physiology) from Penn State. Coach Harrison has been certified as a health/fitness instructor by the American College of Sports Medicine and a certified strength and conditioning specialist by the National Strength and Conditioning Association. He and his wife, Sheri, have three sons, Mark, Troy, and Stevie.

Brian D. Johnston is the founder and president of the International Association of Resistance Trainers (IART), an educational institute providing advanced certification for coaches and personal trainers. He is the author of *Strength Training: Objective Principles of an Exact Discipline* and is coauthor of the IART's *Reference Manual* and *Master Training Specialist Manual*. Mr. Johnston is also the editor-in-chief of *Exercise Protocol* (formerly the *Heavy Duty Bulletin*) and of the Canadian publication the *Fitt Quarterly* (formerly the *Fitt Health Journal*). He and his wife, Wendy, live in North Bay, Ontario, Canada.

Tom Kelso, M.S., C.S.C.S., is the strength and conditioning coach at Southeast Missouri State University in Cape Girardeau, Missouri. Previously, he served as the head strength and conditioning coach at the University of Florida where he began as a graduate assistant in 1984. From 1985 to 1988, Coach Kelso was also a weight training instructor for the Department of Physical Education at the University of Florida. A track and field athlete at the University of Iowa, he later received his master's degree in physical education from Western Illinois University, where he served as a graduate assistant track and field coach. He has authored numerous articles that have appeared in *Scholastic Coach, Hard Training,* and the *National Strength and Conditioning Association Journal.* Coach Kelso also has copyright claims to several unpublished manuals including *Athletic Physical Development, Total Conditioning, Bigger and Stronger,* and *5-Star Weight Training Workouts.*

Jim Kielbaso, M.S., C.S.C.S., is the strength and conditioning coach at the University of Detroit–Mercy in Detroit, Michigan. He earned his bachelor of science in exercise science from Michigan State University and his master of science in kinesiology from the University of Michigan. Coach Kielbaso was voted the 1998 Strength and Conditioning Professional of the Year for the Midwestern Collegiate Conference by the National Strength and Conditioning Association. He and his wife, Elaina, live in Plymouth, Michigan.

Ted Lambrinides, Ph.D., is the Director of Exercise Science at Thomas More College in Krestview Hills, Kentucky. Dr. Lambrinides also serves as a research and design consultant for MedX®, Inc., the editor of *Hard Training,* and a consultant to several teams in the National Football League (NFL). He and his lovely wife, Kim, have two daughters, Kristin and Rebecca.

Ken E. Leistner, D.C., M.S., is a practicing chiropractor and former owner of the renowned Iron Island Gym in Oceanside, New York. He has authored more than 600 articles on strength training, conditioning, injury rehabilitation, and injury prevention. As a collegiate football player, competitive powerlifter, and judo player, "Dr. Ken" experienced many of the injuries that he now treats. He and his wife, Kathy, have four children, all of whom have competed successfully in a variety of athletic pursuits.

Ken Mannie, M.S., C.S.C.S., is the strength and conditioning coach at Michigan State University in East Lansing, Michigan. He joined the Spartans in 1995 after serving nine seasons in the same capacity at the University of Toledo. A 1974 graduate of the University of Akron, he earned three letters in football and started on the 1971 Zips team that was ranked number 8 nationally in Division II. Coach Mannie received his master's degree in health, physical education, and recreation from the Ohio State University in 1985, where he was directly involved in the strength and conditioning program of the school's 1984 Big Ten champion football team. He also taught and coached at the high school level for ten years. Coach Mannie is a certified strength and con-

ditioning specialist and has authored more than 60 articles on strength and fitness. He and his wife, Marianne, live in East Lansing with their daughter, Alaina.

Mickey Marotti, M.S., M.A., C.S.C.S., is the head strength and conditioning coordinator at the University of Notre Dame in Notre Dame, Indiana. In this role, he is responsible for the total development of sport-specific strength and conditioning programs for all 26 varsity sports. Prior to this, Coach Marotti served eight years at the University of Cincinnati, where he coordinated the strength and conditioning programs for 20 varsity sports. He also worked in the areas of diet analysis and planning and assisted in student-athlete rehabilitation. From 1988 to 1990, he was an assistant strength coach at West Virginia University. Coach Marotti spent 1987–1988 as a graduate assistant strength coach at Ohio State, at the same time serving as head strength coach at Grove City High School. A native of Ambridge, Pennsylvania, he earned four letters in football as a fullback at West Liberty State (WV), serving as tri-captain in 1986 and winning first-team academic All-American honors in 1987. Born December 24, 1964, he earned his bachelor of science degree in exercise science from West Liberty State in 1987, a master of arts in strength training and athletic conditioning from Ohio State in 1988, and a master of science in sports medicine from West Virginia in 1990.

M. Doug McGuff, M.D., is the president of Ultimate Exercise, Inc., in Seneca, South Carolina. He earned his bachelor's degree in biology from St. Mary's University (TX) in 1984 and his M.D. from the University of Texas Health Science Center at San Antonio Medical School in 1989. Dr. McGuff received his residency training in emergency medicine at the University of Arkansas for Medical Sciences where he served as chief resident from 1991 to 1992. He then served three years in the Air Force at Wright-Patterson Medical Center where he was an assistant professor of emergency medicine in the Wright State University Emergency Medicine program and director of medical student education. In 1995, Dr. McGuff moved to Seneca, South Carolina, where he became a partner in Blue Ridge Emergency Physicians, P.A., practicing full-time emergency medicine. In 1997, he fulfilled a lifelong dream when he opened Ultimate Exercise, a one-on-one, high intensity training center and licensed SuperSlow® facility. Dr. McGuff conducts ongoing research and writes extensively on issues pertaining to high intensity exercise. Dr. McGuff lives in Seneca with his wife, Wendy.

James A. Peterson, Ph.D., FACSM, is a sports medicine specialist in Monterey, California.

Previously, he served as a faculty member of the United States Military Academy at West Point for 19 years. During his tenure at West Point, Dr. Peterson conducted extensive research into a variety of subjects, including how to design strength training programs, the physiological differences between men and women and their effect on performance, and the treatment and prevention of back pain. From 1990 to 1995, he served as the director of sports medicine for StairMaster® Sports/Medical Products, Inc., in Kirkland, Washington. A fellow of the American College of Sports Medicine and a member of the National Strength and Conditioning Association, Dr. Peterson has authored more than 50 books and 150 articles on sports medicine and fitness. Currently, he lives in Monterey, California, with his wife, Susan. In his spare time, Dr. Peterson enjoys writing, reading, and jogging.

Bill Piche, M.S., received his bachelor of science degree in electrical engineering from Michigan Technological University in 1985 and his master of science degree in electrical engineering from Iowa State University in 1989. That same year, Mr. Piche deadlifted 600 pounds in competition in the 198-pound weight class, which ranked him in the Top 50 in the United States by the American Drug-Free Powerlifting Association. Mr. Piche has authored numerous articles which have appeared in *Powerlifting USA, Master Trainer,*

Hard Training, and *Hardgainer*. He and his wife, Kim, live in Marion, Iowa, with their two children, Ryan and Amanda.

Rachael E. Picone, B.S., is a graduate student pursuing a master of science degree in exercise physiology at the University of Massachusetts–Amherst, where she also manages the Body Shop, a student fitness center. A fitness instructor for more than a decade, her professional career has spanned gymnastics instruction, personal training, cardiac rehabilitation, and health promotion. Specifically, Ms. Picone has served as the assistant recreational fitness director at Princeton University and a health fitness specialist at the AT&T Health Fitness Center in Somerset, New Jersey. She received her bachelor of science from Rutgers University in exercise science and sports studies. Ms. Picone is certified by the American Council on Exercise as a group exercise instructor and the American College of Sports Medicine as an exercise test technologist. She is an author and presenter specializing in strength training, children's fitness, and women's health. Ms. Picone resides in Sunderland, Massachusetts, and enjoys hiking, art, writing, and community volunteer work.

Liza Rovniak, B.S., is a graduate student specializing in clinical health psychology at Virginia Tech in Blacksburg, Virginia. Her research interests are in the areas of health promotion and human motivation. Ms. Rovniak has conducted research on exercise motivation, promoting healthier eating habits and self-regulation. In her spare time, Ms. Rovniak enjoys fitness walking, biking, reading, and surfing the Internet.

W. Daniel Schmidt, Ph.D., is an assistant professor of physical education at the University of Wisconsin–Oshkosh, where his research has focused on the effects of multiple, short-bout exercise versus continuous exercise as it pertains to aerobic fitness and weight loss. During the mid- to late 1980s, Dr. Schmidt worked as the director of fitness for the United States Navy in Norfolk, Virginia, and the Royal Saudi Air Force in Dhahran, Saudi Arabia. He received his doctoral degree in exercise physiology from Purdue University in 1992. Dr. Schmidt was an assistant professor of physical education at Trenton State College (now the College of New Jersey) from 1992 to 1997. He and his wife, Lisa, reside in Oshkosh, Wisconsin, with their three children, Zach, Seth, and Jaime.

Jeremy Scott, M.Ed. is the assistant strength and conditioning coach (football) at Penn State in University Park, Pennsylvania.

John Thomas, B.S., is the strength and conditioning coach (football) at Penn State in University Park, Pennsylvania. Previously, he was the strength and conditioning coach at the United States Military Academy. He and his wife, Kim, have two sons, Jake and Logan.

Kevin C. Tolbert, B.S., is the strength and conditioning coach (basketball) at the University of Miami in Coral Gables, Florida. A 1981 graduate of the United States Naval Academy, he served as a commissioned officer in the United States Navy (achieving the rank of lieutenant). Since his departure from the military, Coach Tolbert has been employed in the field of strength and conditioning in a variety of capacities. Currently, he and his wife, Meg, live in Miami, Florida, with their three children, Kaitlin, Courtney, and Matthew.

Tim "Red" Wakeham, M.S., C.S.C.S., is the assistant strength and conditioning coach at Michigan State University in East Lansing, Michigan. He also instructs classes in strength and conditioning as a member of the university's faculty. Coach Wakeham earned his bachelor of science degree from Northern Michigan University and his master of science degree from the University of North Dakota. Prior to his current position, he served as the strength and conditioning coach at an Olympic Training/ Education Site and the coordinator of strength and conditioning at Michigan Technological University. Coach Wakeham is a certified strength and conditioning specialist and has been a featured speaker at conferences and seminars throughout the midwestern United States.

Steve Weingarten, B.A., is an award-winning freelance writer, National Physique Committee (NPC) nationally qualified bodybuilder, and personal trainer in Louisville, Kentucky. Mr. Weingarten placed first in the middleweight division at the 1998 NPC Louisville Bodybuilding Championships and also was the overall champion among all of the weight classes. In addition, he finished second in the middleweight division at the 1998 NPC Kentucky Bodybuilding Championships. Mr. Weingarten began bodybuilding at age 13. A prototypical hard gainer, he trained for many years with little success until he learned about and refined the principles of high intensity training (HIT). Mr. Weingarten earned his bachelor of arts degree from the University of Kentucky. He lives in Louisville with his wife, Joni, and sons Evan and Nathan.

Wayne L. Westcott, Ph.D., C.S.C.S., is the fitness research director at the South Shore YMCA in Quincy, Massachusetts. He is a strength training consultant for numerous national organizations such as the American Council on Exercise, the National Sports Performance Association, and the National Youth Sports Safety Foundation. In addition, Dr. Westcott is an editorial adviser for many magazines including *Shape, Prevention, Club Industry,* and *Men's Health.* He has also authored more than 300 articles in professional journals and several popular fitness books including his two most recent releases: *Building Strength and Stamina* and *Strength Training Past 50.* Dr. Westcott was recently honored with the Lifetime Achievement Award from IDEA and the Healthy American Fitness Leader Award from the President's Council on Physical Fitness and Sports. His wife, Claudia, also works at the South Shore YMCA.

Bob Whelan, M.S., M.S., C.S.C.S., is the strength coach/owner of Whelan Strength Training in Washington, D.C., where he trains a diverse group of individuals, including many professional athletes from the National Basketball Association (NBA) and the National Football League (NFL). He earned a master of science degree in exercise science and health from George Mason University (VA) and is a certified strength and conditioning specialist. Previously, Mr. Whelan was an exercise physiologist at the National Aeronautics and Space Administration (NASA). A former military powerlifting champion, he was undefeated during a three-year span and bench pressed twice his bodyweight. Mr. Whelan has authored more than 50 articles that have appeared in numerous publications including *Hard Training* and *Hardgainer.*

Jessica A. Whiteley, B.S., is entering her third year of the clinical psychology doctoral program at Virginia Tech in Blacksburg, Virginia. Her specialization is in the area of health psychology with a primary interest in women's health issues. Currently, Ms. Whiteley is researching the psychological and social cognitive factors related to physical activity in women. She also enjoys nature photography, hiking, and gardening.

Richard A. Winett, Ph.D., is a professor of psychology, director of the Center for Research in Health Behavior, and director of the clinical psychology program at Virginia Tech in Blacksburg, Virginia. He has published more than 150 peer-reviewed papers and received more than $7 million in funding, primarily from the National Institutes of Health. Dr. Winett is the publisher of *Master Trainer* (which began with the February 1991 issue) and writes the "High Intensity Training" column for *IronMan* magazine.

About the Editor

Matt Brzycki, B.S., is the coordinator of health fitness, strength and conditioning programs at Princeton University in Princeton, New Jersey. He received his bachelor of science degree in health and physical education from Penn State in 1983. Mr. Brzycki represented the university for two years in the Pennsylvania State Collegiate Powerlifting Championships and was also a place-winner in his first bodybuilding competition. He served as a health fitness supervisor at Princeton University from 1983 to 1984. From 1984 to 1990, Mr. Brzycki was the assistant strength coach at Rutgers University. In 1990, he returned to Princeton University as the school's strength coach and health fitness coordinator. Mr. Brzycki was named to his current position in 1994.

At Princeton University, he teaches a variety of strength and fitness classes for students, faculty, and staff including Adult Fitness, Strength Training, Total Body Fitness, and Women-n-Weights. Mr. Brzycki developed the Strength Training Theory and Applications course for exercise science and sports studies majors at Rutgers University and has taught the program since March 1990 as a member of the faculty of Arts and Sciences. He has also taught the same course at the College of New Jersey since 1996. All told, more than 600 university students in fitness-related majors have received academic credit in his courses.

Mr. Brzycki has been a featured speaker at local, regional, state, and national conferences and clinics throughout the United States and Canada. He has authored more than 175 articles that have been featured in 33 different publications. Mr. Brzycki has written three books—*A Practical Approach to Strength Training, Youth Strength and Conditioning* and *Cross Training for Fitness*—and coauthored *Conditioning for Basketball* with Shaun Brown, the strength and conditioning coach of the Boston Celtics. He also developed a highly popular correspondence course in strength training that is offered through Desert Southwest Fitness in Tucson, Arizona.

Prior to attending college, Mr. Brzycki served in the United States Marine Corps from 1975 to 1979 which included a meritorious promotion to the rank of sergeant and a tour of duty as a drill instructor (DI). In 1978, at age 21, he was one of the youngest DIs in the entire Marine Corps. Among his many responsibilities as a DI was the physical preparedness of Marine recruits. He and his wife, Alicia, currently reside in Lawrenceville, New Jersey, with their son, Ryan.

Index